Title Withdrawn

Biography Today

Profiles
of People
of Interest
to Young
Readers

Volume 21—2012
Annual Cumulation

Cherie D. Abbey
Managing Editor

Omnigraphics

155 West Congress
Suite 200
Detroit, MI 48226

Cherie D. Abbey, *Managing Editor*

Peggy Daniels Becker, Laurie DiMauro, Joan Goldsworthy, Jeff Hill,
Kevin Hillstrom, Laurie Collier Hillstrom, Justin Karr, Leslie Karr,
and Diane Telgen, *Sketch Writers*

Allison A. Beckett and Mary Butler, *Research Staff*

* * *

Peter E. Ruffner, *Publisher*
Matthew P. Barbour, *Senior Vice President*

* * *

Elizabeth Collins, *Research and Permissions Coordinator*
Kevin Hayes, *Operations Manager*

Shirley Amore, Joseph Harris, Martha Johns, and Kirk Kauffmann, *Administrative Staff*

Special thanks to Frederick G. Ruffner for creating this series.

Copyright © 2012 EBSCO Publishing, Inc.
ISSN 1058-2347 • ISBN 978-0-7808-1256-7

Library of Congress Cataloging-in-Publication Data

Contents

4

Preface

Biography Today is a magazine designed and written for the young reader—ages 9 and above—and covers individuals that librarians and teachers tell us that young people want to know about most: entertainers, athletes, writers, illustrators, cartoonists, and political leaders.

The Plan of the Work

The publication was especially created to appeal to young readers in a format they can enjoy reading and readily understand. Each issue contains approximately 10 sketches arranged alphabetically. Each entry provides at least one picture of the individual profiled, and bold-faced rubrics lead the reader to information on birth, youth, early memories, education, first jobs, marriage and family, career highlights, memorable experiences, hobbies, and honors and awards. Each of the entries ends with a list of easily accessible sources designed to lead the student to further reading on the individual and a current address. Retrospective entries are also included, written to provide a perspective on the individual's entire career.

Biographies are prepared by Omnigraphics editors after extensive research, utilizing the most current materials available. Those sources that are generally available to students appear in the list of further reading at the end of the sketch.

Indexes

Cumulative indexes are an important component of *Biography Today*. Each issue of the *Biography Today* General Series includes a Cumulative Names Index, which comprises all individuals profiled in *Biography Today* since the series began in 1992. In addition, we compile three other indexes: the Cumulative General Index, Places of Birth Index, and Birthday Index. See our web site, www.biographytoday.com, for these three indexes, along with the Names Index. All *Biography Today* indexes are cumulative, including all individuals profiled in both the General Series and the Subject Series.

Our Advisors

This series was reviewed by an Advisory Board comprising librarians, children's literature specialists, and reading instructors to ensure that the concept of this publication—to provide a readable and accessible biographical magazine for young readers—was on target. They evaluated the title as it developed, and their suggestions have proved invaluable. Any errors, however, are ours alone. We'd like to list the Advisory Board members, and to thank them for their efforts.

Our Advisory Board stressed to us that we should not shy away from controversial or unconventional people in our profiles, and we have tried to follow their advice. The Advisory Board also mentioned that the sketches might be useful in reluctant reader and adult literacy programs, and we would value any comments librarians might have about the suitability of our magazine for those purposes.

8

Your Comments Are Welcome

Our goal is to be accurate and up to date, to give young readers information they can learn from and enjoy. Now we want to know what you think. Take a look at this issue of *Biography Today*, on approval. Contact me with your comments. We want to provide an excellent source of biographical information for young people. Let us know how you think we're doing.

Cherie Abbey
Managing Editor, *Biography Today*
Omnigraphics, Inc.
155 West Congress
Suite 200
Detroit, MI 48226
www.omnigraphics.com
editorial@omnigraphics.com

Congratulations!

Congratulations to the following individuals and libraries who are receiving a free copy of *Biography Today* for suggesting people who appear in this volume.

Carol Arnold, Hoopeston Public Library, Hoopeston, IL

Judi Chelekis, Vassar High School Library, Vassar MI

Annie Curtis, Gallatin Pulbic Library, Gallatin, TN

Sharon Curtis, Phelan Newmarket Elementary School, Newmarket, NH

Paul Dicken, Aurora Elementary School, Dillsboro Elementary School, Moores Hill Elementary School, South Dearborn Community Schools, Aurora, IN

Rebecca Foster, Memorial Pathway Academy, Garland, TX

James P. Hibler, Kalkaska County Library, Grand Rapids, MI

Kimberly Lentz, North Rowan High School, Spencer, NC

Beth E. Meier, Hayward Middle School Library, Springfield, OH

Alexis Pedretti, Magnolia Elementary, 6209 Nogales Street, Riverside, CA

Orie Ramos, Lakewood Public Schools, Sunfield, MI

Vicki Reutter, Cazenovia Junior-Senior High School, Cazenovia, NY

Yvette and Marjorie Shanks, O'Fallon, MO

Ashley Squires, Charlotte, NC

Carol Starr, Sarah Banks Middle School, Wixom, MI

Shreya Subramanian, Martell Elementary School, Troy, MI

Sharon Thackston, Gallatin Pulbic Library, Gallatin, TN

Owen V., McKenna Elementary School, Massapequa Public Schools, Massapequa, NY

Sierra M. Yoder, Shipshewana, IN

Alejandro Z., Mid-Valley Regional Branch Library, North Hills, CA

Adele 1988-

British Singer and Songwriter
Grammy-Award Winning Creator of the Hit Albums
19 and *21* and the Songs "Chasing Pavements,"
"Someone Like You," and "Rolling in the Deep"

BIRTH

Adele Laurie Blue Adkins was born on May 5, 1988, in the Tottenham section of North London, England. Her mother, Penny Adkins, was 18 years old when Adele was born. Her mother held various different jobs, including masseuse, artist, and furniture maker. Adele's father, Mark Evans, was a Welsh dockworker who was not involved in raising Adele. She has one half-brother, Cameron, on her father's side.

YOUTH

Adele spent her early childhood years in the Brixton area of South London, near where her mother's family lived. She remembers spending a lot of time with her aunts, uncles, and cousins. "I had, like, 30 cousins living down the road, so I'd go and see them, always arguing and hating to share, then I'd be back home to my tidy room and unbroken toys and no fighting over my Barbie. It was like I had the best of both worlds." When Adele was 11 years old, she and her mother moved to the West Norwood area of South London.

> *Adele grew up as an only child. "I had, like, 30 cousins living down the road, so I'd go and see them, always arguing and hating to share, then I'd be back home to my tidy room and unbroken toys and no fighting over my Barbie. It was like I had the best of both worlds."*

Music was one of Adele's biggest interests while she was growing up. She loved to sing and learned to play guitar and clarinet. "I've always liked being the center of attention," she said. When she was about five years old, she entertained her mother's friends by climbing up on the dinner table and singing "Dreams," a song that was a hit for British pop singer Gabrielle in 1993.

As a young girl, Adele explored a wide variety of music. She liked all sorts of different artists, including Aerosmith, the Backstreet Boys, Mary J. Blige, Billy Bragg, Jeff Buckley, The Cure, Destiny's Child, Aretha Franklin, Marvin Gaye, Korn, the Spice Girls, and Suzanne Vega. Adele never thought about having a career as a singer until she first heard Etta James, an American soul and blues singer. Adele came across an Etta James CD in the bargain bin at a local music store and bought it because she liked the picture on the front. She wanted to show James's hairstyle to her own hairdresser. "Then one day I was cleaning my room and I found it and put it on. When I heard the song 'Fool That I Am,' everything changed for me. I never wanted to be a singer until I heard that."

James became an important influence on Adele. "Etta James is my favorite singer. I've loved her since I was 15," Adele recalled. "Initially it was because I loved the way she looked—the big kinda white-woman weave and

Performing live at the BBC studios, December 2007.

her beautiful, catty eyes! But then, once I actually listened to her, though she didn't really even write any of her own songs, I found that her delivery was just so sincere that she really could convince me she was singing directly to me. Which is something I've never ever found in any other artist. She was the first time a voice made me stop what I was doing and sit down and listen. It took over my mind and body."

For Adele, listening to classic singers like Etta James and Ella Fitzgerald was a revelation. "There was no musical heritage in our family. Chart music was all I ever knew. So when I listened to the Ettas and the Ellas, it sounds so cheesy, but it was like an awakening. I was like, oh, right, some people have proper longevity and are legends. I was so inspired that as a 15-year-old I was listening to music that had been made in the 1940s. The idea that people might look back to my music in 50 years' time was a real spur to doing this."

After that, Adele immersed herself in the music of Etta James and other jazz, soul, and rhythm and blues stars like Ella Fitzgerald, Roberta Flack, Jill Scott, and Peggy Lee. She was fascinated by their talent for vocal improvisation, or scat singing. Scat singing is the art of singing with nonsense syllables, or sounds with no words at all. This gives the singer the ability to improvise a vocal solo performance. Adele wanted to learn the technique, and she studied the way these singers used improvisation to add to their recordings.

EDUCATION

Adele attended public schools in London, England. In secondary school, she wanted to join the school choir but was told by the music director that she was not good enough. A friend of her mother's suggested that Adele apply to attend The BRIT School for Performing Arts in London. This prestigious school for the arts was attended by many famous British musicians, including Amy Winehouse and Leona Lewis.

"When I was 14, all my friends were getting pregnant. I panicked, and I was like, 'I don't want this to happen to me.' I applied to school more as a way out than anything," Adele recalled. "As soon as I got a microphone in my hand, when I was about 14, I realized I wanted to do this. Most people don't like the way their voice sounds when it's recorded. I was just so excited by the whole thing that I wasn't bothered by what it sounded like."

Adele auditioned for and was accepted to The BRIT School. She has suggested that enrolling in courses there changed her life and set her on the right path to build a successful career as a singer and songwriter. "I think I do owe it completely to The BRIT School for making me who I am today, as cheesy and embarrassing as it may sound. Because, while my mum is the most supportive mum on Earth, she wouldn't have known how to channel me. With her I'd probably have gone down the classical music route, or maybe Disney, or musical theater ... but at The BRIT School I found my direction, because the music course was really wicked. It had free rehearsal rooms with free equipment, where I was listening to music all day for years. It's not your typical stage-school full of kids that are pushed into it by their parents. It's a school full of kids that will dance at a freezing cold town hall barefoot for eight hours solid. And, whereas before I was going to a school with bums and kids that were rude and wanted to grow up and mug people, it was really inspiring to wake up every day to go to school with kids that actually wanted to be productive at something and wanted to be somebody." Adele graduated from The BRIT School in 2006.

CAREER HIGHLIGHTS

A few months after graduation, Adele posted some of her original songs on the web and began to attract attention. Soon she was performing small gigs around London. She first appeared on stage in 2006 as the opening act for her friend Jack Peñate, a British singer and songwriter. There were about 100 people in the audience. "I went on first and I was on my own, and the whole room was packed. It was hot. It was disgusting," Adele remembered. She started to sing, and "the whole room was silent, and I saw these random girls just, like, crying. That was the time I was like, 'Oh my

God, this is amazing, can't live without it.' There's nothing more freeing than playing live, nothing."

Adele signed her first recording contract in 2006. A year later she released her debut singles, "Hometown Glory" and "Chasing Pavements." Adele wrote "Hometown Glory," one of the first songs she ever wrote, as an ode to the city of London. She was inspired to write "Chasing Pavements" after a horrible breakup with her boyfriend. They got into an argument in a bar and Adele ran out. "I was running down these gigantic, wide sidewalks that stretch on for miles, thinking to myself, 'Where are you going? What are you doing? You're just chasing pavements … that you're never going to catch.' Then, I went straight home and wrote the song."

A Successful Debut Album: *19*

In 2008, Adele released *19,* her first full-length album. The album's title refers to her age at the time. Though she had written a few songs when she was younger, Adele did not have the confidence to create a whole album until after she signed her recording contract. "I didn't realize this was something I could do until I got my record deal," she explained. "When I was signed at 18, I only had three songs to my name. But yet, literally within a month of turning 19, a load more just suddenly came out of me."

"My debut album is about being between 18 and 19, about love," Adele said. "It's quite a sad album, being cheated on and not getting what you want." The songs on *19* are about love, loss, and the thoughts and feelings that come after a relationship ends. "Apart from 'Hometown Glory', 'Daydreamer', and 'My Same'—which were all written earlier, when I was between 16 and 18—the whole album is all about one boy. So I was very sad when I wrote it. And I think that genuinely does come through in the music."

19 was an instant success in the United Kingdom. The album debuted in the No. 1 position on the British music charts, and Adele sold out her first

"

*"At The BRIT School I found my direction, because the music course was really wicked. It had free rehearsal rooms with free equipment, where I was listening to music all day for years….
It was really inspiring to wake up every day to go to school with kids that actually wanted to be productive at something and wanted to be somebody."*

"

15

Appearing on "Saturday Night Live," her first big introduction to the U.S. audience, October 2008.

United Kingdom tour as a headlining act. In recognition of her success, she received the first ever Critics' Choice Brit Award in 2008. *19* was released in the United States six months later, and Adele began her first U.S. tour.

American music fans were slower to embrace Adele, until she was the musical guest on an episode of the popular television show "Saturday Night Live" in October 2008, shortly before the 2008 presidential election. Adele had the good fortune of appearing on the same episode of the show as Sarah Palin, who was at that time the Republican candidate for vice president. A controversial candidate, Palin had been the subject of several sketch parodies by Tina Fey on "Saturday Night Live." So when Palin herself appeared on the show, millions of extra viewers tuned in to see the politician—and also heard the new singer Adele. After the show aired, her album quickly rose to No. 10 on the *Billboard* 200 music chart. *19* soon became a Top Internet Album and a Top Digital Album as well.

As *19* grew in popularity, Adele attracted fans across musical genres. Her soulful delivery of bluesy songs captivated listeners looking for something different. Adele attributed the success of *19* to the widespread accessibility and appeal of soul music. "What I particularly like about soul and blues is its honesty, sincerity, and depth. While with pop, though you do have the entertainment factor, when you scratch away the surface there's very little underneath. Whereas with soul you can constantly trawl through it and find great new things. To me the most important thing, in terms of longevity, is to be real in your music. And soul and blues are filled with real, proper emotions. Like every time I hear Lauryn Hill's voice, she makes me cry."

19 ultimately earned four Grammy Award nominations in 2009: Best New Artist, and Best Female Vocal Pop Performance, Record of the Year, and Song of the Year, all for "Chasing Pavements." Adele was shocked to find that she won the Grammy Awards for Best New Artist and Best Female Vocal Pop Performance. Sitting in the audience during the long awards program, Adele was so convinced that she would not win that by the time her name was called, she had already taken off her shoes and her belt.

The runaway success of *19* caught Adele by surprise. "It didn't even occur to me that a million-plus people would hear my record, and that people were gonna love it and criticize it. And it kind of frightens me sometimes 'cause I think my record's really honest—there's things in it that I'd never admitted to myself, that I would never just say in conversation. But then the other side of it is that I always get people coming up to me after shows and telling me that it helped them through their relationship at the time, which is an amazing feeling," she said. "It's really cheesy, but I feel like I'm living the dream. Even if nothing at all happened for me after 2008, I can say I've done it once and it's been amazing."

A Record-Breaking Follow-Up: *21*

In 2011, Adele released *21*, her second album. The album's title again reflected her age at the time. *21* quickly became the biggest selling album of the year, with millions of copies sold in the first few months alone, and followed that up by becoming the best-selling album of 2012 also. By July 2012, *21* had spent a total of 70 weeks at the top of the American music charts. *Daily Variety* music reviewer A.J. Marechal acknowledged Adele's star power by writing, "Whether in the recording studio or on stage, Adele belts with the kind of emotional depth seldom seen in today's era of mega-production tours. The lyrical honesty of such heartbreak-inspired songs as 'Someone Like You' paired with a powerful voice known to hush celeb-filled rooms has translated into big numbers."

The single "Rolling in the Deep" became a huge crossover hit on Adult Contemporary, R&B/Hip Hop, and Alternative radio stations. The song occupied the No. 1 position on the *Billboard* Hot 100 music chart for eight weeks. With record-breaking digital sales, "Rolling in the Deep" propelled

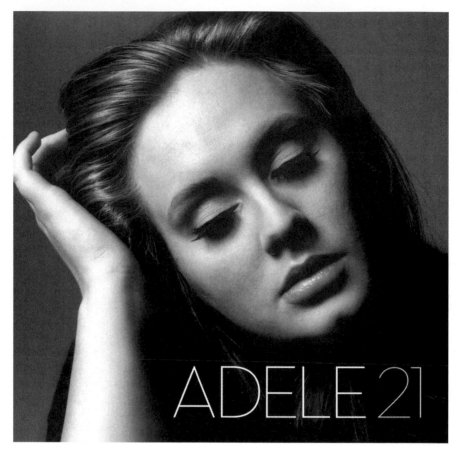

21 was Adele's big breakthrough album.

21 to Top Digital Album status. Music lovers around the world bought more than 10 million copies of *21*. More than 15,000 cover versions and remixes of "Rolling in the Deep" were uploaded to YouTube. The official music video for "Rolling in the Deep" was viewed more than 121 million times on YouTube. These numbers were not only record-breaking, but unprecedented. National Public Radio commentator Sami Yenigun observed, "Simply put, 'Rolling in the Deep' is a heart-stopping, chart-topping, YouTube popping, cover-propping, booty-dropping jam. The song of the summer."

Music critics were generous in their praise. *San Francisco Chronicle* reviewer David Wagner praised Adele's talent by writing, "This is a voice with such emotional resonance that it could sing the Oscar Mayer bologna jingle and still reduce hardened criminals to tears." *Minneapolis Star-Tribune* reviewer Jon Bream noted that "Adele favors a less-is-more style…. She's all about making the listener feel the pain—all her songs are sad except for one or two—without her screaming. It's controlled anger, delivered with deeply soulful aches, an occasional crack and a hint of weariness. She knows how to hold her notes a beat longer to underscore the fervor of her emotion."

In recognition of her phenomenal success with *21*, Adele was nominated for four American Music Awards in 2011, including Artist of the Year. She won the awards for Favorite Pop/Rock Female Artist, Favorite Adult Contemporary Artist, and Favorite Pop/Rock Album, for *21*. In 2011, Adele received three Teen Choice Awards, including Choice Music Female Artist, Choice Breakout Artist, and Choice Break Up Song, for "Rolling in the Deep." "Rolling in the Deep" was named MTV's Song of the Year for 2011, and was nominated for seven MTV Video Music Awards, winning three. Adele was also nominated for four 2012 People's Choice Awards, including two for "Rolling in the Deep" and one for the album *21*.

——— *"* ———

"What I particularly like about soul and blues is its honesty, sincerity, and depth. While with pop, though you do have the entertainment factor, when you scratch away the surface there's very little underneath…. To me the most important thing, in terms of longevity, is to be real in your music. And soul and blues are filled with real, proper emotions."

——— *"* ———

A Health Crisis

During her 2011 tour, Adele began to suffer from a mysterious vocal ailment. Her voice had been weakened when she came down with the flu in late 2010, and in early 2011 she found that she suddenly could not sing at all. She was diagnosed with severe laryngitis and ordered to rest her voice completely for 10 days. (Laryngitis is swelling of the voice box, or larynx, that results in extreme hoarseness or loss of voice.) Her voice improved with rest and Adele was able to speak and sing again, as long as she followed a strict program of vocal rest, vocal warm up exercises, and specific food and drinks.

But just a few months later, in the middle of a conversation, Adele's voice simply "switched off like a light." Unable to speak or sing, she was diagnosed with a hemorrhage on her vocal cords. (A hemorrhage refers to bleeding caused by a broken blood vessel.) Her doctors told her that if she continued trying to sing, she might do permanent damage and lose her

Adele is known for her powerful singing style in live performances.

voice forever. This terrible news came in the middle of her U.S. tour. Adele reluctantly canceled performances and took a month off to rest. Writing on her blog, she explained, "Singing is literally my life, it's my hobby, my love, my freedom, and now my job. I have absolutely no choice but to recuperate properly and fully, or I risk damaging my voice forever."

After that period of rest, Adele was able to continue on with her tour performances and other commitments. In late 2011, however, she experienced another hemorrhage and was forced to cancel the rest of her tour in the U.S. and the United Kingdom. Adele underwent surgery on her vocal cords in November 2011. Within a month after the surgery, she resumed vocal training and was able to begin singing again, with strict limitations. "The surgery couldn't have gone better. But because I was singing with damaged vocal cords for three or four months and because of the surgery and because of the silence after the surgery I now have to build myself back up vocally. It's gonna be a lot easier for me to sing now."

By February 2012, Adele's recovery was complete and she was able to return to the stage. Her first public performance after surgery was during the 2012 Grammy Awards show, where she gave a powerful performance of "Rolling in the Deep" that brought the Grammy audience—filled with top performers—to its feet. She also collected six Grammy Awards: she won the awards for Record of the Year, Song of the Year, and Best Short Form Music Video for "Rolling in the Deep," Album of the Year and Best Pop Vocal Album for *21*, and Best Pop Solo Performance for "Someone Like You." She went on to win two Brit Awards, for British Female Solo Artist and British Album of the Year, for *21*.

Adele's future plans include writing new songs and recording a new album. She plans to take as much time as she needs to make the best record she can. "I imagine I'll be 25 or 26 by the time my next record comes out, as I haven't even thought about my third record yet. I'll disappear and come back with a record when it's good enough. There will be no new music until it's good enough and until I'm ready."

HOME AND FAMILY

In June 2012, Adele announced on her website that she and her boyfriend, Simon Konecki, were expecting their first child. Konecki is the chief executive of a charitable foundation, Drop4Drop, that works on the global water crisis. He is divorced with a daughter from a previous marriage.

SELECTED RECORDINGS

19, 2008
21, 2011

HONORS AND AWARDS

Brit Awards (British Phonographic Institute): 2008, Critics' Choice; 2012 (two awards), British Female Solo Artist and British Album of the Year, for *21*

Grammy Awards: 2009 (two awards), Best New Artist Award and Best Female Vocal Pop Performance, for "Chasing Pavements"; 2012 (six awards), Record of the Year, Song of the Year, and Best Short Form Music Video, for "Rolling in the Deep," Album of the Year and Best Pop Vocal Album, for *21*, Best Pop Solo Performance, for "Someone Like You"

American Music Awards: 2011 (three awards), Favorite Adult Contemporary Artist, Favorite Pop/Rock Female Artist, and Favorite Pop/Rock Album, for *21*

MTV Song of the Year: 2011, for "Rolling in the Deep"

MTV Video Music Awards: 2011 (three awards), Best Art Direction in a Video, Best Cinematography in a Video, and Best Editing in a Video, all for "Rolling in the Deep"

Teen Choice Awards: 2011 (three awards), Choice Music Female Artist, Choice Breakout Artist, and Choice Break Up Song, for "Rolling in the Deep"

FURTHER READING

Periodicals

Billboard, Dec. 17, 2011
Current Biography Yearbook, 2009
Entertainment Weekly, Apr. 15, 2011, p.56; July 1, 2011, p.16
Glamour, Dec. 2008, p.270
Marie Claire, Feb. 2011, p.113
People, May 16, 2011, p. 56
Rolling Stone, Apr. 28, 2011, p.52; Sep. 15, 2011, p.13
USA Today, Feb. 18, 2011
Vogue, Apr. 2009, p.198

Online Articles

www.bbc.co.uk
    (BBC News, "How Has Adele Become So Successful?" Mar. 28, 2011)
www.billboard.biz
    (Billboard, "21 and Up: Adele's Billboard Cover Story," Dec. 8, 2011)
www.bluesandsoul.com
    (Blues and Soul, "Adele: Up Close and Personal," no date)
www.mtv.com/music/artists
    (MTV, "Adele," no date)
www.rollingstone.com
    (Rolling Stone, "Adele Opens Up about Her Inspirations, Looks, and Stage Fright in New *Rolling Stone* Cover Story," Apr. 13, 2011)
www.vh1.com/artists/az/adele/artist.jhtml
    (VH1, "Adele," no date)

ADDRESS

Adele
Columbia Records
550 Madison Ave., 24th Floor
New York, NY 10022

WEB SITE

www.adele.tv

Rob Bell 1970-

American Religious Leader, Author, and Speaker
Founding Pastor of the Mars Hill Bible Church

BIRTH

Robert Holmes Bell Jr., known as Rob, was born on August 23,
1970, in Ingham County, Michigan. He grew up in Okemos,
not far from Michigan's capital, Lansing. His parents are
Helen and Robert Holmes Bell. He has a brother, Jonathan,
and a sister, Ruth.

YOUTH

Bell's father was a judge in Michigan's Ingham District Court and the Ingham County Circuit Court. In 1987, he was nominated to the U.S. District Court by then-president Ronald Reagan and confirmed for the position by the U.S. Senate. The Bell children grew up in a household where they were challenged to think deeply and critically. Dinner was not just a time for eating, but was also a time for meaningful conversation among the family. The parents expected their children to read certain books, including the fiction and nonfiction of C. S. Lewis, author of the "Narnia" series. Lewis's writing frequently explores Christian themes.

———— " ————

"My parents were intellectually rigorous," Bell remembered. *"Ask questions, explore, don't take things at face value. Stretch. I've always been interested in the thing behind the thing."*

———— " ————

The Bells raised their children with conservative Christian values and beliefs, but they didn't discourage them from challenging those beliefs. "My parents were intellectually rigorous," Bell remembered. "Ask questions, explore, don't take things at face value. Stretch. I've always been interested in the thing behind the thing."

Bell's father remembered that even when his son was only about 10 years old, he demonstrated an unusual interest in, and understanding of, people and their problems. "There he'd be, riding along with me, ... going to see sick folks or friends who were having problems, and he would get back in the truck after a visit and begin to analyze them and their situation very acutely. He had a feel for people and how they felt from very early on."

EDUCATION

Bell graduated from Okemos High School in 1988. He then enrolled at Wheaton College, a highly ranked, private, Christian, liberal arts school located just west of Chicago, Illinois. Unsure about what he really wanted to do with his life, Bell decided to major in psychology, but his main interest was music. He sang and played guitar in a rock band called ___ ton bundle, an alt-rock group whose guitar player dressed as a pirate. The band's name starts with an underlined space that was filled in with words that changed from time to time. "Rapunzel ton bundle" and "nun ton bundle" were two examples Bell remembered.

Bell has admitted that he was not an outstanding musician, but that didn't dampen his enthusiasm. "What I lack in talent, I make up in volume and passion," he said. He had always felt he had a lot of creative energy, but he didn't know what to do with it until he started playing with the band. Performing was a lot of fun, and it taught him to express himself, "writing and playing, working with words and images and metaphors. You might say the music unleashed a monster," he reflected. Being in a rock band might seem an unlikely way to prepare for a career as a church pastor, but both require "taking a statement, crafting it, delivering it," Bell explained. "Something was birthed there. It was all a warm-up for the first time I ever preached."

Rob with his baby brother.

At that time, however, Bell still had no thought of becoming a pastor, or any other ideas about his life path other than making music with ___ ton bundle. The band was moderately successful, playing in clubs around the Chicago area; but during Bell's senior year at Wheaton, ___ ton bundle fell apart, for various reasons. Bell became seriously ill with viral meningitis, a life-threatening inflammation of the tissues around the brain. His recovery required a long stay in the hospital, and by the time he was ready to play again, ___ ton bundle's guitarist had moved on to study at a seminary. The band never came back together.

In 1992, Bell graduated with a Bachelor of Arts (BA) degree. That summer, he worked as a water-skiing instructor at Honey Rock Camp, which is run by Wheaton College. One day, when no one else was available, Bell was asked to preach a message to a group of counselors. This spur-of-the-moment experience transformed his life. "I thought, 'This is what I'm supposed to do,'" he recalled. Other people had already suggested to him that he should consider being a pastor, but he had never agreed with them. Now he believed it was his calling, and he enrolled at the Fuller Theological Seminary, a Protestant divinity school in Pasadena, California.

Bell wanted to be a pastor, but he knew he'd always do things a little differently than the norm. He wanted his ministry to be "vibrant and subversive," and he constantly searched for creative new ways to get his points across. His efforts did not earn him good grades, but he did complete his master of divinity degree. During his time at Fuller, he worked as a youth intern at the Lake Avenue Church in Pasadena. He also got some new

Rob with his band, __ton bundle.

ideas about how worship services might be conducted when he and his wife Kristen, whom he had met while at Wheaton, attended Christian Assembly, a progressive church in Eagle Rock.

FIRST JOBS

Following his graduation from Fuller, Bell was invited to be an intern at Calvary Church in Grand Rapids, Michigan. Like Lake Avenue Church and Christian Assembly, Calvary Church falls into the "megachurch" category, meaning the weekly attendance averages more than 2,000 people. At the time of Bell's internship, Calvary was under the direction of Reverend Ed Dobson, who had became well known as one of the leaders of the Moral Majority, a political action group that lobbied on behalf of conservative causes.

Soon Bell had taken over the Saturday night services at Calvary, which had a more casual, modern feel than the Sunday morning service. He was popular, but he wasn't satisfied. He kept looking for new ways to present the Bible and its message. One of his goals was to reach people who might be uncomfortable at a traditional church service. "Most understandings of preaching/teaching have a whole bunch of fundamental assumptions about how it's done," he argued. "You are fitting truth into a prescribed format—generally, a person standing behind a podium, reading the Bible and talking. And so the deepest truths of the universe then are going to need to get run through a very narrow funnel." Bell felt very strongly that "there was a whole generation of people hungry for Jesus, but unable to connect with the churches they had experienced." In 1998, this feeling led him to start a totally new church group. He had "a defining moment" when he realized "If nobody comes, it's still a success. Because we tried something new."

CAREER HIGHLIGHTS

Founding Mars Hill Bible Church

Bell decided to call his new church Mars Hill Bible Church. Like Calvary Church, it would be nondenominational. This means that while its members identify themselves as Christians, the church is not part of any officially organized branch of Christianity. The name refers to a hill near Athens, Greece, known as the Areopagus, or Mars Hill. It was the site of an altar dedicated to "an unknown god," a figure that represented all the gods not known or recognized in the Greek pantheon. It is recorded in the Bible that upon seeing this altar, Paul, one of the Apostles of Jesus, proclaimed: "What you worship as something unknown I am going to proclaim to you. The God who made the world and everything in it is the Lord of heaven and earth and does not live in temples built by hands."

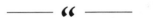

"Jesus is more compelling than ever," Bell has said. "More inviting, more true, more mysterious than ever. The problem isn't Jesus; the problem is what comes with Jesus."

The first meetings of the Mars Hill Bible Church were held in February 1999, in a school gym in Wyoming, Michigan. More than 1,000 people showed up at the church's first worship service. The group soon began meeting in a large warehouse space owned by a church member, with some 4,000 people visiting each week. They were drawn in by Pastor Bell's energetic, casual, humorous style; his youthful, modern mindset; and the upbeat music used in worship.

Numbers continued to swell, and within a year, the congregation was preparing to move to a much larger, permanent location. A benefactor had given Mars Hill an abandoned shopping mall in nearby Grandville. Funds were raised to buy the land around the building, and the space that had formerly served as the mall's main store was converted into a place for worship. The first services were held there in July 2000. Church membership

*Bell has often taken his message on the road,
as in this sermon in Ann Arbor, Michigan.*

grew very rapidly, and by 2005, an estimated 11,000 people attended services at Mars Hill each week. Some 30,000 more visited the church's web site to watch Bell's sermons and downloaded them and other features.

Bell's intense attitude towards his work was summed up in his statement: "A good sermon will exhaust and inspire you.... You'll say 'Whoa—that's a full meal. It'll take me a week to recover from that.'" During this period of explosive growth at Mars Hill, however, he did much more than merely write and deliver dynamic sermons. He threw himself into every aspect of running the church and serving the congregation.

Eventually, the hectic pace and the demands of being spiritual leader to so many people took their toll. One Sunday morning, about five years after the church got started, Bell found himself hiding in a storage room at the church shortly before his 11:00 service. He was afraid to face the crowd and wondering what would happen if he ran for his car at that moment and drove away as fast as he could. He didn't go through with his fantasies of escape, but he did visit his doctor, who told him he was badly overworked and needed a break.

Bell took 10 weeks off, spending much of that time alone and in the outdoors. Upon reflection, he said that one of the things he needed to do at that point was to get past the feeling that he had to prove himself. He returned to Mars Hill, but turned most of the pastor's duties over to other people. He focused his own energies on his sermons and writing. Bell also vowed to make every Friday a kind of retreat day, on which he disconnects from technology—cell phone, e-mail, and social networking sites—and focuses on things other than his work.

Reaching Out to the World

One aspect many people find appealing about Mars Hill is its emphasis on making a real difference in the world, both locally and globally. The church has a mentoring program designed to help the inner-city youth of Grand Rapids. The church also helps refugee families who are starting new lives in Michigan make the adjustment to their new home and its culture. Mars Hill also participates in programs to bring clean water to underprivileged areas in the African country of Rwanda, and it supports a program that makes small-business loans available to people in need around the world. It is typical of the church's priorities that they have continued to meet in their no-frills setting—the old shopping mall—rather than investing funds in a new church building.

"[Bell has] figured out how to convey basic Christian doctrine in a highly skeptical culture," said Quentin J. Schultze, a professor of communication at Calvin College. "He's very challenging in his sermons. There's no appeal for money. You get a sense of intellectual substance and depth of the faith."

Bell spreads the Mars Hill message in other ways, too. The church, like many megachurches, makes extensive use of modern technology. Many people download Mars Hill podcasts and access other features the church makes available through the Internet. Music and inspirational CDs are also available for purchase on the church's web site. The church's basic message of acceptance for all is summed up in the bumper stickers given away after each service, which state simply: "LOVE WINS."

Writing books provided another way for Bell to reach people. His first was *Velvet Elvis: Repainting the Christian Faith,* published in 2005. Its title came from an old ___ ton bundle song, "Velvet Elvis." The themes in the book are closely related to the ideas that inspired Bell to found Mars Hill Bible

Church. The book is aimed at people who feel drawn to Jesus Christ, but who have difficulties dealing with traditional religious worship. Bell states that Christianity needs to be continually re-imagined and re-invented. He feels that this keeps Christianity from becoming stuck in outdated traditions and stagnant systems. As Cindy Crosby wrote in *Christianity Today,* "Joy, awe, raw honesty, and an appreciation for the mystery of faith permeate the pages." Another reviewer, James D. Davis, wrote in the *South Florida Sun-Sentinel,* "If you want brutal honesty, you've come to the right book with *Velvet Elvis.* It's a sensitive yet radical plea for simple Christian living, as stripped down as the alternative rock music Bell once played."

Taking His Message on the Road

On June 30, 2006, in Chicago, Bell began a speaking tour of the United States, with a theme of "Everything Is Spiritual." The tour was a great success, with tickets selling out everywhere. Besides helping to spread Bell's message, the tour also provided a big boost for a charity called WaterAid, which helps to improve and expand access to safe water supplies around the world. All profits from ticket sales to the "Everything Is Spiritual" tour were given to WaterAid.

In March 2007, Bell published his second book, with the attention-grabbing title *Sex God: Exploring the Endless Connections between Sexuality and Spirituality.* In this book, he discusses human urges and physical relationships and the ways they reflect the kind of love that exists between God and humankind. A reviewer for *Publishers Weekly* said that Bell "does a fine job using the Bible and real life to show that our physical relationships are really about spiritual relationships. This book joyfully ties, and then tightens, the knot between God and humankind." Bell made personal appearances on six college campuses to support *Sex God,* hosting sessions for questions and open conversation.

In addition to his books and tours, Bell began work on a series of inspirational videos known as NOOMA. Aimed at people ages 18 to 34, these short films combine music, narration, and visually striking locations—often in western Michigan—to promote spiritual responses to life situations and challenges. A small booklet is also included with the DVDs, which have such simple titles as *Trees, Rain,* and *Luggage.* Topics include love, death, faith, and forgiveness. The title NOOMA comes from the Greek word *pneuma,* which means spirit. Bell said the name reflected the "desire to be ancient while at the same time pushing forward." NOOMA videos increased Bell's following greatly, with approximately 1.2 million copies sold in more than 80 countries. In addition to being viewed by indi-

NOOMA® Rain | 001 Rob Bell

One of the inspirational NOOMA videos.

viduals, NOOMA films are also used by drug-recovery groups, professional sports teams, and other organizations, and in locations as far away as Morocco and India.

In June 2007, Bell went on a short tour of the United Kingdom and Ireland, speaking on the topic "Calling All Peacemakers." In November 2007, he launched his "The Gods Aren't Angry" tour in the United States, traveling to 22 cities to spread his message. Like his other tours, it was a sellout. His principal theme was that God only asks for faith and that requiring sacrifices to make God happy is a reflection of outdated ways of thought. All proceeds from "The Gods Aren't Angry" were given to Turame Microfinance, which helps to establish business ventures among underprivileged people in the country of Burundi. Religious speakers usually appear in churches or at religious festivals, but Bell broke with tradition and gave many of his talks in nightclubs or bars. He stated that he wanted to be booked into places where he might have a better chance of reaching "so many people [who have] been turned off by the packages Jesus has been presented in."

Bell and Don Golden, one of Bell's associates at Mars Hill, worked together to write *Jesus Wants to Save Christians: A Manifesto for the Church in Exile*, published in 2008. The book's message is that Christianity should be a means for helping people, not for justifying political ends, especially violence or war. Although it features the same brief sentences, eye-catching typography, and clever chapter titles as Bell's earlier books, *Jesus Wants to Save Christians* "offers more serious theological reflection and biblical commentary," said a reviewer for *Christianity Today*. "Bell and Golden draw readers into wrenching experiences such as Egyptian slavery, Babylonian captivity, and Roman tyranny."

Drops Like Stars: A Few Thoughts on Creativity and Suffering was published in 2009. It is a collection of brief anecdotes, which Bell uses to explore suffering, creativity, and the connection between them. Bell never attempts to answer a question that has troubled many people throughout the centuries: Why would a loving, all-powerful God allow creatures to suffer? Instead, he draws on his own experience as a pastor to comment on the good that frequently comes out of suffering. Examples could include the chance to make a new start, increased empathy for other people, or personal growth. Once again Bell toured to support the publication of *Drops Like Stars*.

Controversy over the Book *Love Wins*

With his book *Love Wins: A Book about Heaven, Hell, and the Fate of Every Person Who Ever Lived*, Bell expanded on the phrase "Love Wins," the message that Mars Hill Bible Church spreads on its bumper stickers. He sought to defuse the negative image of God as an angry, authoritarian figure who is intent on punishing those who don't measure up. He wanted to replace that image with one of a peaceful, loving, forgiving God. In his book, Bell looked at the many different ways that hell has been envisioned and described, yet, he did not state that any of them are correct. Instead, he expressed a hope that, in fact, the love of God is so great that no one can be outside it, and that in the end, all will be brought to heaven because of God's great love. He asserted that heaven is a real place, but expressed some doubts about hell.

This message was very controversial, especially to the Protestant evangelical tradition from which Bell came. For the most part, evangelical Christianity places utmost importance on the belief that the soul can only reach heaven through a belief in and acceptance of Jesus Christ as the son of God and the savior of humanity. Hell, in that tradition, is very real. Bell's suggestion that everyone might be saved and spend eternity in heaven, no matter how they lived their life or what they believed, was offensive to some Christians. They felt that it ignored or distorted Bible teachings, as well as minimizing the importance of Jesus. Some people felt that Bell had moved from an evangelical Christian stance to one of Universalism, a body of religious thought that suggests that many belief systems hold core truths and are valid. Some Christians feel this is a dangerous school of thought, because it dilutes the importance of the truths revealed in the Bible.

"Our founding pastor, Rob Bell, has decided to leave Mars Hill in order to devote his energy to sharing the message of God's love with a broader audience.... While we recognize that no one person defines a community, we acknowledge the impact of Rob's leadership, creativity, and biblical insights on our lives, and face a deep sadness at the loss of their presence in our community."

Bell had denied that his thought was Universalist in nature, however. He has said that he believes that Jesus is the key to salvation, and yet he has also maintained that Jesus must be bigger than any religious differences found in the world. "I affirm the truth anywhere in any religious system, in any worldview," Bell has said. "If it's true, it belongs to God." He has said that he believes it is crucial to acknowledge that there are mysteries about the world and God, which humans are incapable of understanding completely. He is more interested in asking questions than in having all the answers. "I like to say that I practice militant mysticism," he explained. "I'm really absolutely sure of some things that I don't quite know."

In his sermons, Bell has expressed views that have attracted many followers, but some have proven controversial.

Despite the controversy over Bell's message, many Christians did accept and praise *Love Wins.* "Bell's writing can be choppy at times," Peter W. Marty wrote in *Christian Century.* "Seven consecutive incomplete sentences hardly make for grammatical coherence. But these deficiencies do not distract from the force of the larger argument. Bell has given theologically suspicious Christians new courage to bet their life on Jesus Christ." Richard Mouw, the president of Fuller Theological Seminary, wrote in his blog: "Rob Bell is calling us away from a stingy orthodoxy to a generous orthodoxy."

"Jesus is more compelling than ever," Bell has said. "More inviting, more true, more mysterious than ever. The problem isn't Jesus; the problem is what comes with Jesus." He preaches that instead of focusing on complicated belief systems with rigid rules, people should work to help other people in whatever ways they can. "We're rediscovering Christianity as an Eastern religion, as a way of life," he said. "We grew up in churches where people knew the nine verses why we don't speak in tongues, but had never experienced the overwhelming presence of God."

"Rob Bell is a central figure for his generation and for the way that evangelicals are likely to do church in the next 20 years," said Andy Crouch, an editor at *Christianity Today*. "He occupies a centrist place that is very appealing, committed to the basic evangelical doctrines but incredibly creative in his reinterpretive style."

"He's figured out how to convey basic Christian doctrine in a highly skeptical culture," said Quentin J. Schultze, a professor of communication at Calvin College in Grand Rapids. "He's very challenging in his sermons. There's no appeal for money. You get a sense of intellectual substance and depth of the faith."

In 2011, Bell surprised many when he announced that he was leaving his position at Mars Hill. In a statement, the church announced that "Our founding pastor, Rob Bell, has decided to leave Mars Hill in order to devote his energy to sharing the message of God's love with a broader audience.... While we recognize that no one person defines a community, we acknowledge the impact of Rob's leadership, creativity, and biblical insights on our lives, and face a deep sadness at the loss of their presence in our community." Bell revealed that he was working on writing a spiritual TV drama called "Stronger" that would be loosely based on his own life. The show would focus on Tom Stronger, a musician and teacher, and his spiritual journey as he works with other people. Music is expected to be a big part of the show. Bell and his family will be moving to Los Angeles, where he will also continue to write books and speak on tour.

As Bell faces new challenges, he is likely to keep looking for new ways to spread a positive message: That God loves the world, and people should try to be more Godlike in their love of each other. "For many people, there's a widespread, low-grade despair at the heart of everything," he noted. "If we can tilt things a few clicks in the hope direction, that would be beautiful."

HOME AND FAMILY

Bell and his wife Kristen have three children. Currently, they make their home in a renovated house in the inner city of Grand Rapids.

HOBBIES AND OTHER INTERESTS

Bell takes part in soccer games twice a week, goes to boxing lessons, and likes to water-ski, snowboard, and skateboard. He enjoys cooking and eating healthful food. He loves to read books and magazines on all subjects. "Economics, art, politics. I get on a subject and learn everything I can about it," he said.

Music is very important to him. In addition to playing with ___ ton bundle, from 1995 until 1997 Bell was part of a Christian punk rock band called Big Fil, which recorded two CDs: *Big Fil* and *Via de la Shekel.*

CREDITS

"NOOMA" video series, 2001-2009
Velvet Elvis: Repainting the Christian Faith, 2005
Sex God: Exploring the Endless Connections between Sexuality and Spirituality, 2007
Jesus Wants to Save Christians: A Manifesto for the Church in Exile, 2008 (with Don Golden)
Drops Like Stars: A Few Thoughts on Creativity and Suffering, 2009
Love Wins: A Book about Heaven, Hell, and the Fate of Every Person Who Ever Lived, 2011

HONORS AND AWARDS

100 Most Influential People in the World (*Time* magazine): 2011

FURTHER READING

Periodicals

Christian Century, May 17, 2011
Christianity Today, Mar. 24, 2009, pp.22-24; May 17, 2011, p.22
New York Times, July 8, 2006, p.A10; Mar. 5, 2011, p.A12
St. Petersburg Times, June 5, 2011, p.5P
USA Today, May 23, 2011, p.A11

Online Articles

www.bpnews.net
(Baptist Press, "Rob Bell Book *Love Wins* Stirs Controversy, Denies Core Christian Beliefs," Mar. 15, 2011; "Hard-Hitting Rob Bell Interview Goes Viral," Mar. 16, 2011)
www.christianitytoday.com/ct/special/robbell.html
(Christianity Today, "Rob Bell," multiple articles, various dates)

mlive.com
   (Mlive, "Profile: Mars Hill Bible Church Pastor Rob Bell," Mar. 23, 2008;
   "Profile: U.S. District Court Judge Robert Holmes Bell," Feb. 13, 2011;
   "Trendy Grand Rapids Pastor Leaving Church He Founded to Pursue
   'Strategic Opportunities,'" Sep. 23, 2011)
topics.mlive.com/tag/Rob%20Bell/index.html
   (Mlive, "Rob Bell," multiple articles, various dates)
www.time.com
   (Time, "Pastor Rob Bell: What If Hell Doesn't Exist?," Apr. 14, 2011;
   "Rob Bell," Apr. 21, 2011)
www.usatoday.com
   (USA Today, "Megachurch Pastor Rob Bell Seeks Life Beyond the Pul-
   pit," Sep. 23, 2011)

ADDRESS

Rob Bell
Author Mail, 11th Floor
HarperCollins Publishers
10 East 53rd Street
New York, NY 10022

WEB SITES

www.robbell.com
marshill.org

BIG TIME RUSH
**Logan Henderson 1989-
James Maslow 1990-
Carlos Pena Jr. 1989-
Kendall Schmidt 1990-**
American Pop Music Group and TV Actors
Stars of the Nickelodeon Series "Big Time Rush"

EARLY YEARS

Big Time Rush is a pop music group whose members also star in a television series. The group includes four musicians/actors: Logan Henderson, James Maslow, Carlos Pena Jr., and Kendall Schmidt.

Logan Henderson

Logan Phillip Henderson was born on September 14, 1989, and raised in North Richland Hills, Texas, which is part of the Dallas-Fort Worth metropolitan area. He started singing at a young age and was surrounded by music in his home. "My family is pretty musical," he said. "Growing up, I'd listen to blues and old rock on the radio with my dad. I got a lot of my musical influences from older artists." Among the musicians that he admires are Aerosmith, the Beatles, B. B. King, Billie Holiday, Elvis Costello, and Prince. Henderson also became interested in acting and began attending an acting studio in the Dallas-Fort Worth area. Fellow Texans Demi Lovato and Selena Gomez were in some of his classes. Henderson became friends with both girls, and they have remained close as they have pursued their show-business careers.

> "We got along like brothers from the start and have only grown closer since then," Maslow said. "In the show, as our characters, we have a very high energy and let problems like girls separate us, but in real life in the band we are all much more laid back."

At age 16, Henderson landed his first notable role when he was cast for a small part in the TV series "Friday Night Lights," which was filmed in Texas. His next big break came when he took part in one of the auditions for "Big Time Rush" that were held all around the country, but it would be over 18 months before the producers made their final choices for the show. In the meantime, he made the decision to move to California to pursue his acting career, with the approval of his mom and dad. "I remember my parents saying, 'As long as you're doing something and giving it your all, we're going to back you up,'" Henderson said. He left home at age 18 and arrived in Los Angeles, joining the thousands of other young people in that city seeking a place in the entertainment industry.

James Maslow

James David Maslow was born in New York City on July 16, 1990. During his early childhood, his family lived in Florida and Chicago before settling in La Jolla, California, when he was six years old. That same year, his mother signed him up for the San Diego Children's Choir. "I didn't like it at first," he remembered, "but within two weeks I totally fell in love with it and then knew I'd be performing in some way all my life." Maslow learned

Big Time Rush on location in Santa Monica: (from left) Carlos Pena Jr., James Maslow, Logan Henderson, and Kendall Schmidt.

to sing and act by attending the San Diego School of Creative and Performing Arts and the Coronado School of the Arts, and he learned to play both guitar and piano. He is also a skilled athlete and was a member of the soccer, baseball, and basketball teams at his high school.

An experienced stage performer, Maslow appeared in *La Boheme* with the San Diego Opera and also in productions of *Les Miserables* and *Grease*. His first big break on TV was in a 2008 episode of the "iCarly" series, when he played Shane, a cute boy who sparks a fight between Carly and her friend Sam. Though his parents played an important role in his career, he prides himself on his independence and has lived on his own since age 17.

Carlos Pena Jr.

Born on August 15, 1989, Carlos Roberto Pena Jr. hails from a diverse Hispanic background. His mother is from the Dominican Republic, and his fa-

41

ther is of Spanish and Venezuelan heritage. He spent his early youth in Columbia, Missouri, before moving to Weston, Florida. There, he joined a boy's choir, was trained in musical theater, and learned to play guitar and piano. His love of acting began at age 13, when he appeared in a school musical version of *Titanic* while a student at the American Heritage School in Plantation, Florida. At about the same time, he won a part in a Super Soaker water gun advertising campaign, and that work helped him focus his attention on a career in show business. "From [that point on,] I wanted TV, film, acting, singing, theatre … anything," he said.

Around the time he was 15, Pena began to land guest roles on a number of different TV series, including "E. R.," "Judging Amy," and "Summerland." Another big break was winning a recurring part in "Ned's Declassified School Survival Guide" on the Nickelodeon cable network. The series was created by Scott Fellows—the man who would soon start work on "Big Time Rush"—and the role helped make Pena a familiar face to young viewers. In 2007, he got his first taste of what it might be like to be in a "boy band," when he was one of the 15 performers chosen to appear on the MTV reality show "Making Menudo." The program sought to create a new version of the popular 1980s Latino singing group Menudo, and Pena made it to the final nine contestants before being eliminated. He built a solid list of TV acting credits while in his teens and spent a lot of time in California working on programs. But he decided to complete his high school studies back home in Weston at the Sagemont School, graduating in 2008. He then set his sights on attending the Boston Conservatory, one of the country's elite schools for the performing arts. His plans to earn a degree there were interrupted after he became involved in the auditions for "Big Time Rush."

Kendall Schmidt

Kendall Francis Schmidt was born on November 2, 1990, in Wichita, Kansas, and was raised in the nearby town of Andover. He was the youngest of three sons in a family that became very involved in the entertainment industry. Both of his brothers, Kenneth and Kevin, became child actors, and his parents, Kent and Kathy Schmidt, supported their sons as they sought to establish themselves in the business. As a result, the family lived in New York City for a time and frequently traveled back and forth between Kansas and California. Wishing to follow in his older brothers' footsteps, Kendall began attending auditions and got his first acting job at age six, when he appeared in a cereal commercial along with Kenneth and Kevin.

The Schmidt family moved to the Los Angeles area when Kendall was ten years old, and they lived for five years at the Oakwood apartment complex, which is home to many aspiring actors. As a result, Kendall got to know many people who would go on to become stars. Actresses Kirsten Dunst and Christina Milian were his babysitters, and he was also acquainted with Hilary Duff. He soon began winning roles in such TV programs as "E. R.," "Mad TV," and "Frasier," and he was a recurring character on "General Hospital," "Gilmore Girls," "CSI: Miami," and other shows. He has also worked on films and was a double on the film *A. I.: Artificial Intelligence*, directed by Steven Spielberg. Schmidt's success, as well as that of his brothers, stemmed from assistance they got from their parents, and he has given a lot of credit to his mother and father. "I really couldn't have done anything if it wasn't for my parents being very supportive," he said in the *Boston Herald*. "It's not very often that parents drop everything and take their kids where they want to go to do what they want to do. I gotta give my dad a lot of props for holding strong."

FORMING THE BAND

Unlike most musical acts, Big Time Rush existed as a concept well before it had any actual members. The original idea for the band and TV program was hatched by Scott Fellows, who created "Ned's Declassified School Survival Guide" and has been a writer and producer on many Nickelodeon series. Because "Big Time Rush" is a TV show as well as a musi-

——— **"** ———

When asked who in the band is the biggest star, Schmidt responded that "it really depends on where we are, state by state. We did a promo tour across the U.S. and every state seems to like one of us more than the others. I would say that it evens out and it's pretty hard to say who is the most popular guy in the band!"

——— **"** ———

cal ensemble, it was put together the same way that TV shows are created: the producers held auditions to find an actor to fill each role in the group. That process took a long time. Auditions began around 2007 and continued for more than a year and a half, with some 15,000 young performers trying to become part of Big Time Rush.

The slow pace was caused in part by the fact that the people chosen for the group had to be skilled both as actors and singers, had to have the "look" that the producers were seeking, and had to have good on-camera chemistry with one another. Henderson and Maslow had taken part in some of the first auditions for the show, so they faced many months of waiting before they got the good news that they had made the cut. According to one

Big Time Rush came together as a band in 2009, and their TV show debuted in November that year. From left: Kendall Schmidt, Carlos Pena Jr., Logan Henderson, and James Maslow.

source, Pena was initially not very interested in the program but finally decided to send in an audition tape and was offered his part a month later. Schmidt was the last of the four to be cast.

Once the lineup was set, Fellows shaped the characters in the show to create a good fit for the actors. "We didn't want four kids who looked alike," said Marjorie Cohn, a Nickelodeon executive. "Each one brought some of their personality to the table, which in turn inspired (creator) Scott (Fellows)." In the process of building the show, Fellows decided to use the first name of each actor as the name of their TV character. Kendall Schmidt plays Kendall Knight, the leader of Big Time Rush. Logan Henderson portrays Logan Mitchell, the "brain" of the band, who helps the members find their way out of trouble. James Maslow has the part of James Diamond, the egotistical "pretty boy" of the ensemble. And Carlos Pena plays Carlos Garcia, the fun-loving jokester who is always ready to stick up for his friends.

CAREER HIGHLIGHTS

The plot of the "Big Time Rush" TV show concerns four hockey-playing friends from Minnesota who suddenly find themselves in Los Angeles, striving to become a successful boy band singing group. Their adventure begins when Kendall is accidentally discovered by a record producer during a nationwide casting call for singers. Not wishing to leave his friends behind, he talks the producer into allowing Logan, Carlos, and James to become part of the act. Soon, they are in California, where they work to establish themselves in the music industry.

In creating a show for young viewers that centers on pop music, the producers were carrying on a recent trend that had been established with the success of "Hannah Montana" as well as series such as "Jonas" and "Glee!" that debuted just months before the "Big Time Rush" premier. An important part of the marketing plan for such programs is to make the performers successful in two different media: as TV actors and as musical artists. In that way, the TV show helps promote the music, the music helps promote the show, and both—hopefully—make money.

The series was also influenced by several other factors. Fellows was inspired by the pop band the Monkees. The group was created in the late 1960s to star in its own TV series but also became a popular act in its own right, with numerous hit records. In addition, the decision to make Big Time Rush a boy band built on the success of similar groups, including *N Sync and Backstreet Boys, both of which became popular in the 1990s. Of course, the importance of having four cute performers in the band to appeal to young female fans was lost on no one. As Henderson observed in an interview with *Seventeen*, "a lot of our show takes place in or around a pool, so there's not always a lot of clothes on us."

Big Time Success

After months of preparation and production, "Big Time Rush" debuted on Nickelodeon in November 2009 with a special two-hour preview episode and then began its regular schedule in January 2010. It was clear from the outset that the show was going to be a success. When the first January episode was broadcast, it became the highest rated premier for a live-action series in the history of Nickelodeon, drawing 6.8 million viewers, and it has averaged a healthy audience of 3 million per episode ever since.

The group's music proved popular as well. Big Time Rush began releasing singles for digital download shortly after the show went on the air: its first album, *BTR*, came out in October 2010 and went gold, meaning it sold more than 500,000 copies. A Christmas-themed extended play (EP) release, *Holiday Bundle*, followed in late November of that year.

Big Time Rush began working up a stage act for concert performances soon after being formed. Their live shows began in May 2010 but were limited at first to brief promotional appearances. Their later concerts included a series of special appearances at schools around the United States, with the locations being decided by contests in which the students sent in text messages to show their school spirit. In 2011, the band made appearances in Europe and then embarked on its first U.S. tour as a headline act, with the majority of the shows taking place at fairs around the country.

Truth or Fiction?

On the one hand, Big Time Rush is a group of actors playing made-up characters on a TV show. On the other hand, the band puts out real recordings and plays real concerts. That combination can make it difficult for fans to figure out where make-believe ends and reality begins. In many ways, the two are mixed together, and the show's plot mirrors some of the real-life experiences of the actors. This is especially true of the scenes in which the members undertake "pop 101" studies to learn about the music industry. "The first episode is a caricature of what actually happened," said Maslow. "We went through boy band boot camp.... In real life it doesn't have the same over-the-top energy we have on the show but, that's actually our lives."

It would be a mistake, however, to think that the actors are exactly the same as the people they play on the show. "I'm actually completely opposite of my character," explained Pena, who plays the freewheeling Carlos Garcia. "He has fun and does whatever he wants ... [but] I think that out of all four of us in real life, I'm the calmest." Maslow has made a similar point. "We're very different," the actor said, referring to his character. "James Diamond is really motivated by material objects and rewards, money and cars. I am motivated by the opportunity to do this, to perform, and to do it forever." Maslow also noted that "I don't usually care as much as [James Diamond] does about my hair or what I'm wearing."

One of the biggest questions about the blurring of real and imaginary elements concerns the band's music: are they really musicians or are they actors pretending to be musicians? Henderson addressed that issue by explaining that "we are actors making a show, but we are a real band in real life.... The music is all from us. Everything you hear is actually us."

The group does have help in creating its records. They draw on the expertise of a number of well-known producers and songwriters who have worked with such artists as Katy Perry, Kelly Clarkson, and Britney Spears. "All the producers we work with have been extremely cool," noted Schmidt. "I don't think we've come across anyone that hasn't let us have our input. We'll throw a harmony or something in there, and they'll love it so they put it in there." The members have also gotten involved in song-

The band's first album debuted in 2010 and went gold.

writing, contributing to the creation of the song "Oh Yeah." Moreover, several of the members have other outlets for their musical talent, including Schmidt, who is part of the electro-rock duo Heffron Drive.

Keeping It Friendly

On the TV show, the members of Big Time Rush play a group of good friends, which leads to the question of how close the performers are in real life. Since they hailed from different parts of the country, they did not know one another before becoming involved in Big Time Rush. Even though they were suddenly thrown together, there have been few problems. "We got along like brothers from the start and have only grown closer since then," Maslow said. "In the show, as our characters, we have a very high energy and let problems like girls separate us, but in real life in the band we are all much more laid back." The members of the group have admitted that they sometimes argue over small matters, largely as a result of having to spend so much time together, but are united by their desire to succeed. "We've been lucky enough to stay out of fights," said Henderson. "You learn to work stuff out. It's not only sunshine and rainbows. But we have one singular vision of what we want this to be."

Jealousy among musicians can also sink a band in short order. Thus far, the four members seem to receive roughly equal attention in the media, and each has his devoted fans, which has helped to keep things on an even keel. When asked who in the band is the biggest star, Schmidt responded that "it really depends on where we are, state by state. We did a promo tour across the U.S. and every state seems to like one of us more than the others. I would say that it evens out and it's pretty hard to say who is the most popular guy in the band!"

Building the Brand

In spring 2011, Big Time Rush had good news on two fronts. Nickelodeon ordered a third season of the program, which will begin airing in January 2012. In addition, the song "Boyfriend" climbed to No. 72 on the *Billboard* Hot 100 list, making it the band's biggest hit to date and the second time they had placed a song on that elite chart. The popularity of "Boyfriend" was helped along by a music video that included an appearance by hip-hop star Snoop Dogg. This unusual pairing came about, in part, because of one of the rapper's children. "He told us that his daughter was a big fan [of Big Time Rush] and that once he knew that, it was a done deal," explained Pena. "Working with Snoop was just as awesome as anyone might think. He met all of our expectations and more. He's just as cool and relaxed as he appears."

The band members are looking ahead to other projects in addition to the series. There is a possibility that they will star in a made-for-TV movie, and their second full-length album was released in 2011. The performers have also used their fame to help others. They have taken part in fund-raising events for the T. J. Martell Foundation, which seeks cures for cancer, leukemia, and AIDS, and they also appeared in public service announcements for the Presidential Active Lifestyle Award program that promotes exercise.

As they focus on building the popularity of the group, the band members are finding that being pop stars can be exhausting. Between shooting the TV episodes, recording songs, appearing at concerts, and meeting various other commitments, they put in very long hours. "I feel like for us, it's become like a lifestyle," noted Pena. "There's so much going on. I sleep, eat,

Performing at the 2011 Nickelodeon Kids' Choice Awards.

drink, wake up, everything—Big Time Rush." They have also found that, as celebrities, the attention they now attract has forced them to change the way they live. "You give up a piece of stuff you normally would do," explained Henderson. "But that's part of the show. That's why we are entertainers, why we do what we do." And some parts of fame are more pleasant than others. As Maslow said, "It's not that bad of a thing to have thousands of girls chasing you.... Most guys dream of that." Taking the bad with the good, the band members seem to be intent on making the most of their opportunity and to have a great time doing so. "I think this is going to go on for as long as we have fun," said Maslow, "and as long as our fans enjoy it."

HOBBIES AND OTHER INTERESTS

All of the members of Big Time Rush live in the Los Angeles area, with the exception of Maslow, who continues to reside in nearby San Diego but is considering moving to LA. In their spare time, they enjoy a variety of athletic activities. Water sports are especially popular. Maslow and Schmidt are into surfing, Henderson enjoys wake boarding, and Pena is a scuba enthusiast and a certified rescue diver. In addition, Henderson, Maslow, and Schmidt take part in other outdoor activities such as hiking, mountain climbing, and rock climbing, and all three are also avid skateboarders. Pena studies Tae Kwan Do and, like his character, is into hockey, though he plays on roller blades rather than on ice skates.

CREDITS
TV
"Big Time Rush," 2010-

Recordings
BTR, 2010
Holiday Bundle, 2010
Elevate, 2011

FURTHER READING
Periodicals
Boston Herald, Dec. 4, 2010, p.21
New York Daily News, May 24, 2011
New York Times, May 16, 2010, p.ST9

Online Articles
www.billboard.com
  (Billboard, "Big Time Rush Brings Boy Bands Back," Oct. 13, 2010)
www.kidzworld.com
  (Kidzworld, "Big Time Rush Q&A," Apr. 12, 2011; "Carlos Pena Bio," "Kendall Schmidt Bio," "Logan Henderson bio," "James Maslow Bio," "Q&A with James Maslow from BTR," all no date)
www.mtv.com
  (MTV, "Big TimeRush, Full Biography," no date)
www.seventeen.com
  (Seventeen, "Meet the Cast of Big Time Rush," Nov. 23, 2009; "Big Time Rush Answers 17 Questions," no date)

ADDRESS
Big Time Rush
Nickelodeon
4401 Sunset Blvd.
Los Angeles, CA 90027

WEB SITE
www.nick.com/btr
www.btrband.com

Judy Blume 1938-

American Author of Juvenile, Young Adult, and Adult Fiction

Award-Winning Writer of the Best-Selling Books *Are You There God? It's Me, Margaret; Deenie; Blubber; Forever; Tiger Eyes;* the *Fudge* Series; and Many More

BIRTH

Judy Blume (born Judy Sussman) was born on February 12, 1938, in Elizabeth, New Jersey. Her father, Rudolph Sussman, was a dentist. Her mother, Esther Sussman, was a homemaker. She has one older brother, named David.

YOUTH

Blume grew up in Elizabeth, New Jersey. She described herself as a shy, quiet, and anxious child. She was very close to her father, who was known for his warm, outgoing personality. "My father was fun. Everybody loved him…. He taught me about classical music."

As a child, Blume liked going to the movies, listening to the radio, and roller skating. She also liked dancing, singing, and painting. But reading books was her favorite thing to do, and she loved visiting the public library. "I not only liked the pictures and the stories but the feel and the smell of the books themselves. My favorite book was *Madeline* by Ludwig Bemelmans. I loved that book! I loved it so much I hid it in my kitchen toy drawer so my mother wouldn't be able to return it to the library…. I thought the copy I had hidden was the only copy in the whole world. I knew it was wrong to hide the book but there was no way I was going to part with *Madeline*," Blume said. "When I was older I liked the Betsy-Tacy books by Maud Hart Lovelace, and the Oz Books, and Nancy Drew mysteries. But I didn't find real satisfaction in reading until I was older. Because there weren't any books with characters who felt the way I did, who acted the way I did, with whom I could identify. I think I write the kinds of books I would have liked to read when young."

———— **"** ————

"My favorite book was **Madeline** *by Ludwig Bemelmans," Blume recalled. "I loved that book! I loved it so much I hid it in my kitchen toy drawer so my mother wouldn't be able to return it to the library…. I thought the copy I had hidden was the only copy in the whole world. I knew it was wrong to hide the book but there was no way I was going to part with* **Madeline***."*

———— **"** ————

Blume was also very imaginative. "I was a great pretender, always making up stories inside my head … but I never told anyone." Though she loved reading and making up her own stories, Blume did not think about becoming a writer. "When I was growing up, I dreamed about becoming a cowgirl, a detective, a spy, a great actress, or a ballerina," she explained. "I never really thought of writing professionally. I never knew it was a possibility."

During her childhood, Blume and her mother and brother lived for two years in Miami Beach, Florida. They moved there in the hope that the

Blume at a book signing with some of her fans.

warm climate would improve her brother's health. They lived with Blume's grandmother, while her father stayed in New Jersey. "As much as I missed my father, I loved it there. I played outside until dark. I was coming out of my shell. When I got back to New Jersey, I was a changed person, much more social."

As a teenager, Blume struggled with the social and emotional challenges of adolescence. She recalled being confused about her changing body and tumultuous feelings. "My father delivered these little lectures to me, the last one when I was 10, on how babies are made. But questions about what I was feeling, and how my body could feel, I *never* asked my parents," she said. "We kept our feelings to ourselves."

EDUCATION

Blume attended public schools in Elizabeth and Miami Beach. She was a good student and liked English and journalism classes the best. She was an editor of the school newspaper, sang in the chorus, and studied dance. Blume graduated with honors from Battin High School in Elizabeth, New Jersey.

After high school, Blume enrolled in Boston University. Only two weeks into her first year, she was diagnosed with mononucleosis and had to leave school. (Mononucleosis is an infectious disease that can cause fever, aches and pains, and tiredness. In extreme cases, it can take several months to recover from mono.) Blume enrolled in New York University the following year. She earned a bachelor's degree in early childhood education in 1961.

CAREER HIGHLIGHTS

Blume is widely recognized as one of the most popular and successful authors of fiction for children and young adults. Over the course of her long career, she has published more than 25 books. She has written picture books for very young children, chapter books for beginning readers, and novels for middle-grade readers, teens, and adults. Early in her career, Blume gained a reputation for being unafraid to tackle difficult and often taboo subjects like puberty, teenage sex, peer pressure, bullying, sibling rivalry, divorce, illness, and death.

Blume's readers often identify with the characters in her books, who face common issues like clueless parents, annoying siblings, problems at school, and feeling that they don't fit in. As a result, her books have remained extremely popular for generations of readers. Her books have been translated into 31 different languages; more than 80 million copies have been sold around the world; and 14 of her books are on the *Publishers Weekly* list of the all-time best-selling children's books.

Becoming a Writer

Blume described her decision to write books for young people as an accident. "My kids were about three and five and I wanted to do something, but I didn't want to go back to classroom teaching, which is what I was qualified for. I read my kids a lot of books, and I guess I just decided—Well, I could do that too. So when I washed the dinner dishes at night I would do imitation Dr. Seuss rhyming books; and each night by the time I'd done the dishes I would have a whole book. I would send some of them in to publishers and they would be rejected. They were terrible. That's how I started."

After two years of publishers' rejections, Blume enrolled in a graduate course at New York University on writing for young people. She enjoyed the class so much she took it twice. During this time, she published some short stories and finished the first draft of *The One in the Middle Is the Green Kangaroo*. This picture book for young children told the story of a middle child who feels left out of the family. In 1969, *The One in the Middle Is the Green Kangaroo* became Blume's first published book. She remembered her reaction to the news that it was going to be published as "overjoyed, hysterical, unbelieving! I felt like such a celebrity."

Writing for Middle-Grade Readers

Some of Blume's most popular books describe the everyday problems, struggles, and concerns of upper elementary and middle school readers. "The child from 9 to 12 interests me very much," she offered. "And so, those were the years that I like to write about." Her books for this age group focus on the experiences of growing up, including everyday problems and challenges often faced by many readers.

In 1970, Blume published *Iggie's House*, her first book for middle-grade readers. "*Iggie's House* was my first long book. I wrote it week by week, a chapter at a time, while taking a writing course at NYU," she said. *Iggie's House* tells the story of the racial tension surrounding the arrival of the Garbers, the first African-American family to move into an all-white neighborhood. Sixth-grader Winnie quickly becomes friends with the Garber children. But Winnie soon discovers that not everyone in the neighborhood shares her excitement to have new neighbors. Conflict grows as some of the long-time residents try to pressure the Garbers to leave the neighborhood. Winnie struggles to understand why some people seem to hate the Garbers without knowing anything about the family. As events unfold, Winnie learns about the lasting effects of racism on a community.

> **"**
>
> *"Margaret is fiction, but based on the kind of 12-year-old I was," Blume said about the book* **Are You There God? It's Me, Margaret.** *"Sitting down to write Margaret was just remembering what it was like for me, when I was Margaret's age. And you know, yeah for a while in my life I was totally obsessed by breast development and the idea of getting my period. And maybe that's because I was the late bloomer. I was sick of being the smallest in the class and the skinniest."*
>
> **"**

Are You There God? It's Me, Margaret

In 1970, Blume also published *Are You There God? It's Me, Margaret,* the book that launched her reputation for creating frank stories about everyday concerns for kids. The story begins as 12-year-old Margaret's family moves from the city to the suburbs, where she will have to start sixth grade in a new school. Margaret is worried about being accepted in the new

JUDY BLUME

Are You There God? It's Me, Margaret
was Blume's first major novel for young readers.

neighborhood and making new friends. She is preoccupied with her own physical development and getting her first period. Margaret is also struggling with a crisis of religious identity—her mother is Christian and her father is Jewish. Confused about where she belongs, Margaret decides to visit as many different places of worship as she can in order to discover where she fits in.

Are You There God? It's Me, Margaret is regarded as a revolutionary and pioneering book because of its honest handling of the real-life concerns of pre-teen girls. It was first published during a time when books for young readers simply did not take on such taboo subjects as puberty, young girls getting their first period, and buying training bras. The book's realism and honesty won fans among critics and young readers. *Publishers Weekly* noted, "With sensitivity and humor Judy Blume has captured the joys, fears, and uncertainty that surround a young girl approaching adolescence." *New York Times Book Review* critic Dorothy Broderick called *Are You There God? It's Me, Margaret* "a warm, funny, and loving book, one that captures the essence of adolescence." The book became an instant phenomenon among young readers, particularly with girls around Margaret's age. Soon after its publication, Blume began receiving thousands of letters from readers who told her that Margaret's story was just like their own lives. "Margaret brought me my first and most loyal readers. I love her for that," Blume said.

"Margaret is fiction, but based on the kind of 12-year-old I was. Growing up, we did have a club like The PTSs [Pre-Teen Sensations]. And Margaret's interests and concerns were similar to mine. I was small and thin when thin wasn't in. I was a late developer and was anxious to grow like my friends. Margaret was right from my own sixth grade experience. I wanted to tell the truth as I knew it," Blume said. "Sitting down to write Margaret was just remembering what it was like for me, when I was Margaret's age. And you know, yeah for a while in my life I was totally obsessed by breast development and the idea of getting my period. And maybe that's because I was the late bloomer. I was sick of being the smallest in the class and the skinniest."

Are You There God? It's Me, Margaret is also noteworthy because of its direct handling of religious conflict during a time when religion defined social life in many communities. In the book, all of Margaret's friends belong to either a church or a synagogue. Her family doesn't observe any religion, so she belongs to neither. In *The Half-Jewish Book*, Daniel M. Klein and Freke Vuijst write, "The book actually talked frankly about young girls getting their first period! And about their fervent desire to start growing breasts!

So much did these shocking topics dominate discussions of this novel for children between 10 and 12 that hardly anything was said about the title character's perplexity concerning religious identity—a theme that runs through the book as dominantly as matters of maturing bodies do." As Blume observed, "I thought I was writing about organized religion, yet the book has become famous for dealing with puberty. Hardly anyone ever mentions religion or Margaret's very personal relationship with God."

More Books for Middle-Grade Readers

Blume's next book, *Then Again, Maybe I Won't*, was published in 1971. It tells the story of 12-year-old Tony, whose family is suddenly rich from the sale of his dad's new invention. Tony's family moves to a big house in a new neighborhood, and his life is turned upside down. People in the new neighborhood are very different from their old neighbors. His father sells the family's truck because the neighbors make comments about it being parked in their driveway. His mother lets the neighbors call her "Carol" because her real name—Carmella—is too hard to remember. Meanwhile, Tony's grandmother is acting strangely and refusing to come out of her room. As the story unfolds, Tony must face the challenges of his new school, a friend's shoplifting habit, and his own confusion over the sexual dreams he's begun to have almost every night. The book was another sensational success with young readers and critics alike. The *New York Times Book Review* noted, "Judy Blume is on target. Her understanding of young people is sympathetic and psychologically sound; her skill engages the reader in human drama."

In 1972, Blume published *It's Not the End of the World*. In this book, 12-year-old Karen must work through her emotions and navigate changes at home as her parents get divorced. Her parents fight all the time, but Karen thinks she can save their marriage. She tries plan after plan but nothing seems to work—her parents are still splitting up. The situation gets worse when her brother runs away, and again when Karen finds out she's moving to a new place with her mother and siblings. Karen has no choice but to find a way to adjust to it all.

At the time it was published, *It's Not the End of the World* was one of the first books for young readers that focused on the painful topic of divorce and its effect on children. By writing honestly about Karen's experiences, Blume once again gave voice to the fears and concerns of many young readers. *It's Not the End of the World* was praised by *Horn Book Magazine* as "A brisk, first-person narrative [that] believably delineates the bewilderment and anxiety affecting children of about-to-be-divorced parents.

JUDY BLUME

It's Not the End of the World
was one of the first books for young adults to deal with the topic of divorce.

Honest, but not depressing, [the book] explores with precision and sympathy the distinctive personality of a 12-year-old."

Blume's next book, *Deenie,* was published in 1973. This book tells the story of Deenie, a beautiful 13-year-old girl who is on her way to a modeling career at the insistence of her mother. Deenie's life changes forever when she is diagnosed with scoliosis, a condition in which a person's spine is curved from side to side. Deenie learns that she must wear a metal body brace that stretches from her neck to her hips. She will have to wear the brace almost all the time for the next four years. Her ability to move her body will be severely restricted, and her modeling career is over before it even begins. As Deenie learns to accept her situation, her sister and parents must also come to terms with changes in their lives.

According to Blume, Deenie and her story were based on a family she knew. "I met a lively 14-year-old girl with scoliosis. She seemed to be adjusting well to her condition and her brace but her mother was in tears over the situation," Blume confided. "The basic idea for the book came from that meeting. Everything else about the family is fiction. I set the book in the town where I grew up—Elizabeth, New Jersey—and sent Deenie and her friends to my junior high school. I think of the story as one about parental expectations. Deenie's mother says: *Deenie's the beauty, Helen's the brain.* What happens when a parent pigeon-holes her children that way?"

Blubber, published in 1974, focuses on the effects of bullying. The story is told from the point of view of Jill, a fifth-grader who joins several classmates in the merciless and cruel bullying of Linda, an overweight and awkward girl. Jill finds it amusing to come up with new ways to be cruel to Linda. But as the story unfolds, an unexpected turn of events changes things for Jill. As she tries to resolve her own problems at school, Jill learns some important lessons about how to treat others.

Blubber became an immediate success with young readers as well as book reviewers. "Some adults are bothered by the language and the cruelty, but the kids get it. They live it," a reviewer observed in *School Library Journal.* "This is an accurate, entertaining, warts-and-all picture of under-12 social dynamics." Since its publication, the story has remained relevant and continues to affect readers. One fan is Diablo Cody, the author of the screenplays for the movies *Juno* and *Young Adult.* As she commented in *Entertainment Weekly,* "I didn't know whom to relate to as I read *Blubber;* I wanted to believe that I wasn't like Jill, but at the same time, Linda was infuriatingly weak. The book, unlike others written for girls my age, refused to tell me how to feel. And yet, looking back, it's rich with revealing symbolism."

In 1977, Blume published what she describes as her most autobiographical novel. *Starring Sally J. Freedman as Herself* is the story of a 10-year-old girl named Sally who moves with her family from New Jersey to Miami Beach in 1947. American adults are returning to their normal lives after the end of World War II, but Sally has lingering fears about the war. She is convinced that Mr. Zavodsky, a man who lives in her apartment building, is actually Adolph Hitler disguised and in hiding. Sally knows that Hitler wanted to kill all Jewish people, and since she is Jewish, she believes Mr. Zavodsky is trying to poison her. She wonders what to do about Mr. Zavodsky, but at the same time, her year in Miami Beach also includes new friends and experiences, her first crush on a boy, and many other adventures.

"Sally J. Freedman is my most autobiographical character," Blume revealed. "She is the kind of child I was at nine and ten, when I was the most interesting." That connection was noted by the reviewer for *School Library Journal.* "Clearly there is much of Judy Blume in the main character and her affection for Sally shines through. The novel is as pertinent today as it was when first published."

———— **"** ————

"Judy Blume excels at describing how it feels to be invisible," Diablo Cody wrote in **Entertainment Weekly.** *"Every other book written for kids my age was sunny, upbeat, and about as subtle as a bullhorn-wielding camp counselor. Blume's stuff had an edge; it was grimly hilarious and worthy of my attention."*

———— **"** ————

Blume published *Just as Long as We're Together* in 1987. In this book, she tells the story of Rachel and Stephanie, best friends who share everything. Then in seventh grade, Alison moves into the neighborhood. Stephanie wants to include Alison in things that she used to share only with Rachel, and that's when things start to get complicated. *Washington Post Book World* reviewer Beryl Lieff Benderly observed, "While apparently presenting the bright, slangy, surface details of life in an upper-middle class suburban junior high school, she's really plumbing the meaning of honesty, friendship, loyalty, secrecy, individuality, and the painful, puzzling question of what we owe those we love."

In 1993, Blume published *Here's to You, Rachel Robinson* as a companion book to *Just as Long as We're Together.* This book revisits the characters in-

Blume has acknowledged that Sally J. Freedman is her most autobiographical character, based on herself as a child.

troduced in *Just as Long as We're Together*, picking up the story at the end of seventh grade. Perfectionist Rachel is stressed out about school and problems at home. Her older brother Charles has been kicked out of boarding school and is causing all kinds of trouble. Everyone keeps telling Rachel to "lighten up" but that isn't so easy to do. *Here's to You, Rachel Robinson* and *Just as Long as We're Together* continue to appeal to readers, and in 2007 they were republished as a two-book edition titled *BFF**.

As a reviewer noted in *Publisher's Weekly*, "Rachel's incisive, first-person narration easily draws readers into her complicated world as she learns to cope with the pressures brought on by her relentless quest to be the best at everything and by her troubled family situation. Perceptive, strong storytelling ensures that other characters' points of view (particularly Rachel's brother's) can also be discerned. Blume once again demonstrates her ability to shape multidimensional characters and to explore—often through very convincing dialogue—the tangled interactions of believable, complex people."

Books for Younger Readers

Along with her many novels for teens and pre-teens, Blume has also published books for younger readers. Some of her most beloved books are those about Fudge, with stories derived from her own family. According to Blume, "Fudge is based on my son, Larry, when he was a toddler." *Tales of a Fourth Grade Nothing* (1972) is the first of a five-book series about Peter and his little brother Fudge. Everyone else seems to think Fudge is so cute, but to Peter, Fudge is nothing but an annoying little troublemaker. That resonated with *Entertainment Weekly* contributor Diablo Cody, who wrote this about *Tales of a Fourth-Grade Nothing*: "Judy Blume excels at describing how it feels to be invisible.... Every other book written for kids my age was sunny, upbeat, and about as subtle as a bullhorn-wielding camp counselor. Blume's stuff had an edge; it was grimly hilarious and worthy of my attention."

Blume followed that with the second book in the Fudge series, *Otherwise Known As Sheila the Great* (1972). This installment focuses on Peter's nemesis Sheila Tubman as she grapples with the challenges of scary dogs and the dreaded swimming lessons. In *Superfudge* (1980), Peter learns that a new baby will soon join the family. Now Peter will have to deal with many big changes at home in addition to putting up with Fudge. A *New York Times Book Review* called *Superfudge* "a genuinely funny story ... dealing with the kinks and knots of modern family life." Things only get worse for Peter as the story continues with *Fudge-a-Mania* (1990). In this book, Peter learns that his family is going on summer vacation to a cottage right next door to Sheila Tubman's family. *Publishers Weekly* praised *Fudge-a-Mania* as a "fast-pitched, funny novel…. The colorful antics of all members of the two families makes reading these pages a treat." Blume wrote *Double Fudge* (2002), the final book in the Fudge series, at the request of her grandson. Now in seventh grade, Peter must cope with the usual annoyances plus the antics of his eccentric cousins.

In 1984, Blume published *The Pain and the Great One*, a picture book for very young readers. She later developed a new series based on that picture book—chapter books for readers aged five to eight that featured the same characters as those in *The Pain and the Great One*. The books in this series include short stories about the adventures of eight-year-old Abigail and her six-year-old brother Jake. *Soupy Saturdays* was published in 2007, followed by *Cool Zone* and *Going, Going, Gone* in 2008, and *Friend or Fiend?*, the last *Pain and the Great One* book, in 2009. A *Booklist* review noted, "Blume's singular ability to portray the minutiae of a child's everyday life with humor is perfectly complemented by … occasional line drawings that extend the story's charm and fully shaped characters." *Kirkus Reviews* observed, "Once again, Blume shows off her pitch-perfect understanding of childhood anxieties and family dynamics."

Books for Teens

Like her books for middle-grade readers, Blume's novels for teens have remained popular with generations of readers. In *Forever* and *Tiger Eyes*, she explored the coming-of-age stories of teen characters who must navigate through difficult emotional situations. These books focus on mature themes such as teenage sexuality, death, and the grief process. Blume's direct, honest writing about teens struggling with critical life experiences added to her reputation for taking on taboo subjects.

Blume published *Forever,* her ground-breaking and perhaps most controversial book, in 1975. *Forever* is the story of Katherine, a high school senior who falls in love for the first time. Katherine meets Michael at a New Year's Eve party and the two quickly become devoted to each other. As their relationship develops, they make a conscious decision to have sex. When they finally do, they both pledge to love each other "forever." But as time passes and the two are separated for the summer, Katherine begins to see things differently.

Forever caused a stir when it was first published, primarily due to Blume's frank and direct writing about sex between two teenagers. Blume did not

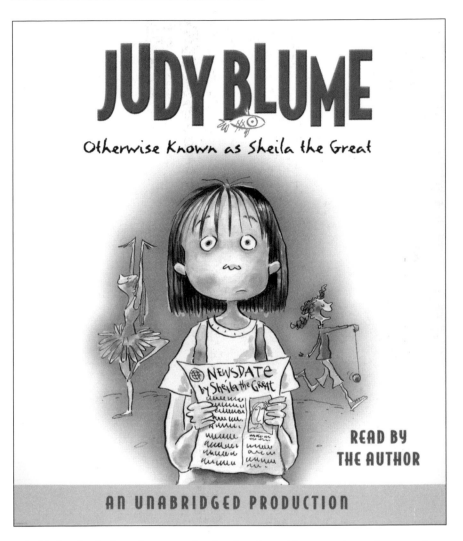

JUDY BLUME

Otherwise Known as Sheila the Great

NEWSDATE
by Sheila the Great

READ BY
THE AUTHOR

AN UNABRIDGED PRODUCTION

The Fudge *books have been popular for decades, with generations of new readers enjoying them in print, as audio books, and as e-books.*

set out to write a controversial book, and was somewhat surprised by the response *Forever* received from some adults. "My 14-year-old daughter was reading a lot of books that equated sex with punishment. She said, 'Couldn't there ever be a book about two nice, smart kids who do it, and nobody has to die?' I thought, yeah, we're not doing anybody any favor by all of this sex linked with punishment. That's really why I wrote it," Blume explained. "I wanted to present another kind of story—one in which two seniors in high school fall in love, decide together to have sex, and act responsibly."

———— " ————

"I believe that censorship grows out of fear, and because fear is contagious, some parents are easily swayed," Blume argued. *"Book banning satisfies their need to feel in control of their children's lives.... They want to believe that if their children don't read about it, their children won't know about it. And if they don't know about it, it won't happen."*

———— " ————

Some adults saw *Forever* as a realistic portrayal of teen romance, what the *New York Times Book Review* called "a convincing account of first love." Others protested that the book was too explicit and that it sent the wrong message to teens. They argued that the book made it acceptable for teens to be sexually active, Fueled by these objections, *Forever* became one of the most banned books in America. Since 1990, *Forever* has consistently been ranked among the top 10 on the American Library Association's list of the 100 Most Challenged Books.

That controversy continues today, as seen in this recent remark by NPR commentator J. Courtney Sullivan. "What shocks me is that in the age of sexting, Bristol Palin, and online porn, *Forever* is still considered controversial. At its core, it's about female teenagers who make responsible birth control choices—who, when they're ready, have sex on their own terms, instead of for the gaze or approval of men. What's so shocking about that?" *Seattle Post-Intelligencer* book reviewer Cecelia Goodnow noted, "*Forever*, a teen novel that was deemed racy in the 1970s, is undeniably frank about a teenage girl's sexual initiation. But there's also something wistfully innocent, from today's vantage point, in a girl who dates and falls in love instead of 'hooking up.' Katherine even introduces her boyfriend Michael to her parents. What a concept, and one that's bound to give contemporary parents a pang for the good old days."

In 1981, Blume published *Tiger Eyes,* another book for teens. *Tiger Eyes* is the story of Davey, a young girl whose father is tragically killed in a robbery. Soon after, Davey goes with her mother and younger brother to visit relatives in New Mexico. Struggling with grief over her father's death, Davey becomes friends with a young man who helps her find the strength to begin to heal. "Although there's a violent crime at the center of the story, *Tiger Eyes* isn't about violence," Blume explained. "It's about the sudden, tragic loss of someone you love. I lost my beloved father suddenly, when I was 21. He died, not as the result of a violent crime, but of a heart attack at

#1 *NEW YORK TIMES* BESTSELLING AUTHOR

judy blume

forever...

Is there a difference between first love and true love?

Forever, *a portrayal of teen romance, is Blume's most controversial work and a frequent target of censorship. The novel is one of five of her books on the American Library Association's list of the 100 most challenged books.*

home. I was with him. I still can't write this without choking up, remembering. Davey's feelings about her father's sudden death were based on mine, though I'm not sure I was aware of it while I was writing the book.

"I lived in Los Alamos, New Mexico, the setting of the book, for two years. My teenaged children went to school there. It wasn't a happy experience.... It allowed me to write about a world I would never have known, about characters I'd never have imagined. Yet I didn't start to write this book until I'd left the town (and the relationship that took me there) and was able to look back. Someday, I hope, Larry will direct the film version." Indeed, Blume worked with her son Lawrence to produce a feature film based on *Tiger Eyes*. The movie premiered at the 2012 International Film Festival in Sonoma, California. *Filmmaker Magazine* movie critic Lauren Wissot praised *Tiger Eyes* as "the rarest of family films, smart and nuanced, with an attention to detail in images that mirrors what is Ms. Blume's strength with words."

Responding to Censorship

During the 1980s, several of Blume's books became the target of organized book-banning campaigns in schools and public libraries across the country. Some adults objected to her use of profanity in her books, the mature themes of some stories, and the straightforward discussions of sexuality. Others found fault with the books' ambiguous or unresolved endings, which left readers to form their own conclusions. Unlike most previously published novels for younger readers, Blume's books did not provide simple or clear solutions to characters' problems. For these reasons, some parents felt that her books were inappropriate and even harmful for young people to read.

Blume disagreed strongly with those who felt her books were wrong for kids. "I believe that censorship grows out of fear, and because fear is contagious, some parents are easily swayed," she argued. "Book banning satisfies their need to feel in control of their children's lives. This fear is often disguised as moral outrage. They want to believe that if their children don't read about it, their children won't know about it. And if they don't know about it, it won't happen."

"I wrote these books a long time ago when there wasn't anything near the censorship that there is now. I wasn't aware at the time that I was writing anything controversial. I just know what these books would have meant to me when I was a kid," Blume explained. "I knew intuitively what kids wanted to know because I remembered what I wanted to know. I think I write about sexuality because it was uppermost in my mind when I was a kid: the need to know, and not knowing how to find out."

Blume is shown here in her tap dance class, one of her many hobbies.

Blume has been a fixture on the American Library Association's list of the most-challenged authors since the early 1980s. From 1982 to 1996, Blume was ranked the number one Most Challenged Author. Five of her books are on the American Library Association's list of the 100 Most Challenged Books (*Forever, Blubber, Deenie, Tiger Eyes,* and *Are You There God? It's Me, Margaret*). The campaigns against her books inspired Blume to work with the National Coalition against Censorship to protect the freedom to read.

In 1996, Blume won the Margaret A. Edwards Award for *Forever* from the Young Adult Library Services Association (YALSA), a division of the American Library Association. For Blume, whose books have won a lot of awards, this one was particularly gratifying. "Winning an award is always an honor but it doesn't always affect your personal or professional life. Winning the Margaret A. Edwards Award has made a profound difference for me, both personally and professionally. By honoring a controversial book like *Forever* YALSA has sent a message—We're not afraid of challenges. We're prepared to defend books that teens want to read. It gives me heft when I speak out in defense of someone else's book. It reminds me that I'm far from alone in the fight for intellectual freedom.... I'm deeply grateful to YALSA for recognizing my work. To have an award that's described as 'honoring writers whose work has helped YA readers understand themselves and their world ...' well, it's enough to make you want to sit down and start another novel."

> "I wasn't aware at the time that I was writing anything controversial. I just know what these books would have meant to me when I was a kid," Blume explained. "I knew intuitively what kids wanted to know because I remembered what I wanted to know. I think I write about sexuality because it was uppermost in my mind when I was a kid: the need to know, and not knowing how to find out.

Some of Blume's books continue to be challenged or restricted in schools and public libraries, but her popularity with readers and critics has remained strong. That's because her work reflects real life, according to Natalie Babbitt, author of the children's classics *Tuck Everlasting* and *The Eyes of the Amaryllis*. "Some parents and librarians have come down hard on Judy Blume for the occasional vulgarities in her stories," Babbitt wrote in the *New York Times Book Review*. "Blume's vulgarities, however, exist in real life and are presented in her books with honesty and full acceptance." Blume has received a host of awards over her long career, including several recent prestigious awards. In 2000, she was honored by the Library of Congress with a Living Legends Award. In 2004, she received the National Book Foundation award for distinguished contributions to American letters. This was the first time that this prestigious award was given to an author of books for children and young adults. In 2011, Blume was recognized by the Smithsonian Associates with the John P. McGovern Award for contributions to the American family.

Blume and her work have been greeted with controversy and book banning as well as popular and critical acclaim. But controversy hasn't changed Blume—and neither have honors and awards. "I don't think people change," she explained. 'Everything around us changes, but the human condition doesn't change. What's important to us remains the same, and that's what links everyone together. It's that inside stuff: the need for love and acceptance, and getting to know yourself and your place in the world."

MARRIAGE AND FAMILY

In 1959, Blume married her first husband, John Blume. They had two children, a daughter named Randy Lee, born in 1961, and a son named Lawrence Andrew, born in 1963. The couple divorced in 1975. In 1976, Blume married Thomas Kitchens, and the marriage ended in divorce in 1979. In 1987, Blume married George Cooper, with whom she has a step-daughter named Amanda.

Blume currently lives with her husband George. They spend most of the year in Key West, Florida, and also own homes in New York City and Martha's Vineyard, an island off the coast of Massachusetts.

HOBBIES AND OTHER INTERESTS

Blume founded the non-profit KIDS Fund in 1981. KIDS Fund is an organization that contributes thousands of dollars each year to programs that help children talk with their parents. In her spare time, Blume enjoys going to the movies, seeing plays, reading, dancing, kayaking, bicycling, needlepoint, and baseball. She is a fan of the New York Mets.

SELECTED WRITINGS

For Young Readers

The One in the Middle Is the Green Kangaroo, 1969
Freckle Juice, 1971
Tales of a Fourth Grade Nothing, 1972
Otherwise Known as Sheila the Great, 1972
Superfudge, 1980
The Pain and the Great One, 1984
Fudge-a-Mania, 1990
Double Fudge, 2002

Soupy Saturdays with the Pain and the Great One, 2007
Cool Zone with the Pain and the Great One, 2008
Going, Going, Gone! With the Pain and the Great One, 2008
Friend or Fiend? With the Pain and the Great One, 2009

For Middle-Grade Readers

Iggie's House, 1970
Are You There God? It's Me, Margaret, 1970
Then Again, Maybe I Won't, 1971
It's Not the End of the World, 1972
Deenie, 1973
Blubber, 1974
Starring Sally J. Freedman as Herself, 1977
Just as Long as We're Together, 1987
Here's to You, Rachel Robinson, 1993
BFF*, 2007 (includes *Just as Long as We're Together* and *Here's to You, Rachel Robinson*)

For Teens

Forever, 1975
Tiger Eyes, 1981

For Adults

Wifey, 1978
Smart Women, 1983
Summer Sisters, 1998

HONORS AND AWARDS

Outstanding Book of the Year (*New York Times*): 1970, for *Are You There God? It's Me, Margaret*; 1974, for *Blubber*
Eleanor Roosevelt Humanitarian Awards: 1983
Children's Choice Awards (International Reading Association and Children's Book Council): 1981, for *Superfudge*; 1985, for *The Pain and the Great One*
Best Books for Young Adults (*School Library Journal*): 1981, for *Tiger Eyes*
Books for the Teen Age (New York Public Library): 1982, for *Tiger Eyes*
Dorothy Canfield Fisher Children's Book Award: 1983, for *Tiger Eyes*
National Hero Awards (Big Brothers/Big Sisters): 1992
Parents' Choice Awards (Parents' Choice Foundation): 1993, for *Here's to You, Rachel Robinson*
Margaret A. Edwards Awards for Outstanding Literature for Young Adults (YALSA-American Library Association): 1996, for *Forever*
Living Legends Award (Library of Congress): 2000

Medal for Distinguished Contribution to American Letters (National Book Foundation): 2004

All-Time 100 Novels List (Time magazine): 2005, for *Are You There God? It's Me, Margaret*

John P. McGovern Award (Smithsonian Associates): 2011, for contributions to the American family

FURTHER READING

Periodicals

Cosmo Girl, June 2002

Entertainment Weekly, Oct. 3, 2008, p.32

Instructor, May/June 2005, pg.37

New York Times, Nov. 16, 1997; Nov. 14, 2004, p.L1

Newsweek, June 1990

School Library Journal, June 1996, p.24

Seattle Post-Intelligencer, Sep. 13, 2007

Seventeen, Oct. 2007

Smithsonian, Jan. 2012

Online Articles

bookclubs.barnesandnoble.com/t5/The-NOOK-Blog/Guest-Author-Judy-Blume/ba-p/1225280
   (Barnes and Noble, "Guest Author: Judy Blume," Dec. 7, 2011)

www.januarymagazine.com/profiles/blume.html
   (January Magazine, "Judy Blume," no date)

www.kindlepost.com/2012/01/guest-blogger-judy-blume-.html
   (Kindle Daily Post, "Guest Blogger: Judy Blume," Jan. 27, 2012)

www.npr.org/2011/11/28/142859819/judy-blume-banned-often-but-widely-beloved
   (NPR, "Judy Blume: Often Banned, But Widely Beloved," Nov. 28, 2011)

www.randomhouse.com/boldtype/0698/blume/interview.html
   (Random House, "Alison Dorfman Interviews Judy Blume," no date)

www.scholastic.com/teachers/article/judy-blume-interview-transcript
   (Scholastic, "Judy Blume Interview Transcript," no date)

ADDRESS

Judy Blume
Children's Publicity
1745 Broadway
New York, NY 10019

WEB SITE

www.judyblume.com

Cheryl Burke 1984-

American Dancer and Choreographer
First Professional Dancer to Win Back-to-Back
"Dancing with the Stars" Championships

BIRTH

Stephanie Cheryl Burke was born on May 3, 1984, in Atherton, California. Her mother, Sherri Bautista Burke, was born in the Philippines and worked as a nurse before opening her own medical staffing agency. Her father, Stephen Burke, is an attorney. They divorced before she was one year old, and her mother remarried in 1993. Burke has an older stepsister and a younger half-sister.

———— " ————

*"I shared the trauma of
being molested as a child
because I wanted other
victims to know that it's okay
to feel sad and angry and
confused," Burke revealed.*

———— " ————

Burke switched the order of her first and middle names in a legal name change when she was in the first grade. She explained, "My parents thought it would be cute to give me names that were similar to theirs but unique enough to be my own.... But for a long time, they couldn't decide if I was more of a Stephanie or a Cheryl. Finally, when I was in first grade, I made the decision for them. 'From now on I want to be Cheryl. No more Stephanie,' I declared ... and that's who I've been ever since."

YOUTH

Burke grew up in Atherton, California. She was an extremely shy child who did not begin speaking until she was much older than the typical age for this milestone. In an attempt to draw her out of her shell, her mother enrolled her in ballet lessons when she was four years old. She was soon dancing in performances throughout the San Francisco Bay area.

When Burke was five years old, she was molested by a neighborhood handyman that her mother and stepfather had hired to do some work at their home. The man had also molested other children in the neighborhood and was arrested once the children's parents discovered the abuse. When she was in kindergarten, Burke testified against the man at his court trial. Her statements helped to send him to prison.

Though the incident happened long ago, it is still difficult for Burke to talk about that time of her life. But she feels that it is important for her to tell her story, and she wrote about it in her autobiography *Dancing Lessons*. "I shared the trauma of being molested as a child because I wanted other victims to know that it's okay to feel sad and angry and confused," she revealed. "It's not easy, nor is healing an overnight process. But I want people to know that it is possible to move beyond those feelings and begin to win back your life from those memories. I'm living proof of that.

"I've thought a lot about that time in my life. I've been able to look back with a clearer understanding of what happened and how it affected many years of my life," Burke wrote. "I understand that many people have a very difficult time overcoming an experience like this. It's not easy. It takes time to heal. Although I am one of countless victims of that kind of crime, I made a concerted choice several years ago that I would not let it stop me from living my life—the life that I deserve. No longer would I allow this experience to control me." Burke also wrote about how she learned to deal with it. "I have learned that the molestation was not my fault. I did nothing wrong. As a child, it was normal for me to trust a grown-up," she explained. "Letting go of the resentment has been a gradual process, but it's very empowering. Every time I talk about it, it makes me stronger and more aware of what has made me who I am."

Discovering Ballroom Dance

Burke continued studying ballet throughout her childhood. She liked dancing, but as she grew up she began to realize that ballet might not be right for her. Her parents enjoyed ballroom dancing as a hobby, and she went to see a local dance competition with her mother. "I went to a competition and saw the costumes, heard the music, and loved that the dancers had partners," she recalled. That competition changed Burke's opinion of ballroom dancing. Before that, she had thought it was only for "old people" since her parents liked it. She began to take ballroom dance lessons when she was 12 years old.

By the time Burke was 13 years old, she was participating in as many ballroom dance competitions as she could. She travelled extensively and entered competitions all over the world. Once she became serious about ballroom dancing, her family all became more interested in the hobby. Her parents converted their home's living room into a small dance studio, and everyone spent most of their free time dancing there. Having a dance space at home also made it easier and more convenient for Burke to practice. Instead of driving back and forth to a dance studio in a nearby town, she could practice any time right in her own home.

"It's not easy, nor is healing an overnight process. But I want people to know that it is possible to move beyond those feelings and begin to win back your life from those memories. I'm living proof of that."

When she was a teenager, Burke and some of her friends decided they wanted to go to London, England, for the summer, to train and enter competitions. Her mother agreed to the plan, but said that she would have to raise part of the money to pay for the trip herself. Burke and her friends set to work immediately. They organized a dance camp for local kids and also danced for tips as street performers in San Francisco's Union Square. They raised enough money to pay for their air fare and to rent rooms in a small house in London.

EDUCATION

Although Burke spent a lot of time travelling to dance competitions while she was in high school, she was able to complete her studies on time. She graduated from Menlo-Atherton High School in 2002. After graduation, she wanted to focus on dancing full time, but her mother insisted that she go to college. Burke attended a local community college for one year, but she ended up leaving school to become a professional ballroom dancer.

CAREER HIGHLIGHTS

As a professional ballroom dancer, Burke spent her time in dance lessons, rehearsals, and competitions. She continued to travel all over the world to enter competitions and became known for her bubbly personality, creative choreography, and dazzling costumes. Though she competed in many forms of ballroom dance, her specialty was Latin dances. "For me, they are the most fun. They're energetic and the music and costumes are great."

In 2005, when she was 20 years old, Burke had her best year of competition ever. She won the San Francisco Open Latin Competition, the Ohio Star Ball Rising Star Competition, and the World Cup Professional Rising Star Latin Championship. She also won several other championships in the United States and the United Kingdom.

"Dancing With the Stars"

Burke's competition performances soon attracted the attention of talent scouts for a new reality competition show called "Dancing with the Stars." The new show was based on a British television show that paired star athletes, actors, musicians, and other public figures with professional dancers in a weekly competition. When she was 21 years old, Burke was invited to join the show's cast of professional dancers.

Burke's shy personality made her hesitant to consider the offer at first. "My immediate reaction was to turn them down because of my strong fear of cameras. But the more I thought about it, the more I figured, 'Why not? Give it a chance, at least, before you turn them down,'" she said. "I know it sounds unbelievable to say that I almost turned down the opportunity to star as a professional dancer on the hit reality dance show, but that's the truth." It was a decision that changed her life.

Dressed to dance.

Burke practicing with her season 2 partner, Drew Lachey. Lengthy rehearsals have been an important part of "Dancing with the Stars."

On "Dancing with the Stars," competition focuses on the ten basic styles of ballroom dance. In the Standards category, competitors perform the waltz, tango, Viennese waltz, slow fox-trot, and quick-step. The Latin category includes cha-cha, samba, rumba, paso doble, and jive. The show produces two seasons of competition each year. To prepare for each season, professional dancers and their celebrity partners begin training for four hours each day. As the competition goes on, training time increases to eight to ten hours each day, seven days a week. Burke explained that the grueling schedule is necessary for competitors to perform at their best. "Practice makes perfect. It takes a lot of time and energy to get it right and to go out there and perform. On the show you see celebrities who have no dance experience learn a dance in four or five days. They put in the time, and you see them exceed and improve every day. It all has to do with devotion and motivation."

Burke joined "Dancing with the Stars" for its second season, in 2006, and she quickly became a favorite of the TV viewing audience. She enjoyed choreographing the dances and teaching the moves to her partner, and she was also at home when performing the dances during the live competition shows. But Burke had trouble adjusting to one aspect of being a part of a hit TV show. "I was terrified of the cameras. The fame was new to me, and the whole idea of talking to the press was the scariest thing I could imagine, because I've always been a very shy and private person."

Burke credits her first celebrity partner, singer Drew Lachey, with helping her overcome some of her fears. "'Just focus on me,' Drew said. 'When you're talking to me, look at me and ignore the crew.' So I did," Burke wrote in her autobiography. "Thanks to Drew's constant efforts at drawing me out of my shell, I was able to let my personality start to emerge while the camera crews were there."

———— " ————

"I do have curves—women are supposed to have curves. I always have, and I always will. I will never be the skeletal supermodel of magazines and runways and, frankly, I'm a lot healthier because of it. When the gossip magazines fixated on my weight, I eventually moved past being hurt just for myself.... I started to get angry for every 15-year-old girl who wants to try out for the cheerleading squad but is afraid because she worries she won't look good in the uniform."

———— " ————

Though Burke wasn't always sure of herself in front of the camera, she was completely confident on the dance floor. Burke won the "Dancing with the Stars" championship in her first two seasons on the show. In season two, she shared the honors with Drew Lachey. In season three, former NFL football player Emmitt Smith was her championship-winning partner.

This achievement made Burke the first professional dancer to win two championships and the first to win two in a row. These wins meant that she was starting to be recognized outside the small community of professional ballroom dancers. "It was a lot of fun but overwhelming at times, too, as I skyrocketed from being 'just a dancer' to 'that girl on "Dancing with the Stars."'" Burke began to get requests for more interviews and was a featured guest star on "The Suite Life of Zack and Cody."

Dealing with Criticism

Burke's success on "Dancing with the Stars" helped to raise the status of professional ballroom dancers and also attracted more interest in Burke herself. As she became more well-known, she often found herself being followed by paparazzi photographers. Stories about her began to appear in tabloid newspapers and gossip magazines. She had a hard time dealing with the unwanted attention, especially after an incident in 2008 when a tabloid published photos of her wearing a bikini. The photos set off a flurry of public commentary about her weight and her figure. People said that Burke was fat and began to speculate that she might even be pregnant.

> "
>
> *"I wanted to learn again and be a student, instead of always teaching.... I miss learning and sweating. I miss just going home and thinking about my dance and being inspired again, being coached. I love to teach, but I still feel like I have so much more to learn."*
>
> "

Burke took the comments hard. "It messed me up," she said. "I took the bloggers' criticism and negative comments personally, and I had a hard time maintaining a positive attitude." But she was also angry that people felt it was acceptable to make such comments. "No sane person thinks that a woman who is size four is overweight," she asserted. "I do have curves—women are supposed to have curves. I always have, and I always will. I will never be the skeletal supermodel of magazines and runways and, frankly, I'm a lot healthier because of it. When the gossip magazines fixated on my weight, I eventually moved past being hurt just for myself and became indignant for every woman out there who is perfectly normal yet fears that her body isn't beautiful. I started to get angry for every 15-year-old girl who wants to try out for the cheerleading squad but is afraid because she worries she won't look good in the uniform.

"I think a lot of young women struggle with taking compliments well. We find it easier to receive—and believe—criticism than a compliment. But that shouldn't be the case," Burke argued. "We should learn how to shake off negative comments that are intended to bruise our minds and instead allow ourselves to accept genuine compliments and constructive criticism. Compliments are a form of congratulations, celebrating something special about you," she said. "I just want everyone to know that, you know, you're beautiful in your own skin. You do not have to be anorexic or a size zero to feel great about yourself."

Branching Out

Burke's success on "Dancing with the Stars" has provided her with many opportunities to grow both personally and professionally. "The doors that have opened for me because of "Dancing with the Stars" and the perspective I have gained completely changed the way I view my life, my art, and my reason for dancing," she shared. "These opportunities have given me a new sense of strength and purpose that I believe can help to encourage other people to overcome the past, relate in new ways to the present, and reach for the future. It's made it possible to tell my story. All the hard things? You can move on from them. It's your choice."

Burke has toured the country with "Dancing with the Stars" and performed for sold-out crowds in many different cities. In 2006, her work on "Dancing with the Stars" was recognized with Emmy award nominations for Outstanding Choreography for Paso Doble and Outstanding Choreography for Freestyle. She received the Filipino/American Library's Role Model Award in 2007 and the Asian Excellence Viewer's Choice Award for Favorite TV Personality in 2008. Burke has also produced a dance exercise DVD and developed her own line of clothing for FitCouture.com. Demand was so high for her active wear that the retailer's web site crashed on the first day that the clothing was available for purchase.

At the request of her fans and with her mother's encouragement, Burke also achieved her lifelong dream of opening her own dance studio. The first Cheryl Burke Dance location opened in California in 2008. "I've wanted to open my own school since I was a little girl, and I got a lot of emails from fans asking when I would. They want to learn how to dance! And I really want to get young people into it, too, not just adults. It's fun, and kids can do it as a hobby or seriously," Burke explained. "I really want to promote physical fitness. And, you know, dancing is a way of life for me. And it's a great way to exercise."

Burke's "Dancing with the Stars" experience helped her to eventually overcome her fear of being on camera. In 2009, she became a correspondent reporter for the E! cable TV network and the show "Extra" and co-hosted the TV broadcast of the Citrus Bowl Parade in Orlando, Florida. In

*Burke performing with Rob Kardashian during the finals of season 13,
when they came in second.*

2010, her choreography was featured in the movie *Toy Story 3*. She and "Dancing with the Stars" co-star Tony Dovolani choreographed the Latin dance number performed by characters Buzz Lightyear and Cowgirl Jessie in the movie. For this project, Burke and Dovolani performed the dance for the film's design crew, who used their moves to create the animation for Buzz and Jessie.

Burke achieved another of her lifelong dreams when she joined the *Forever Tango* touring stage show in 2010. *Forever Tango* showcases the Argentinian tango dance style and features performances by individual couples and groups. The show has been in production off and on since 1994. "Since I was a little girl, I've been a huge fan," she commented. "When they were here in San Francisco performing, I remember my mom and dad taking me to their performance and I fell in love with it right away. It's part of how I got started into ballroom dancing, even though Argentine tango and ballroom dancing are completely separate styles." To prepare for *Forever Tango*, Burke spent three weeks studying the dance in Argentina. "On ["Dancing with the Stars"] they added the Argentine tango a few seasons ago, and ever since I've been really interested in learning how to dance it properly. None of us ballroom dancers really know the actual technique of it. And I wanted to be re-inspired—I wanted to learn again and be a student, instead of always teaching…. I miss learning and sweating. I miss just going home and thinking about my dance and being inspired again, being coached. I love to teach, but I still feel like I have so much more to learn."

Throughout all of these new opportunities, Burke has continued competing on "Dancing with the Stars." Since partnering with Drew Lachey in season two and Emmitt Smith in season three, she has also danced with actor Ian Ziering; singer Wayne Newton; actor Cristián de la Fuente; track and field sprinter Maurice Greene; actor Gilles Marini; political leader Tom DeLay; football player Chad Ochocinco; basketball player Rick Fox; WWE wrestler Chris Jericho; reality TV star Rob Kardashian; and actor William Levy.

After finding success in her dream field, Burke offers these words of advice. "You have to have a passion for what you do," she suggested. "If you don't, it won't work. Set goals in life. Follow your dreams and love what you do. Go for it 100 percent. Don't look back; keep looking forward."

HOME AND FAMILY
Burke has a home in the Hollywood Hills area of Los Angeles, California.

SELECTED CREDITS
"Dancing With the Stars," 2006- (TV show)
Dancing with the Stars: Latin Cardio Dance, 2008 (exercise DVD)
Forever Tango, 2010-2011 (stage show)
Dancing Lessons, 2011 (autobiography)

HONORS AND AWARDS
World Cup Professional Rising Star Latin Champion: 2005
San Francisco Open Latin Champion: 2005

Ohio Star Ball Rising Star Champion: 2005
Dancing with the Stars Championship: 2006 (season two)
Dancing with the Stars Championship: 2006 (season three)
Role Model Award (Filipino/American Library): 2007
Viewer's Choice Award (Asian Excellence Award): 2008, for Favorite TV
    Personality

FURTHER READING

Books

Burke, Cheryl. *Dancing Lessons*, 2011

Periodicals

Dance Magazine, Mar. 2008
Dance Spirit, Sep. 2008, p.140
Los Angeles Magazine, Oct. 2007, p.40
People, Oct. 20, 2008; Feb. 7, 2011
San Francisco Chronicle, Dec. 30, 2010, p.F1
USA Today, Mar. 26, 2007, p.D1; Oct. 16, 2007, p.D3

Online Articles

www.dancespirit.com
    (Dance Spirit, "Dancing with the Stars' Cheryl Burke Is Back," Sep. 1,
    2006; "A Q&A with Cheryl Burke from Dancing with the Stars," Sep. 21,
    2008)

ADDRESS

Cheryl Burke
"Dancing with the Stars"
CBS Television City
7800 Beverly Blvd., Bungalow #1
Los Angeles, CA 90036

WEB SITES

www.strictlycheryl.com
abc.go.com/shows/dancing-with-the-stars/bios

Chris Daughtry 1979-

American Rock Musician
Lead Singer of the Group Daughtry
Finalist on "American Idol"

Editor's Note: Daughtry is the leader of the rock group of the same name, so using that name can be confusing. Throughout this article, the name "Chris" is used to refer to the individual, and the name "Daughtry" is used to refer to the group as a whole.

BIRTH

Christopher Adam Daughtry was born on December 26, 1979, in Roanoke Rapids, North Carolina, just south of the Virginia border. His parents, Pete and Sandra Daughtry, raised Chris and his older brother, Kenneth, in Lasker, North Carolina.

YOUTH

Chris was raised in the backwoods of North Carolina. From the time he was a toddler, he grew up picking potatoes and corn on the family farm, where his family kept chickens, goats, ducks, and hunting dogs. As a child, he was interested in martial arts and dreamed of starring in action movies like Jean-Claude Van Damme. He was also a fan of professional wrestling, which he would watch on television with his dad. In addition, he was an avid reader of comic books and showed some artistic talent. He spent his spare time drawing in hopes of becoming a comic book artist.

When Chris was 14, the Daughtry family moved to Lake Monticello, Virginia. As a teenager, he enjoyed a range of music. He started listening to 1990s grunge and rock bands like Pearl Jam, Alice in Chains, Soundgarden, Stone Temple Pilots, and Live. He also admired rap music by Public Enemy, N.W.A., and the Beastie Boys and enjoyed heavy metal music by Guns n' Roses and Skid Row. At age 16 he learned to play the guitar and started to take his singing voice seriously, performing in various rock bands during his high school years.

EDUCATION

Chris attended Fluvanna County High School in Palmyra, Virginia, graduating in 1998. He found his calling as a performer in school productions of the musicals *The Wiz* and *Peter Pan*. His first live solo performance was at his grandfather's bar, where he sang "Achy Breaky Heart" for a crowd of locals. During his junior year, his math teacher offered extra credit to any student who wrote something math-related—such as a poem—and shared it with the class. Chris and his friend Rob Nesbit wrote and performed a math song; it was such a hit that they were asked to perform it for other math classes. Nesbit told the *Fluvanna Review* that he taught Chris "some chords and how to put songs together" on the guitar. Soon after, Chris formed the band Cadence, for which he sang lead vocals and played rhythm guitar. The band recorded a very rare album entitled *All Eyes on You* in 1999 and performed live on a local college radio station.

FIRST JOBS

Chris held several jobs as a teenager. He started working with his father in a sawmill at age 14 and later worked at McDonald's, Lowe's Home Improvement, and an appliance rental center. After high school, he moved to

McLeansville, North Carolina, and got a job behind the service desk at a Honda dealership in Greensboro. "I got on my boss's nerves a lot. I'd always be in my own head, trying to write a song," he remembered. At that time, he was the front man for his band, Absent Element, which recorded an album, *Uprooted,* in 2005. The CD includes the tracks "Conviction" and "Breakdown," which the singer would later combine and re-record as "Breakdown" on his self-titled debut album.

Absent Element performed regularly at several local bars. Despite these weekend gigs, Chris's day job and family commitments prevented him from taking the conventional route to a career in the music business. "I couldn't just hop in a van and play places until you get noticed," he explained. "I didn't have that luxury. It was just, 'I'm gonna play here, and hopefully somebody that means something will come along and snag me up.' But that never happened, so it was, 'All right, I gotta do it on TV instead.'" In 2005 he auditioned for "Rock Star: INXS"—a reality-show competition to discover a new lead singer for the Australian rock band INXS—but did not advance to the televised round.

> "
>
> *As a struggling musician, Chris couldn't afford to quit his day job. "I couldn't just hop in a van and play places until you get noticed," he explained. "I didn't have that luxury. It was just, 'I'm gonna play here, and hopefully somebody that means something will come along and snag me up.'"*
>
> "

CAREER HIGHLIGHTS

"American Idol"

In winter 2006 Chris and approximately 9,000 other contestants auditioned for the fifth season of the Fox television talent show "American Idol" in Denver, Colorado. "I thought to myself, 'How am I gonna stand out?'" he recalled. He passed the preliminary round in front of the show's producers and then was invited to sing for a minute or so in front of the judges, Paula Abdul, Simon Cowell, and Randy Jackson. His goal at that stage was to wow the judges and earn a ticket to Hollywood to appear on the show. Chris chose to sing "The Letter," written by country musician Wayne Carson Thompson. The song has been performed by several artists, including British rock singer Joe Cocker, upon whose rendition Chris based his performance. Jackson immediately liked him, complimenting his voice and his stylistic choices. Cowell, however, criticized him for rushing

Chris with the cast of "American Idol," season five.

the song and showing a lack of charisma. "I'm not sure I'm looking at a standalone star," he observed, voting against Chris. Abdul agreed with Jackson: "I heard talent, and I saw nerves. But I like you." With the support of Abdul and Jackson, Chris advanced to the televised competition. He left the audition room with a golden ticket to Hollywood tucked under his cowboy hat.

Season Five of "American Idol" began in February 2006, and Chris quickly became a fan favorite. He performed Bon Jovi's "Dead or Alive" for his first national TV appearance and songs by the rock bands Fuel and Seether the following two weeks. "He was different than the typical 'Idol' style," said executive producer Ken Warwick in *Entertainment Weekly*. "Chris had attitude and credibility. He didn't sell himself out during the show." Later in the competition, he performed a hard rock version of Johnny Cash's "Walk the Line" as well as hits by Stevie Wonder, Louis Armstrong, Bryan Adams, and Styx. As a reviewer said in *Entertainment Weekly*, "The bald boy can tackle the perilous theme nights—from Stevie Wonder to country—and still give performances that are undeniably his.... Chris gives us what we are hungry for." The judges and audience embraced him, and the tabloid press predicted he would win the competition based on both talent and his physical resemblance to action film star Vin Diesel. As Chuck Arnold and Carrie Borzillo-Vrenna stated in *People*, "His cred as a bona-fide rocker—plus that whole Vin Diesel thing—many give him the best shot at true idoldom."

After competing for 13 weeks, Chris was one of four singers still standing in the contest that *Entertainment Weekly* deemed "the biggest 'Idol' (season) ever." Indeed, Season Five lacked a clear frontrunner, featuring such gifted performers as Elliott Yamin, Katharine McPhee, Kellie Pickler, and Taylor Hicks. During the semi-finals on May 9, 2006, Chris sang the Elvis Presley hits "Suspicious Minds" and "A Little Less Conversation," drawing rave reviews from the judges. "See ya in the finals," Abdul hinted after his stirring performances. The next night, however, "American Idol" host Ryan Seacrest delivered the news that shocked the contestants, judges, and viewers. "A lot of people predicted, Chris, that you could be the next 'American Idol,'" Seacrest announced. "Chris, you are going home tonight. This journey ends."

> *"He was different than the typical 'Idol' style," said executive producer Ken Warwick. "Chris had attitude and credibility. He didn't sell himself out during the show."*

Chris finished the "American Idol" competition in fourth place. After the surprising revelation that viewers had voted him off the show, several audience members booed the decision. His fans were in tears, as was one of the judges. "Randy was pretty much saying, 'Don't worry about it, you're going to be fine.' Paula was crying too much to say anything," Chris recalled. "And Simon was shocked. He said he didn't see this coming and wished me the best of luck and totally believes in me." Although Chris has admitted that it was a gut-wrenching, unexpected moment, he did not dwell on his loss for long. "It didn't feel good but I try to look at the positive and see the bigger picture and say, 'You know what? Maybe this is the right thing. Maybe this is just a big opportunity for many doors to open,'" he said.

Chris did not have to wait long for the next opportunity to present itself. Hours after he was eliminated from "American Idol," he got a surprising proposal: members of the band Fuel made a pitch to him on the TV show "Extra" and offered him a job as their lead singer. During the second week of "American Idol," Chris had sung a rendition of the Fuel song "Hemorrhage (In My Hands)" that caught the band's attention and renewed the public's interest in the group. Although Chris was flattered by the offer and seriously considered it, he ultimately decided to turn it down in favor of

Performing live on "American Idol," March 2006.

launching a solo career. "Deep down, I knew it wasn't for me," he admitted. "I wasn't comfortable being the guy who replaced the other guy or being limited to their success. I wanted to create my own. If I failed, I could blame myself." The media has often asked him whether he regrets any of the choices he made on "American Idol," to which he has responded,

"Nothing on the show hurt my confidence.... That's one reason I did so well. I didn't let them sway me or change me in any way. I think that's the key to anything in life: You have to know who you are."

Daughtry

Chris was soon glad he trusted his instincts, when he was asked to perform the original song "Home" for legendary record producer Clive Davis in his office at 19 Recordings/RCA Records. "He was the first Idol that I'd ever met who had material that he had written," Davis said in *Entertainment Weekly.* "That was compelling." In July 2006 Chris signed a contract with Davis's record label and began working on material for his debut album in collaboration with such A-list songwriters as Rob Thomas of Matchbox Twenty, Mitch Allan of SR-71, and Carl Bell of Fuel. Meanwhile, his rendition of Bon Jovi's hit "Wanted Dead or Alive" was released as a single, debuting at No. 43 on *Billboard*'s Hot 100 list and No. 16 on its Hot Digital Tracks list.

The self-titled debut *Daughtry* was released in November 2006, just six months after he left "American Idol." Featuring 12 tracks, all but two of which Chris had a hand in writing, *Daughtry* became the fastest-selling rock debut album in Nielsen SoundScan history. *Billboard* magazine declared it the top-selling album of 2007 with almost 2.3 million copies sold. Moreover, the album reached No. 1 on the *Billboard* Top 200 chart and spawned three No. 1 singles: "It's Not Over," "Home," and "Feels Like Tonight." By 2008 *Daughtry* had sold more than four million copies.

Despite impressive sales figures, critical reviews of Daughtry were mixed. Although most commentators praised Chris's voice and songwriting abilities, some characterized the album as monotonous and generic. For example, critic Henry Goldblatt deemed the song "It's Not Over" "ridiculously catchy" in *Entertainment Weekly,* describing Chris's voice as "a confident sultry growl that's not pitch-perfect, but pretty close." Later in the review, however, he lamented the album's lack of variety. Likewise, commentator Stephen Thomas Erlewine in *All Music Guide* extolled Chris's vocal range and the sensitivity in his singing, describing his songs as "sturdier than most post-grunge, with big, anthemic hooks on the choruses." Chris received some recognition at the 2007 American Music Awards where he received three awards, for favorite contemporary artist, favorite breakthrough new artist, and favorite pop/rock album. "We were certainly new to the industry, but getting recognized for your hard work is a pretty big deal," he acknowledged. The following month he was nominated for four Grammy awards.

Chris had recorded his debut album using studio musicians. But as he prepared to go out on tour to promote the album, he held auditions for permanent band members. The group, which goes by the name Daughtry, features Josh Steely and Brian Craddock on guitar, Josh Paul on bass, and Robin Diaz on drums (original guitarist Jeremy Brady and drummer Joey Barnes are no longer in the band). "We're just normal guys who are doing what we've always wanted to do and what we love to do," Chris affirmed. Asked why he named the band Daughtry, he joked, "Because I'm conceited. Just kidding. It was more about name recognition than anything else." The band has been performing live all over the world since 2007, embarking on a sold-out tour with Bon Jovi in 2008. Opening for Bon Jovi was a turning point for Chris. "At the end of the tour Jon did this speech in Atlanta ... and at the end of it he says, 'This man will never open for another band again.' To get that respect from someone who has obviously stayed relevant for that amount of time? It felt really good."

Leave This Town

While on the road, Chris and the band began working on songs for the next Daughtry record. The resulting album, *Leave This Town,* was released in July 2009. In addition to powerful anthems, quiet ballads, and emotional mid-tempo tracks, the album includes a country-influenced tune, "Tennessee Line," which features harmonies by country music sensation Vince Gill. The album's title comes from a line in the song "September," a bittersweet ballad inspired by Chris's childhood experiences growing up with his brother in small-town North Carolina. The anthem "No Surprise" became the group's fourth No. 1 single.

Chris worked with band members Steely and Craddock to write many of the tunes on *Leave This Town,* and he also collaborated with Mitch Allan from SR-71 and Chad Kroeger from Nickelback. "We went in together as a band and wrote the record together, arranged the songs together in rehearsals, and recorded them all together," Chris remarked. "It was very much a collaborative effort, as opposed to ... having to rush to record [the first album] with studio musicians." His vision guided each recording and he co-wrote all 12 of the songs on the album. Still, Chris emphasized that "[*Leave This Town*] will definitely show people that it is a band and not a one-man show.... It's a rock band, it's definitely not all me up there."

Leave This Town opened at the top of the *Billboard* 200 chart upon its release in July 2009, selling 269,000 copies in its first week. As a result, Chris became the first "American Idol" contestant to produce two consecutive No. 1 albums. Again, critical reviews were mixed. "*Leave This Town* might not make an impression on those not already inclined to love it," wrote

Daughtry's 2009 album Leave This Town.

Ann Powers in the *Los Angeles Times,* "but Daughtry is still a major architect in mainstream rock, and his music is part of an important shift in the genre.... Dismiss him at your peril." Reviewers also acknowledged that he was attuned to his audience. "[Chris Daughtry] is a man of straightforward meat-and-potatoes rock principle, and so far it's served him very well," Leah Greenblatt argued in *Entertainment Weekly.* "One may search *Town* in vain for a flash of something raw and off-the-script, a moment that does not feel both scrupulously test-marketed and impeccably (over)produced, but Daughtry's relentless competence as a mainstream-rock artist likely serves him far better than any radical departure ever could."

In 2009 the band made a number of high-profile appearances, including performances at the American Music Awards, the Country Music Awards, Dick Clark's New Year's Rockin' Eve with Ryan Seacrest, and the Dallas

Chris with the band Daughtry.

Cowboys game on Thanksgiving Day. In fall 2009 they launched a headlining arena tour across the United States.

Break the Spell

The third album, *Break the Spell,* came out in November 2011. "We came up with some pretty interesting tunes that sound nothing like anything we've done before," Chris pointed out. "Even though some of them didn't make the album, the process stretched us and took us to new places. It was an absolutely inspirational experience." In spite of the lukewarm reception by critics, the album debuted at No. 8 on the *Billboard* 200 with sales of 129,000 in its first week.

Again, reviews were mixed. Brian Mansfield of *USA Today* argued that "*Break the Spell* doesn't break the Daughtry mold, but it does find the group stretching out a bit. The earnest, angst-ridden rockers are still there, in the title track and early single 'Crawling Back to You,' but songs like 'Rescue Me' and 'Gone Too Soon' broaden the band's sound." Writing in *Billboard,* music critic Gary Graff commented that "[*Break the Spell*] isn't quite all things for all people. But it comes pretty close. The quintet brings its best Bon Jovi-style power drive on rockers like 'Renegade,' 'Outta My Head,' and 'Louder Than Ever.'… The real wrinkle on *Break the Spell,* however, is a more substantive and deliberate embrace of country crossover…. It all sounds sturdy and fits comfortably down the middle, more dependable than daring." Other commentators were less generous. Jonathan Keefe argued in *Slant Magazine* that "[*Break the Spell*] reaffirms that the band is defined by competence rather than ambition or creativity, by rote expressions of overwrought emotions rather than insight or depth." Despite such comments, Daughtry has remained a big hit with fans and has sold more than seven million albums.

> *Chris is regarded as a devoted family man. Now that he has a successful career in music, his biggest challenge is balancing fame and family. "I don't want to look back and think that I missed opportunities to make memories with my kids," he stated.*

MARRIAGE AND FAMILY

Chris has been married to Deanna Robertson since he was 20 years old. The couple met at a party and wed six months later, on November 11, 2000. "We had an instant connection," he recalled. At the time of their marriage, Deanna, a massage therapist, had two children from previous relationships: Hannah, born in 1996; and Griffin, born in 1998. In 2010, Chris and Deanna welcomed fraternal twins, daughter Adalynn Rose and son Noah James. As a father of teens and toddlers, Chris says, "It's pretty crazy having to take [Hannah and Griffin] to this lesson and see this friend, and this and that. And then you have the one-year-olds, who are completely needy! They can't do anything for themselves—it's ridiculous! They're so

97

awesome, though." The family lives in Oak Ridge, North Carolina, with three dogs, a guinea pig, and chickens as pets.

Chris is regarded as a devoted family man, and many consider this to be one of his most admirable qualities. "It wasn't like, 'This is cool that I'm a rock guy taking on two kids,'" he explained. "It just felt like that was what I was supposed to do." Now that Chris has a successful career in music, his biggest challenge is balancing fame and family. "I don't want to look back and think that I missed opportunities to make memories with my kids," he stated. Although he has an impressive list of accomplishments, he has cited "teaching my son to ride a bike" as one of his proudest moments. He has acknowledged that being away from home has been difficult.

HOBBIES AND OTHER INTERESTS

Chris values quality time spent with his family above all else. He enjoys such family activities as taking his kids to the movies and helping them make Halloween costumes; he is even known to dress up like Batman from time to time. He still enjoys drawing, painting, and comic books, especially the Spider-Man and Batman franchises. He is very active on Twitter, where he converses with friends, family, and fans.

Since becoming a celebrity, Chris has demonstrated a commitment to giving back to the community through charitable work. He has been involved in a number of fundraisers, including the ONE Campaign to fight poverty and AIDS in Africa. He has given special concerts for a variety of groups, including the ONE Campaign, children's hospitals, and servicemen and women on military bases all over the world. Despite this demanding schedule, Chris has insisted that he is "just an easygoing, lighthearted guy." Of his life as a rock star, he has said: "It's go, go, go, but I wanted to do this my whole life, so I'm enjoying every minute of it."

RECORDINGS

Daughtry, 2006
Leave This Town, 2009
Break the Spell, 2011

HONORS AND AWARDS

American Music Awards: 2007, Favorite Adult Contemporary Artist, Favorite Breakthrough New Artist, Favorite Pop/Rock Album, for *Daughtry*; 2008, Favorite Pop/Rock Band/Duo/Group
People's Choice Awards: 2008, Favorite Rock Song, for "Home"

FURTHER READING

Books

Marcovitz, Hal. *American Idol Superstars: Chris Daughtry,* 2010

Periodicals

Billboard, Dec. 22, 2007, p.54; June 20, 2009, p.21
Entertainment Weekly, Feb. 23, 2007, p.72
Newsweek, July 20, 2009, p.66
Rolling Stone, Apr. 5, 2007, p.30
Time, Jan. 21, 2008, p.19
Today's Woman, Dec. 2009, p.66
USA Today, Mar. 21, 2007, p.D1

Online Articles

www.allmusic.com
    (Allmusic, "Artist: Daughtry," undated)
www.billboard.com
    (Billboard, "The *Billboard* Q&A: Chris Daughtry," Dec. 22, 2007)
www.ew.com
    (Entertainment Weekly, "The Anti-Idol," Feb. 23, 2007)
www.gibson.com
    (Gibson, "It's Daughtry's World; We Just Shop in It," Sep. 17, 2007; "The Gibson Classic Interview: Chris Daughtry," Feb. 19, 2011)
www.knowtheartist.com
    (KnowTheArtist, "Daughtry to *Leave This Town,*" Aug. 14, 2009)
www.time.com
    (Time, "Q & A: Talking with Chris Daughtry," Jan. 21, 2008)

ADDRESS

Chris Daughtry
RCA Records
550 Madison Ave.
New York, NY 10022

WEB SITES

www.daughtryofficial.com
www.rcarecords.com/artists/daughtry
www.americanidol.com/archive/contestants/season5/chris_daughtry

Ellen DeGeneres 1958-

American Actor, Comedian, and Talk Show Host
Award-Winning Host of the Hit TV Talk Show "The
Ellen DeGeneres Show"

BIRTH

Ellen DeGeneres was born on January 26, 1958, in Metairie,
Louisiana. Her father, Elliot, sold insurance. Her mother, Betty,
worked as a secretary. She has one older brother, named Vance.

YOUTH

As a child, DeGeneres was shy and quiet. She loved animals
and thought of becoming a veterinarian. But she gave up on

this idea when she realized that she wasn't "book smart" enough for veterinarian school. She liked to spend time alone, writing and dreaming of becoming a singer. "I wanted to be a singer and a songwriter. I love music and singing, and like a lot of young girls who are lonely, I sat at home and wrote songs and poetry, and that's something I could do. And then it turned out I was better at being funny."

When DeGeneres was growing up her family moved around a lot, and they lived in different places in and around the city of New Orleans. "We never owned a house when I was growing up," she recalled. "We rented, and we moved about every two years, just far enough to have to start at a new school." Her parents divorced when she was 13 years old. After the divorce, DeGeneres and her brother moved with their mother to the small town of Atlanta, Texas.

> "I wanted to be a singer and a songwriter," DeGeneres said about her childhood plans. "I love music and singing, and like a lot of young girls who are lonely, I sat at home and wrote songs and poetry, and that's something I could do. And then it turned out I was better at being funny."

DeGeneres's mother married again, but the relationship lasted only a few years. When Ellen was 16 years old, she was molested by her stepfather. She did not tell anyone about the abuse right away, because her mother was undergoing treatment for breast cancer at the time. Many years later she explained that decision. "I really didn't want to have to talk about it, but at the same time, the statistics are that one in three women have been molested in some way, and that's a pretty high statistic. And there should be more people talking about it; it shouldn't be a shameful thing. It is never your fault. So I don't mind talking about it. He did horrible things to me and he was a bad man. I should have told Mother right away.... You should always, always tell somebody."

EDUCATION

DeGeneres attended public elementary schools in New Orleans and went to high school in Atlanta, Texas. After graduating from high school in 1976, she moved back to New Orleans. She enrolled in the University of New Orleans but only attended classes for half of one semester. "I hated school. I started college because everyone else was going. I majored in communications, I think. Or communications and drama. And I just remember sit-

DeGeneres performing stand up at The Improv comedy club in the 1980s.

ting in there, and they were talking about the history of Greek theater or something, and thinking, 'This is not what I want to know.'"

CAREER HIGHLIGHTS

After dropping out of college, DeGeneres supported herself by working at a variety of different jobs. She worked as a waitress, a bartender, and a house painter. At one point, she had a job shucking oysters. She sold clothing and vacuum cleaners, and was a legal secretary for a short time. DeGeneres was good at some of these jobs, but she always ran into problems following rules. "I realized I needed to find something where I didn't have to answer to a boss. I slowly started to discover what I wanted."

DeGeneres had always had a talent for making people laugh. When she was 23 years old, she began performing stand-up comedy at the open mic night at a local coffee house. From there, she went on to perform stand-up comedy gigs at area colleges and universities. Her stand-up comedy routines were based on her funny observations of normal, everyday life. "I watch people's behavior and I notice things. I think that's why I became a comedian. I notice how stupid the things we do are."

Becoming a Comedian and an Actor

In 1981, DeGeneres landed a job as the emcee at Clyde's Comedy Club in the New Orleans entertainment district known as the French Quarter. At that time, Clyde's was the only comedy club in the city. As the club's emcee, DeGeneres performed stand-up comedy routines and introduced the other comedians who appeared at the club.

DeGeneres moved to Los Angeles, California, after Clyde's Comedy Club closed. She performed in stand-up comedy clubs around Los Angeles, refining her jokes and developing new comedy routines. One of her most well-known comedy bits from this time period was titled "Phone Call to God." In this monologue, DeGeneres pretends to call God to ask about things that had always bothered her, such as why God created fleas. "Phone Call to God" quickly became her most popular comedy routine and soon led to bigger opportunities.

DeGeneres began performing at the Los Angeles comedy club The Improv, a famous comedy club (now a chain of clubs) where many comedians got their start. "I had a friend in L.A. who knew the owner of the Improv," she recalled. "We went to see him, I auditioned, and he gave me some great spots. Instead of having to wait around for hours like the rest of the beginning comics, he had me booked into good time slots." In 1982, DeGeneres was named the Funniest Person in America by the cable television channel Showtime. She went on to become the opening act for Jay Leno. This was earlier in Leno's career, when he was one of America's top stand-up comedians and was not yet a late-night TV host.

DeGeneres made her TV debut in 1986 on "The Tonight Show Starring Johnny Carson." This was a different era in TV, a time when there were very few TV networks and very few choices about what to watch. As the king of late-night TV, Carson was one of the most influential people in the entertainment industry. DeGeneres's first stand-up comedy performance on "The Tonight Show" was a huge success. She was surprised and thrilled when Carson invited her over to sit on the couch and chat after she finished her monologue. That was an honor usually reserved for the very best comedians; in fact, DeGeneres was the first female comedian he had ever invited over. Carson's endorsement led to appearances on several comedy specials produced by the HBO cable TV network. Throughout the late 1980s, DeGeneres made regular appearances on HBO.

DeGeneres made the transition from stand-up comedian to actor in 1989. She had small roles in several different situation comedies, beginning with "Open House" on the Fox network. In 1991, she won the American Comedy Award for Best Female Comedy Club Stand-Up Performer. She had a recurring role in the 1992 ABC series "Laurie Hill" and appeared in the 1993 movie *Coneheads*.

A cast shot from the TV series "Laurie Hill," an early acting job.
DeGeneres is second from the right.

"Ellen"

In 1994, DeGeneres landed her first major acting role as part of the ensemble cast of the ABC situation comedy "These Friends of Mine." DeGeneres played Ellen Morgan, a clerk in a bookstore coffeehouse who was always preoccupied with making a good impression on everyone around her. Over the course of the first season, her character grew into a leading role. After the first season, the network renamed the show "Ellen" and made DeGeneres the star.

Beginning in the second season of "Ellen," the focus shifted to highlight DeGeneres's humor and comedic delivery. She patterned her performances on Lucille Ball in "I Love Lucy," a popular TV comedy series that aired in the late 1950s. "I knew what I could do with it," she remarked. "I wanted to do a smarter, hipper version of 'I Love Lucy.' I wanted a show that everybody talks about the next day."

Episodes of "Ellen" were based on Ellen Morgan's adventures and mishaps at work, in relationships, and funny situations and circumstances. DeGeneres described Ellen Morgan as "this person who's desperate to make everyone happy. Unfortunately, when she does that, she ends up putting her foot in her mouth."

"Ellen" became an instant hit show that attracted record-breaking ratings week after week. As the popularity of "Ellen" grew, DeGeneres became more recognizable and more well-known. She had mixed feelings about her rise to fame. In a 1994 interview in *TV Guide*, DeGeneres said, "If the show is successful, then you're reaching millions of people. But you're also standing there naked, saying, 'What do you think of me?' And there are mean people who just want to tear you apart. That kind of frightens me.... I try not to, but I worry about everything."

For her work on "Ellen," DeGeneres received multiple Golden Globe and Screen Actors Guild nominations, and was nominated for the Emmy Award for Best Actress for every season of the show. In 1995, while continuing work on "Ellen," DeGeneres published her first book, *My Point ... And I Do Have One*. This collection of some of her better-known comedy sketches debuted at number one on the *New York Times* Bestseller list.

In 1996, DeGeneres landed her first starring role in a movie. In the dark romantic comedy *Mr. Wrong*, she played Martha, a woman who falls in love with a handsome stranger, played by Bill Pullman. But Martha's life is turned upside down as she soon discovers that her dream man is not as perfect as she thought he was. *Mr. Wrong* was panned by critics and was only moderately successful with moviegoers.

A Turning Point

During the fourth season of "Ellen," DeGeneres made an important personal and professional decision. She decided that it was time for both herself and her character Ellen Morgan to come out as lesbian. This was a risky decision because the only gay characters seen on TV were in supporting roles. At that time, homosexuality was not widely accepted. Most gay and lesbian entertainers were in the closet, or secretive, about their sexual orientation. Very few entertainers were open about being gay, and there were no leading characters that were gay. In spite of the risk involved, DeGeneres felt that it was something she needed to do.

"I mean, you get used to living with secrets, because I did," DeGeneres explained. "There are people out there hiding all kinds of things. People who have all this success and all this fame and all this money, and yet there are secrets that they think if we found out about, it would be over for them. And it's a horrible way to live whether you're famous or not. You could just be somebody at home with a bunch of kids, and hiding something from the ladies at the PTA. That's a horrible way to live."

DeGeneres worked with the writers of "Ellen" to create the episode in which her character would reveal that she was gay. Titled "The Puppy

A scene from "The Puppy Episode": DeGeneres with Laura Dern at the airport, standing at the microphone.

Episode," it features a mix of serious themes and humor. The story revolves around Ellen Morgan's growing realization that she is attracted to Susan, a woman she recently met (played by Laura Dern). Ellen struggles with this new awareness and talks to a therapist (played by Oprah Winfrey). Thinking that Susan is leaving town, Ellen follows her to the airport. When she tries to talk to Susan, Ellen accidentally announces that she is gay over a loudspeaker in the crowded airport. She is then afraid to tell her friends, but eventually does with the help of one of her neighbors.

"The Puppy Episode" aired in 1997 and was the highest-rated episode of "Ellen," drawing a record 46 million viewers. DeGeneres won the prestigious Peabody Award and an Emmy Award for the critically acclaimed episode. She was named the Entertainer of the Year for 1997 and 1998 by *Entertainment Weekly* magazine and received the 1998 GLAAD Stephen F. Kolzak Award.

Controversy and Consequences

But "The Puppy Episode" was also very controversial. DeGeneres's public confirmation that she was gay in real life became national headline news. She came under attack from political and religious conservative groups who accused her of promoting homosexuality. She was also criticized by some in the gay community. "There were extreme groups that didn't think I was gay enough. There were other groups of people who thought I was too gay. It didn't occur to me that when I announced I was gay I would have to clarify just how gay I was," DeGeneres said. "I never wanted to be the lesbian actress. I never wanted to be the spokesperson for the gay community. Ever. I did it for my own truth."

The controversy over DeGeneres's decision to come out on national TV proved to be too much for the network. "Ellen" was cancelled in 1998. DeGeneres was out of a job, and she also found herself suddenly and unexpectedly without any prospects for work. In spite of her past success, no one would hire her. The backlash also affected actor Laura Dern, who played Ellen's love interest in "The Puppy Episode." Dern was unable to find work as an actor for almost a year after the episode aired.

"Even though I had a big foundation with my career and years of work, it just divided everyone when I came out," DeGeneres revealed. "Simply my saying I was gay—even though I was the exact same person—divided everyone. People stopped watching the show, so some advertisers pulled out. It didn't matter that I was a good, devoted, loyal employee. I mean, I showed up on time. I never did anything wrong. I was kind. I was easy to work with. And yet it was the dollar that mattered more. It was just a huge dose of reality for me. But losing it all really gave me time to realize that all this stuff is very fleeting. If success is really dependent on someone liking you or not liking you, and you have to teeter on that kind of tightrope of how you're supposed to act and how you're supposed to look and who you are, it's just not a healthy way to live. Now I get to be me every single day and not have to worry about hiding anything at all."

By 1999, DeGeneres was starting to rebuild her career. That year, she appeared in two movies, *The Love Letter,* a romantic comedy about mistaken identity, and *EDtv,* a comedy about a reality show taken to the extreme. In 2000, she was featured in the HBO production *If These Walls Could Talk II,* a set of three separate stories of lesbian couples in different time periods. She also appeared as a guest on "The Larry Sanders Show," a role for which she received an Emmy nomination.

In 2001, DeGeneres created and starred in the CBS situation comedy "The Ellen Show." She played Ellen Richmond, an entrepreneur who returns to her small hometown after her company fails. She gets a job as a counselor at the local high school and learns to adjust to the slower pace of life in the small community. Though "The Ellen Show" was critically acclaimed, ratings were low and only 18 episodes were produced. "The Ellen Show" was cancelled in its first season.

DeGeneres dancing with First Lady Michelle Obama on "The Ellen DeGeneres Show."

"The Ellen DeGeneres Show"

DeGeneres found success once again with "The Ellen DeGeneres Show," a daily TV talk show that began airing in 2003. "The Ellen DeGeneres Show" is described on its web site as "the daytime destination for laughter and fun." Each episode of the show begins with DeGeneres talking for a few minutes about whatever is on her mind that day, often including her personal observations on current events or topics of everyday life. This segment of the show is always followed by DeGeneres dancing through the studio—she is known for her love of dancing—with the whole audience dancing along with her.

Episodes of "The Ellen DeGeneres Show" typically feature a mix of entertainment and interviews with popular celebrities, musicians, politicians, and other notable people. Her interviews include a playful quality that seems to put people at ease and encourages her guests to relax and chat. She sometimes appears star-struck, as awed by her famous guests as her audience would be. "The Ellen DeGeneres Show" often showcases performances by both established stars and unknown musicians. DeGeneres has gained a reputation for finding talented performers on the Internet and inviting these new artists to appear on her show. Other popular features are the frequent audience participation contests, games, and prize give-aways. She has also created special segments of the show that highlight funny photos and text messages sent in by viewers.

―――― " ――――

"I think we need more love in the world. We need more kindness, more compassion, more joy, more laughter," DeGeneres stressed. *"The most important thing for me is to know that I represent kindness. I'm glad I'm funny. I'm glad I make people happy, because that's very important. But I'm proud to be known as a kind person."*

―――― " ――――

"The Ellen DeGeneres Show" quickly became a hit with daytime viewers as well as TV critics. "Ellen just gets people—whether they're celebrities or plain folks," wrote *Redbook* TV critic John Griffits. "It's no wonder that millions of people tune into 'The Ellen DeGeneres Show' each day, or that Hollywood's biggest stars are jumping at the chance to be her guests. She says what we're thinking. She zeroes in on all the weird and wonderful things that make life great—like bells on bicycles, singing parrots, and good, old-fashioned sneakers." Since its debut in 2003, "The Ellen DeGeneres Show" has earned numerous Daytime Emmy Awards and People's Choice Awards, a Teen Choice Award, a Genesis Award, and a GLAAD Media Award.

The popularity of "The Ellen DeGeneres Show" propelled DeGeneres back to the top of the entertainment industry. She has been named among the *Forbes* 100 Most Powerful Women, *Time* magazine's 100 Most Influential People, and *Entertainment Weekly*'s 50 Most Powerful Entertainers. She has hosted the Primetime Emmy Awards broadcast three times, the Grammy Awards show twice, and the Academy Awards TV broadcast.

A Versatile Entertainer

DeGeneres is a versatile entertainer who has stayed active in many entertainment arenas in addition to her TV talk show. She returned to movie acting as the voice of Dory, a fish who has trouble remembering things, in the 2003 animated feature *Finding Nemo.* She also published her second book *The Funny Thing Is ...* that year. This collection of short stories and essays was an immediate best-seller. DeGeneres was nominated for a 2005 Grammy Award for Best Comedy Album for her reading of the

DeGeneres voiced the character of Dory in Finding Nemo.

audio version of the book. In 2010, she was a judge on the popular TV singing competition show "American Idol" for one season. Also in 2010, she founded the eleveneleven record label with the goal of discovering new musical talent. DeGeneres published her third book *Seriously ... I'm Kidding* in 2011. This collection of photos, quotes, and stories from her life includes her thoughts on meditation, gambling, pets, the importance of being on time, and more.

Throughout the ups and downs of her long career, DeGeneres has managed to maintain perspective. "I'm definitely happier than I've ever been. I assume tomorrow I'll be happier than today, because things are great. I have a great career and I have wonderful fans who really are supportive and loyal—because I'm not hiding anything from them. So, on the spectrum of happiness, I'm pretty high up there."

"I believe everything in life is energy. If we're destroying our trees and destroying our environment and hurting animals and hurting one another and all that stuff, there's got to be a very powerful energy to fight that. I think we need more love in the world. We need more kindness, more compassion, more joy, more laughter. I definitely want my time here to be positive and productive," DeGeneres stressed. "The most important thing for me is to know that I represent kindness. I'm glad I'm funny. I'm glad I make people happy, because that's very important. But I'm proud to be known as a kind person."

MARRIAGE AND FAMILY

DeGeneres married actor Portia de Rossi in 2008. They live in Beverly Hills, California.

HOBBIES AND OTHER INTERESTS

DeGeneres is active in many humanitarian causes, particularly campaigns against bullying. She works closely with The Trevor Project and the Pacer Center to educate and raise awareness about bullying. She founded the United Against Bullying campaign to promote the message "be kind to one another." DeGeneres also promotes animal welfare through her work with animal rescue organizations such as Gentle Barn.

In her spare time, DeGeneres enjoys gardening, hunting for antiques, and interior design. "Designing is my hobby. If I didn't do what I do for a living—at some point when I don't do this for a living—I'll probably just do design work.… I enjoy putting rooms together." She collects old paintings and photographs of people, and enjoys spending time with her many pets.

SELECTED CREDITS

Books

My Point … And I Do Have One, 1995
The Funny Thing Is …, 2003
Seriously … I'm Kidding, 2011

Movies

Mr. Wrong, 1996
EDtv, 1999
The Love Letter, 1999
Finding Nemo, 2003

Television

"Ellen," 1994-1998 (series)
If These Walls Could Talk II, 2000 (special)
"The Ellen Show," 2001-2002 (series)
"The Ellen DeGeneres Show," 2003- (talk show)

HONORS AND AWARDS

Funniest Person in America (Showtime): 1982
American Comedy Awards: 1991, Best Female Comedy Club Stand-Up Performer

Golden Apple Awards (Hollywood Women's Press Association): 1994, Female Discovery of the Year

Entertainer of the Year (*Entertainment Weekly*): 1997 and 1998

Peabody Awards: 1998, for writing of "The Puppy Episode" of "Ellen"

Stephen F. Kolzak Awards (GLAAD): 1998

Annie Awards (International Animated Film Association): 2004, Outstanding Voice Acting, for *Finding Nemo*

Daytime Emmy Awards (National Academy of Television Arts and Sciences): 2004, Outstanding Talk Show; 2005 (3 awards), Outstanding Talk Show, Outstanding Talk Show Host, and Outstanding Special Class Writing; 2006 (3 awards), Outstanding Talk Show, Outstanding Talk Show Host, and Outstanding Special Class Writing; 2007 (3 awards), Outstanding Talk Show, Outstanding Talk Show Host, and Outstanding Special Class Writing; 2008 (2 awards), Outstanding Talk Show and Outstanding Talk Show Host; 2010, Outstanding Talk Show; 2011, Outstanding Talk Show

Kids Choice Awards (Nickelodeon): 2004, Favorite Voice from an Animated Movie, for *Finding Nemo*

Saturn Awards (Academy of Science Fiction, Fantasy & Horror): 2004, Best Supporting Actress, for *Finding Nemo*

People's Choice Awards: 2005 (2 awards), Favorite Funny Female Star and Favorite Talk Show Host; 2006 (2 awards), Favorite Funny Female Star and Favorite Talk Show Host; 2007 (2 awards), Favorite Funny Female Star and Favorite Talk Show Host; 2008 (2 awards), Favorite Funny Female Star and Favorite Talk Show Host; 2009, Favorite Talk Show Host; 2010 (2 awards), Favorite Talk Show Host and Favorite Talk Show; 2012, Favorite Daytime TV Host

Genesis Awards (The Humane Society of the United States): 2009 (two awards), Best Talk Show and Gretchen Wyler Award (shared with Portia de Rossi); 2011, Best Talk Show

Woman of the Year (PETA): 2009

Teen Choice Awards: 2010, Choice Comedian; 2011, Choice Comedian

TV Guide Award: 2011, Favorite Host

FURTHER READING

Periodicals

Entertainment Weekly, Feb. 2, 2007, p.96; Jan. 15, 2010, p.26

Good Housekeeping, Oct. 2003, p.130; Oct. 2011

Hollywood Reporter, Feb. 23, 2007, p.O12

Newsweek, Sep. 15, 2008, p.103

People, Sep. 19, 2011, p.176

Publishers Weekly, Sep. 26, 2011, p.59
Redbook, Jan. 2006, p.88
Teen People, Feb. 2006, p.46
Time, Feb. 23, 2004, p.8
USA Today, Jan. 8, 2010

Online Articles

www.biography.com
   (Biography, "Ellen DeGeneres," no date)
ellen.warnerbros.com/about/bio.php
   (Ellen DeGeneres Show, "Ellen DeGeneres Bio," no date)
www.nytimes.com/pages/topics
   (New York Times, Times Topics, "Ellen DeGeneres," multiple articles,
   various dates)
www.people.com/people/ellen_degeneres/0,,,00.html
   (People, "Ellen DeGeneres," no date)

ADDRESS

Ellen DeGeneres
The Ellen DeGeneres Show
PO Box 7788
Burbank, CA 91522
ATTN: Fan Mail

WEB SITE

ellen.warnerbros.com

Drake 1986-

Canadian-American Rapper and Actor
Creator of the Hit Records *Thank Me Later* and *Take Care*
Played Jimmy Brooks on "Degrassi: The Next Generation"

BIRTH

Aubrey Drake Graham, known professionally as Aubrey Graham and also as Drake, was born on October 24, 1986, in Toronto, Ontario, Canada. His mother, Sandi, is a Canadian teacher. His father, Dennis, is an African-American musician from Memphis, Tennessee. As the son of an American and a Canadian, Drake has dual citizenship. This means that he is a citizen of both the U.S. and Canada.

YOUTH

Drake's parents divorced when he was five years old. His mother raised him in the Jewish faith of her family. He grew up celebrating Jewish holidays and had a *bar mitzvah* when he was 13 years old. (A *bar mitzvah* is a Jewish ceremony that formally marks the age at which a Jewish male assumes the responsibilities of observing the Jewish faith. It typically includes a religious ceremony and a party in the young man's honor.)

> "At the end of the day, I consider myself a black man because I'm more immersed in the black culture than any other," Drake commented. "Being Jewish is kind of a cool twist. It makes me unique."

Drake grew up dividing his time between two very different worlds. For most of the year, he lived with his mother in an upper-class Jewish neighborhood in Toronto. As the only biracial person in the community, he often felt like an outsider. Summer vacations were spent with his father, aunts, uncles, and cousins in Memphis. Drake explored the Memphis music scene and often went to gigs with his musician father. Though Drake was very close to his mother, he felt more at home with his father's side of the family. "At the end of the day, I consider myself a black man because I'm more immersed in the black culture than any other," he commented. "Being Jewish is kind of a cool twist. It makes me unique."

EDUCATION

Drake attended Forest Hill Collegiate Institute in Toronto. He was often the only black student in his classes at school and sometimes had difficulties with other students because of that. "Going to Forest Hill was definitely an interesting way of growing up," he acknowledged. "When you're young and unaware that the world is made up of different people, it is tough growing up. But me being different from everyone else just made me a lot stronger."

Drake became interested in acting when he was young, working occasionally as a child model during elementary school and participating in his

A cast shot from "Degrassi: The Next Generation,"
with Drake in the front in a wheelchair.

high school's drama program. During high school, he was known for making people laugh. The father of one of his classmates was an acting agent, and he invited Drake to audition. He landed his first acting job when he was 14 years old, a small role in the 2002 movie *Conviction*. As an actor, he was known by his full name, Aubrey Graham.

This role led to Drake being cast in the Canadian teen drama series "Degrassi: The Next Generation." This television show was part of a series of popular and respected shows that had appeared on Canadian television, first "The Kids of Degrassi Street" (1979-1986), then "Degrassi Junior High" (1987-1989), followed by "Degrassi High" (1989-1991). The Degrassi shows followed the lives of a group of kids who lived on or near Degrassi Street in Toronto, Canada. Episodes of "Degrassi Junior High" and "Degrassi High" often included controversial subject matter, including teen sexuality, AIDS, teen pregnancy, abortion, drug abuse, racism, and teen suicide. TV critics applauded the Degrassi lineup, calling it "a series that dispenses with tidy morality and goes for the gut" and "a tough, compelling slice of life." Ten years after the end of "Degrassi High," the creators developed a new series, "Degrassi: The Next Generation," which focused on the stories of a new group of teens. When he was 16 years old, Drake dropped out of high school to begin filming "Degrassi: The Next Generation."

CAREER HIGHLIGHTS

"Degrassi: The Next Generation" began airing in the U.S. and Canada in 2001. The plot of the show focused on the lives of a group of students at

117

Degrassi Community School. Weekly episodes followed the experiences, challenges, and adventures of the group as they dealt with high school life. Drake played Jimmy Brooks, a wealthy, well-liked star player on the school's basketball team. In 2002, he and his "Degrassi: The Next Generation" costars won the Young Artist Award for Best Ensemble in a TV Series (Comedy or Drama).

During the fourth season of the series, as part of a storyline about school violence, Drake's character Jimmy is shot in the back by another student. Permanently injured by the shooting, Jimmy begins to use a wheelchair. Basketball was an important part of Jimmy's life, but he can no longer play on the school team. As the story develops, Jimmy must learn to adjust to new limitations in his abilities as he discovers who he is without sports to define him. In an interview shortly after the episode in which his character was shot, Drake said, "I took it very seriously. I spent a lot of time with someone in a wheelchair, and I also have a friend who had been shot. Playing Jimmy all day and being able to get up and walk away is weird; I appreciate things a lot more now."

Becoming a Rapper

While he was filming "Degrassi: The Next Generation," Drake had also been writing and recording his own raps in his spare time. "The reason it was rap was because in my mind I told myself, 'you're not a good enough singer,'" he admitted. "My father, actually, was always like, 'you've got a great tone ... man, you gotta sing.'" Drake had appeared as an actor under the name Aubrey Graham. To keep his creative interests separate, he decided to use only his middle name to identify himself as a rapper. He recorded and released a series of mix tapes under the name Drake and sometimes using the nickname Drizzy Drake.

Drake released his first mix tape, *Room for Improvement,* in 2006. This collection of tracks featured guest performances by well-known artists who were also Drake's friends, including Trey Songz, Lupe Fiasco, and the Clipse. In 2007, Drake released *Comeback Season,* his second mix tape. Trey Songz appeared once again as a guest performer and was featured on the single "Replacement Girl."

Drake posted his mix tapes on his web site as free downloads. As people began to listen to his tracks, word spread quickly among music fans. Soon his mix tapes were being downloaded at a record-breaking pace. This attracted the attention of professionals in the music and entertainment industry. "Replacement Girl" was featured on BET's "106 & Park" program

Drake performing with his mentor, Lil Wayne, in 2009.

as a Joint of the Day, giving Drake a huge amount of exposure. He also received a 2008 BET Award for Best Male Hip-Hop Artist.

Around this time, the producers of "Degrassi: The Next Generation" became aware of Drake's growing success as a rap artist. During the final season of the series, a plot twist was written in to the show to have his character Jimmy writing and performing his own rap songs. All of Jimmy's raps were written by Drake.

119

Breakout Success

In 2008, Drake captured the attention of rap superstar Lil Wayne. A friend had given Lil Wayne a copy of one of Drake's mix tapes. After listening to the first few tracks, Lil Wayne invited Drake to fly to Houston for a meeting. The result of that meeting was Drake's 2009 mix tape, *So Far Gone*.

With another round of guest performances by well-known rap artists, including Lil Wayne, *So Far Gone* became an instant sensation. The single "Best I Ever Had" reached No. 1 on the *Billboard* Hot R&B/Hip-Hop Songs chart. Drake won two Juno Awards in 2008, one for Best New Artist and another for Rap Recording of the Year for *So Far Gone*. This was an amazing accomplishment for Drake, an independent artist with no recording contract who was giving his music away for free on the Internet. Seemingly overnight, he went from underground rapper to mainstream recording artist.

Drake left "Degrassi: The Next Generation" in 2009 when his character graduated from high school. Soon after, he signed a recording contract with Lil Wayne's Young Money Entertainment label. Around that time, he also went on tour with Lil Wayne. This gave Drake the opportunity to perform in front of thousands of fans. He attracted new fans at every show and his mix tapes became even more popular.

In late 2009, Drake released an EP version of his mix tape *So Far Gone*. It debuted at No. 6 on the U.S. *Billboard* 200 chart. Drake won two *Billboard* Music Awards in 2009. He won the *Billboard* Top New Hip Hop/R&B Artist Award and the Top Rap Song Award, for "Best I Ever Had." BET also honored Drake with two awards in 2009: he was named the BET Hip-Hop Rookie of the Year and also received the BET Hip-Hop Track of the Year Award for his single "Every Girl."

Drake was nominated for two 2010 Grammy Awards for *So Far Gone* and performed with Lil Wayne and Eminem on the Grammy Awards TV broadcast. This caused a stir in the music industry because he had not yet released an official studio album. At that time it was completely unprecedented for an artist to be recognized with Grammy nominations for a mix tape. Though Drake did not win a Grammy that year, his appearance on the TV broadcast set the stage for his first major record release.

Thank Me Later

Drake released his debut album *Thank Me Later* in 2010. This highly anticipated album featured collaborations with such rap superstars as Kanye West, Jay Z, and Lil Wayne. On the day the record was released, Drake planned to give a free concert in New York City. When more than 25,000 fans showed up, things quickly got out of control. The New York City police department cancelled the concert because the unruly crowd was too large for the location.

Thank Me Later was a phenomenal hit with music fans and critics alike. With *Thank Me Later*, Drake introduced a new style of hip-hop that blended rap and R&B singing styles. According to *Billboard* magazine contributor Mariel Concepcion, "As hip-hop continues to drift further away from rap's basic elements and seeks to re-energize and expand its fan base with a new, hybrid sound that blends rap, R&B, dance, even alt-rock … this half-singing, half-rapping, half-Jewish, half-black former actor and current heartthrob is helping change the face of the genre firsthand."

The success of *Thank Me Later* brought Drake more in touch with mainstream music listeners. As Kelley L. Carter wrote in *Jet*, "Drake isn't exactly the archetype emcee. He's less

——— " ———

"Drake isn't exactly the archetype emcee. He's less about bling and more about interesting wordplay…. You won't find him talking much about illegal activities in his music. Instead, you'll find him making humorous, clever digs at popular culture and addressing his love of the ladies and how he's handling his newfound fame."
—Kelley L. Carter, Jet

——— " ———

about bling and more about interesting wordplay. He doesn't exactly know what it's like to walk on the seedier side of life, so you won't find him talking much about illegal activities in his music. Instead, you'll find him making humorous, clever digs at popular culture and addressing his love of the ladies and how he's handling his newfound fame." *Washington Post* music reviewer Chris Richards said, "He's tugging on a strand of pop music that feels both magical and rare—the kind that brings us all together by reminding us that we're all alone." Drake ended 2010 with a performance on "Dick Clark's Rockin' New Year's Eve" TV program, broadcast to viewers around the world. In 2010, Drake received the BET Hip-Hop MVP Award and was also named Man of the Year by *GQ* magazine.

In 2011, Drake received the BMI Urban Award for Songwriter of the Year and the Hal David Starlight Award from the Songwriters Hall of Fame. Also in 2011, he appeared on "Saturday Night Live" where he performed his single "Make Me Proud" with Nicki Minaj. Sales of "Make Me Proud" skyrocketed in the weeks after the program aired. During the "Saturday

Drake performing with Nicki Minaj on "Saturday Night Live," 2011.

Night Live" episode, Drake also performed in several comedy sketches. He later said that being on "Saturday Night Live" made him want to return to acting. "I caught that acting bug again," he admitted. "I'm dying to be on sets and be part of some movies. So hopefully I'll find some time for that amidst all the touring. It was nice to show people in those skits that I can get out of rapper mode and just be funny."

Take Care

Drake released his second album, *Take Care,* in 2012. This record included tracks that were more introspective and emotional than his previous recordings. On this album he once again used a blend of rapping and singing, and the track lyrics gave listeners a glimpse into his private life. *Take Care* was almost like a musical version of his diary, as he rapped and sang about romance, the downside of fame, and his feelings about specific events in his life.

"Music is the only way that I can really vent and tell my story. It's definitely personal. It's definitely very vivid, detailed, and I feel it's an incredible chapter of my life documented. All these albums and mix tapes are just time markers for me. Pictures and social media are great, but I think the best way for me to remember real feelings that I've experienced is to make music about it," Drake said. "I always feel that with each new project, a new group of people are dying to see what my next move is. With that comes pressure, but it also creates excitement and makes me want to work harder. I still feel that I am new and I have something to prove with this album."

Take Care was received warmly by fans and critics, who praised Drake's ability to cross musical genres with ease. *New York Times* music reviewer Jon Caramanica wrote, "*Take Care* isn't a hip-hop album or an R&B album so much as an album of eccentric black pop that takes those genres as starting points, asks what they can do that they haven't been doing, then attempts those things. In the future an album like this will be common-place; today, it's radical." Also writing in the *New York Times*, Nate Chinen said, "Rapping well, singing even better and erasing distinctions between the two, Drake made the sleekest, most self-aware pop album of the year."

Drake's rapid rise to fame seemed to surprise even the most seasoned music industry professionals. As Benjamin Meadows-Ingram wrote in *Billboard,* "In his short career, he's already appeared on the *Billboard* Hot 100 with 30 different songs and cracked the top ten seven times, the best performance by any rapper in the chart's history besides Lil Wayne, who's tallied 49 songs on the chart and eight top tens." *Take Care* received a 2012 Juno Award for Rap Recording of the Year.

Other Plans

Drake has managed to remain grounded even as his reputation and success as an artist continue to grow. "My life has changed, but I have a great grasp on it," he pointed out. "By no means have I paid my dues yet. But I think I've put in enough work where people understand that I'm here to stay." His future plans include more acting projects—he appeared as a voice actor in the 2011 video game *Gears of War 3* and the 2012 animated movie *Ice Age: Continental Drift.* Drake also plans to develop a line of personal fragrances and scented products for the home, including candles and incense. *Fame: Drake,* a comic book about Drake's life, was published in 2012.

Though he has earned his reputation as a talented songwriter and recording artist, Drake is sometimes still surprised by his own success. "I'm accepted by fans, accepted by my peers. It's crazy. The images that exist of me pre-2007 are, like, horrendous, like Phat Farm velour suits, big afro, like, it's terrible. So just the fact that the world allowed me to grow—I grew up in

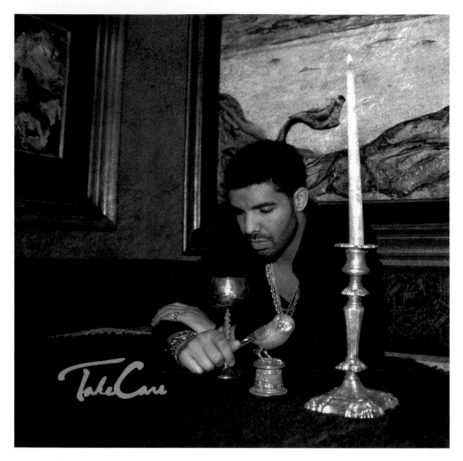

Take Care, *Drake's second album, showed his growth as an artist.*

front of the world and they watched it, and now they want to hear my story," Drake said. "I get respect from the guys who are respected for being real rapper's rappers. I get respect from women. I get respect from mothers, fathers, and kids. It's very humbling and flattering and incredible, and I'm honored to be in this position because I get to be myself. And I get a lot of love for it."

Still, Drake acknowledged that "Real, legendary status can't be dictated by the people who are still here witnessing it. Legendary status is when the next generation comes up. The kids that are 15 right now and will be going to college in five or six years—if they say, 'Yo, I remember when Drake came to this school. That's one of the most legendary shows ever,' that's when you're a legend. I'm young. I'm 23. This is too soon. I really want to grow and be that guy."

"I want to encourage my generation to love, to be happy. I want to encourage open communication. And even though it's not always a good thing—some things are better kept to yourself—but I want to encourage my generation to be honest, to be yourself. If you don't like doing drugs or you don't want to fight people in the street, it's OK. That's never been cool anyway. To me, losers do that. It's way cooler to be yourself. If you're good at math, be good at math. If you're good at acting or drama, just be you. Just be what you're good at."

HOME AND FAMILY

When he is not travelling or on tour, Drake divides his time between homes in Toronto and Miami, Florida.

SELECTED CREDITS

"Degrassi: The Next Generation," 2001-2009 (TV series)
Room for Improvement, 2006 (mix tape)
Comeback Season, 2007 (mix tape)
So Far Gone, 2009 (mix tape)
So Far Gone, 2009 (EP)
Thank Me Later, 2010 (album)
Take Care, 2012 (album)

HONORS AND AWARDS

Young Artist Award: 2002, Best Ensemble in a TV Series (Comedy or Drama) for "Degrassi: The Next Generation"
BET Hip Hop Award: 2008 (two awards), Best Male Hip-Hop Artist and Best Group; 2009 (two awards), Rookie of the Year and Track of the Year, for "Every Girl"; 2010, MVP Award
Juno Award: 2008 (two awards), Best New Artist, and Rap Recording of the Year, for *So Far Gone*; 2012, Rap Recording of the Year, for *Take Care*
Billboard Music Award: 2009 (two awards), Top New Hip Hop/R&B Artist, and Top Rap Song, for "Best I Ever Had"
GQ Award (*GQ*): 2010, Man of the Year
BMI Urban Award: 2011, Songwriter of the Year
Hal David Starlight Award (Songwriters Hall of Fame): 2011

FURTHER READING

Periodicals

Billboard, May 29, 2010, p.20; Nov. 19, 2011
Ebony, Mar. 2010, p.38

Jet, Sep. 20, 2010, p.28; Dec. 5, 2011, p.22
Maclean's, June 22, 2009; June 28, 2010, p. 44; Jan. 16, 2012
Newsweek, Nov. 21, 2011
Rolling Stone, Aug. 2, 2009, p.31; Sep. 30, 2010, p.30
USA Today, Nov. 17, 2011
Wall Street Journal, Nov. 11, 2011
Word Up!, Jan. 2011, p.28

Online Articles

www.billboard.com/#/artist/drake/855020
    (Billboard, "Drake," no date)
www.biography.com/people
    (Biography, "Drake," no date)
www.cbc.ca/archives
    (CBC Digital Archives, "The Degrassi Approach to Children's Drama,"
    no date)
www.kidzworld.com
    (Kidz World, "Drake Biography," May 8, 2012)
www.mtv.com/music/artist/drake/artist.jhtml
    (MTV, "Drake," no date)
www.rollingstone.com
    (Rolling Stone, "Artist to Watch 2009: Drake," Aug. 7, 2009; "Drake,"
    Sep. 29, 2010)

ADDRESS

Drake
Universal/Republic
1755 Broadway, 8th floor
New York, NY 10019

WEB SITE

www.drakeofficial.com

Kevin Durant 1988-
American Professional Basketball Player
Forward for the Oklahoma City Thunder

BIRTH

Kevin Wayne Durant was born in Suitland, Maryland, on September 29, 1988. His mother, Wanda (Durant) Pratt, is a postal worker, while his father, Wayne Pratt, works as a federal law enforcement officer with the Library of Congress. At the time of Kevin's birth, his parents were unmarried, so he was given his mother's maiden name. His father was not involved in his upbringing for most of his childhood. Instead, his mother raised him and his older brother, Tony, as a single mom with the help of his grandmother, Barbara Davis. Durant's parents reunited and married in 2001. "My wife did a tremendous job with those boys," Wayne Pratt explained in the *Dallas Morning News*. She is the rock and the strength of our family." Durant has two brothers, Tony and Rayvonne, one sister, Briana, and a stepbrother, Cliff Dixon.

YOUTH

Kevin grew up in the Suitland-Silver Hill area of Prince George's County, Maryland, just outside Washington, DC. During his elementary school years, he participated in a range of after-school sports at the Boys & Girls Club program in Capitol Heights, including playing lineman on the football team. A hard worker with natural athletic ability, he was also a thoughtful and respectful young boy. His mother told the *New York Times* about a football practice during which the coach challenged a less-athletic teammate to tackle him. After the practice, Kevin revealed to his mother that he had let his teammate tackle him—had purposely risked his own humiliation—to save the young teammate from being bullied. "'Mom, he couldn't knock me down,'" he confessed. "'I let him knock me down because I didn't want anybody to hurt him.'"

―――― **"** ――――

"It was tough," Durant said about his training regime. "I didn't like it at all, I wanted to play with my friends. [Coach Brown] told me that I would pick up bad habits by playing 5-on-5, so every day I just did the drill work. It was like boot camp every day. It made me cry all the time—I just told myself not to be a quitter."

―――― **"** ――――

Kevin and his brother Tony spent a lot of time at the Seat Pleasant Activity Center near his grandmother's house. Kevin joined the PG Jaguars, an Amateur Athletic Union (AAU) youth basketball team, and played alongside future Minnesota Timberwolves forward Mike Beasley. According to Beasley, the Jaguars were the "best nine-year-old team in Prince George's County." As Beasley told the *Minneapolis Star Tribune*, "That jump shot Kevin's got? Kevin's had that his whole life. Every time I grabbed a rebound, I'd just throw it out to Kevin." Beasley's mom would take Mike to Kevin's house in the mornings. They would eat breakfast, ride the bus, and play basketball after school together. "I love him like a brother," Durant said as he reflected on Beasley's success in the NBA. "We worked so hard…. Playing each other on the highest stage of basketball is an unbelievable feeling. It's just a blessing."

Durant was a quiet boy with a vivid imagination. His mother recalled that he was always capable of entertaining himself, often disappearing into a corner of his grandmother's house to play. "It was just a penny and a clothespin," she told the *Washington Post*. "That's what he was playing with. And he'd spend hours … just sitting there, playing with a penny and a clothespin." When she asked him what he was doing, he told her that he was making up basketball plays. Around that same time, when Durant was nine or ten years old, he greatly admired NBA player Vince Carter of the Toronto Raptors. His mother bought him a Vince Carter uniform that he insisted on wearing to all of his games. "I always wanted to play the way he did, so I would always want to wear his uniform," he explained. "I still call myself a big Vince Carter fan."

At age 11 Durant knew he wanted to be a professional basketball player. He told his mother about his dream after a big game with the Jaguars—a tournament final—in which he scored 18 points in the second half to secure the championship for his team. "I don't know if she thought I was serious or not," Durant admitted, "but she said, 'All right, if that's what you want, then you've got to work hard and commit to it.'" AAU coach Taras Brown agreed to train him, and the two began meeting daily to practice drills that would improve his form, agility, strength, accuracy, and endurance. Durant recalls sprints up and down steep hills and long afternoons in the gym doing hundreds of laps, crab-walk exercises, and drills to hone his shooting, dribbling, passing, and defensive skills. He lovingly refers to Brown as his godfather, and he credits him with shaping his dream into a reality. Brown was a strict coach, however, forbidding Durant from playing in pickup games on the playground so that he could focus on technique. He also challenged him by making him write essays on basketball and diagram the mechanics involved in a jump shot. Brown's motto was "Hard work beats talent when talent fails to work hard."

From age 11 to age 16, Durant trained with Brown for several hours every day. His routine consisted of attending school, completing his homework, running to the gym, and then working out late into the evening. His grandmother would bring his dinner to the gym and he would scarf it down between drills. Training for a basketball career required extraordinary mental and physical discipline. "It was tough," Durant admitted. "I didn't like it at all, I wanted to play with my friends. He told me that I would pick up bad habits by playing 5-on-5, so every day I just did the drill work. It was like boot camp every day. It made me cry all the time—I just told myself not to

Durant was a basketball prodigy even in high school, the MVP of the McDonald's High School All-American Game, 2006 (shown here).

be a quitter." In retrospect, he has said that "Honestly, I don't know how I did all of those things when I was younger. I just wanted to be great."

EDUCATION

Durant spent his freshman and sophomore years of high school at National Christian Academy in Fort Washington, Maryland, playing point guard on the junior varsity team before being upgraded to the varsity team midway through his freshman season. During his sophomore year he became the team's leading scorer, playing guard, forward, and center. He led the team to 27 victories, a school record. His National Christian coach, Trevor Brown, described him as both modest and driven. "He was never a kid who needed to play in front of big crowds, who needed to be a star, who needed all the accolades," he told the *Washington Post*. "That's not him. He was always more concerned with being the best player possible."

For his junior year, Durant attended Oak Hill Academy in Mouth of Wilson, Virginia, a school renowned for its basketball program. He started in every game, helping the team advance to the national championship with a 34-2 record. For his senior year, he transferred to Montrose Christian Academy in Rockville, Maryland, to play on the team of Stu Vetter, a seasoned coach who had trained multiple future NBA players and had led many high school teams to the national championships. Durant took an hour-long train ride every morning to school, and then at 7:30 a.m. he fit in a 45-minute workout before the beginning of the school day. After afternoon basketball practice ended, he would stay 45 minutes for additional training. As Durant approached graduation, he was getting attention as one of the top high school players in the nation, averaging 23.6 points and 10.2 rebounds per game. He received handwritten letters from college coaches and was named the 2006 All-Met Player of the Year by the *Washington Post*. He also earned Most Valuable Player honors for his performance in the 2006 McDonald's High School All-American Game.

Meanwhile, Durant remained active in AAU basketball at Seat Pleasant Activity Center. During his high school years, he played on the DC Blue Devils alongside future Denver Nuggets point guard Tywon Lawson. Coaches with the Blue Devils have described Durant as a likeable teen with a positive attitude who achieved success through old-fashioned hard work. He was particularly close to his AAU coach and mentor Charles Craig, whom he affectionately called "Big Chuckie." Coach Craig, he has stated, taught him "how to be tough, how to go out there and play with passion and play with heart." In April 2005, however, when Durant was a junior in high school, Craig was murdered at the age of 35. "I didn't know what to think," Durant lamented. "He's a person that died for no reason." Since Craig's death, Durant has worn the number 35 in tribute to him. "He was just a caring and loving person that everybody would love to meet," he said. "Every time I step on that floor, I do it to win games and make him proud."

As the annual NBA draft approached, Durant was considered the number-two recruit in the nation in the class of 2006. That year, however, the NBA increased the age requirement from 18 to 19, requiring players to play at least one year beyond high school before being eligible for the NBA draft. Multiple colleges attempted to recruit him, but Durant chose the University of Texas because of his respect for coaches Russell Springman and Rick

Texas Longhorns player Durant (35, left) goes for a rebound against Oklahoma Sooners player Nate Carter (24, right), 2007. Durant won multiple major awards for his performance at the University of Texas.

Barnes. He moved to Austin and began preparing for his freshman season with the Longhorns. Many predicted that he would enter the NBA draft after just one year of college ball, but he was reluctant to declare himself a one-year-and-out student athlete, focusing instead on the hard work ahead of him in the classroom and on the court.

To the delight of his parents and coaches, Durant excelled at the university both academically and athletically. He became a two-time member of the

University of Texas Athletics Director's Honor Roll, which requires a minimum 3.0 grade point average, and cited his anthropology course as a favorite class. He enjoyed learning about different cultures around the world, both past and present. "The rituals of how they found food were just amazing to me," he remarked. "They had to catch it, cook it, make sure it's not poisoned—all that different type of stuff."

At the same time, Durant participated in what he refers to on his website as "one of the greatest seasons in the history of college basketball." He set records in both scoring and rebounds in the Big 12 college athletic conference, averaging 25.8 points and 11.1 rebounds per game. He also set the University of Texas record for total points and total rebounds in a single season. Coach Rick Barnes called him the best player in the history of the Longhorns, citing his versatility and spot-on instincts. Durant earned the Most Valuable Player Award for the Big 12 conference and was named National College Player of the Year by the National Association of Basketball Coaches, the U.S. Basketball Writers Association, *Sporting News,* and the Associated Press (AP). He also won three major awards for outstanding college basketball player of the year—the Adolph Rupp Trophy for NCAA basketball player of the year, the Naismith Award, and the John R. Wooden Award—and was the first freshman in NCAA history to win any of those awards. Despite this recognition, he maintained his humility, declining to pose for the cover of *Dime* magazine unless the other four starting Longhorns were pictured alongside him. He was also selected to appear on the cover of the March Madness 2008 video game.

CAREER HIGHLIGHTS

The Seattle Sonics

In June 2007 Durant started his professional career when he was chosen by the Seattle SuperSonics as the second overall draft pick. Ohio State University player Greg Oden was selected as the first pick by the Portland Trailblazers, but Durant's supporters believed that he deserved top billing. As coach Barnes told the *Dallas Morning News,* "Kevin's the best player in the draft—period, at any position." Durant's father agreed, telling the *Seattle Times,* "You haven't seen anything yet. He's prepared almost his entire life for this and he's only going to get better." But Durant shied away from claims that he would save the Seattle franchise. "I don't think I'm the face of the franchise like everybody has been saying," he stated. "I don't think I'm going to be the star. I just want to play within the flow of the team."

Members of the press and professional basketball community had high expectations for Durant, who at age 19 was the youngest player in the NBA.

———— " ————

"If you would have told me a couple of years ago that I would be the NBA Rookie of the Year, to be in the same company as LeBron James, Larry Bird ... I would have told you you were crazy," Durant said in amazement.

———— " ————

Despite his humble demeanor, he was an intimidating addition to the league. "His length, his height," Timberwolves Coach Kurt Rambis marveled in the *Star Tribune,* referring to Durant's six-feet, nine-inch frame and wingspan of seven feet, five inches. Fran Blinebury of the *Houston Chronicle* lauded his diverse skill set and ability to transcend the requirements of a single position. "If Durant were a restaurant, he'd be an all-you-can-eat buffet, where the only things that matter are appetite and imagination," Blinebury wrote. "He has the splendid athleticism of the greatest small forwards and brings guard skills that boggle the mind. He has an impressive shooting range and the height, wingspan, and shot-blocking ability of a center." Sportswriter Jerry Brewer of the *Seattle Times* echoed these comments. "Don't characterize him as either a small forward or power forward. Just consider him, as many experts do, a prodigy capable of redefining how we label players." From his first day as a Sonic, Durant expressed his willingness to work hard to live up to their expectations. "I'll play all five positions if my team needs me to," he said. Sonics Coach P. J. Carlesimo likened his enthusiasm to that of Magic Johnson and Michael Jordon when they were his age, while others compared him to Hall of Fame scoring champion George Gervin.

Durant made his NBA debut on October 31, 2007, in a game against the Denver Nuggets. Although the Sonics lost, Durant made a solid first impression with 18 points, five rebounds, and three steals. On November 16, 2007, during his tenth professional game, he scored his first game-winning basket—a three-pointer in double overtime—to beat the Atlanta Hawks. "Every game I play in, it's like I'm star-struck," he said during his rookie season. "But once the ball is tipped, you've got to get all that out of your mind. It's fun playing against the best players in the world." Durant averaged 20.3 points per game, becoming the third teenager in the history of the NBA with a per-game scoring average above 20. He was the only rookie to lead his team in five different categories: points, blocks steals, free throws made, and free throw percentage. He also blocked more shots than any other guard in the league. He was selected as a member of the NBA All-Rookie First Team and was named Rookie of the Year, the first Sonics player to receive this honor. "If you would have told me a couple of years

*In his rookie season in the NBA, Durant may have been a little
starstruck by some of his superstar opponents, including
Grant Hill (shown here) of the Phoenix Suns.*

ago that I would be the NBA Rookie of the Year, to be in the same company as LeBron James, Larry Bird … I would have told you you were crazy," he said in amazement. Always one to keep his success in perspective, he said, "I just can't be complacent with just making it. I've got to keep working and keep getting better."

Unfortunately, Durant's scoring and shot-blocking record could not elevate the Sonics' reputation in 2007-2008. They ended the season with 20 wins and 62 losses, the second-worst record in the NBA. "[To] lose at something you love so much, at something you work so hard at, that makes it that much harder. We didn't lose much when I was at Texas, or in high school or in AAU, so it is not something I am used to.… The guys in our locker room fight so hard in games and work so hard in practice. But you have to take your lumps to become great." Despite the team's losses that year, Durant rose in fame and popularity, signing endorsement deals with Nike, the videogame developer EA Sports, and Gatorade.

The Oklahoma City Thunder

In July 2008, the Sonics announced their relocation to Oklahoma City, Oklahoma, where they were renamed the Thunder. Durant was in Austin taking summer classes at the University of Texas when the announcement was made. "I thought we would be [in Seattle] for at least two more years," he stated. "I got a phone call—the team is moving to Oklahoma City, this year, now. I was shocked." During the Thunder's inaugural 2008-2009 season, Durant ranked sixth in the NBA for scoring, averaging 25.3 points per game despite spending eight games on the sidelines due to an injury. In February 2009 he returned to the University of Texas for a ceremony in which officials retired his No. 35 jersey. "It was really emotional," Durant recalled. "[The No. 35] represents one of my closest friends, my AAU coach, Charles Craig.… It means more than just my jersey number hanging up in the rafters. It is everything he's done for me in my life, everything he did to help … the kids who played for him.… My coach is going to be up there forever." That same month, he earned MVP honors in the Rookie/Sophomore T-Mobile Challenge after scoring 46 points. His impressive performance captured the attention of commentators, who began calling him by the nickname "Durantula."

In summer 2009, Durant again returned to his college campus to take classes toward a degree in education, a dream he says he plans to accomplish no matter how many summers it takes. In addition to studying, he spent the summer doing strength training and defensive drills in preparation for his third year in the NBA. His hard work paid off during the 2009-2010 season, when he led the Thunder in steals and averaged 30.1 points per game to become the NBA's scoring champion. At age 21, Durant was the youngest player ever to earn this distinction. He was selected for the Western Conference All-Star team in 2010, and he enjoyed a scoring streak of 25 or more points in 29 consecutive games. He capped off the season by leading the Oklahoma City Thunder to the playoffs with a 50-32 record.

Durant drives against the Minnesota Timberwolves in 2010, when he led the league in scoring.

Although the Thunder lost to the Los Angeles Lakers in the first round of the postseason, Durant earned NBA Western Conference Player of the Month honors for April.

In July 2010, Durant signed a five-year contract extension worth $86 million with the Thunder. "I just told everybody I wasn't talking about it, really. I just kept it to myself. That's just the type of person I am. I don't like the attention around me," he said of the low-profile deal. Considering his scoring performance, the deal received very little hype and fanfare in the press, which Jack McCallum of *Sports Illustrated* attributed to the fact that Durant is "seemingly uncorrupted by what we consider the me-first culture of the NBA." In his fourth season with the Thunder, he led the NBA in scoring and was named to the All-NBA First Team for the second year in a row. Fans voted him to the NBA Western Conference All-Star Team for a second time, this year as a starting player. The Thunder won 55 games during the regular season and advanced to the Western Conference Finals before being defeated by the Dallas Mavericks.

The International Spotlight

Durant was chosen to play on the U.S.A. Basketball team for the 2010 FIBA World Championship tournament. "He's the whole package," explained U.S.A. Basketball's Managing Director Jerry Colangelo in the *New York Times*. "This is his opportunity to come forth on an international stage." Seizing that opportunity, Durant led his team to victory over Turkey in the finals, securing the world championship title for the U.S.A. for the first time since 1994. "My only option was to come out here and get a gold, and it feels really good to bring this back to the States," he said. He claimed the Most Valuable Player award for his solid performance throughout the tournament, especially the final three games in which he scored 33, 38, and 28 points against Russia, Lithuania, and Turkey, respectively. Overall, he averaged 22.8 points and 6.2 rebounds per game, propelling the undefeated Team U.S.A. to its World Championship gold-medal finish and paving their way to the 2012 Olympics.

During the summers of 2010 and 2011, Durant traveled to China as a spokesperson for Nike Basketball. There he participated in basketball clinics, charity events, and Nike store appearances while meeting his fans overseas. In July 2011 he joined a star-studded team of NBA players in the Philippines for a pair of exhibition games to benefit the MVP Sports Foundation. Meanwhile, NBA owners and the players' union were in the midst of a lockout because they could not reach a new collective bargaining agreement. The stall in labor negotiations delayed the start of the 2011-2012 NBA season by two months and reduced the number of games from 82 to 66. Late in the summer of 2011, Durant considered opportunities to play basketball in Turkey, Spain, and Russia before turning instead to the Hollywood spotlight. That September, when he would ordinarily be preparing for training camp, he began filming a Warner Brothers movie. The yet-to-be-released *Thunderstruck* is a family-friendly basketball comedy about a klutzy young fan who magically switches talents with Kevin Durant—his hero—to become the star of his high school team. Durant, meanwhile, cannot make a basket to save his life.

The 2011-2012 season presented yet another opportunity for Durant to shine. On February 19, 2012, he scored a career-best 51 points in a game against the Denver Nuggets. The crowd chanted "MVP!" as he made two free throws in the final seconds of the game to solidify the Thunder's 124-118 win. A week later he played in his third NBA All-Star game. He scored 36 points and grabbed seven rebounds to usher the Western Conference team to a 152-149 victory, a performance that earned him the All-Star MVP award. By the end of the regular season he had improved his game in several areas, setting career highs in assists per game (3.5) and rebounds per game (8.0), and improving his defense. For the third year in a row, he was the NBA scoring champion, averaging 28 points per game. "If Durant hasn't fully come into his own, the rest of the NBA should really be afraid. He can already do it all," wrote commentator Sean Gregory in *Time*.

That spring, Durant ushered the Thunder into the postseason, carrying the team to victory over the Dallas Mavericks, the Los Angeles Lakers, and the San Antonio Spurs in the playoffs. The Thunder than faced LeBron James and the Miami Heat in the 2012 NBA Finals. As the press analyzed the exciting matchup between star players Durant and James, they predicted that it could blossom into the NBA's next great rivalry. "A new era in the NBA arrived at long last, and it took two men to deliver it," Ian Thomsen wrote in *Sports Illustrated* as the Finals began. "[James and Durant] are the seminal players of this post-Kobe era, and each is seeking his first title at the other's expense. The last Finals to launch a new generation with so much anticipation and promise was the showdown of the Lakers and the Celtics in 1984, when Magic Johnson succumbed to Larry Bird over seven memorable games....

—— " ——

"[James and Durant] are the seminal players of this post-Kobe era, and each is seeking his first title at the other's expense," Ian Thomsen *wrote in* **Sports Illustrated.** *"Neither Durant nor James can know for sure what the other is capable of accomplishing in this series, because they've never put each other to the ultimate test. And so the new era begins."*

—— " ——

Durant is a naturally ruthless finisher, a closer who is every bit as mean in the final minutes as he is nice off the court. James is at heart a playmaker who was blessed with the physical gifts of Michael Jordan yet desired instead to fulfill his own egalitarian vision of Magic creating for himself and others. Lately, the two have been trying to emulate each other's games: Durant has become a better defender and passer as well as OKC's leading re-

Durant chasing LeBron James in the 2012 NBA Championships,
which Miami won four games to one.

bounder, while James has shown more willingness to hunt for his shot in the game's final minutes rather than play the playmaker."

"These Finals defy prediction," Thomsen continued. "In its initiation of a rivalry that has been long anticipated, there is no history from which to draw. Neither Durant nor James can know for sure what the other is capable of accomplishing in this series, because they've never put each other to the ultimate test. And so the new era begins." Unfortunately for Durant and the Thunder, the series did not live up to the hype. The Thunder won Game 1 105-94, but then went on to lose the next four games in a row. Durant turned in an excellent performance, averaging 30.6 points a game in the Finals while shooting 54.8 percent from the field, but James was unstoppable. Oklahoma City lost the championship to Miami in Game 5.

The 2012 Olympics

Durant was selected as part of the U.S. basketball team for the 2012 Olympic Games, held in London, England. The U.S. team was made up of professional players from many different NBA teams, giving the athletes the chance to play with their usual rivals while representing the United States. The U.S. team was expected to dominate the competition, and it did. In the preliminary round, a series of 5 games, the U.S. knocked out each of their rivals, beating France 98-71; Tunisia 110-63; Nigeria 156-73; Lithuania 99-94; and Argentina 126-97. The game against Nigeria was perhaps their easiest win, a blowout in which the U.S. set an all-time Olympic scoring record. The game against Lithuania was by far their toughest battle, with Lithuania answering every U.S. score with one of their own. With the USA trailing 82-80 in the fourth quarter, LeBron James scored 9 of his 20 points in the last 4 minutes to help the team outlast Lithuania.

With their undefeated record, the U.S. moved on to the quarterfinals as the No. 1 seed. The team faced Australia, which put up a tough contest. Durant managed five 3-pointers during the 42-point third quarter and helped the team take control during the second half. He shot 8-of-10 3-pointers to lead the team with 28 points, helping the U.S. defeat Australia 119-86. The U.S. then advanced to the semifinals against Argentina. Once again 3-pointers were a big factor. With the U.S. leading by seven points at halftime, Durant sank two 3-pointers in an 8-0 run in the third quarter that gave the team some breathing room, and then sank 2 more to help the team take a 74-57 lead into the fourth quarter. He finished with 19 points, and the U.S. knocked out Argentina 109-83 to advance to the gold medal game.

The gold medal game was seen as a rematch of the final game of the 2008 Beijing Olympic game against Spain. It was an exciting, hard-fought game that featured 16 lead changes and 6 tied scores. According to the AP, "This was no Dream Team. This was reality. The gold medal was in doubt for the U.S. men's basketball team. The Americans led Spain by only one point after three quarters, a back-and-forth, impossible-to-turn-away-from game that almost anyone would hope for in an Olympic final." Durant scored 30 points and led a balanced attack that helped the undefeated U.S Olympic Men's Basketball Team fight off Spain for a 107-100 win to capture the Olympic gold medal. Durant's 30-point game tied the third-highest total in U.S. Olympic history. He grabbed 9 rebounds and shot 5-of-13 3-pointers to set a U.S. Olympic single-game record for 3-pointers attempted. He also drew 9 Spanish fouls to finish 9-of-10 from the free throw line.

"They are a tough team," Durant said about the Spanish team. "They made it tough for us all night. Fourth quarter, we were able to pull away, make some big shots. We have so many weapons on this team that can take over a game, but everybody chipped in tonight, and we got a really good win." And not just a win—an Olympic gold medal. "I have a gold

*U.S. players Durant (left), Carmelo Anthony (center left),
LeBron James (center right), and Kobe Bryant (right)
pose with their gold medals at the 2012 Olympics in London, England.*

medal," he exclaimed. "It's unbelievable, man. I couldn't sleep last night waiting for the game. I'm glad we came out and got the W."

After the game, Durant talked about his time at the Olympics. "I put everything aside. I put the NBA season aside," he said. "I just wanted to come out here and play my role for this team. I had a great year. A really fun year. I'm so blessed to be healthy and play the game that I love every day. I could have been at home working out, but I was here, fighting for my country, and it's a great feeling."

During the eight Olympic games, Durant led Team USA in scoring with 156 total points (19.5 points per game) and was second in rebounding with 46 total offensive and defensive rebounds (5.8 rebounds per game). He also had a team-high five blocks. His 156 total points in the Olympic tournament set a new U.S. record and inspired a lot of praise. "As potent a scorer as Durant was last NBA season—he led the league with 28 points a game—he was even more deadly in the Olympics," Robert Klemko wrote in *USA Today.* "He set a Summer Games record with 34 three-pointers, shooting 52% from beyond the arc in London. A prolific shot-maker in those playoffs, Durant took on a new identity early in the Games, passing up shots to get his well-decorated peers involved. On a team stacked with scorers, Durant stressed unselfishness, and then teammates started begging him to shoot." With this new style of play, many commentators looked forward to the next NBA season to see if Durant can continue his outstanding Olympic play and turn it into an NBA championship.

In spite of his quick ascent to the top, Durant is still described by his coaches and fellow players as humble, loyal, and down to earth. As former NBA coach Jeff Van Gundy told *Time*, "I have no question that with his work ethic, and sense of team, Durant is going to go down as one of the greatest of the greats in the NBA." When asked about the future, Durant stated, "I just see myself as a good pro, a great vet who helps a lot of guys out, and a champion."

HOME AND FAMILY

Durant shares a close bond with his mother, whom he credits with teaching him the importance of a strong work ethic. "I can't explain how important my mom is in my life," he said. He has respect for the hard work she did when he was a boy, working the midnight shift to make ends meet for their family. While his mom was at the post office, he spent time with his grandmother, with whom he is also very close, and his mother's sister, Aunt Pearl, who died of breast cancer when he was 11. To honor his aunt's memory, he scribbles "Aunt Pearl" on his sneakers. He recently worked with Nike on a special-edition shoe, the Nike Zoom KD IV "Aunt Pearl," as a tribute to her. The sneaker features a hidden inscription that reads "In memory of Aunt Pearl, who inspired us all to continue the fight for a cure."

When Durant signed with the Seattle Supersonics, his mother moved to Mercer Island, Washington, so she could cook for him and help him gain weight. "She can make me a better person and make the transition easier, so why not," he reasoned. He recently purchased a home in the upscale Gaillardia section of Oklahoma City, which he shares with his brother Tony and his dogs, Diego and Capone. His parents, though frequent visitors to Oklahoma City, maintain their permanent residence near Washington, DC. When Durant scored a career-best 51 points in early 2012, his family members were courtside to celebrate. "They've been there with me ever since I was eight trying to play this game," he said. "To score 50 points with them on the sideline at the highest level of basketball is a dream come true and a blessing."

HOBBIES AND OTHER INTERESTS

Although Durant is a self-proclaimed basketball fanatic, he also has a passion for music. An aspiring music producer and sound engineer, he has a home studio where he spends time rapping and mixing music. In addition to making music, he enjoys playing video games like "NBA Live" and "March Madness." He also likes to shop for clothes and has unexpectedly become a style icon for sporting black-rimmed glasses, a plaid button-up dress shirt, and his signature accessory—the backpack—in which he keeps a Bible, sneakers, headphones, his iPad, and other gadgets. After he created a buzz by wearing the book bag into his press conferences in 2011, Nike announced a new line of limited edition Kevin Durant backpacks that were an instant hit.

Durant is known for interacting with his fans via social media. He has more than one million followers on Twitter. On October 31, 2011, four months into the NBA lockout, he tweeted, "Anybody playing flag football in [Oklahoma City]? I need to run around or something." Oklahoma State University student George Overbey responded by inviting Durant to an intramural game that evening. A few messages later, Durant was on his way to campus to pick up Overbey at his house and drive him to the football field. "I think people were skeptical that he was actually going to come. I was trying to keep it as low-key as I could. But that didn't work so well," Overbey explained in *Tulsa World*. Playing quarterback, Durant threw four touchdowns, and he picked off four passes while playing defense. "He's such a good, quality guy. It's just unbelievable to see someone that successful, that admired to be so humble," Overbey said. "It really is incredible. It speaks volumes about his character." Attendees of the game described Durant as patient and generous as he posed for photos and signed autographs after the game.

In addition to being an all-star on the court, Durant has established himself as a community leader with a generous heart and boundless energy. He has hosted numerous charity events, teaches kids in a summer basketball Pro-Camp in Oklahoma City, and has taught youth basketball clinics all over the country. He returns home to the Washington, DC area as much as he can and has given back to his hometown community by funding major renovations at his old childhood hangout, the Seat Pleasant Activity Center.

HONORS AND AWARDS

Adolph Rupp Trophy: 2007, for NCAA basketball player of the year

John R. Wooden Award (Los Angeles Athletic Club): 2007, for the outstanding college basketball player in the United States

Naismith Award (Atlanta Tipoff Club): 2007, for men's college player of the year

NCAA Division 1 Player of the Year (National Association of Basketball Coaches): 2007

Oscar Robertson Trophy (U.S. Basketball Writers Association): 2007, for
   NCAA basketball player of the year
Player of the Year (*Sporting News*): 2007
Player of the Year (Associated Press-AP): 2007
Rookie of the Year Award (National Basketball Association): 2007-2008
T-Mobile Rookie Challenge Most Valuable Player Award: 2009
FIBA World Championship Most Valuable Player Award (International
   Basketball Federation): 2010
All-Star Game Most Valuable Player Award (National Basketball Associa-
   tion): 2012
Olympic Men's Basketball: 2012, gold medal (with USA Men's Olympic
   Basketball Team)

FURTHER READING

Books

Doeden, Matt. *Kevin Durant: Basketball Superstar,* 2012 (juvenile)
Sandler, Michael. *Kevin Durant,* 2012 (juvenile)
Savage, Jeff. *Kevin Durant,* 2012 (juvenile)

Periodicals

Current Biography Yearbook, 2010
Men's Fitness, Nov. 2009, p.33
New York Times, Dec. 13, 2007, p.D4; July 8, 2010, p.B13; Aug. 15, 2010,
   p.SP5; Sep. 13, 2010, p.D2
Seattle Times, July 1, 2007
Sporting News, Mar. 30, 2009, p.40; Aug. 17, 2009, p.80; June 21, 2010, p.22;
   June 6, 2011, p.15
Sports Illustrated, Feb. 19, 2007; Nov. 12, 2007, p.52; Dec. 24, 2007, p.72;
   Sep. 20, 2010, p.12; June 18, 2012
Washington Post, Aug. 15, 2011, p.D6

Online Articles

www.espn.com
   (ESPN, "Kevin Durant Splits from Longtime Agent," Feb. 17, 2012;
   "Kevin Durant Wins All-Star Game MVP," Feb. 26, 2012; "Kevin Durant,
   U.S. Pull through in Final as Spain Can't Rain on Parade," Aug. 12, 2012)
www.chron.com
   (Houston Chronicle, "Stock Is Soaring: The Skinny on Kevin Durant,"
   June 26, 2007)
sportsillustrated.cnn.com
   (Sports Illustrated, "Phenomenal Freshman," Feb. 19, 2007; "The Kid
   Enters the Picture," Nov. 12, 2007; "All Hail a King without the Bling,"

Sep. 20, 2010; "Immune to Hype, Humble Durant Following His Own Path to Greatness," June 13, 2012; "Let the Rivalry Begin," June 18, 2012; "Durant, James Lead USA Past Spain 107-100 for Hoops Gold Medal," Aug. 12, 2012)

www.time.com

(Time, "Q&A: Kevin Durant on NBA Draft Day," June 28, 2007; "How Team USA Won Men's Hoops—and the Entire Olympics," Aug. 12, 2012)

www.usatoday.com

(USA Today, "Durant Scores 51 as Thunder Top Nuggets in OT," Feb. 19, 2012; "Thunder Top Lakers, Tie Miami as NBA's Best," Feb. 24, 2012; "Durant Earns MVP Honors," Feb. 27, 2012; "Kevin Durant Drops 38, Thunder Beat Magic," Mar. 1, 2012; "USA Men Survive Spain to Win Basketball Gold Medal" and "Durant Sinks Shots, Spain in Finale," Aug. 12, 2012)

ADDRESS

Kevin Durant
Oklahoma City Thunder
Two Leadership Square
211 North Robinson Ave., Suite 300
Oklahoma City, OK 73102

WEB SITES

kevindurant35.com
www.nba.com/playerfile/kevin_durant

Dale Earnhardt Jr. 1974-

American Professional Race Car Driver
Nine-Time Winner of NASCAR's Most Popular
Driver Award

BIRTH

Ralph Dale Earnhardt Jr. (known to auto racing fans as Dale Jr. or just Junior) was born on October 10, 1974, in Kannapolis, North Carolina. His parents were Ralph Dale Earnhardt Sr. (known as Dale), a professional race car driver, and his second wife, Brenda Gee Earnhardt. Dale Earnhardt Sr. was married three times and had four children. Dale Jr. has a sister, Kelley, who is two years older. He also has an older half-brother,

147

Kerry, from his father's first marriage, and a younger half-sister, Taylor, from his father's third marriage.

YOUTH

Auto racing was a huge part of Dale Jr.'s life from an early age. The town where he was born, about 30 miles outside of Charlotte, was nicknamed "Car Town" because all of the streets were named after car models or engine parts. In addition, many of the people who lived and worked in the area were involved with the National Association for Stock Car Auto Racing (NASCAR).

> "[Dad] never really did anything with me. He never told me things. We were raised by six or seven nannies. I always thought he felt I wasn't much like him," Dale Jr. recalled. "He was intimidating, like they say. He was like that as a father when he was at home. You wanted to please him all the time, make him happy, and you wanted to somehow get a response from him."

Stock car racing got its start in the American South after World War II ended in 1945. Young men bought regular street cars and modified the engines to make them go faster. Then they held informal races on country roads and oval dirt tracks across the region. This type of racing was called "stock" car racing because the cars were souped-up versions of the ones sold in automobile dealerships, rather than specially built racing machines. In the late 1940s, a group of racers formed NASCAR to organize races and award prizes to the winners. NASCAR eventually grew into the largest sanctioning body for the sport of stock car racing, with drivers in various divisions competing in 1,500 races at 100 different tracks each year. NASCAR's highest division is the Sprint Cup (formerly known as the Winston Cup and the Nextel Cup), followed by the Nationwide Series (formerly known as the Busch Series).

Dale Jr. was born into a NASCAR family. His paternal grandfather, Ralph Earnhardt, was a legendary driver who won more than 500 races in the early days of NASCAR. His maternal grandfather, Robert Gee, was a well-known car builder and mechanic for NASCAR race teams. His father, Dale Sr., was an up-and-coming young driver at the time of Dale Jr.'s birth. He eventually became one of the most popular and successful drivers in NASCAR history, winning 76 Winston Cup races and seven champi-

Dale Sr. and family celebrating a win in 1985. From left: Kelley, Dale Jr.'s sister; Dale Sr.; Teresa, Dale Jr.'s stepmother; and Dale Jr.

onships during his 25-year career. Several uncles, cousins, and other members of the extended family worked in the racing industry as well.

Feeling Distant from His Famous Father

Despite his many connections to NASCAR, Dale Jr. did not spend much time at racetracks as a kid. His parents divorced in 1978, when he was four years old. He and Kelley lived with their mother until 1982, when their home was destroyed by a fire. Then the children moved in with their father and his new wife, Teresa Houston, in Mooresville, North Carolina. By this time Dale Sr. had worked his way up through NASCAR's racing divisions and won his first Winston Cup championship. His no-nonsense personality and aggressive driving style made him a fan favorite and earned him the nicknames The Intimidator and The Man in Black.

Dale Sr.'s racing career kept him extremely busy. He competed in races on more than 30 weekends per year and spent countless hours making public appearances on behalf of corporate sponsors. He also owned several Chevrolet dealerships and ran his own NASCAR race team, Dale Earnhardt Inc. (DEI). As a result, Dale Sr. did not spend much time with his children. "Dad was away racing most of the time," Dale Jr. remembered.

"He was so focused on winning that even when he was home between races, his mind was still at the racetrack instead of at home with us."

Although Dale Jr. admired his father and was proud of his racing successes, he felt very distant from Dale Sr. through most of his youth. "[Dad] never really did anything with me. He never told me things. We were raised by six or seven nannies. I always thought he felt I wasn't much like him," Dale Jr. recalled. "He was intimidating, like they say. He was like that as a father when he was at home. You wanted to please him all the time, make him happy, and you wanted to somehow get a response from him."

Dale Jr.'s mother, meanwhile, lived in Virginia and only managed to see the children on occasional weekends. "When she left, she'd cry," he related. "It tore us up." With neither of his parents around much, Dale Jr. relied on his sister Kelley for emotional support. She defended him when he was teased by other kids who were jealous of their father's fame and wealth. "Kids bullied him," Kelley acknowledged. "He was a lot smaller than they were. He was shy and sensitive and easily intimidated. He didn't stand up for himself. I never thought he'd race cars."

EDUCATION

By the time Dale Jr. reached his teen years, he had grown angry and resentful. He had trouble getting along with his stepmother and obeying his father's strict rules. They responded to his difficult behavior by sending him away to Oak Ridge Military Academy near Greensboro, North Carolina. Dale Jr. struggled to fit in at the school and was eventually kicked out. He returned home and graduated from Mooresville High School in 1992.

Since Dale Sr. had always placed a strong emphasis on education, Dale Jr. felt deeply disappointed when his father failed to attend his graduation ceremony. "Education. Yeah, it was such a big thing," he said. "So I graduated from high school, and where was my father? He didn't come to graduation. He was in a race somewhere. I understand now, of course, but I was looking forward to holding that diploma in his face. Except he wasn't there." Dale Jr. went on to earn an associate's degree in automotives from Mitchell Community College in Statesville, North Carolina.

CAREER HIGHLIGHTS

Breaking into Stock Car Racing

Earnhardt Jr. began to dabble in auto racing around the time he graduated from high school. He and his brother Kerry and sister Kelley bought a 1978 Chevrolet Monte Carlo at a junkyard, fixed it up, and took turns driving it in short-track races in NASCAR's Street Stock division. Their father never attended their races or offered them advice. Although Earnhardt Sr. had won four Winston Cup titles and earned millions of dollars in prize money by the time his children got involved in the sport, he did not think that they should receive any special treatment. He wanted them to work their way up through the ranks of NASCAR like other young drivers.

Earnhardt Jr. continued racing on weekends during college and afterward, while he worked as an auto mechanic and oil-change man at one of his father's Chevrolet dealerships in Newton, North Carolina. He learned a great deal about racing and steadily gained confidence as a driver. "I helped put together, work on, and set up my cars," he noted. "I learned from my mistakes. I wasn't a dominating driver, didn't win many races, but I was consistent."

Earnhardt Jr. impressed people in the racing industry with his talent and composure on the track. In 1994 Gary Hargett, a former driver and longtime friend of his father, offered

> "
>
> *Earnhardt Jr. revealed that gaining his father's attention was an important factor in his decision to race. "I wanted to impress him," he said. "I could have went and done other things, but no matter how successful I'd been ... it wouldn't have been as impressive to him as winning a race."*
>
> "

him an opportunity to move up to the Late Model division. Earnhardt Jr. competed in 113 races over the next three seasons. Although he only chalked up three victories, he finished in the top 10 an impressive 90 times because he rarely crashed. His strong performance earned him several opportunities to compete in the Busch Series, which was considered NASCAR's training ground for future Winston Cup drivers. Earnhardt Jr. appeared in one Busch race in 1996 and eight more in 1997.

Winning Back-to-Back Busch Series Titles

As Earnhardt Jr. worked his way up through the NASCAR divisions, Earnhardt Sr. gradually began to take notice of his son's abilities as a driver. Earnhardt Jr. acknowledged that gaining his father's attention was an important factor in his decision to race. "I wanted to impress him," he said. "I could have went and done other things, but no matter how successful I'd been ... it wouldn't have been as impressive to him as winning a race."

Earnhardt Jr. discussing preparation for a race with his father,
after Jr. joined Sr.'s race team, May 1998.

As the start of the 1998 NASCAR race season approached, Dale Earnhardt Inc. had an opening for a Busch Series driver. The crew chief and many other members of the DEI race team encouraged Earnhardt Sr. to offer the job to his son. They argued that Earnhardt Jr. had earned a full-time ride in the Busch Series. Earnhardt Jr. drove the DEI car in pre-season test sessions, but weeks passed without Earnhardt Sr. making a decision. Earnhardt Jr. had almost given up on the idea when he accidentally learned that he would be driving for DEI in 1998. "I didn't know for sure that I was the driver until the name decals came into the shop two weeks before [the season-opening race at] Daytona," he recalled. "I know [my dad] just wants to teach me respect. He didn't want me to assume."

Earnhardt Jr. repaid his father's confidence in him by winning a race at Texas Motor Speedway on April 4, in only his 16th career Busch Series start. When he pulled his car into Victory Lane to accept his trophy, his father reacted with an uncharacteristic display of affection. Earnhardt Sr. rushed toward him, gave him a big hug, and told him how proud he was. "It stirred memories of the years I had tried so hard to earn my dad's approval. Maybe that did it," Earnhardt Jr. remembered. "It really was a proud moment for him to show that much excitement and happiness over something that I had accomplished."

Earnhardt Jr. went on to win six more races in 1998. He thus earned enough points to claim the Busch Series championship in his first full season of competition on the circuit. (NASCAR drivers earn points based on their finishing position in races, number of laps led, number of pole positions earned, and other criteria. At the end of each season, the drivers who earn the most points in their division are named champions.) Earnhardt Jr. became the first third-generation driver to win the Busch Series points title, following in the footsteps of his father and grandfather. At the conclusion of his highly successful first season with DEI, Earnhardt Jr. signed a five-year sponsorship deal with Budweiser worth $50 million.

As the 1999 season got underway, Earnhardt Jr. emerged as the most popular driver in the Busch Series. NASCAR fans not only recognized his famous name, but they also liked his red number 3 Budweiser Chevrolet and his hard-charging driving style. "I enjoy that kind of racing, hate watching a race that looks like a bunch of toy soldiers marching around," Earnhardt Jr. explained. "Fans like action, even if their favorite driver gets bumped around or spun out." He rewarded fans for their support by claiming six race victories and a second consecutive Busch Series championship. He also appeared in five Winston Cup Series races during the 1999 season, posting a best finishing position of tenth.

Moving Up to Winston Cup

On the strength of his back-to-back titles in the Busch Series, Earnhardt Jr. earned the opportunity to compete in the prestigious Winston Cup Series full-time in 2000. Since his father championed the number 3 in Winston Cup, Earnhardt Jr. chose the number 8, which had once belonged to his grandfather. In the season-opening Daytona 500—the biggest race of the NASCAR season, held in February each year—he finished a respectable 13th and beat his father for the first time. On April 2 Earnhardt Jr. claimed his first victory, at Texas Motor Speedway, in only his 12th career Winston Cup race. "It was fun to get out front and show these guys I could use my head and make smart decisions," he said afterward.

Only a month later, Earnhardt Jr. claimed a second victory at Richmond International Speedway, crossing the finish line only 0.159 seconds ahead of veteran driver Terry Labonte. "We are the first team to take two races this season," he noted. "Rookie team, rookie driver. Winners, not just once, but

*The 2001 Daytona 500, with Jr. in the #8 Budweiser Chevy
and Sr. in the #3 Goodwrench Chevy.*

twice." On the strength of his two wins, Earnhardt Jr. earned enough points to finish 16th in the Winston Cup standings at the end of the season. He narrowly missed winning the Raybestos Rookie of the Year Award, finishing 42 points behind fellow rookie driver Matt Kenseth.

One of the things Earnhardt Jr. enjoyed most about his rookie Winston Cup season, however, was that it brought him closer to his father. Being involved in NASCAR's highest level of racing gave Earnhardt Jr. a new understanding of the pressures and demands that his father had long faced. It also enabled the two men to hang out together at the track and relate to each other as friends and colleagues. Several longtime Winston Cup drivers remarked that the presence of his son seemed to rekindle Earnhardt Sr.'s interest in racing. "It totally changed Dale Sr.'s outlook on things," said racer Dave Marcis. "He became more competitive and rejuvenated."

Dealing with Tragedy

Following his strong rookie year, Earnhardt Jr. eagerly anticipated the start of the 2001 Winston Cup season. As always, the season opened with the biggest race on the NASCAR schedule, the Daytona 500. Earnhardt Jr.'s car ran well throughout the race. With only a few laps to go, he found himself running second behind his DEI teammate, Michael Waltrip, with his father sitting behind him in third place.

Earnhardt Sr. did not seem to have enough power to pass his son or Waltrip, so he tried to prevent other cars from getting by him in order to ensure victory for a member of his race team. His strategy worked, as Waltrip streaked across the finish line to take the checkered flag, followed closely by Earnhardt Jr. in second. As Earnhardt Sr. entered the final turn, however, his car was bumped from behind by fellow driver Sterling Marlin. Earnhardt Sr. lost control of the car and crashed into the concrete barrier on the outside of the track at 180 miles per hour. Although the crash did not initially appear to be life-threatening, NASCAR fans soon learned that Earnhardt Sr. had died instantly from severe head and neck injuries.

The tragic loss of the NASCAR legend shocked and saddened race fans everywhere. Makeshift memorials to Earnhardt Sr. appeared at racetracks across the country, and thousands of people displayed his number 3 on T-shirts, flags, banners, and window stickers. Earnhardt Jr. took the news of his father's death very hard. He struggled to find a way to come to terms with his grief. "I lost the greatest man I ever knew," he stated. "I miss my father, and I've cried for him. I'm trying to maintain a good focus for the future and just remember that he's in a better place, a place we all want to be.... We'll get through this. I'm sure he'd want us to keep going, and that's what we're going to do."

Although Earnhardt Jr. returned to competition the following week, he did poorly over the next few races. He finally broke through for his first victory of the season on July 7, when the Winston Cup Series returned to Daytona for the first time since Earnhardt Sr.'s death. Earnhardt Jr. turned in one of the best performances of his career, leading 116 of 160 laps and fighting his way back from sixth to first with only a few laps remaining. Waltrip, his DEI teammate who had won the Daytona 500, finished second. Earnhardt Jr. claimed that he had felt his father's presence throughout the race. "He was with me," he declared. "I know I did it, but he was there."

Earnhardt Jr. went on to win two more races in the 2001 season, giving him 15 finishes in the top 10 and placing him eighth in the Winston Cup point standings. During the off-season he published a book called *Driver #8*. It describes what it was like growing up as the son of a famous driver, provides a race-by-race chronicle of his rookie season of Winston Cup competition, and concludes with the tragic death of his father. NASCAR fans snapped up copies of the memoir, vaulting it onto the *New York Times* best-seller list. Earnhardt Jr. also joined his stepmother, Teresa, as part-owner of a Busch Series race team called Chance 2 Motorsports. Chance 2 hired a young driver, Martin Truex Jr., who went on to win back-to-back Busch Series championships in 2004 and 2005.

Winning the 2004 Daytona 500

In the 2002 Winston Cup season, Earnhardt Jr. won two races and posted six finishes in the top 10. These results were good enough to claim 11th place in the Winston Cup point standings. Earnhardt Jr. performed more consistently in 2003, winning two races and finishing in the top 10 a career-high 21 times. His strong performance lifted him to an impressive third in the season-ending point standings—the best finish of his career. At the end of the year he was thrilled to receive the NASCAR Most Popular Driver Award from the National Motorsports Press Association.

Prior to the start of the 2004 season, NASCAR introduced a number of changes. It dropped Winston cigarettes as the sponsor of its premier race series in favor of the telecommunications company Nextel, so the Winston Cup became the Nextel Cup. It also created a 10-race playoff system called the Chase for the Cup in an effort to tighten competition and increase fan interest toward the end of the season. Only the 12 drivers ranked highest in the point standings with 10 races remaining would qualify for the Chase and compete for the championship.

As always, though, the 2004 NASCAR season started with the Daytona 500. Earnhardt Jr. made it his personal mission to win the prestigious race as a way to honor his father's legacy. He led the first 29 laps and ran near the front all day. Toward the end of the race, it became clear that the two strongest cars belonged to Earnhardt Jr. and Tony Stewart. Earnhardt Jr. made a daring pass of Stewart with a few laps remaining to clinch the victory. "Every time we come to Daytona, it feels like I'm closer to Dad. But at the same time it's a reminder of losing him. So I wanted to come down here and win," he said afterward. "This is like you can't write a better script.… It's just the greatest race. It's the greatest day of my life. I really can't describe it."

Winning the Daytona 500 turned out to be the beginning of an outstanding season for Earnhardt Jr. He won a total of 6 races that year and posted 21 finishes in the top 10, which easily allowed him to qualify for the inaugural Chase. He actually led the standings briefly with seven races left, but he dropped to second when NASCAR officials penalized him 25 points for swearing in a post-race TV interview. The controversial decision turned out to be a key turning point in his season, and he ended up finishing fifth in the point standings. Still, he won the Most Popular Driver Award for the second straight year.

Earnhardt Jr. celebrating his win at the 2004 Daytona 500.

By the time Earnhardt Jr. completed his fourth full Cup season, he had become one of the most marketable athletes in the United States. NASCAR fans appreciated his good looks, down-to-earth personality, casual style, and hip interests. But his popularity extended well beyond the traditional stock car racing fan base, making him one of the first true crossover stars in NASCAR history. In fact, some observers described him as the "face of NASCAR" because he helped expand interest in the sport nationwide. Earnhardt Jr.'s appeal led to a number of business and endorsement opportunities. He gave an interview on the national TV news show "60 Minutes," hosted his own auto racing shows on cable TV, served as a presenter at the annual Country Music Awards, and developed racing video games. Although he enjoyed some aspects of his fame, Earnhardt Jr. also admitted that he sometimes wished he had more personal privacy and fewer demands on his time.

Leaving His Father's Race Team

The 2005 Nextel Cup season was a disappointing one for Earnhardt Jr. He earned only one victory and 13 top-10 finishes, failed to qualify for the

*Earnhardt Jr. with the Hendrick Motorsports team. From left:
driver Jimmie Johnson; driver Todd Bodine; team owner Rick Hendrick;
driver Mark Martin; driver Jeff Gordon; and Earnhardt Jr.*

Chase, and ended up 19th in the point standings. He performed more consistently during the 2006 season, posting his 17th career victory and earning 17 finishes in the top 10. Although his results were good enough to qualify for the Chase, he only managed to finish fifth in the point standings. He remained a favorite among NASCAR fans, however, and claimed the Most Popular Driver Award in both 2005 and 2006.

As the 2007 Nextel Cup season approached, NASCAR observers noted that Earnhardt Jr.'s contract with DEI was due to expire at the end of the year. Teresa Earnhardt had taken ownership of her husband's race team following Earnhardt Sr.'s death in 2001. Since then, Earnhardt Jr. and his stepmother had disagreed publicly about the future direction of DEI on several occasions. Teresa also claimed that Earnhardt Jr.'s popularity and outside interests distracted him from his job as a driver.

Earnhardt Jr., on the other hand, blamed the team owner and DEI management for not spending the money necessary to build elite race cars. He argued that DEI could not be a top-notch race team with non-racers in charge of the business. He tried to buy a controlling interest in his father's company, but his stepmother refused to consider his offer. Despite the high-profile differences of opinion, however, most observers felt confident that the two sides would eventually iron out their problems so that Earnhardt Jr. could remain with DEI.

During the 2007 Nextel Cup season, however, Earnhardt Jr. failed to win a race for the first time in his career, did not finish a career-high nine races, missed qualifying for the Chase, and ended up a disappointing 16th in the point standings. Midway through the frustrating season, Earnhardt Jr. shocked many NASCAR fans by announcing his decision to leave DEI at the end of 2007. "I had to leave and get out and do my own thing," he declared. "It's time for me to take charge of my career. It's time for me to start winning championships."

A month after announcing his departure from DEI, Earnhardt Jr. shocked NASCAR fans once again by signing a contract with rival Hendrick Motorsports (HMS). HMS was the most dominant team in Nextel Cup competition. Its talented stable of drivers included four-time champion Jeff Gordon and two-time defending champion Jimmie Johnson. HMS drivers had won fully half of the 36 races on the Nextel Cup schedule in 2007. Many fans of Earnhardt Jr. and his father, however, had long viewed Hendrick Motorsports as the bitter enemy of their favorite drivers. They especially disliked the young, clean-cut, California-born Gordon, whom they felt had prevented Earnhardt Sr. from capturing a record eighth career Winston Cup title in the late 1990s.

Still, Earnhardt Jr. found the idea of driving for HMS very appealing. He felt comfortable with the team owner, Rick Hendrick, whom he had known for many years as a friend and competitor of his father. "He's kind of like a father figure to me and has been for a long time," he noted. Earnhardt Jr. also appreciated Hendrick's state-of-the-art race shop and technology-driven approach to racing. He believed that gaining access to HMS equipment and engineers would make him more competitive. "I'm a racer, and I just want to win races and contend for championships. Now that I'm with Rick, that's going to start happening," he stated. "I understand that I

Earnhardt Jr. joined rival team Hendrick Motorsports to become more competitive. "I'm a racer, and I just want to win races and contend for championships. Now that I'm with Rick [Hendrick], that's going to start happening," he stated. "I understand that I have no more excuses. Now I'll have the best equipment and the best people behind me. It's time for me to start winning."

---

have no more excuses. Now I'll have the best equipment and the best people behind me. It's time for me to start winning."

Seeking a Championship

In addition to switching teams, Earnhardt Jr.'s racing effort underwent a number of other changes prior to the start of the 2008 season. His primary sponsor changed from Budweiser to Mountain Dew/Amp Energy Drink and the U.S. National Guard. In addition, the color of his car changed from red to green, and his number changed from 8 to 88. Since NASCAR fans purchase millions of dollars worth of merchandise every year bearing the name and number of their favorite drivers, all of these changes forced Earnhardt Jr.'s many fans to overhaul their wardrobes. NASCAR underwent a change in 2008 as well, as the Nextel Cup became the Sprint Cup.

All of the changes appeared to be positive for Earnhardt Jr. as the 2008 Sprint Cup season got underway. He won the first two races he competed in for HMS, the Bud Shootout exhibition race and the Gatorade Duel qualifying race, which are held as part of the festivities surrounding the Daytona 500 but do not count toward the Sprint Cup point standings. He finished ninth in the big race that weekend, then went on to finish in the top 10 in three of the next four races. Earnhardt Jr. notched the 18th race victory of his 10-year Cup career at Michigan International Speedway on Father's Day. "It's special—my daddy meant a lot to me," he said afterward. "I know I can't tell my father 'Happy Father's Day,' but I get to wish all fathers a happy day. I mean it." His one victory and 16 top-10 finishes enabled him to qualify for the Chase, but he ended up 12th in the final point standings. He still won his sixth consecutive Most Popular Driver Award, while his HMS teammate Johnson claimed his third straight Sprint Cup title.

Earnhardt Jr. hoped to improve his results in 2009, but he struggled throughout his second season with HMS. He was assigned a new crew chief, Lance McGrew, to replace his cousin, Tony Eury Jr. Eury Jr. had moved from DEI to Hendrick along with Earnhardt Jr., but he had trouble fitting into the disciplined, high-tech atmosphere at HMS. As Earnhardt Jr. and McGrew tried to establish a good working relationship, the 88 car's performance on the track suffered. Earnhardt Jr. failed to win a race for only the second time in his Cup career, posted only five top-10 finishes, and finished a career-worst 25th in the point standings. Meanwhile, Johnson won a fourth consecutive Sprint Cup championship, and two other HMS drivers (Mark Martin and Gordon) finished second and third in the points. "Maybe Junior has struggled a little to adapt to the culture of Hen-

Earnhardt Jr. in #88 comes in for a pit stop during a race.

drick," Johnson said. "It's a demanding place, and if you're not totally committed, you might struggle."

Earnhardt Jr. took a break at the end of the 2009 season to recharge his batteries, and he came back in 2010 with an improved attitude. "This was the best off-season of my life because it was the first time I can remember that I got away from the sport," he explained. "I just stayed at home and remembered that I've won races, a lot of big trophies, and that I know how to drive these cars. My confidence came back." Earnhardt Jr. demonstrated his newfound confidence at the Daytona 500. In what some observers described as the best driving of his life, he passed eight cars in the final two laps to finish in second place. "It was a blur," he said afterward. "I just held the gas pedal down and prayed."

Unfortunately, Earnhardt Jr.'s struggles continued later in the 2010 season. He went winless for the second straight year, only managed to finish in the top 10 eight times, failed to qualify for the Chase, and ended up 21st in the point standings. His teammate Johnson had another great year and claimed his fifth straight Sprint Cup title, while Earnhardt Jr. won the Most Popular Driver Award for the eighth time.

In 2011 Earnhardt Jr. changed crew chiefs again and began working with Steve Letarte, who had formerly been Gordon's crew chief. "Confidence breeds confidence," Letarte stated. "I know he can drive, I know he can win, I know our cars can win, and I'm excited to give him a platform week in and week out that he can display his talents." Rick Hendrick also moved the 88 car into the same race shop as Johnson's 48 team, in hopes that Earnhardt Jr.'s crew might benefit from knowing the five-time champion's strategy and setup.

The changes seemed to help, as Earnhardt Jr. ran well through much of the 2011 season. Although he did not win a race, he came close on several occasions. He was poised to win the Coca-Cola 600 at Charlotte Motor Speedway in May, for instance, until his car ran out of gas in the final turn. He ended up with 11 finishes in the top 10, qualified for the Chase, and finished ninth in the point standings. In accepting the Most Popular Driver Award for the ninth consecutive year, Earnhardt Jr. expressed satisfaction with the improvement in his results and optimism about his chances for 2012. "I'm happy to be competing again and I feel like I'm almost where I want to be," he said. "This year it turned all around, 180 degrees, and I'm enjoying it again and I didn't want the season to come to an end.... I feel much more excited about my future."

Earnhardt Jr. was off to a great start in the 2012 Sprint Cup season. In his first 25 races for points, he had top 5 finishes in 10 of the 25 races, and top 10 finishes in 17. His first win of the season came in May 2012 in the Sprint Showdown race at Charlotte Motor Speedway, a qualifying race for the Sprint All-Star Race. While the Sprint Showdown does not count toward the Sprint Cup point standings, it was a satisfying win nonetheless. Earnhardt Jr. led all 40 laps of the race and broke his winless streak. He then placed 5th in the All-Star Race.

Earnhardt Jr. won his second race of the 2012 season in June at the Quicken Loans 400 at Michigan International Speedway. It was his first NASCAR Sprint Cup Series victory in four years—and oddly, at the same racetrack where he won four years ago. He dominated the race, leading a race-high 95 laps and beating runner-up Tony Stewart with a more than 5-second lead. After the win, Earnhardt Jr. was quick to give credit to his fans. "[To win] for my fans that stuck behind me for all these years, and I know exactly what they've been thinking about and how long they've wanted us to get to victory lane, this is for them," he said. "I appreciate their loyalty and we wouldn't have made it back to victory lane without them so that's who we've got to give all the credit to." Some commentators believed that Earnhardt Jr. and team were concerned less with winning individual races and more with earning points with the ultimate goal of winning the Sprint Cup Series Championship. And indeed, as of August 2012, Earnhardt Jr. led the Sprint Cup standings.

Dealing with High Expectations

According to race car enthusiasts, Earnhardt Jr. has shown real improvement during the 2011 and 2012 Sprint Cup seasons, his best seasons since joining Hendrick Motorsports. Still, most feel that he has not yet lived up to the high expectations that accompanied his move. After all, Earnhardt Jr. enjoys access to the same engineering expertise and well-prepared cars as Johnson and the other HMS drivers, yet he has only produced one victory and has never contended for the Cup championship in four seasons. By the end of 2011, his winless streak extended to more than 120 races. Although he remains a huge favorite among NASCAR fans, critics claim that his on-track performance does not support his popularity.

Few people question that Earnhardt Jr. has talent as a driver, but some people wonder whether he possesses the dedication and focus necessary to compete at the highest level. "It was eye-opening for Dale, the level of intensity at HMS," said Gordon. "How hard everyone works. Jimmie [Johnson] works out at a gym five times a week. He pays attention to details." Earnhardt Jr. acknowledges that he does not maintain as rigorous a training schedule as some other NASCAR drivers. "I try to keep in shape, eat right, lift weights. But I don't do it all the time," he admitted. "Jimmie hardly ever makes a step without thinking how it's gonna affect his racing. But I don't believe in living like that. I'd have to become a different person. I'm not willing to devote that much to it."

Other observers claim that the problem lies not with Earnhardt Jr., but with the unreasonably high expectations he has faced throughout his career as the son of a legendary seven-time Cup champion. "Dale Jr. has never gotten a fair shake from the start because, guess what, he's not his father," said fellow driver Kevin Harvick. "He was always sup-

Earnhardt Jr. has acknowledged that living up to his father's legacy is a difficult task. "I still love racing, still love the challenge. I really want to win a championship one day, but if that never happens, I'll still be happy," he stated. "You know, I never thought I'd accomplish everything that I have in racing. I may have this name, but I never thought of myself being like my father. He was just so big, man, larger than life. It's a damn tough act to follow."

Nine-time Most Popular Driver winner Earnhardt Jr. signing autographs for fans.

posed to have been someone else. The pressure he's under is unreal." Even though he has not captured a title of his own, Earnhardt Jr. has accumulated a respectable 18 Cup wins and $58 million in race earnings in 10 full seasons on the circuit. In addition, he has accomplished these things while facing more intense fan pressure and media scrutiny than any other driver.

Earnhardt Jr. recognizes that living up to his father's legacy is a difficult task. "I still love racing, still love the challenge. I really want to win a championship one day, but if that never happens, I'll still be happy," he stated. "You know, I never thought I'd accomplish everything that I have in racing. I may have this name, but I never thought of myself being like my father. He was just so big, man, larger than life. It's a damn tough act to follow."

HOME AND FAMILY

Earnhardt Jr. lives on 140 acres of land near Mooresville, North Carolina. His property features a six-hole golf course, three go-kart tracks, a regulation boxing ring, and a replica Western frontier town with a saloon, a hotel, and a jail. He shares his home with a variety of pets, including dogs, cats, and a pair of bison.

Earnhardt Jr. has never been married, and he has always kept his personal relationships strictly private. In late 2011, however, he introduced his girlfriend Amy Reimann to the media after dating her for more than a year.

HOBBIES AND OTHER INTERESTS

In his spare time, Earnhardt Jr. enjoys hanging out at home, playing video games, and tinkering with computers. He also maintains a wide variety of business and charitable interests. He owns a Nationwide race team called JR Motorsports, which signed Danica Patrick to its roster of drivers in 2010. He also owns a bar and nightclub called Whisky River in Charlotte. In 2007 he launched the Dale Jr. Foundation to help underprivileged youth gain confidence through education. The foundation lends support to 700 local and national youth organizations. Finally, Earnhardt Jr. is active with the Make-a-Wish Foundation.

HONORS AND AWARDS

Busch (Nationwide) Series Champion: 1998, 1999
NASCAR Most Popular Driver (National Motorsports Press Association): 2003-2011

FURTHER READING

Books

Earnhardt, Dale Jr., with Jade Gurss. *Driver #8,* 2002
Hillstrom, Laurie Collier. *People in the News: Dale Earnhardt Jr.,* 2009 (juvenile)
MacDonald, James. *Dale Earnhardt, Jr.: Racing's Living Legacy,* 2008 (juvenile)

Periodicals

Current Biography Yearbook, 2007
New York Times, Jan. 20, 2008, p.3
New York Times Magazine, Aug. 8, 2010, p.22
Sporting News, August 6, 2001, p.48; Feb. 14, 2011, p.48
Sports Illustrated, July 1, 2002, p.60; May 26, 2004, p.12; Dec. 5, 2007; Feb. 18, 2008, p.72; Nov. 25, 2010, p.62

Online Articles

www.notablebiographies.com/news/Ca-Ge/Earnhardt-Dale-Jr.html (Encyclopedia of World Biography, "Dale Earnhardt Jr. Biography," no date)

espn.go.com/racing
   (ESPN, "Dale Earnhardt Jr.," multiple articles, various dates)
espn.go.com/racing/nascar
   (ESPN, "Dale Earnhardt Jr.'s Confidence Surging," Feb. 7, 2012; "Dale Earnhardt Jr. Wins at Michigan," June 18, 2012)
www.nascar.com/news
   (NASCAR, "The Drought Is Over! Junior Back in Victory Lane," June 19, 2012)
topics.nytimes.com/pages/topics
   (New York Times, "Dale Earnhardt Jr.," multiple articles, various dates)
sportsillustrated.cnn.com
   (Sports Illustrated, "Dale Earnhardt Jr.: A Junior Renaissance," Jan. 12, 2012)
www.usatoday.com
   (USA Today, "Adulation Follows Dale Earnhardt Jr.'s Drought-Snapping Win," June 18, 2012)

ADDRESS

Dale Earnhardt Jr.
Hendrick Motorsports
4400 Papa Joe Hendrick Blvd.
Charlotte, NC 28262

WEB SITES

www.dalejr.com
www.nascar.com
www.hendrickmotorsports.com

Zaha Hadid 1950-

Iraqi-Born British Architect and Designer
First Female Winner of the Pritzker Prize,
Architecture's Highest Honor

BIRTH

Zaha Hadid was born on October 31, 1950, in Baghdad, Iraq.
Her father, Muhammad Hadid, was an economist, business-
man, and politician who co-founded the progressive Iraqi National Democratic Party. Her mother did not work outside the
home, but raised Hadid and her two brothers: Haytham, 15
years older, and Foulath, 12 years older.

YOUTH

When Hadid was a child, during the 1950s and early 1960s, Iraq was different than it is today. At that time Iraq was a modern, liberal country with a secular, Westernized outlook. Hadid's father had studied at the London School of Economics and was involved in progressive politics, serving as Iraq's Minister of Finance in the late 1950s. Hadid was an active child, "asking questions all the time," she recalled. Although her family was Muslim, Hadid attended a convent school in Baghdad, where her fellow students came from various religious backgrounds. She grew up believing there were few limits to what a girl could achieve. "There was never a question that I would be a professional," she recalled. For a time she wanted to become a singer, and she also considered becoming a politician or a psychiatrist.

> *Hadid grew interested in historic architecture when her father took her to visit the ancient cities of Sumer. "I was amazed,"* she recalled. *"We went by boat, and then on a smaller one made of reeds, to visit villages in the marshes. The beauty of the landscape—where sand, water, reeds, birds, building, and people all somehow flowed together—has never left me."*

It was design and architecture that claimed her imagination. "Architecture was used as part of nation-building in Iraq then," Hadid said of her childhood, and "I saw this great modern architecture every day." Her school sat across from a building designed by Italian architect Gio Ponti, while her family owned one of the earliest Iraqi houses built in the Bauhaus fashion, a modernist style that emerged from Germany in the 1920s and 1930s. Her aunt built a modern house in northern Iraq, and Hadid was nine when her father took her to an exhibition that featured it. Afterwards, she recalled, "I became obsessed by the topic." She also grew interested in historic architecture. Her father took her to visit the ancient cities of Sumer, which flourished over 4,000 years ago in what is now southern Iraq. "I was amazed," she recalled of the trip. "We went by boat, and then on a smaller one made of reeds, to visit villages in the marshes. The beauty of the landscape—where sand, water, reeds, birds, building, and people all somehow flowed together—has never left me." She was 11 or 12 when she decided she wanted to be an architect.

Hadid in her London office, 1985.

EDUCATION

Hadid completed her secondary education at a boarding school in Switzerland, then entered the American University of Beirut, Lebanon. She received her Bachelor of Science degree (BS) in mathematics in 1971, and the following year she moved to London, England, to study at the Architectural Association (AA). Her instructors there supported experimental design, but also insisted she master draftsmanship, the art of drawing architectural plans. Hadid graduated in 1977, receiving the school's Diploma Prize for her graduation portfolio. The portfolio featured a striking design for a 14-story hotel on London's Hungerford Bridge, in the middle of the River Thames. One critic later said of the design: "It really was one of these very rare moments when a fissure opens up in architecture, and a different way of seeing emerges. We no longer have to be bound by gravity. We don't have to accept reality—she will unfold her own reality."

CAREER HIGHLIGHTS

A Frustrating Start

Today, Zaha Hadid is a world-renowned architect known for her influential and revolutionary structures. She struggled for years to achieve success, however. Her early career was marked by building plans that people admired but would not construct, and it took two decades before her designs were in demand.

After Hadid completed her architecture degree in 1977, she was invited by one of her instructors, Dutch architect Rem Koolhaas, to join his company, the Office of Metropolitan Architecture. Koolhaas would eventually design award-winning buildings around the world. He was linked with architecture's "deconstructivism" movement, which emphasized unusual shapes, such as curves or jagged lines, over more traditional rectangular shapes. Hadid's designs were also in the deconstructivist tradition; they were rendered as oil paintings that were impressionistic, with an emphasis on unusual shapes and shadows that seemed to move fluidly. The curves of Arabic calligraphy and intricacies of Persian carpet patterns also influenced her architectural ideas. Sometimes her designs were so abstract that people who saw them doubted they could be translated into real buildings.

In 1980, Hadid left the Office of Metropolitan Architecture to found her own practice in conjunction with the AA. She spent the next decade or more establishing and building her practice. To support herself, she also taught architecture at the AA and later lectured at Harvard University, the University of Illinois, and Yale University. In 1982 she beat more than 500 other entrants to win her first design competition, for Hong Kong's Peak Leisure Club. Her design, a "horizontal skyscraper" that featured four huge beams that looked as if they were emerging from a mountainside, was never built. Nevertheless, her designs were catching international attention; they were exhibited in New York, Tokyo, and London, including shows at the Guggenheim Museum in 1978 and the Museum of Modern Art in 1988. In 1987 she established Zaha Hadid Associates in London and soon hired her long-time business partner, Patrik Schumacher. Some of her early work included interior design work for apartments in London and a restaurant in Sapporo, Japan, as well as several temporary art installations. Her interior work also included designing furniture. In 1989, Hadid became a British citizen.

In 1993, Hadid finally completed her first building project, a fire station for the Vitra Furniture Company in Weil am Rhein, Germany. The Vitra Fire Station showcased a sharply angled roof that resembled a wing in flight. Large glass windows set into angled concrete walls put the fire engines on display. The client was thrilled with the completed design, noting that Hadid was his first choice "because we felt that her architectural vision was very dynamic, daring, and also evinced danger." After a few years, however, Vitra's fire company was moved to another facility, and the building was turned into a museum.

The Vitra Fire Station in Weil am Rhein, Germany, was Hadid's first completed building project.

In 1994, Hadid seemed to have broken through with a winning design for the Cardiff Bay Opera House, in the capital city of Wales in the United Kingdom. Her design called for a glass courtyard to surround the auditorium. The design took spectacular advantage of the waterfront site, but public opinion turned against the project. Critics called the design too modern and elitist for a construction project funded by lottery money. The local government decided to build a stadium instead. Hadid believed her background as a foreign-born woman created resentment toward her design. "When I was in Cardiff they didn't talk to me. Literally. They looked at me sideways, or behind me. Not all of them, but some quite specific people," she recalled. "I don't know whether people responded to me in a strange way because they just thought I was one of those eccentric people, or they thought I was a foreigner or behaved funny or I'm a woman." The debacle in Cardiff seemed to confirm her reputation as an architect who created interesting designs but could not turn them into real buildings.

Pushing the Boundaries of Building

At first the Cardiff rejection made Hadid believe her career was over, but she was able to change her attitude. "I made a decision that I wasn't going to be bitter," she explained. "And you know what? It made us tougher as a practice." During the 1990s, advances in computer-aided design made it easier for her striking designs to be translated into workable building plans. In the latter part of the decade Hadid continued teaching and submitting designs to competitions. As technology caught up to her

———— " ————

*"[The Rosenthal Center] is
an amazing building, a work
of international stature that
confidently meets the high
expectations aroused by this
prodigiously gifted architect,"
Herbert Muschamp stated.
"Might as well blurt it out:
the Rosenthal Center is the
most important American
building to be completed
since the end of the
cold war."*

———— " ————

imagination, more of her projects reached the construction stage. In 2001, her design for a combination tram station and parking lot, the Hoenheim-Nord Terminus and Car Park, was completed in the city of Strasbourg, France. The design made use of parallel lines—angular columns in the terminus, perfectly cylindrical lights, even the lines to designate parking spaces—to create a sense of overlapping fields knitted together into a whole. The result resembled a forest, something growing organically from the site. The project earned the Mies van der Rohe Award, the European Union's Prize for Contemporary Architecture.

Hadid was also honored for a project completed in 2002, the Bergisel Ski-Jump and Lodge in Innsbruck, Austria. The former host city of the Winter Olympics decided to upgrade their ski jump on Bergisel Mountain and selected a design by Hadid that incorporated spaces for public facilities, including a café and viewing terrace. At 295 feet long and almost 165 feet high, the new facility was part tower, part bridge, and its sinuous shape led some to nickname it the "Cobra." The cobra's "head," comprising both the public spaces and the top of the jump, provided spectacular views of the surrounding Alps mountain range. The design won awards from both regional and national governments of Austria, as well as a Gold Medal for Design from the International Olympic Committee.

In 2003, Hadid completed her first building in the United States, the Lois and Richard Rosenthal Center for Contemporary Art, in Cincinnati, Ohio. The building was the first major American museum to be designed solely by a woman and made the most of its relatively small space on a city corner. The exterior was an irregular arrangement of blocks made from concrete and translucent glass. The interior used concrete as well, continuing the outside sidewalk into a concrete path that curved into the wall, creating an "urban carpet" that connected the interior spaces. Combined with an atrium and staircases that played with vertical space, the interior created a sense of movement that invited visitors into the variously sized exhi-

The Lois and Richard Rosenthal Center for Contemporary Art in Cincinnati, Ohio.

bition galleries. "It is an amazing building, a work of international stature that confidently meets the high expectations aroused by this prodigiously gifted architect for nearly two decades," architecture critic Herbert Muschamp stated in the *New York Times.* "Might as well blurt it out: the Rosenthal Center is the most important American building to be completed since the end of the cold war." The building earned Hadid the International Award from the Royal Institute of British Architects (RIBA), her first recognition from this respected group.

The recognition helped Hadid feel more accepted by the architectural community, but awards were not the goal of her work. "No matter how many prizes you get, you are still walked all over by your clients," she commented. "It's a very tough profession, and so it brings you down to earth." Instead, Hadid worked to inspire imaginations through her designs. "People don't want to be in the kind of space that they inhabit every day," she explained. As her career developed, she had to combat the pressure of always being new and innovative. "There's a point when you have to try to always be inventive—out of that you do discover things that you would have never thought possible. On the other hand, you have to build on your repertoire and make it fresh in different ways." One common thread she saw in her work was "the connection between project and site." Tailoring each project to fit within its environment—city corner, factory site, urban center—made her work very interesting.

Earning the Prestigious Pritzker Prize

Hadid had completed only a few projects during her early career, but she was widely acknowledged as having a great influence on modern architecture, through both her designs and her teaching. In 2004, the jury for the Pritzker Architecture Prize, architecture's equivalent to the Nobel Prize, selected Hadid to receive the honor. In their announcement, the jury noted, "Clients, journalists, fellow professionals are mesmerized by her dynamic forms and strategies for achieving a truly distinctive approach to architecture and its settings. Each new project is more audacious than the last and the sources of her originality seem endless." Hadid felt particularly gratified by the award, which she was the first woman to receive. "I think it shows that you can actually break through the glass ceiling," she said. Although she didn't want to be thought of as a "woman architect," she added that she was glad to be a role model for up-and-coming women in the field. "When I lecture all over the world, women come up to me all the time to tell me how encouraged they are."

After winning the Pritzker Prize, Hadid's practice grew even faster. Her staff increased rapidly—from five people in 1985 to more than 300 in 2010—and the firm was able to complete more buildings. In 2005 she finished two buildings in Germany, the Phaeno Science Center in Wolfsburg and the BMW Central Building in Leipzig. The Phaeno Science Center resembled a massive three-sided concrete boulder, pocked with irregularly shaped windows, while the interior had curving floors like sand dunes. The BMW Central Building was part of a campus that included three factories, and her design called for the assembly line to travel through the central management building. Rubberized pathways on the floor were included to

The MAXXI Museum for XXI Century Art in Rome, Italy—a view of the main entrance showing stairways and bridges.

resemble roadways and encourage movement within the building. "Our work has always been influenced by ideas of movement," Hadid noted of the design. "There's always a desire to achieve buildings with fluidity and complexity." Office cubicles were open to outside areas, and company executives noted that communications between factory workers and management increased after the building opened. The BMW building earned a prize from the German government, while both of Hadid's German buildings won the RIBA Europe Award.

By this point Hadid had worked around the world, but not in her adopted country. She had become a British citizen in 1989 and had been recognized in 2002 with a Commander of the British Empire honor. Despite her growing international reputation, however, it was not until 2006 that she completed her first building in the United Kingdom. That project was relatively small, a Maggie's Cancer Care Centre in Fife, Scotland. Some critics attributed Hadid's slow path to acceptance in Britain to her reputation as a diva, someone who can be difficult to work with. The architect herself admitted that "I don't have the patience, and I'm not very tactful. People say I can be frightening." Another explanation, she suggested, was that her designs tended to be radical and intimidating. "In another way, I can be my own worst enemy," she explained. "As a woman, I'm expected to want everything to be nice, and to be nice myself. A very English thing. I don't design nice buildings—I don't like them. I like architecture to have some raw, vital, earthy quality." Despite the potential for culture clash, Hadid chose to stay in Britain throughout her career to take advantage of the country's rich tradition of skilled engineers, an important factor in realizing some of her designs.

Gaining World Renown

In 2009, Hadid completed her largest project to date, the 30,000-square meter (almost 323,000-square foot) MAXXI Museum for XXI Century Art in Rome, Italy. Her design called for a "confluence of lines" to blur the boundaries between indoor and outdoor spaces; winding lines of concrete, steel, and glass moved and intersected to draw in the visitor. *New York Times* architecture critic Nicolai Ouroussoff noted that "its sensual lines seem to draw the energy of the city right up into its belly, making everything around it look timid.... The idea is to weave her buildings into the network of streets and sidewalks that surround them—into the infrastructure that binds us together. But it is also a way of making architecture—which is about static objects—more dynamic by capturing the energy of bodies charging through space." Ouroussoff added that the museum "will only add to [Hadid's] legacy." In 2010, the MAXXI Museum earned Hadid RIBA's highest honor, the Stirling Prize for building of the year, as well as the RIBA Europe Award.

———— " ————

"[Hadid's] recent buildings have proved a revelation, confounding her critics and cementing her reputation ... as one of the very few who are genuinely attempting something new," wrote Edwin Heathcote. "Her buildings are fluid, theatrical and sculptural—structurally daring and spatially inventive, they sweep you up and astound you."

———— " ————

In 2010 Hadid also completed her first permanent structures in Asia and the Middle East. The Guangzhou Opera House became a feature of Guangzhou (formerly known as Canton), China's third largest city. The building contained an exterior featuring a multitude of triangular windows as well as ramps and staircases that connected performance spaces to plazas, a reflecting pool, and the park outside it. Hadid's design won the RIBA International Award. *New York Times* critic Ouroussoff called the building "the most alluring opera house built anywhere in the world in decades.... [The design] establishes the opera house and its grounds as part of the public realm—something that belongs to

The Riverside Museum:
Scotland's Museum of Transport and Travel in Glasgow, Scotland.

everyone, not just elite opera fans." Another work completed in 2010, the Sheikh Zayed Bridge, was a wavelike structure connecting Abu Dhabi Island to the mainland of the United Arab Emirates. The curved design of the arches is said to evoke sand dunes in the desert.

By the time she turned 60 in 2010, Hadid was widely acknowledged as one of the world's preeminent architects. "Her recent buildings have proved a revelation, confounding her critics and cementing her reputation not only as the world's foremost female architect but also as one of the very few who are genuinely attempting something new," Edwin Heathcote wrote in the *Financial Times.* "Her buildings are fluid, theatrical and sculptural—structurally daring and spatially inventive, they sweep you up and astound you."

In 2011 Hadid completed a smaller but still celebrated project: the Evelyn Grace Academy in Brixton, a lower-income neighborhood of London. Her design used sleek lines and a Z-shape to integrate classrooms and athletic fields, while still dividing the building into four sub-schools. The architect felt very strongly that interesting, beautiful buildings should be available to everyone. "Part of architecture is about making people feel good in their space," she noted, especially in areas where people may not have many resources. "It's important to think about architecture in a way that inspires people in their locale—because not everyone is privileged enough to travel the world and see the great wonders." The Evelyn Grace Academy earned Hadid her second Stirling Prize for building of the year as well as the RIBA London Award.

The Evelyn Grace Academy was the first in a run of completed projects in Hadid's adopted country. "Something has changed radically here recently," she noted. "There is no resistance to the new any more. Eventually this will filter through into building. England being part of Europe is the most positive thing that could have happened." In 2011, another unique Hadid design opened in the United Kingdom, the Riverside Museum: Scotland's Museum of Transport and Travel. The building featured an irregular zigzag of a roof, which resembled a river and echoed the corrugated roofs of Glasgow's old industrial sheds. The design encouraged a sense of motion—ideal for a transport museum—and helped tie together the building with its surroundings. That year Hadid also completed her first major commission in England, the London Aquatics Centre. Her design resembled a wave or sea creature and was the most notable structure completed for the Olympic Games of 2012.

Bringing Design to the World

In 2012, Hadid's firm had projects under construction all over the world. These included an art museum on the campus of Michigan State University; a spiral tower in Barcelona, Spain; a museum and cultural center in Baku, Azerbaijan; an office and retail complex in Beijing, China; and an oyster-shaped ferry terminal in Salerno, Italy. In 2012 she also signed a contract to design the new Iraq Central Bank, her first building for her native country of Iraq.

Hadid has maintained a busy schedule as head of a globally influential architecture firm but has also continued devoting time to lecturing and edu-

Hadid at the opening of her art exhibit at the Design Museum in London, 2007.

cation. She served as a professor at the University of Applied Arts in Vienna, Austria, and often lectured at conferences and exhibitions. She herself was the focus of retrospective exhibitions at New York's Guggenheim Museum in 2006, London's Design Museum in 2007, and the Pallazzo della Ragione in Padua, Italy in 2009. Her work was also made part of the permanent collections at New York's Museum of Modern Art and the German Architecture Museum (Deutches Architektur Museum). Hadid has earned numerous honorary doctorates and fellowships, including membership in the American Institute of Architects and the American Academy of Arts and Letters, and she was named a United Nations Education, Scientific and Cultural Organization (UNESCO) Artist for Peace in 2010.

In addition to designing buildings, Hadid has occasionally dabbled in interior and fashion design. She has created handbags, shoes, furniture, vases, wallpaper, shelving units, and cutlery. "For an architect, everything connects," she explained. "The design of a handbag, or furniture, or cutlery have their challenges, and they're fun to do. I'd love to get some designs into mass, low-cost production. I want to be able to touch everyone, not just the educated and cultural elite, with a little of what we can do. One of the things I feel confident in saying we can do is bring some excitement, and challenges, to people's lives. We want them to be able to embrace the unexpected." Hadid has said that she creates her designs "so that people can experience things they wouldn't otherwise. Whether it's a good school, or a nice museum, or a concert hall, or having a nice street or street furniture or a lamp, I think all these things need to be very inspiring."

HOME AND FAMILY

Hadid, who has never married, has made her home in London since moving there in the early 1970s to study architecture. She owns the top floor loft in a five-story building, and it is decorated with her own paintings and furniture designs. She spends time with her brother Foulath, a historian at England's Oxford University, and his family. As of 2012 she had not returned to her childhood home of Iraq since 1980—most of the people she knew growing up left the country during its various wars over the past 30 years. She looked forward to a possible return to her native country after signing a contract in 2012 to design the new Central Bank of Iraq.

HOBBIES AND OTHER INTERESTS

As the head of a busy architectural firm, Hadid has had precious little free time for hobbies, often working late into the night on her projects. Nevertheless, she has always been interested in style and fashion—her own personal style extends to a fondness for wearing capes—and occasionally she designs wearable items for various fashion companies. Her work has included an experimental handbag for Louis Vuitton; limited edition shoes for Lacoste; and necklaces, rings, and cuffs for Swarovski crystal. In 2008, she designed a traveling exhibition space for noted fashion company Chanel, at the request of head designer Karl Lagerfeld.

SELECTED WRITINGS

Zaha Hadid: The Complete Buildings and Projects, 1998, 2nd ed., 2009
Zaha Hadid: Thirty Years of Architecture, 2006 (with Detlef Martins and Patrik Schumacher)
Zaha Hadid: Complete Works, 2009

HONORS AND AWARDS

Commander of the Order of the British Empire: 2002
Austrian State Architecture Prize: 2002, for Bergisel Ski Jump
Mies van der Rohe Award-European Union Prize for Contemporary Architecture (European Commission/Fundació Mies van der Rohe): 2003, for Hoenheim-Nord Terminus and Car Park
International Award (Royal Institute of British Architects): 2004, for Lois & Richard Rosenthal Center for Contemporary Art; and 2011, for Guangzhou Opera House
Pritzker Prize for Architecture (Hyatt Foundation): 2004
Europe Award (Royal Institute of British Architects): 2005, for BMW Central Building; 2006, for Phaeno Science Centre; 2008, for Nordpark Railway Stations; and 2010, for MAXXI Museum
Deutscher Architekturpreis-German Architecture Award (German Architecture Association): 2005, for BMW Central Building
Thomas Jefferson Foundation Medal in Architecture (Thomas Jefferson Foundation and University of Virginia): 2007
Praemium Imperile (Japan Art Association): 2009
Stirling Prize (Royal Institute of British Architects): 2010, for MAXXI Museum; and 2011, for Evelyn Grace Academy
Artist for Peace (United Nations Education, Scientific and Cultural Organization—UNESCO): 2010
Commandeur de l'Ordre des Arts et des Lettres (Republic of France): 2010, for services to architecture
London Award (Royal Institute of British Architects): 2011, for Evelyn Grace Academy
Global Road Achievement Award for Design (International Road Federation): 2012, for Sheikh Zayed Bridge

FURTHER READING

Periodicals

Architectural Digest, Oct. 2004, p.110
Architectural Record, Aug. 2005, p.82; Oct. 2010, p.82
Architectural Review, Aug. 10. 2011
Building Design, Feb. 4, 2005, p.8
Current Biography Yearbook, 2003
Financial Times (London), June 29, 2002, p.7; May 25, 2004, p.13; Oct. 17, 2006, p. 10; June 30, 2007, p.15
Guardian (England), Oct. 8, 2006
Interview, Feb. 2005, p.132
New York Times, June 8, 2003, p.1; Mar. 28, 2004; June 2, 2006; Nov. 12, 2009; July 5, 2011
New York Times Magazine, May 16, 1993, p.33
New Yorker, Dec. 21, 2009, p.112; July 24, 2011, p.80
Newsweek, May 19, 2003, p.78; Sep. 26, 2011, p.52
Progressive, June 2008, p.33
Time, Apr. 29, 2010
Times (London), May 16, 2009, p.3

Online Articles

www.guardian.co.uk/artanddesign
   (Guardian, England, "Space Is Her Place," Feb. 1, 2003)
www.pritzkerprize.com/laureates/2004
   (Pritzker Architecture Prize, "Zaha Hadid: 2004 Laureate," accessed April 2, 2012)
www.scotsman.com
   (Scotsman, Edinburgh, "Interview: Zaha Hadid, Architect Who Builds the Unbuildable," June 9, 2011)
www.telegraph.co.uk/culture/art/architecture
   (Telegraph, England, "Zaha Hadid's Fantastic Future," Jan. 1, 2012)

ADDRESS

Zaha Hadid Architects
10 Bowling Green Lane
London EC1R 0BQ
United Kingdom

WEB SITE

www.zaha-hadid.com

Josh Hamilton 1981-

American Professional Baseball Player with the Texas
Rangers
American League MVP and Batting Champion in 2010

BIRTH

Joshua Holt Hamilton was born on May 21, 1981, in Raleigh,
North Carolina. His father, Tony Hamilton, worked as a supervisor in factories that produced Wonder Bread baked goods
and Ditch Witch construction equipment. His mother, Linda
(Holt) Hamilton, worked for the North Carolina Department
of Transportation. Josh has an older brother, Jason.

YOUTH

Josh grew up as part of a family that loved sports, especially baseball. "Life in the Hamilton household revolved around family and baseball," he recalled. "You couldn't tell where one started and the other stopped—not on a dare." Both of his parents played in their youth, and they actually met for the first time at a softball game.

Josh showed exceptional ability as a baseball player from an early age. From the time he began playing Little League as a five-year-old, he frightened other players by hitting and throwing the ball much harder than they could handle. When Josh was seven, he could hit a ball 200 feet and clear the outfield fence. His talent was so remarkable that other parents began calling the commissioner of the league to express concern about the safety of their children. The commissioner responded by moving Josh up to the 12-and-under league, where he played with boys who were five years older than he was—but much closer to his own skill level.

> "Life in the Hamilton household revolved around family and baseball," he recalled. "You couldn't tell where one started and the other stopped—not on a dare."

From the beginning, Josh's parents supported his interest in baseball by signing him up for leagues, coaching his teams, attending all his games, and teaching him the importance of discipline and hard work. Although his parents were a constant presence throughout his youth baseball career, Josh insisted that he never felt forced to play. "I was never pressured to play ball," he stated. "The perception of my parents as hard-driving stage parents was never accurate. I played because I loved to play, and because I was good at it."

EDUCATION

Hamilton attended Athens Drive High School in Raleigh. He made the varsity baseball team as a freshman, playing pitcher and center field. During his junior year in 1998, he posted an amazing .636 batting average with 12 home runs and 56 runs batted in (RBIs). As a senior in 1999, Hamilton batted .529 with 13 home runs and 35 RBIs, and he added 20 stolen bases. On the mound, he earned an 18-3 won-loss record for those two years, striking out 230 hitters in 143 innings. His achievements earned him the Gatorade High School Player of the Year Award for North Carolina in both his junior and senior seasons. He was also named the national High School Player of the Year by *Baseball America* for 1999.

By the end of his high school baseball career, Hamilton's talents had captured the attention of college coaches as well as Major League Baseball (MLB) scouts. As many as 60 professional scouts would attend his games—especially on the days when he pitched—armed with radar guns, stopwatches, and video cameras. They considered Hamilton to be a rare "five-tool prospect," meaning that he excelled in all five fundamental baseball skills that are typically evaluated by scouts: hitting for power, hitting for average, fielding, throwing, and speed. Everyone was certain that Hamilton would be selected in the 1999 MLB draft—the only question was whether he would be drafted as a pitcher or as an outfielder. "My preference was to be an outfielder, so I could play every day and do what I loved best—hit," he explained.

As draft day drew closer, several major-league teams evaluated Hamilton's off-the-field performance as well. They sent scouts to interview his teachers, friends, and teammates and even asked the young prospect to undergo psychological testing to predict how well he would handle stress. The MLB representatives were reassured to find Hamilton universally described as a polite, clean-cut, grounded kid from a good family. They learned that he was well-liked by teammates and even made a ritual of kissing his mother and grandmother for luck before every game. Shortly before graduating from Athens Drive High in the spring of 1999, Hamilton officially gave up his college baseball eligibility and made himself available for the MLB draft. "Faced with the possibility of being given the job of my dreams after high school graduation, choosing professional baseball over college was an easy decision," he noted.

CAREER HIGHLIGHTS

Turning Pro

The first overall pick in the 1999 draft was held by the Tampa Bay Devil Rays. Virtually all experts agreed that the club would use the choice to select either Hamilton or another prospect named Josh—a hard-throwing (and hot-headed) young pitcher from Texas named Josh Beckett. Partly on the basis of Hamilton's squeaky-clean image, the Devil Rays selected the big hitter from North Carolina instead. "Character may have been the determining factor," said Tampa Bay scout Mark McKnight. "You read so many bad things about pro athletes these days, but I don't think you ever will about Josh." Hamilton was determined to live up to the high expectations that came with being "one-one," or the first player selected in the first round of the draft. "I understood that being one-one came with a cer-

Tampa Bay general manager Chuck LaMar and draft pick Josh Hamilton hold up his new Devil Rays jersey after he was the first player taken in the draft in 1999.

tain responsibility that extended far beyond draft day," he acknowledged. "It was my responsibility to dictate whether the label would become a source of pride, or a burden."

Hamilton quickly reached an agreement with the Devil Rays on a lucrative contract that included a $4 million signing bonus. He launched his professional baseball career by playing for a Rookie League team based in Princeton, West Virginia, where he batted .347 with 10 home runs, 48 RBIs, and 17 steals. In 2000 he moved up to play for Tampa Bay's Class A affiliate, the Charleston River Dogs of the South Atlantic League. Hamilton continued his march toward the big leagues by batting .302 with 13 home runs, 61 RBIs, and 14 stolen bases in 96 games. During one game, he hit a towering home run that was measured at 549 feet—only 16 feet shorter than Hall of Fame great Mickey Mantle's all-time record. Although Hamilton's season was cut short by a knee injury, he was still named Most Valuable Player (MVP) of the league and Minor League Player of the Year. "That guy was a man among boys," recalled one of his Charleston teammates, Delvin James. "Some guys, you hear the hype and know it's just hype. But I'll tell you, you'll never see a more gifted, more skilled player than Josh Hamilton."

Team management's only concern about Hamilton involved his continued high level of dependence on his parents. He had used part of his signing bonus to pay off his parents' debts, which allowed them to retire from their jobs. Tony and Linda Hamilton decided to spend their newly acquired free time supporting their 18-year-old son. They followed Josh around the minor leagues, attended all of his games, offered him guidance, and even prepared his meals and did his laundry. Some people in the Tampa Bay organization worried that the constant presence of his parents would prevent Hamilton from maturing as a player and as a person. "The folks who ran the Devil Rays thought my parents' involvement was getting in the way of my becoming a man and learning to cope with life on my own. They also thought it was an obstacle to my bonding with my teammates," Hamilton explained. "I looked at it differently. They were here to make the transition easier, and we couldn't see how that could be seen as anything but positive."

> "
>
> *"From the moment I tried cocaine, I became a different person," Hamilton related. "I became the coke-sniffing baseball player. I was a guy who was in violation of my contract, a guy who was willing to take a huge chance with his talent and his career, a guy who was willing to trade everything he'd achieved for temporary acceptance from a bunch of guys he didn't really know."*
>
> "

Descending into Drug Addiction

Hamilton's life reached a turning point in March 2001, when he and his parents were involved in a serious car accident. A dump truck sped through a red light and hit their vehicle broadside, sending it spinning more than 100 feet. His parents suffered head and neck injuries and returned home to North Carolina to recover. Although Josh initially seemed unhurt, he soon began experiencing a stabbing pain in his lower back that affected his swing. He appeared in only 23 games for the Devil Rays' Class AA affiliate in Orlando during the 2001 season, and his batting average dropped to a dismal .180. Placed on the injured reserve list, Hamilton struggled with boredom and loneliness. "I won't downplay the importance of finding myself alone for the first time in my life. I've always struggled with free time," he admitted. "These events—the accident, my parents' leaving, my back hurting—created an environment where one bad decision could lead to many more."

Hamilton in the dugout during spring training in March 2003. He suited up for spring training but behaved erratically and ended up leaving the team. By this point he had started getting tattoos.

Hamilton took refuge from his feelings of uncertainty in an unusual place—a tattoo parlor. He started out by having his childhood nicknames ("Hambone" and "Hammer") tattooed on his biceps. These tattoos quickly led to more, and before long Hamilton was spending much of his free time hanging out at the tattoo parlor. He eventually ended up with close to 30 tattoos. "For me, the [tattoo] chair was an escape," he remembered. "I could sit there and escape from baseball and the people who wondered why I wasn't playing and the whispers that suggested I wasn't really injured and had lost my drive for the game. With my eyes closed and the ink taking shape under my skin, the world got a lot smaller. There were no expectations, nobody telling me how great I was or how great I could be."

Many people in the Devil Rays organization and in the media were shocked and dismayed to see the formerly straight-laced player covering his skin with designs and symbols. Some people wondered whether Hamilton was reacting to his sudden freedom from his parents' influence. "People say I was rebelling against my parents. That's not true. If my parents had been with me, none of this would have happened. I needed something, and I looked in the wrong place," he explained. "Clearly, the designs that kept springing up on my body, working from the top down, were an exterior sign of my interior confusion. In a sense, I became addicted to the feeling of getting tattoos—the first sign of my addictive personality."

While hanging out at the tattoo parlor, Hamilton was exposed to alcohol and drugs for the first time. The tattoo artists initially convinced the struggling young ballplayer to have a few drinks with them. Before long, Hamilton began snorting cocaine with his new "friends," and he quickly became addicted. "From the moment I tried cocaine, I became a different person," he related. "I became the coke-sniffing baseball player. I was a guy who was in violation of my contract, a guy who was willing to take a huge chance with his talent and his career, a guy who was willing to trade everything he'd achieved for temporary acceptance from a bunch of guys he didn't really know."

Deep in denial about his growing drug problem, Hamilton recovered from his back injury and returned to minor-league baseball in 2002. Playing in California for the Advanced Class A Bakersfield Blaze, he batted a solid .303 with 9 home runs and 44 RBIs before shoulder and elbow injuries ended his season prematurely on July 10. Although Hamilton did not know it at the time, that would be the last time he played in a professional baseball game for nearly four years. A short time later, he failed two consecutive drug tests and was suspended for 25 days for violating the MLB substance abuse policy. The Devil Rays sent him to the famous Betty Ford Clinic in California, named after its founder, former first lady Betty Ford, who courageously discussed her addiction publicly at a time when people hid such problems. A number of big-name athletes and movie stars have received treatment for addiction to drugs and alcohol at the Betty Ford Clinic. Hamilton insisted that he did not have a problem, though, and he left after a few days.

Hamilton's next three years deteriorated into a blur of failed drug tests, season-long suspensions from baseball, visits to various rehabilitation centers, brief recoveries, and repeated relapses. During this period he poured most of his $4 million signing bonus into drugs. In one six-week binge he threw away an estimated $100,000 on crack cocaine. His priorities changed so that baseball lost its meaning and drugs became all-important. "Drugs had taken over," he acknowledged. "They'd gone from a recreational mistake, something I stupidly thought I could control or ignore or deny, to a full-blown personal disaster. It was astonishing and perfectly natural how quickly drugs and the drug culture had taken up residence in my life."

Hitting Rock Bottom

In 2004, during one of his few extended periods of sobriety, Hamilton married Katie Chadwick. The couple had met through her father, Michael "Big Daddy" Chadwick, a former drug dealer and user who later became a successful home builder and youth minister. Hamilton had approached the elder Chadwick for help in beating his addiction, and he managed to stay sober for several months before he relapsed and began using drugs again.

Hamilton's addiction took a terrible toll on his wife. When Katie gave birth to their daughter in 2005, Hamilton left the house on an errand to pick up supplies for the newborn, ended up buying drugs instead, and did not return home for four days. On one occasion he even sold her wedding ring to buy drugs. Finally, after Hamilton flew into a violent rage while under the influence of drugs, his wife kicked him out of the house and took out a restraining order against him. "I'd been in rehab five or six times—on my way to eight—and failed to get clean. I was a bad husband and a bad father, and I had no relationship with God. Baseball wasn't even on my mind," he recalled. "Drugs had destroyed my body and my mind and my spirit. I could no longer experience happiness or surprise. I couldn't remember the last time I felt spontaneous joy. Why was I even alive?"

Hamilton finally hit rock bottom in October 2005. He awoke from a crack-cocaine binge in a dingy trailer surrounded by strangers and realized that he would not live much longer if he did not beat his addiction. "I prayed to be spared another day of guilt and depression and addiction," he remembered. "I couldn't continue living the life of a crack addict, and I couldn't stop, either. It was a horrible downward spiral that I had to pull out of, or die." Having alienated his wife and parents, Hamilton went to the only safe place he could think of—the home of his maternal grandmother, Mary Holt. When he showed up on her doorstep, he was dirty and unshaven, his nose was bleeding, he was coughing up a sticky black substance, and he had dropped 50 pounds from his once-muscular 230-pound frame. Nevertheless, his grandmother took him in, cleaned him up, fed him, and supported him as he started on the long road to recovery.

An important factor in Hamilton's recovery from drug addiction was reconnecting with his Christian faith. He turned his problems over to God, began attending church regularly, and devoted countless hours to Bible study. "I had been sober only a short time, but this time felt different," he explained. "When I surrendered to God, He took care of the rest. I had a peacefulness inside me, a calm that I hadn't felt since I started using." When he had remained clean for several months, Hamilton was able to reconcile with his wife and family. Then he began working himself back into playing shape at The Winning Inning, a baseball training academy that makes extensive use of Christian teachings.

> *An important factor in Hamilton's recovery from drug addiction was reconnecting with his Christian faith. "I had been sober only a short time, but this time felt different," he explained. "When I surrendered to God, He took care of the rest. I had a peacefulness inside me, a calm that I hadn't felt since I started using."*

Making a Comeback

By the spring of 2006, Hamilton felt secure enough in his recovery—and confident enough in his physical skills—to seek a return to professional baseball. He sent a heartfelt letter of apology to Devil Rays management and MLB officials, along with a formal request for early reinstatement. He also sent along glowing testimonials from friends, relatives, religious leaders, drug counselors, and doctors to support his claims that he had finally beaten his drug addiction. In June 2006 Hamilton received news that he would be reinstated by MLB and allowed to participate in spring training. He returned to professional baseball that summer by playing 15 games for the Hudson Valley Renegades in a short-season Class A league.

In December 2006 Hamilton received more good news. The Cincinnati Reds had selected him in the Rule 5 draft, an annual event that is intended

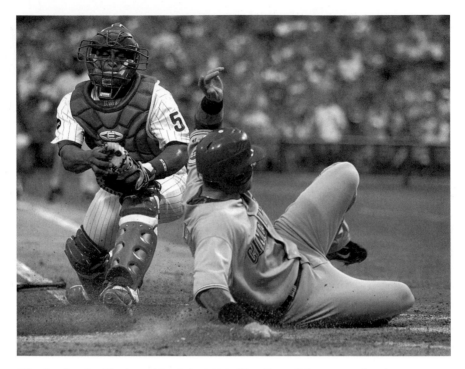

Playing for the Cincinnati Reds in 2007, Hamilton slides across the plate to score, beating the tag by Philadelphia Phillies catcher Carlos Ruiz.

to prevent teams from hoarding major-league caliber players in their minor-league farm systems. Any young player that is not listed on a team's extended, 40-man roster can be picked up by another team for a small fee—as long as the acquiring team agrees to keep that player on its regular, 25-man roster for a full season. In effect, this development gave Hamilton a great shot at playing for the Reds in the big leagues during the 2007 season. "This was the kind of news I was afraid to pray for. This was sent directly from heaven, a phenomenal opportunity," he stated. "Number-one draft pick or not, I was a 25-year-old man with a history of serious drug problems and less than a hundred at-bats above Class A. In the past four years, I had played a total of 15 games, all at low-level Class A. And now I was being given the opportunity to make a major-league 25-man roster."

Hamilton rewarded the Reds' faith in him from the very beginning, posting an impressive .403 batting average in spring training. He made his long-awaited major-league debut on April 2, 2007, when he came in as a pinch hitter and hit a line drive that was caught for an out. A week later, on April 10, Hamilton made his first career start in a game against the Arizona

Diamondbacks and tallied his first career hit, a two-run homer off pitcher Edgar Gonzalez. Hamilton finished his rookie season with a .292 batting average, 19 home runs, and 47 RBIs in 90 games.

Throughout the 2007 season, Hamilton stayed clean and sober with the help of an extensive support system. He kept in constant touch with a group of "accountability partners" that included his wife, his father-in-law, his grandmother, Raleigh pastor Jimmy Carroll, televangelist James Robison, and Christian sports agent Mike Moye. "It is very important to my recovery and my walk with Christ that I have people like that around me," he noted. "They always call or text at the right time."

Hamilton's closest supporter was Johnny Narron, a former MLB first baseman who had been his youth basketball coach in Raleigh. Officially hired as an assistant batting coach for the Reds, Narron became Hamilton's mentor, confidant, chaperone, and friend. He kept track of Hamilton's whereabouts at all times and ensured that the recovering addict never carried credit cards or more than $20 cash, never went out alone at night, and rarely socialized with teammates after games. As a final precaution, the team required Hamilton to submit to a drug test every three days. "It reassures the people who made the decision to let me back in the game that things are good," he explained.

Joining the Texas Rangers

Following his successful rookie season, Hamilton was traded to the Texas Rangers in December 2007 for pitchers Edinson Volquez and Danny Herrera. The Rangers scouted Hamilton extensively and consulted with experts about drug addiction and recovery before making the deal. Hamilton made an immediate impact on his new team. He earned a position as the Rangers' starting center fielder by hitting an incredible .556 with 13 RBIs in 14 games during spring training. His impressive performance continued during the early regular season, when he became the first American League (AL) player to be named Player of the Month for two consecutive months.

While Rangers' fans recognized Hamilton's talent from the beginning, he only came to national attention at mid-season, when his statistics earned him a spot in the 2008 MLB All-Star Game. His remarkable comeback story attracted a great deal of media attention and fan interest, and people across the country enjoyed watching him rise above his troubled past to finally reach his potential. Invited to compete in the annual Home Run Derby as part of the All-Star festivities, Hamilton hit a record 28 home runs in the first round, including 13 in a row and 3 blasts longer than 500 feet. Although he finished with a total of 35 home runs, he lost in the final round of competition to slugger Justin Morneau of the Minnesota Twins.

Hamilton's bat cooled off a bit during the second half of the season, but he still finished with an impressive .304 average, adding 32 home runs and an AL-leading 130 RBIs. His strong performance helped the Rangers finish second in the AL West Division with a 79-83 record. At the end of the season Hamilton published a book about his life experiences, entitled *Beyond Belief,* co-authored by sportswriter Tim Keown.

In 2009 Hamilton endured several injuries that had a negative impact on his offensive numbers. He still managed to hit .268 with 10 home runs and 54 RBIs in 89 games, and he was selected to the All-Star team for the second time. The Rangers ended the season with an 87-75 record, which once again resulted in a second-place finish in the division. The most disheartening part of the season for Hamilton occurred in August, when the media revealed that he had relapsed and used alcohol several months earlier. Photographs appeared on the Internet that showed the Rangers star clearly intoxicated and behaving inappropriately with women in a bar. Hamilton admitted that he had made a mistake and said that he had already apologized to his wife, his teammates, and Rangers management. "You have to look at the positives," said Texas general manager Jon Daniels. "It was a reminder to Josh that he can't sneak off, that this can't happen privately. It made his system for dealing with it that much stronger."

Earning MVP Honors

Hamilton bounced back in 2010 to have one of the best offensive years in Rangers history. He was named Player of the Month for June after batting .454 with 9 home runs and a franchise record 49 hits, and he was selected to the All-Star team for the third consecutive season. Late in the season Hamilton collided with an outfield fence while trying to run down a fly ball. The collision resulted in broken ribs that forced him to miss 25 of the last 30 games of the season. Nonetheless, Hamilton still led the majors with a .359 batting average. He also added 32 home runs and 100 RBIs, and he led the majors in slugging percentage (a measure of power hitting that is calculated by dividing total bases by at-bats) with .633. The Baseball Writers Association recognized his stellar season by naming him Most Valuable Player in the American League, and he also received MLB Player of the Year honors from the *Sporting News* and *Baseball Digest.*

Hamilton's contributions helped the Rangers win the AL West Division with a 90-72 record and make the playoffs for the first time since 1999. "We have more fun than any team in baseball, and I think it's evident in

Hamilton making a diving catch during the 2010 World Series.

the way we play," he declared. "We never give up until the last out is made. We always feel like we have a chance to win the game."

In the first round of the AL playoffs, Texas defeated Hamilton's former team, Tampa Bay, in 5 games. Still recovering from his rib injury, Hamilton hit a disappointing .143 with 2 hits in 14 at-bats during the series. He came back strong in the American League Championship Series (ALCS), when the Rangers defeated the defending champion New York Yankees in 6 games to claim the first pennant in franchise history. Hamilton was named ALCS Most Valuable Player for his performance, which included 4 home runs, 7 RBIs, and an ALCS-record 5 intentional walks. Unfortunately, the Rangers lost the 2010 World Series to the San Francisco Giants in 5 games. Hamilton managed only 2 hits (including a home run) in 20 at-bats against the Giants.

Facing Tragedy and Disappointment

Prior to the start of the 2011 season, Hamilton signed a two-year, $24 million contract extension with the Rangers. Although he was pleased with the deal, the year proved to be a difficult one for him. In April he broke his upper right arm while sliding headfirst into home plate, putting him out of action for more than a month. In July Hamilton was involved in a tragic accident. He casually tossed a foul ball into the stands, as players routinely do. A fan leaned out to try to catch it for his young son and fell to his death from the upper deck. Hamilton recognized that what happened was not his fault, but he felt terrible about it nonetheless. "It was a traumatic event. It's going to be around for a while," he acknowledged. "Just a random act of kindness turned tragic. It just lets you know how quickly life can change, just in the blink of an eye."

> "My story is bigger than me. Every time I go to the ballpark, I talk to people who are either battling addictions themselves or trying to help someone else who is. They want to confide in me, to share, to see if something I experienced can help them succeed as well.... They know where I've been. They look to me because I'm proof that hope is never lost. They remind me that this isn't really about baseball."

The Rangers moved past the tragedy to have a tremendous season, defending their AL West Division title with a franchise-best 96-66 record. Hamilton batted .298 with 25 home runs during the regular season and was voted to the All-Star Team for the fourth straight year. Texas then marched through the first two rounds of the playoffs, defeating Tampa Bay 3-1 in the divisional series and besting the Detroit Tigers 4-2 in the ALCS, to make a second consecutive trip to the World Series.

This time, Hamilton and his teammates faced the St. Louis Cardinals. After trading victories with their rivals in the first four games, the Rangers managed to take a 3-2 lead and seemed poised to win the first world championship in franchise history. In the potentially deciding Game 6, Texas came within one strike of victory on two different occasions. Instead, the Rangers suffered a heartbreaking 10-9 defeat in an 11-inning thriller. They could not overcome their disappointment in Game 7, and St. Louis won the clincher by a score of 6-2 to claim the World Series title.

Despite a painful sports hernia that limited his postseason performance, Hamilton managed to bat .271 during the playoffs, with 1 home run and 13 RBIs. "I've been hurt the last two years in the playoffs," he said after-

*Hamilton hitting a two-run home run off a pitch by the Cardinals'
Jason Motte during the 2011 World Series.*

ward. "I could either be really resentful and mad, and grow apart from
[God], or I could be satisfied that He got me through it again and grow
closer to Him. I'm not mad, I'm not upset. I did what I could do."

The lead-up to the 2012 season was a tough period for Hamilton, who had
a relapse with alcohol one night in February. Afterwards he made a public
statement, saying that he had been hurtful toward his family and he regret-
ted the behavior. "It was just wrong," he said. "That's all it comes down to. I
needed to be in a different place. I needed to be responsible at that moment, that day, period, and I was not responsible. Those actions of mine
have hurt a lot of people that are very close to me." Hamilton also added
these thoughts: "My life in general is based on making the right choices,
everything as far as my recovery, as far as my baseball goes, it's all based
around my relationship with the Lord. And I look at it like that, you all
know how hard I play on the field and I give it everything I absolutely have.
When I don't do that off the field, I leave myself open for a weak moment."

When the 2012 season began, it turned into a rollercoaster ride. Hamilton had a great start: in April and May, hitting .368 with 21 HRs and 57 RBIs. His performance during the beginning of his season—when he hit .402 with 18 home runs and 41 RBIs in his first 31 games—marked the best start by a hitter since 1932. During one May game he belted 4 home runs, and during one seven-day period in May he hit .467 with 9 homers, 43 total bases and 18 RBIs. But then he went into a batting slump for two months. In June and July, he was hitting .160 to .180, with 8 HRs and 27 RBIs. "Hamilton has endured the ultimate Jekyll and Hyde season in 2012," Jesse Pantuosco wrote for the Sports Network. "He went from awesome to terrible almost overnight. It's inexplicable." By early August, when this edition went to press, his hitting seemed to be improving. But the remainder of the season—and beyond—was a question mark. Hamilton's contract with the Rangers is due to expire at the end of the 2012 season, when he will become a free agent. Given the recent turmoil, some have questioned whether the team will sign him again.

Providing a Positive Example

Hamilton remains dedicated to serving God by providing a positive example and a message of hope for others who are fighting addictions. "My mission is to be the ray of hope, the guy who stands out there on that beautiful field and owns up to his mistakes and lets people know it's never completely hopeless, no matter how bad it seems at the time. I have a platform and a message, and now I go to bed at night, sober and happy, praying I can be a good messenger," he explained. "My story is bigger than me. Every time I go to the ballpark, I talk to people who are either battling addictions themselves or trying to help someone else who is. They want to confide in me, to share, to see if something I experienced can help them succeed as well.... They know where I've been. They look to me because I'm proof that hope is never lost. They remind me that this isn't really about baseball."

Hamilton feels pleased that he is able to inspire others with his story. He believes that his struggles have made him a better person, given him a sense of purpose, and allowed him to make a difference in people's lives. "This may sound crazy, but I wouldn't change a thing about my path to the big leagues," he noted. "If I hadn't gone through all the hard times, this whole story would be just about baseball. If I'd made the big leagues at 21 and made my first All-Star team at 23 and done all the things expected of me, I would be a big-time baseball player, and that's it." Hamilton frequently expresses gratitude that he was able to turn his life around and return to professional baseball. "I just feel so blessed that God allowed me to keep my skills, allowed me to not be brain-dead or dead period or in jail, that He allowed me the grace to be able to come back and be able to share my story and be able to play the game," he stated.

MARRIAGE AND FAMILY

Hamilton married Katie Chadwick in November 2004. Although he and his wife went to the same high school, they did not really know each other until Hamilton approached her father for help in conquering his drug addiction. Katie had a daughter, Julia (born in 2001), from a previous relationship when they got married. They also have two daughters together, Sierra (2005) and Michaela (2008).

HOBBIES AND OTHER INTERESTS

Hamilton and his wife formed a charitable foundation called Triple Play Ministries "to spread the word of God and assist others in overcoming obstacles and challenges." The organization is involved in sports ministry, community outreach, and mission projects. Hamilton enjoys using his talents in baseball and his life experiences as a platform to share his faith and spread his message of hope.

HONORS AND AWARDS

Gatorade High School Player of the Year (North Carolina): 1998, 1999
High School Player of the Year (*Baseball America*): 1999
Minor League Player of the Year (*USA Today*): 2000
Silver Slugger Award: 2008
American League All-Star Team: 2008, 2009, 2010, 2011
American League Most Valuable Player (Baseball Writers Association): 2010
American League Championship Series (ALCS) Most Valuable Player: 2010
Major League Baseball Player of the Year (*Sporting News* and *Baseball Digest*): 2010

FURTHER READING

Books

Hamilton, Josh, with Tim Keown. *Beyond Belief: Finding the Strength to Come Back,* 2008

Periodicals

Baseball Digest, Sep./Oct. 2010, p.14; Jan./Feb. 2011, p.24
Christianity Today, June 2011, p.34
Current Biography Yearbook, 2011

ESPN The Magazine, June 24, 2004; July 16, 2007
Sporting News, Sep. 27, 2010, p.34
Sports Illustrated, Apr. 12, 2004, p.56; June 2, 2008, p.30

Online Articles

www.dallasnews.com
   (Dallas News, "Josh Hamilton Finds Strength after Misstep in Recovery
   from Addiction," Oct. 4, 2010)
espn.go.com
   (ESPN, "Hell and Back" and "I'm Proof that Hope Is Never Lost," July
   15, 2008; "Josh Hamilton Rips Four 2-Run HRs," May 9, 2012; "Josh
   Hamilton Leaves Rangers in Awe," May 9, 2012)
mlb.com
   (MLB, "On and Off Field, Hamilton Finds Ways to Inspire," May 8,
   2012)
www.sportsillustrated.cnn.com
   (Sports Illustrated, "The Curse of Bigness," June 11, 2012; "The Legendary Tales of a Carolina Kid Named Hambone," July 2, 2012)

ADDRESS

Josh Hamilton
Texas Rangers Baseball Club
PO Box 90111
Arlington, TX 76004-3111

WEB SITES

tripleplayministries.com
texas.rangers.mlb.com

Heidi Hammel 1960-

American Scientist and Planetary Astronomer
Pioneering Researcher in Astronomical Observation
of the Planets Neptune and Uranus

BIRTH

Heidi Hammel was born on March 14, 1960, in Sacramento,
California. Her father, Bob, worked a variety of different jobs,
and her mother, Phyllis, was a homemaker and former nurse.
Hammel has an older brother named Hazen and a younger
sister named Lisa.

YOUTH

Hammel's family moved around a lot when she was young,
moving to a new location whenever her father changed jobs.

By the time Hammel was six years old, her family had lived in five homes in three different cities in California. They relocated to Pennsylvania and moved two more times before finally settling in Clarks Summit, Pennsylvania, in 1970, when she was ten years old.

No matter where the family lived, their house was always full of books and magazines. Hammel loved to read, especially science fiction stories. She was a fan of the television show "Star Trek" and spent hours studying blueprints of the "Star Trek" spaceship, Enterprise. She liked to climb trees and go exploring with her brother. She took swimming lessons and piano lessons, built things with Lego blocks, and loved music and singing in the church choir. Her parents encouraged her creativity and imagination and provided plenty of opportunities for Hammel to learn new things. Family vacations were spent visiting museums and other places that taught about nature, history, or culture. One of her favorite things to do was to invent new games to play with her best friend. She would combine different card games to create a new game, like putting three or four Monopoly sets together with the Game of Life, or figuring out how to play Gin Rummy with five decks of cards.

> "I used to get car sick, and my parents used to take us on trips a lot in the car and so I had to lie on the back seat being sick, and the only thing I could do was look out the window and see the stars. And so I learned the constellations, I learned what the bright stars were, and so that's what kept me going on those long car trips."

Hammel was not particularly interested in science or astronomy when she was growing up. "I spent far more time playing Monopoly or card games or riding a bike than anything science-related," she recalled. "I was not an amateur astronomer as a child.... I used to get car sick, and my parents used to take us on trips a lot in the car and so I had to lie on the back seat being sick, and the only thing I could do was look out the window and see the stars. And so I learned the constellations, I learned what the bright stars were, and so that's what kept me going on those long car trips."

"The second thing I remember, when I was a kid, is going to a planetarium, and they would do a star show about what the stars were looking like and what was 'up'—the planets—and that was all kind of boring, but then at some point during the show a comet would streak across the sky with flames and a roar that was really loud, and you never knew when it was going to happen, and it was really exciting. And I would go back to the planetarium again and again and again just to wait for that comet to come. And I think I probably picked up a little astronomy along the way when I was doing that."

Hammel's parents divorced when she was in middle school. After that, she lived with her mother, brother, and sister, and saw her father occasionally.

EDUCATION

Hammel went to Abington Heights Middle School and Abington Heights High School in Clarks Summit, Pennsylvania. She was good at math and enjoyed science classes. She was a member of the school band and played percussion instruments, including drums, xylophone, and chimes. She also liked to sing and act, and she performed in school plays. She was a good student who usually got high grades in all of her classes. Hammel graduated from high school in 1978.

After high school, Hammel began studying at the Massachusetts Institute of Technology (MIT) in Cambridge, Massachusetts. A research university that focuses on science and technology, MIT is one of the premier universities in the United States—and one of the most difficult. Though Hammel had always done well in her courses in high school, she found her classes at MIT to be extremely challenging. "MIT was just an awful, awful experience for me. You get to MIT and you work and work and work and then you fail. And work-work-work harder, and you fail," she recalled. "I struggled so hard. Nobody seemed to be working as hard as I did and they were getting much better grades. I was not a very happy person there. I learned how to work hard and how to cope with failure. I learned you couldn't let things get you down. If you persevere, the rewards will come later on." Hammel was committed to succeeding at MIT and managed to pass her freshman year.

In her sophomore year, Hammel impulsively decided to take an observational astronomy course. Observational astronomy is the study of space and objects such as planets, stars, and galaxies through the use of telescopes and other scientific devices. Though she knew nothing about astronomy, she thought the course sounded like fun. The coursework turned out to be very difficult and Hammel considered dropping out of the class. She decided to finish the course with the encouragement and support of her professor. By the end of that semester, she had decided to major in astronomy.

As she continued in the astronomy program, Hammel quickly found that she had a natural talent for understanding the data she gathered in her research. She also discovered a talent for creative problem-solving. If her research data was not exactly what she needed, she would come up with

Hammel shown with images taken with a space telescope.

ways to improve the performance of her research equipment. For example, Hammel found that the telescope she was using was not producing images that were clear enough for her work. She made a tube that fit on the end of the telescope to block out the stray light that was making her images blurry. She also created a special filter that allowed the telescope to detect more kinds of light, helping her to gather even more information about the stars and planets she was observing.

Though Hammel continued to work hard in her classes, she did not limit her time at MIT to just studying. She joined MIT's musical theater guild and played percussion in the orchestra that accompanied theater performances. She also sang in a local church choir and had a part-time job playing guitar in a bluegrass band that performed in a coffee shop in MIT's student center.

In 1982, Hammel earned a Bachelor of Science degree (BS) in Earth and Planetary Science from MIT. She immediately enrolled in graduate school at the University of Hawaii, planning to earn her doctorate, or PhD.

An advanced degree in astronomy requires courses in math, statistics, data analysis, and physics. Hammel had a talent for working with data and numbers, but she found the physics classes to be extremely difficult. After her first two years at the University of Hawaii, she needed to pass qualifying exams in order to continue in the graduate program. These tests included an extensive oral exam, during which a panel of professors could ask her about any aspect of astronomy. Hammel did not pass the qualifying oral exam the first time she took it. The doctoral committee gave her an opportunity to retake the oral exam, and she passed the test on her second try.

Passing the qualifying exam meant that Hammel would be allowed to finish her graduate degree. To do this, she needed to complete a new, original research project. Though she didn't know it at the time, the research she chose to conduct would mark the beginning of her career as a pioneer of astronomy.

CAREER HIGHLIGHTS

The Ice Giants

Hammel's astronomy career actually began while she was still in graduate school. For her doctoral research project, she decided to study the planets Uranus and Neptune. These are the two planets in the solar system that are located the farthest away from Earth. They are known as Ice Giants. Ice Giants are massive planets with atmospheres made of various types of gases that are poisonous to humans. Ice Giants are believed to have slushy surfaces and icy or semi-molten rocky cores. Many details of the nature and composition of Ice Giants are unknown because of their remote location and inhospitable atmospheres.

Hammel's graduate research project included the use of astronomical imaging to study the atmospheres of Uranus and Neptune. Astronomical imaging uses special telescopes equipped with filters that can separate the different types of light waves that reflect off of a planet, to make images that show each type of light individually. This kind of information helps astronomers to determine the elements or materials that make up a planet, because each element or material reflects light in a different way.

In her research, Hammel wanted to learn about the clouds, winds, and weather on the two planets, and how these things changed over time. She knew that up to that time, no one had studied Uranus and Neptune in this way. No matter what she discovered in her research, all of it would be new information. She would be a pioneer in this area of astronomy.

"One thing that we all care about is the weather," Hammel explained. "And we care about the weather on the Earth the most. But what makes weather is gases and clouds. And the reason the weather on the Earth is hard to predict is because we have oceans and continents that interact with our atmosphere. That makes it very hard to predict the weather, as we all know. But if you take a planet like Jupiter or Neptune, you don't have continents and you don't have oceans. All you have is gas. All you have is atmosphere. And therefore it is a lot easier to model the weather on those planets. But it's the same physical process, it's the same kind of thing happening whether it happens on the Earth or whether it happens on Neptune. Therefore, by studying weather on Neptune we learn about weather in general, and that helps us understand the weather on Earth better."

Hammel began her research by collecting images of Uranus using a huge, powerful telescope owned by the University of Hawaii. This telescope was located at the top of Mauna Kea. As the tallest mountain in Hawaii, Mauna Kea stands more than 13,000 feet above sea level. At this extremely high altitude, the thin, dry air can cause headaches and drowsiness, and the increased atmospheric pressure can make people feel nauseous. But that same thin air provides an ideal environment for astronomical observation. Mauna Kea is considered one of the best sites in the world for astronomers, and demand for telescope time there is high. Astronomers often get to use the telescope for only a few hours at a time to make their observations.

The images Hammel collected at Mauna Kea provided a wealth of new information about Uranus. As she analyzed the data from her images, she gained a better understanding of the planet's cloud patterns, weather systems, wind speeds and directions, and how all of these changed over time. But there was only so much data that Hammel could gather with a telescope located on the ground. In order to learn more, she would need to see data collected closer to the distant planet.

In 1986, Hammel got a unique opportunity to do just that. She was among a group of young scientists who were invited by NASA to study close-up

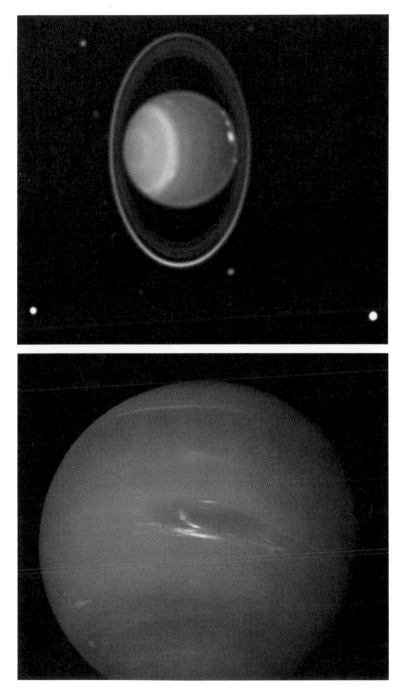

*Photos of Uranus and Neptune, the Ice Giants
that Hammel has spent years studying.*

images of Uranus as they were transmitted back to Earth by the Voyager 2 spacecraft. The mission of Voyager 2, which was launched in 1977, was to explore the farthest reaches of the solar system and send information about deep space back to Earth. By 1986 Voyager 2 had reached Uranus, and it collected a series of images and other data as it flew by. Hammel was excited at the chance to be among the first to see what Voyager 2 had found.

Voyager 2 collected a huge amount of previously unknown information about Uranus. The data and images provided new insight on Uranus's moons, rings, and magnetic field. But there was very little information about the atmosphere of Uranus. Though she could appreciate the importance of the other data, Hammel was disappointed at the lack of atmospheric information.

Becoming an Expert

As Voyager 2 continued on its exploration, it left Uranus and headed towards Neptune. The data it collected about Neptune was expected to reach Earth in three years. Hammel hoped that Voyager 2 would provide more substantial data about Neptune's atmosphere, which was very difficult to observe using telescopes on Earth. While she waited to see what Voyager 2 discovered about Neptune, Hammel decided to focus her own astronomical observations on that planet. She wanted to learn as much as she could about Neptune so that she would be prepared to analyze the data from Voyager 2.

Hammel began collecting images of Neptune using the big telescope on Mauna Kea. To her surprise, her images looked nothing like those taken by other astronomers in previous years. Her images showed that Neptune's atmosphere looked completely different than it had a short time before. Well-known astronomers said that Hammel must have done something wrong to get such radically different images. The controversy grew when she published more of her findings that included data showing that Neptune was rotating faster than previously believed. Hammel defended her work and was eventually able to persuade her critics that she was right.

Throughout this time, Hammel had been a graduate student at the University of Hawaii. In 1988, she received her PhD in physics and astronomy from the University of Hawaii. In 1989, she accepted a post-doctoral position with NASA's Jet Propulsion Laboratory team. This group was working with Voyager 2, and Hammel would be part of the mission team when the spacecraft flew by Neptune. By the time she was 29 years old, she was widely regarded as the expert on Neptune.

Once Voyager 2 began transmitting data about Neptune, Hammel understood why so little had been known about the planet before. As she ana-

A photo of the Hubble Space Telescope drifting over the Earth.

lyzed the data and compared it to images she collected with the Mauna Kea telescope, she saw two very different pictures of the same planet. Voyager 2 provided the first images of Neptune's Great Dark Spot, which could not be seen by telescopes on Earth. Hammel combined the data from her telescope observations with the Voyager 2 data, and for the first time a complete picture of Neptune's atmosphere came into view. Her work provided a new understanding of Neptune's weather, which would help scientists better understand the Earth's weather patterns.

In 1990, Hammel became the Principal Research Scientist in MIT's Department of Earth, Atmospheric and Planetary Sciences. This position allowed her to continue collecting information about Neptune and other giant planets. It also put her in the right place, at the right time, to lead the team that would observe one of the most important astronomical events of her generation—the Great Comet Crash of 1994.

The Great Comet Crash

During the week of July 16-22, 1994, a comet named Shoemaker-Levy 9 was expected to crash into Jupiter, the largest planet in the solar system. Shoemaker-Levy 9 consisted of a string of 21 smaller pieces that had been circling Jupiter on a collision course for some time. This event was highly anticipated by astronomers around the world because it was such a rare occurrence. It would be the first time that people could observe the collision of two planetary bodies and study the impact of such a collision.

"Events like these were critical to the formation and evolution of the planets, and this was the first time astronomers had a chance to observe such an encounter," Hammel explained. Her team would use the Hubble Space Telescope to collect images and data as the crash happened. The Hubble Space Telescope is located in space above Earth's atmosphere, where it can capture images with less distortion than ground telescopes. It's been orbiting around the Earth since 1990, when it was ferried into orbit by a space shuttle.

> "I ran into an amateur astronomer who had a small telescope set up on the sidewalk. I looked through the lens at Jupiter, and I saw the explosions [from the Great Comet Crash]. Something was happening 500 million miles away and I was staring at it on a street corner in Baltimore," Hammel said. "When I saw those black spots, it hit me right in the gut. This wasn't something just for astronomers. It belonged to everyone."

"I just love working with Hubble.... It's incredible to me that there is a robotic telescope in orbit around the Earth, and that you can design a program and send these sequences up and move this telescope around to point anywhere around the sky and do any kind of science and get absolutely fabulous pictures, without the Earth's atmosphere in the way. You just can't do this from the ground," Hammel explained. "But with Hubble you only get one chance, so you've got to do it right the first time. That means you have to work very, very hard to make sure you have everything completely understood and you can't take chances and that makes it hard to use."

Hammel's challenge in preparing the Hubble Space Telescope to observe the Great Comet Crash was that no one knew what to expect, or how to prepare for observing and recording the event. She needed to figure out where to point the Hubble Space Telescope, which filters to use, when to take pictures, and many other details. Without really knowing what the collision would entail, Hammel began making calculations based on her best guesses of what would happen.

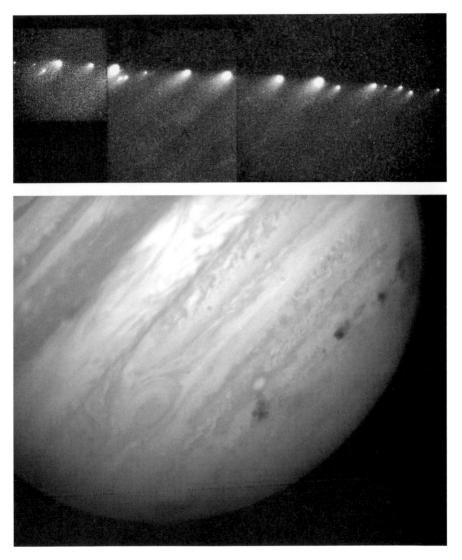

Two images related to the Great Comet Crash: the Shoemaker-Levy 9 comet in space (top) and the impact sites on Jupiter after the crash (bottom). The image of the comet is actually multiple photos pieced together.

Hammel guessed correctly, and her calculations produced more than 400 images from the Hubble Space Telescope of the Great Comet Crash. The images were clear and richly detailed, providing a huge amount of surprising new data. As the team leader, Hammel presented the first images to the world, exclaiming, "In my wildest dreams we couldn't have gotten any better!" Speaking to members of the press from around the world, she became the public face of the team working on the Great Comet Crash. Her excitement and enthusiasm were contagious, and her ability to explain complex astronomical observations in plain language helped non-scientists understand the significance of the collision.

"There's a little bit more to it than just the science," Hammel explained. "Of course, we're interested in science here because that's what we do. But it's a fascinating thing. There are things whizzing around the solar system, smashing into other things with huge explosions, and that's just really incredible to think about. We don't often think about the universe out there. We just sort of look at the sky and stars up there and—big deal. But if we really take a step back, it's a dynamic universe. And this is just a key example of some of the energetics that go on." She continued by explaining the powerful impact of the collision. "It made plumes of gases that rose 1,000 miles high. Jupiter was covered with atmospheric soot. If that impact had happened on Earth, we all would have died. It would have created a major disruption of the biosphere. This is what we think happened to the dinosaurs."

The Great Comet Crash fascinated the entire astronomy community, including amateurs who were able to observe the collision even with their small telescopes. "I ran into an amateur astronomer who had a small telescope set up on the sidewalk. I looked through the lens at Jupiter, and I saw the explosions. Something was happening 500 million miles away and I was staring at it on a street corner in Baltimore. I got a hitch in my chest. I was just amazed," Hammel recalled. "It was just an incredible sight. I had spent months planning the whole thing with Hubble. But I had never physically looked through an eyepiece to see what was happening. When I saw those black spots, it hit me right in the gut. This wasn't something just for astronomers. It belonged to everyone."

Returning to Research

In 1998, Hammel became a Senior Research Scientist at the Space Science Institute in Boulder, Colorado, a position she holds to the present day. In addition, she is also the co-director of the Space Science Institute's Research Branch. Hammel works at her home office in Connecticut and travels extensively to conduct observational research, attend astronomy conferences, and speak on astronomy topics. She continues her research on the Ice Giants Neptune and Uranus.

"I am fascinated by the delicate balance of external radiation from the Sun and the internal heat from these planets.... We do not fully understand the physical processes involved in the balance, and yet it is the same balance that occurs in the Earth's atmosphere. In other words, by studying other planets, we learn about Earth, and knowledge of Earth is incredibly important to us as a species."

"What I like best about the planet Neptune is that every time you look at it, it's different, so Neptune can be *your* planet. The pictures that would be taken of Neptune would be yours. No one else would have seen the clouds that you see and they'll never be seen again probably. And so that means that the pictures of Neptune you take would be absolutely unique."

"With Uranus, now we're rewriting the textbooks on it. Our recent observations are so counter to what we thought.... We thought of Uranus's atmosphere as pretty much dead. And it's not," Hammel said. "Text-books describe Uranus as boring, but that's because the Voyager 2 probe flew by it during an uninteresting season.... We are now seeing the northern hemisphere for the first time, and the seasonal changes are fascinating to watch."

———— " ————

"So many people, especially women, think they're not qualified when it comes to new opportunities," Hammel observed. "You think there is someone who can do a job better, but usually there's not. Those guys who are acting like they are better qualified? They aren't any better qualified. They just think they are. Be willing to take a chance!"

———— " ————

Planning for Deep Space Observation

In addition to conducting her own research, Hammel is a member of the team that is developing the James Webb Space Telescope. This telescope is expected to launch into space in 2018 and is intended to replace the Hubble Space Telescope. "I've been studying these planets for 20, 30 years now," Hammel said, "and we've really pushed the limits of what we can do from the ground and with Hubble." The James Webb Space Telescope will be capable of producing images of longer light wavelengths, allowing astronomers to look more closely at the oldest parts of the universe. Its mission will be to search for the first galaxies that were formed after the Big Bang, and determine how galaxies evolve over time.

"Each new discovery or observation or theory helps us better understand our universe. And that's important, but in some cases the new knowledge can be what we call incremental. It adds just a little bit of new understand-

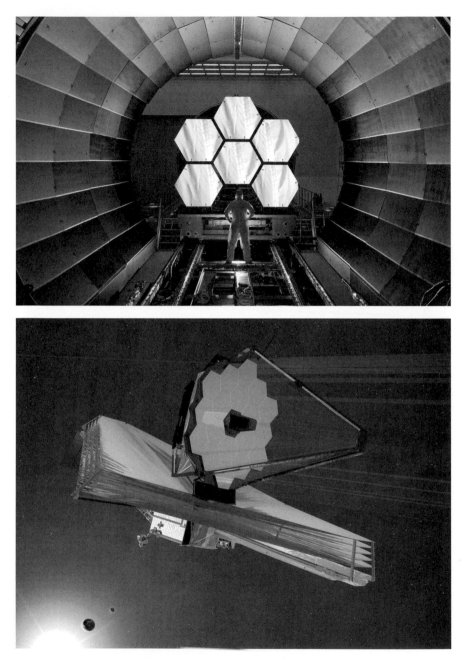

*Two images of the James Webb Space Telescope, now in construction:
a NASA engineer looks at the first six mirror segments, and an artist's vision
of how the telescope will look when complete.*

ing. For example, someone might have a model of the universe that says the universe is getting smaller with time. If your new data show that the universe is getting smaller faster than the other person thought, this is important. But if your new data show that the universe is actually getting BIGGER with time, then that is IMPORTANT. See the difference? To do really IMPORTANT work usually requires either being exceedingly brilliant … or being clever about which problem you choose and how you choose to solve it—like use a brand new instrument or work on a brand new field."

"If I see something that seems out of sync with what's already known, the first thing I do is try to find out what's wrong with the data. Once you've done that, and it still seems wrong, that's when things get interesting. It means you've found something new to understand. So you think about it and go for more data and come up with different models. All real science is like that."

Over the course of her long career, Hammel has established a reputation as one of the foremost planetary astronomers in the world. Planetary astronomers study the formation, development, and evolution of planets, including planetary atmosphere, weather, any satellites (such as moons), and any cosmic events that affect the planet. "You feel like you're exploring when you're doing planetary astronomy," she explained. "Maybe you're not physically walking on the surface of the planet, but you are exploring it for the first time. You're the pioneer."

"To be the best in a field always requires a lot of hard work. There are also still misperceptions that women don't do science, so one is always educating people about that. Girls especially seem to blame themselves if things go wrong (if they fail a test, or don't win a contest), and it takes a long time and plenty of self-coaching to get over that spurious limitation," Hammel said. "Don't turn down an opportunity because you are afraid. That's not a good reason to turn down something. So many people, especially women, think they're not qualified when it comes to new opportunities. You think there is someone who can do a job better, but usually there's not. Those guys who are acting like they are better qualified? They aren't any better qualified. They just think they are. Be willing to take a chance!"

MARRIAGE AND FAMILY

In 1996, Hammel married Tim Dalton, a chemical engineer. They live in Ridgefield, Connecticut, with their children: Beatrix, born in 1997, Tobias, born in 1999, and Lucas, born in 2001.

HONORS AND AWARDS

Harold C. Urey Prize (American Astronomical Society): 1996, for outstanding achievement by a young scientist

Spirit of American Women Award: 1996, for contributions to educational
outreach

Named among the 50 Most Important Women Scientists (Discover): 2002

Carl Sagan Medal (American Astronomical Society's Division for Planetary
Sciences): 2002, for outstanding communication of planetary science to
the general public

FURTHER READING

Books

Beyond Jupiter: The Story of Planetary Astronomer Heidi Hammel, 2005

Periodicals

Astronomy, July 1997, p.50; Dec. 2010, p.50; Aug. 1, 2011
New York Times, Sep. 2, 2008; July 25, 2009, p.1
O, Dec. 2010
Sky & Telescope, Oct. 1995, p.6

Online Articles

www.fredbortz.com/HammelBio/AstroFAQ.htm
    (Dr. Fred's Place, "Heidi Hammel's Astronomy FAQ," Jan. 2006)
www.iwaswondering.org/heidi_homepage.html
    (IWasWondering.org, "Heidi Hammel," no date)
quest.nasa.gov/hst/PA-neptune.html
    (NASA, "Neptune," no date)
jwst.nasa.gov/meet-hammel.html
    (NASA James Webb Space Telescope, "Meet Heidi Hammel: Webb
    Telescope Interdisciplinary Scientist," no date)
www.thedailybeast.com/newsweek/2007/11/17/to-shoot-for-the-stars.html
    (Newsweek, "To Shoot For the Stars," Nov. 17, 2007)

ADDRESS

Heidi Hammel
Space Science Institute
4750 Walnut Street, Ste. 205
Boulder, CO 80301

WEB SITE

www.spacescience.org/about_ssi/staff/hammel.html

Josh Hutcherson 1992-

American Actor
Starred in *Bridge to Terabithia, Journey to the Center of the Earth,* and *The Hunger Games*

BIRTH

Joshua Ryan Hutcherson was born on October 12, 1992, in Union, Kentucky. His father, Chris, works as an analyst for the Environmental Protection Agency. His mother, Michelle, worked for Delta Airlines. He has a younger brother named Connor who is also an actor.

YOUTH AND EDUCATION

Hutcherson knew at a very young age that he wanted to become an actor, though he does not remember exactly when he first had the idea. "I just kind of wanted to do it," he explained. "I felt like this was what I was meant to do." At first, his parents resisted the idea. They thought their son was too young to make a decision like that. "Being from Kentucky, you know, you don't really know much about the business," he acknowledged. "You hear all of the negative connotations that come with the words 'child star' and 'child actor.' They kind of wanted to keep me out of all that stuff. They just wanted me to keep on playing T-ball, but you know, I was ready to move on from T-ball."

> *Hutcherson knew at a very young age that he wanted to become an actor, but his parents thought he was too young. "Being from Kentucky, you know, you don't really know much about the business," he acknowledged. "You hear all of the negative connotations that come with the words 'child star' and 'child actor.' They kind of wanted to keep me out of all that stuff. They just wanted me to keep on playing T-ball, but you know, I was ready to move on from T-ball."*

A few years passed and Hutcherson still had not given up his dream of acting. His parents reconsidered the idea when he was eight years old and allowed him to try out during pilot season, the period when many television networks film the pilot episodes, the first episode of a new TV show. "An acting coach said we should go out to California for pilot season," Hutcherson recalled. "My mom had just taken a leave of absence from Delta Airlines, and we were so confused. We didn't know what a pilot was."

Hutcherson and his mother went to Los Angeles so that he could begin auditioning for acting jobs. By the time he was nine years old, he had hired his first acting agent. With the agent's help, he soon landed roles in TV commercials and also appeared in the pilot episode for a new TV show.

Hutcherson and his mother spent the next few years travelling between California and Kentucky. When he wasn't working, they lived in Kentucky with his family. The family also had an apartment in Burbank, California, where Hutcherson and his mother stayed when he was auditioning for roles or filming in the Los Angeles area.

Hutcherson provided the voice of Markl in Howl's Moving Castle.

By this point Hutcherson was beginning to develop a career as an actor, but as he explained, "I was still a kid. I still had a childhood. It was just a little bit different from a normal one." Whenever he was at home in Kentucky, he liked to be outdoors doing things like looking for snakes in the creek near his home and playing football and soccer. He also enjoyed playing Guitar Hero II with his brother. As a teenager, he liked to compete in triathlons. (A triathlon is a multi-sport event in which participants compete to finish three consecutive races in the shortest amount of time. Triathlons normally include swimming, biking, and running races.)

Between acting jobs Hutcherson attended Ryle High School in Union, Kentucky. Whenever he was working, he studied with a tutor.

CAREER HIGHLIGHTS

Hutcherson's first notable acting job was on a 2002 episode of the TV series "ER." His first movie role was in the 2003 made-for-TV movie *Wilder Days*. In this movie, he played Chris, a boy who goes on an adventurous road trip with his father and grandfather. After that, Hutcherson landed some parts as a voice actor. He provided the voice of Markl in the English-language version of the animated movie *Howl's Moving Castle*. Hutcherson was also the voice of one of many "Hero Boys" in the animated feature film *The Polar Express*. By the time he started high school, he had already appeared in several movies and TV shows.

Hutcherson's first supporting role in a theatrical movie release was in the 2005 sports comedy *Kicking & Screaming*. He played Bucky, the son of demanding soccer coach Buck (played by Robert Duvall) and half-brother of Phil (played by Will Ferrell). Hutcherson's first starring role was as Gabe in the 2005 movie *Little Manhattan*. In this coming-of-age story, 11-year-old Gabe navigates a complicated family life and his first real crush on a girl.

Zathura

Hutcherson's first major role was in the 2005 adventure *Zathura*, based on the picture book by children's author Chris Van Allsburg. *Zathura* was a follow-up to *Jumanji*, also by Van Allsburg. In *Jumanji*, two children find an old board game and decide to play. They are transported into the most astonishing and frightening adventures, and they can't escape until they finish the game. At the end of the story, the children try to get rid of the game, but another child takes it home.

In *Zathura*, Walter (played by Hutcherson) and his brother Danny (played by Jonah Bobo) set off an unexpected chain of events when they decide to play the old board game, which was hidden in the basement of their new house. As the boys begin to play, events in the game come to life. A meteor shower destroys part of the house, killer robots and monsters appear, and the house itself goes flying through space. To set things right, the two brothers must figure out how to stop arguing with each other and work together as a team for the first time in their lives. According to *Entertainment Weekly* movie reviewer Scott Brown, "From a Hollywood that often settles for less in the family department, *Zathura* is a rarity: a stellar fantasy that faces down childhood anxieties with feet-on-the-ground maturity." Hutcherson won a 2006 Young Artist Award for Leading Young Actor for his portrayal of Walter in *Zathura*.

Bridge to Terabithia

Hutcherson next appeared in the 2007 movie *Bridge to Terabithia*, based on the Newbery Award-winning 1977 book by Katherine Paterson. Hutcherson played Jess Aarons, a talented artist who is an outsider at school and within his own family. Tormented by school bullies and his four sisters, and mostly ignored by his father, Jess is lonely and alone. Then he meets Leslie (AnnaSophia Robb), a new girl at school who soon becomes his best friend. Together Leslie and Jess create an imaginary forest kingdom called Terabithia. They begin spending most of their free time in Terabithia, which

Hutcherson with AnnaSophia Robb in a scene from Bridge to Terabithia, *adapted from the novel of the same name by Katherine Paterson.*

can only be reached by swinging across a creek on a rope that hangs from a tree. Jess and Leslie build a tree house where they make up fantastic stories about monsters and dangerous quests. Leslie helps Jess learn about courage, strength, and true friendship. These qualities prove invaluable to Jess when he must come to terms with a terrible tragedy that he feels responsible for causing.

"I read the book when I found out it was getting made into a movie … and as I was reading it, I could see it coming to life off the pages, and I could picture myself as Jess. Then I got the script, I read the script, I loved the script. And I was like, I just read this, I just read the book, it's the exact same thing pretty much. They kept it so true to the book," Hutcherson said. "I think that there are kids who are outcasts, and they get kind of picked on at school. They need to find a good friend to hang out with and create sort of a fantasy world, like we did in the movie."

Bridge to Terabithia earned good reviews from movie critics, as in this comment from *Hollywood Reporter* critic Michael Rechtshaffen: "The fantasy-adventure incorporates the novel's magical and emotional elements without overplaying either—a balance that hasn't always proven easy to maintain in the world of kid-lit adaptation." *New York Times* movie reviewer Jeannette Catsoulis praised *Bridge to Terabithia* as "a thoughtful and extremely affecting story of a transformative friendship between two unusually gifted children.... Consistently smart and delicate as a spider web, *Bridge to Terabithia* is the kind of children's movie rarely seen nowadays. And at a time when many public schools are being forced to cut music and art from the curriculum, the story's insistence on the healing power of a nurtured imagination is both welcome and essential." For his role in *Bridge to Terabithia*, Hutcherson won a 2008 Young Artist Award for Leading Young Actor.

Journey to the Center of the Earth

Hutcherson's next starring role was in the 2008 remake of the adventure story *Journey to the Center of the Earth*, an adaptation of the 1874 novel by French science fiction pioneer Jules Verne. *Journey to the Center of the Earth* was the first live action feature film produced in high-definition 3-D. In this movie, Hutcherson played Sean, whose father has disappeared mysteriously. Sean is sent to visit his uncle Trevor (played by Brendan Fraser), who is a geologist and volcanologist. In a box of his father's papers, Sean discovers a copy of the book *Journey to the Center of the Earth*. The book contains notes written by Sean's father showing that volcanoes could contain a way to reach the Earth's core. Uncle Trevor impulsively sets off with Sean to investigate this theory. In Iceland, Sean and Uncle Trevor team up with Hannah (played by Anita Briem), a mountain guide whose own father believed that it was possible to discover another world at the Earth's center. The team sets off for the mouth of a volcano and soon find themselves immersed in a fantastic and dangerous adventure travelling through the hidden world beneath the surface of the Earth.

Journey to the Center of the Earth was dismissed by most critics, though younger movie fans enjoyed the fast-paced special effects. Still, Hutcherson's performance as Sean increased his popularity with moviegoers and led to him being cast in more starring roles.

Hutcherson returned to the role of Sean in the 2012 adventure movie *Journey 2: Mysterious Island*. This sequel is based on the Jules Verne novel *The Mysterious Island*, published in 1874. This story follows Sean, now 17 years old, as he joins up with his new stepfather Hank (played by Dwayne Johnson) on a mission to find Sean's long-lost grandfather. After Sean and Hank intercept and decode a strange distress signal, they realize that Sean's grandfather may be stranded on a remote island in the South Pacific. They hire a pilot to fly them to the island, where they crash into a spectacular fantasy world where nothing is normal. While navigating many dangerous challenges, everyone must work together to find a way off the island before it sinks into the ocean.

A scene from Journey to the Center of the Earth: *Hutcherson (Sean) with Brendan Fraser (Trevor) and Anita Briem (Hannah).*

Cirque du Freak: The Vampire's Assistant

Hutcherson appeared in the 2009 movie *Cirque du Freak: The Vampire's Assistant.* The movie is based on three books in the series *The Saga of Darren Shan,* a comic-goth series for young adults written by Darren Shan. The story focuses on two teenaged best friends, Darren (played by Chris Massoglia) and Steve (played by Hutcherson). Darren is popular and gets good grades in school, while Steve is a troublemaker who is accused of being a bad influence on Darren. When the two friends decide to visit a travelling circus freak show, their lives are changed forever. Darren and Steve are drawn into a long-running conflict between two rival groups, the Vampires and the Vampaneze. Through a dramatic sequence of events, Darren becomes a Vampire and must begin training as a vampire's assistant. Steve soon becomes a Vampaneze, one of the evil clan fighting against the Vampires. The two must then leave their old lives behind and join the travelling band of freaks. Tension rises as the two former friends, now on opposite sides of an ancient rivalry, must determine whether they are destined to become sworn enemies.

The movie received mixed reviews, with critics finding some elements to praise even when dismissing it overall. As Betsy Sharkey wrote in the *Los Angeles Times,* "The themes in *Cirque* are typical teenage ones—feeling like a freak, unsure of who you are or what you want to be in life, ready to fall in love, kinda, especially when the monkey girl (Jessica Carlson) is so cute, and falling out with your best friend.... So it's a disappointment that *Cirque* isn't better. The look of the film has a great, eerie Victorian story-book quality to it. The story and characters are mostly sized for the 8- to 10-year-old crowd. The action—a lot of rough vampire-versus-vampaneze (the killer vamps) fighting, which entails limb tearing, head butting, and spilled blood—aims a little older. Meanwhile the dialogue is shooting for something akin to the campy cleverness of *Scream.* Unfortunately [director Paul Weitz] can't quite get a handle on what the film should be.... *Cirque* is a harmless bit of fluff with a very cool look, but there's just never enough bite." Hutcherson came in for some praise for his performance as Steve, including these comments from Sandie Angulo Chen on the website Common Sense Media. "Hutcherson, who was brilliant in *Bridge to Terabithia,* nails the insecure, impetuous character of Steve and deserves more leading—not sidekick—roles."

The Kids Are All Right

Hutcherson's next project was the 2010 Academy Award nominated drama *The Kids Are All Right.* He played 15-year-old Laser, who is teetering on the brink of juvenile delinquency, in an all-star cast that included Annette Bening and Julianne Moore, playing his same-sex parents; Mark Ruffalo, playing his sperm-donor father; and Mia Wasikoska, playing his sister Joni. When Joni decides that Laser needs a father figure, she tries to track down their father, an anonymous sperm donor. When he shows up to meet the family, everyone must adjust to the new presence in their lives. As the awkward new relationships develop, the kids, the two mothers, and the father all struggle to fit their lives together in a new way.

Hutcherson's portrayal of Laser brought him to the attention of a larger audience of moviegoers and was seen as a big step in advancing his career. "It's not a movie aimed at a particularly teen audience, and I guess that means an 'acting' breakthrough. I hope so," he remarked. "I just know that I was floored—blown away—when I learned who was going to be in it. I mean, these are heavy hitters. I had to be on my toes this time out." *The Kids Are All Right* was widely praised by critics. *USA Today* film reviewer Claudia Puig noted, "The kids come off wiser and more mature in many ways than the adults responsible for them in the warmly funny and intelligent *The Kids Are All Right.*"

The Hunger Games

Hutcherson next landed the coveted role of Peeta Mellark in the highly anticipated 2012 movie *The Hunger Games.* Based on the first book in the wildly popular three-book series by Suzanne Collins, *The Hunger Games* is set in

Peeta (Hutcherson) in the Capitol with Cinna (Lenny Kravitz, left) and Haymitch Abernathy (Woody Harrelson, center), before the Games.

the brutal world of Panem, a nation that evolved from the remains of North America after a terrible calamity. Most of the citizens of Panem's 12 districts are forced to work to support the wealthy, tyrannical rulers of the Capitol.

Some time in the past, the people in the districts had gone to war against the Capitol but suffered a terrible defeat. As part of their surrender, each district was forced to agree to send one boy and one girl to participate in "The Hunger Games," an annual televised competition. The 24 competitors, known as "tributes," are selected by lottery. They are taken to the Capitol and locked in an arena where they must fight and kill one another until only one is left alive. The winner is awarded riches and freedom. Peeta, the gentle and kind son of his district's baker, becomes a tribute along with Katniss (played by Jennifer Lawrence), an expert hunter and archer. Peeta and Katniss both must fight in the Games, and there can be only one survivor. The movie also featured Liam Hemsworth as Gale, Woody Harrelson as Haymitch Abernathy, Elizabeth Banks as Effie, Lenny Kravitz as Cinna, and Donald Sutherland as President Snow. (For more information on Suzanne Collins, see *Biography Today,* September 2011.)

When Hutcherson learned that *The Hunger Games* would be made into a movie, he knew immediately that he wanted the role of Peeta. "I read the

Hutcherson as Peeta competing during the Games.

whole series in five days. Bam! Bam! Yes, more! Gimme, gimme! Come on!" Hutcherson said, "I don't want to be that actor who's like, 'Yeah, man, the role is so me.' But it is! I am Peeta. His humility, his self-deprecating humor, his way that he can just talk to anybody in any room." Hutcherson was even more confident once filming began. "I've never connected with a character more in my life and felt like I had to act less. It was kind of weird. Like, 'Suzanne Collins, how did you know me? How do you know what I stand for? This is crazy!'"

The Hunger Games was an instant hit with moviegoers and critics alike. Fans flocked to theaters, making *The Hunger Games* the highest earning movie for several weeks after its premiere. *New York Daily News* movie reviewer Joe Neumaier said, "*The Hunger Games*, the highly anticipated movie based on the best-selling teen novel, is as tough-spirited as fans would hope for— and exciting and thought-provoking in a way few adventure dramas ever are.... It's also a far more serious movie than the marketing, and mainstream mania, have led us to believe. It's better and scarier than its source book, and aims an angry eye at our bloodthirsty, watch-anything-and-cheer culture." According to *Rolling Stone* movie reviewer Peter Travers, "Relax, you legions of Hunger Gamers. We have a winner. Hollywood didn't screw up the film version of Suzanne Collins' young-adult bestseller about a survival-of-the-fittest reality show that sends home all its teen contestants, save the victor, in body bags. The screen *Hunger Games* radiates a hot, jumpy energy that's irresistible. It has epic spectacle, yearning romance, suspense that won't quit…. *The Hunger Games* is a zeitgeist movie that captures the spirit of a soul-sucking age in which ego easily trumps common cause." Travers also praised Hutcherson for bringing "humor and a bruised heart to a boy who needs to mature fast."

As one of the stars of the incredibly popular movie, Hutcherson has had to learn to live with fame. So far, he has remained philosophical about all of the extra attention. "I know it's going to be a big change, but I think if you go about it in the right way, you can still have your privacy. You got to just keep on trucking and make sure you're always being true to yourself. Which is so funny be-cause—God bless America!—that's exactly what Peeta would say." His performance as Peeta earned him four MTV Movie Award nominations in 2012, including Best Male Performance, Best Cast (shared with *The Hunger Games* costars), Best Fight (shared with Jennifer Lawrence), and Best Kiss (shared with Jennifer Lawrence). Hutcherson has already signed on to play Peeta in *Catching Fire*, the second *Hunger Games* movie.

———— **"** ————

"I am Peeta. His humility, his self-deprecating humor, his way that he can just talk to anybody in any room," Hutcherson said. *"I've never connected with a character more in my life and felt like I had to act less. It was kind of weird. Like, 'Suzanne Collins, how did you know me? How do you know what I stand for? This is crazy!'"*

———— **"** ————

In 2012, Hutcherson received a Vanguard Award from the Gay and Lesbian Alliance against Defamation (GLAAD). This award recognizes a member of the entertainment industry who has made a significant difference in promoting equal rights for lesbian, gay, bisexual, and transgender people. He is the youngest person to receive the award. Hutcherson was honored for the video he created as part of the Straight But Not Narrow campaign, an educational project that works to reduce homophobia among young heterosexual males.

Future Plans

Hutcherson's next movie role will be in *Red Dawn*, a remake of the 1984 action movie of the same title. The story of a group of teenagers who come together to fight against an invading foreign army as the U.S. stands at the brink of World War III, *Red Dawn* is scheduled to be released in 2012.

Hutcherson plans to continue acting and to become a director someday. "I just sort of followed my passion, and anything I got turned down for, I just kept my head up looking for the next project," he said. "Since I first started, my goal has been to act forever. I knew the transition from child actor into adult actor is one that not everyone gets the luxury of making and some fizzle out. It's about finding the right scripts, doing things that are different."

HOME AND FAMILY

Hutcherson currently lives in California.

SELECTED CREDITS

Kicking & Screaming, 2005
Little Manhattan, 2005
Zathura, 2005
Bridge to Terabithia, 2007
Journey to the Center of the Earth, 2008
Cirque du Freak: The Vampire's Assistant, 2009
The Kids Are All Right, 2010
Journey 2: Mysterious Island, 2012
The Hunger Games, 2012

HONORS AND AWARDS

Leading Young Actor Award (Young Artist Awards): 2006, for *Zathura;* 2008, for *Bridge to Terabithia*
Vanguard Award (Gay and Lesbian Alliance against Defamation—GLAAD): 2012
MTV Movie Awards: 2012 (two awards), Best Male Performance, Best Fight in a Movie (with Jennifer Lawrence and Alexander Ludwig)

FURTHER READING

Periodicals

Current Events, Feb. 12, 2007, p.6
Entertainment Weekly, July 23, 2010, p.67; Aug. 5, 2011, p.44
Girls' Life, Oct./Nov. 2009, p.55
Seventeen, Oct. 2011, p.89
USA Today, Nov. 2, 2005, p.D3

Online Articles

www.allmovie.com/artist/josh-hutcherson-p380181
    (AllMovie.com, "Josh Hutcherson," 2012)

www.kidzworld.com/article/25889-josh-hutcherson-bio
  (Kidz World, "Josh Hutcherson Bio," no date)
movies.yahoo.com/person/josh-hutcherson
  (Yahoo, "Josh Hutcherson," no date)

ADDRESS

Josh Hutcherson
ICM Partners
10250 Constellation Boulevard
Los Angeles, CA 90067

WEB SITES

joshhutcherson.com
www.thehungergamesmovie.com
www.suzannecollinsbooks.com
www.scholastic.com/thehungergames

Steve Jobs 1955-2011
American Technology Pioneer and Business Leader
Co-Founder of Apple Inc. and Pixar

BIRTH

Steven Paul Jobs was born on February 24, 1955, in San Francisco, California. He was adopted by Paul Jobs, a machinist, and his wife Clara Jobs, who worked as an accountant. They raised him with a younger sister, Patty, adopted in 1957.

As an adult, Jobs traced the story of his birth parents. Joanne Schieble was a graduate student studying speech therapy at the University of Wisconsin. She fell in love with Abdulfattah

"John" Jandali, a teaching assistant in political science who was a Muslim from Syria. Schieble's father did not approve of the match, so when Schieble became pregnant she went to California to give the child up for adoption. Soon after, her father died and she and Jandali married. The marriage only lasted six years, and they had a daughter, Mona Simpson. Jobs met his birth mother and sister when he was in his 20s, but never contacted Jandali. His sister Mona remained one of his closest friends for the rest of his life.

YOUTH

Jobs was five when his family moved to the southern end of the San Francisco Bay area, home to so many technology companies that it would soon earn the name of "Silicon Valley." While it was clear young Steve was bright—his mother taught him to read before he started kindergarten—he did not always enjoy school. "When I got there I really just wanted to do two things," he noted. "I wanted to read books because I loved reading books and I wanted to go outside and chase butterflies." Jobs became a mischief maker, until his fourth grade teacher bribed him to complete his math workbook and get it right. "Before very long I had such a respect for her that it sort of re-ignited my desire to learn," he recalled. He skipped fifth grade but had trouble fitting in with his classmates. He was bullied so much in middle school he came home and announced he was never going back. Instead, the family moved to a new home in nearby Los Altos, which had better schools.

Jobs was only 10 or 11 when he was introduced to computers. His father took him to see the NASA Ames Research Center in nearby Sunnyvale, California, which had a computer. "I didn't see the computer, I saw a terminal and it was theoretically a computer on the other end of the wire," he recalled. "I fell in love with it."

Jobs's father supported his son in learning outside the classroom in other ways as well. Paul Jobs rebuilt and sold old cars as a side business and gave his son a special area in his garage workshop to work on his own projects. He introduced his son to the basics of electronics, and young Steve was soon fascinated. He was also encouraged by a neighbor, an engineer for electronics company Hewlett-Packard (HP). The neighbor introduced him to Heathkit-brand do-it yourself electronics projects. Soon Jobs began assembling his own Heathkits. "It made you realize you could build and understand anything," he said. "Once you built a couple of radios, you'd see a TV in the catalogue and say, 'I can build that as well,' even if you didn't. I was very lucky, because when I was a kid both my dad and the Heathkits

---

IMPORTANT COMPUTER TERMS

Application Software: Software that is designed to help the user perform a specific task, such as word processing, designing graphics, or playing music, movies, or games. Often abbreviated to the term App.

Computer Processing Unit (CPU): The key component of all computers that carries out instructions of computer programs. Types of CPUs include circuit boards and microprocessors, also known as chips. A faster CPU makes for a more powerful computer.

Graphical User Interface (GUI): A method for a user to interact with computers by manipulating images (graphics) on the screen, usually with a mouse, rather than by typing text commands onto the screen with a keyboard.

Hardware: The physical "guts" of a computer, which may contain circuit boards, microchips, or similar CPU devices to process and store information.

Memory: Physical devices that can store instructions in a computer; these include magnetic tapes, magnetic disk drives, and optical disc drives, which use lasers. A larger memory makes for a more powerful computer.

Operating System (OS): A set of computer programs that manage a computer's hardware and provide a way for application software to communicate with the hardware. Common operating systems, besides Apple's iOS, include Microsoft Windows, UNIX, Linux, and Android (for mobile devices).

Software: A collection of computer programs that provide a computer with instructions of what tasks to perform and how to perform them. The term is often used to refer solely to application software.

System Software: Software, including operating systems, that manages computer hardware resources, telling them what to do and helping them communicate and run application software smoothly.

---

made me believe I could build anything." Jobs was 13 when, in the middle of building a device to measure electronic signals, he discovered a part missing. He looked up the home phone of William Hewlett, co-founder of HP, and called him directly. After talking to Hewlett for 20 minutes, Jobs secured the part as well as a summer internship on the HP assembly line.

EDUCATION

Jobs attended Homestead High School in Cupertino, California, where he was a member of the electronics club. After graduating in 1972, he enrolled at Reed College, a liberal arts college in Portland, Oregon. After one semester of required classes, he realized he was draining his parents' savings and not learning anything that interested him. Although he withdrew his enrollment, he became a "drop-in" rather than a dropout. He spent the next 18 months auditing classes, attending them without earning any credits toward a degree. He took only classes that interested him, including philosophy and calligraphy (the art of writing).

FIRST JOBS

Jobs came back to Silicon Valley in 1974 and found a job working for Atari, the video game company that had created the first hit video game, "Pong." After a few months he had saved enough money to finance a trip to India. He traveled throughout the country for seven months, exploring Eastern philosophy and seeking spiritual enlightenment. He returned to California in fall 1974 and returned to Atari.

By 1975 Jobs became involved with the Homebrew Computer Club, where he reconnected with Steve Wozniak, an older acquaintance he knew from his high school electronics club. Jobs and Wozniak had first collaborated in 1971 on a "blue box," an illegal device that used sound to fool telephones into giving the user free long-distance calls. They read about the machine, built one, and used it for pranks until Jobs suggested selling them. They sold almost 100 before being robbed of one at gunpoint. Although they quickly got out of the blue-box business, a few years later their common love of electronics would blossom into a partnership that transformed the computer industry.

CAREER HIGHLIGHTS

The Apple Computer Revolution

In the mid-1970s, when Jobs and Wozniak reconnected, computers were huge machines that could take up entire rooms; only businesses and universities could afford to buy and maintain them. Wozniak, however, had designed a simple standalone computer for hobbyists, consisting of a single circuit board as a central processing unit (CPU) that could be used at home with the owner's own video screen and keyboard. At first, Wozniak only intended the computer as a demonstration for the Homebrew Computer Club; it was Jobs who suggested they could sell the machine to computer

Jobs (right) with Apple co-founder Steve Wozniak from the company's early days.

enthusiasts. They founded Apple in 1976, dubbed the computer the Apple I, and Jobs soon got their first order—for 50 computers at $500 each—and financing to buy the parts. Wozniak, Jobs, and assorted friends and family members worked out of the Jobs family garage to complete the order. Jobs soon realized, however, that the do-it-yourself Apple I only appealed to hobbyists; their next product should be ready to run out of the box.

In 1977 the partners incorporated the company, rented offices, hired a president and a marketing firm, and chose the company's distinctive logo, an apple with a bite out of it. The Apple II launched that year and started the personal computer revolution: it included a built-in keyboard and speaker and even featured color graphics. While the insides were the product of Wozniak's electronics genius, the simple design and user-friendly case came from Jobs. When other computers still looked like scientific equipment, the Apple II was electronic equipment for the average consumer. The Apple II earned $2 million in its first year of sales, and by 1981 yearly sales were $600 million. When Apple Computer first began selling shares of the company to the public in December 1980, demand went through the roof. Four years after being founded for just over $5,000, Apple was worth $1.79 billion. At the age of 25, Jobs became a multi-millionaire. Rather than spend his new-found wealth, however, Jobs threw himself into working on two new products: the upgraded Apple III and the Lisa, a more powerful (and more expensive) personal computer.

A New Type of Computer: The Mac

Even as Apple engineers worked on these new—but not revolutionary—products, Jobs had another vision for the company. In 1979 he had visited the research center of Xerox, the copier and computer company, where he saw an experimental computer that used a mouse and a graphical user interface (GUI, pronounced "gooey") instead of typed commands. At this point, there were no computer icons (like the little pictures of a folder, a sheet of paper, and a trash can), no point and click, no drag and drop. Instead, computer users had to type in complicated sequences of commands and hold down multiple keys at a time, including the control, alt, tab, and function keys. It required far more expertise on the part of the user. For Jobs, seeing the new computer was a revelation. "It was one of those sort of apocalyptic moments," he recalled. "I remember within 10 minutes of seeing the graphical user interface stuff, just knowing that every computer would work this way someday. It was so obvious once you saw it. It didn't require tremendous intellect. It was so clear." Jobs went back to the Apple offices and immediately set his engineers to working on an operating system that would feature GUI and mouse.

> *For Jobs, seeing an early computer with a graphical user interface and mouse was a revelation. "It was one of those sort of apocalyptic moments," he recalled. "I remember within 10 minutes of seeing the graphical user interface stuff, just knowing that every computer would work this way someday. It was so obvious once you saw it. It didn't require tremendous intellect. It was so clear."*

Two of the many Apple devices that revolutionized the industry: the Apple II (top), credited with launching the personal computer revolution; and the Macintosh (bottom), with a graphical user interface, mouse, and other features now common to all computers.

An impatient perfectionist, Jobs had a unique management style that developed from his passion for his work. He occasionally gave employees enthusiastic praise, but more often he offered only scornful criticisms or even insults. This was how Jobs tested his employees' enthusiasm for their ideas. One co-worker called his approach the "reality distortion field," because Jobs would refuse to accept scheduling or design limitations. By insisting that something could be done—often faster or better than before—Jobs goaded his employees into rising to the challenge. Some burned out and left the company, but others were inspired.

Under Jobs's direction, Apple engineers created the Macintosh, a simple, easy-to-use computer with a graphical user interface that changed the personal computing market. While Xerox first came up with the idea, Apple was the first to develop it for the personal computer, making the first commercially successful computer with a mouse and the features that are common on modern computers. As Jobs recalled, "The contributions we tried to make embodied values not only of technical excellence and innovation—which I think we did our share of—but innovation of a more humanistic kind."

The Macintosh was unveiled in 1984 with a groundbreaking Super Bowl commercial that portrayed Apple as breaking the conformist "Big Brother" mentality of their main competitor, computer giant IBM. The Mac's small memory meant sales were slow at first, but its graphical user interface, mouse control, and simplicity of use made it appeal to thousands of people who had never considered owning a personal computer before. The Mac changed people's perception of computers, convincing many that there was a market for personal computers for individuals, not just for businesses. The launch of the Mac was the second time that Jobs had changed the computer industry, according to *Fortune* writer Brent Schlender. "[Jobs] twice altered the direction of the computer industry. In 1977 the Apple II kicked off the PC era, and the graphical user interface launched by Macintosh in 1984 has been aped by every other computer since."

Apple's board of directors, however, was impatient. Sales of the error-prone Apple III and the expensive Lisa were dragging, and the Macintosh did not immediately take off. The board took away Jobs's power to make decisions for Apple products. In 1985, a frustrated Jobs was forced to resign from the company he had built.

New Directions: Pixar and the iMac

When Jobs left Apple, he saw a gap in the university market. Many science labs, for instance, needed individual computers more powerful than what the personal computer industry offered. He founded NeXT in 1985 to fill that gap by building a computer—both hardware and operating system—to meet that need. He sold all but one share of his Apple stock and got additional funding from financier (and future independent presidential candidate) Ross Perot. He built a state-of-the-art factory to produce the NeXT computer, a sleek black cube that debuted in 1988 with faster processing speeds, state-of-the-art graphics, and a new optical disc drive to provide computer memory. "I've always been attracted to the more revolutionary changes," Jobs noted. "I don't know why. Because they're harder. They're much more stressful emotionally. And you usually go through a period where everybody tells you that you've completely failed."

> *"I've always been attracted to the more revolutionary changes," Jobs noted. "I don't know why. Because they're harder. They're much more stressful emotionally. And you usually go through a period where everybody tells you that you've completely failed."*

Jobs had always been interested in the intersection between computers and creative arts, once noting that "I actually think there's actually very little distinction between an artist and a scientist or engineer of the highest caliber." In 1986 he bought the graphics supercomputing division of Lucasfilm, the company founded by *Star Wars* director George Lucas, for $5 million. He immediately invested another $5 million in the company, which was incorporated as Pixar and initially developed high-end hardware, computers with powerful imaging capabilities that sold to medical facilities and intelligence agencies. Pixar's animation department, led by John Lasseter, initially existed to create short films that illustrated the capabilities of Pixar systems and software. But as sales of Pixar computers underperformed, the animation division developed a reputation for quality, with clever commercials and short films that won awards. After the Pixar short "Tin Toy" won the 1988 Academy Award for best animated short film, the company signed an agreement with Walt Disney Company, the pioneering animation studio, to produce the first feature-length computer-animated movie.

Disney liked Lasseter's story about two lost toys who try to find their way home, and production on Pixar's first full-length animated movie began in 1991. But the relationship between Disney and Pixar was rocky. Disney executives interfered with Pixar's ideas, so Jobs ran interference and kept

*Woody, Buzz Lightyear, and the gang in Toy Story,
the first full-length Pixar feature film.*

funding going when Disney threatened to pull out of the deal. During Pixar's first 10 years, Jobs spent another $50 million of his own money on the company, an investment that paid off in 1995 with the debut of *Toy Story*. Critics praised the film and audiences loved it; the film made $362 million worldwide and topped the U.S. charts for the year. Pixar also began selling shares of the company to the public in 1995. Their initial public offering (IPO) was the most successful of the year, with trading having to be delayed because of high demand. After the IPO, Jobs's shares—he owned 80 percent of the company—were worth $1.2 billion. Pixar's success resulted from more than Jobs's foresight, Pixar co-founder Edwin Catmull noted, "You need a lot more than vision—you need a stubbornness, tenacity, belief, and patience to stay the course. In Steve's case, he pushes right to the edge, to try to make the next big step forward. It's built into him."

Like Pixar's early imaging computers, the NeXT system did not sell as well as projected. (Nevertheless, it was used by programmer Tim Berners-Lee to create the first version of the World Wide Web in 1990.) Eventually Jobs decided the company should focus on producing operating systems instead of hardware. Its NeXTSTEP system was modestly successful, especially with computer programmers, and Jobs considered selling the company to focus on running Pixar. In the meantime, Apple Computer had suffered a downturn in sales and was behind schedule in developing an operating system for their next generation of computers. They bought NeXT in 1996 for $430 million and Jobs returned to Apple as an adviser. In September 1997 he became interim Chief Executive Officer (CEO) of Apple and faced the challenge of turning around a company whose share of the personal computing market had fallen to only four percent, from a high of 16 percent in the late 1980s.

Jobs set about changing the company's culture, which had chased profits with a confusing array of computers and devices. He decided Apple should focus on four core products: laptop and desktop computers for home and professional users. He found new board members who supported his goals, slashed development programs and personnel, and cut costs. He settled a patent lawsuit with Microsoft, whose GUI-based Windows operating system seemed to copy the Macintosh, and signed an agreement for Microsoft to make popular software programs available to Mac users. Jobs closely oversaw a new "Think Different" ad campaign for the company and drummed up excitement for Apple's new products. He also oversaw the beautiful new iMac, featuring a translucent blue case and a return to the revolutionary all-in-one design that had been popularized by the original Macintosh. When the iMac launched in 1998, it quickly became the best-selling computer in America. The portable iBook, with its bright colors and

Jobs with the iMac, known for its sleek all-in-one design.

distinctive clamshell shape, debuted in 1999 to similar excitement. In 2000, Jobs announced he would officially remain at Apple as its permanent CEO.

Reviving Apple with Music

The year 2001 was a turning point for Apple. Jobs was a firm believer in making products that integrated hardware, operating system, applications, and design to create a seamless experience for the user. In order to demonstrate these systems and provide customers with expert advice, he opened the first Apple store in 2001. While other computer manufacturers had failed with retail stores, Apple's emphasis on service and design— closely supervised by Jobs—made them a hit, grossing $1.4 billion in sales by 2004. Jobs also had a vision that in the future, home computers would serve as a hub, storing and organizing information for many portable digital machines. In fall 2001 Apple debuted the first of these portable devices, a music player dubbed the iPod. When integrated with Apple's free iTunes application, the iPod became an easy-to-use music player that could play any of 1,000 songs with no more than three clicks. With the iPod, Apple transitioned from a computer company to a consumer electronics company. The iPod quickly became a hot seller, but Jobs had a further innovation planned for the music industry.

At that time, in the early 2000s, sharing music illegally on the internet had become widespread, and the music industry was suffering greatly from lost sales. Jobs proposed creating an online store that would sell single songs as well as entire albums, then he convinced nervous music companies to sign on by limiting the service to Apple users. The new iTunes Store was an instant success, selling one million songs in the first six days alone. More record companies signed on to the service, and it was opened to Windows users as well. For each 99-cent song sold on the iTunes store, Apple's share was only about a dime. But with one billion songs sold by 2006, those dimes added up. Internet advocates had predicted since the early 1990s that businesses could profit from these small "micropayments." But as Alan Deutschman argued in *Newsweek,* "It took Jobs and Apple to finally make it happen, and the execution was brilliant."

———— " ————

"[The iPod was not] the truly revolutionary advance that launched Apple on the path to dominance in the Internet era," Alan Deutschman wrote in Newsweek. *"The greatest breakthrough was really the iTunes store. ... The debut of iTunes marked the beginning of one of the most incredible winning streaks in the history of modern business, a breathtaking eight-year run."*

———— " ————

By 2008, Apple was the largest music retailer in the United States, with its music division providing almost 50 percent of company revenues. To date, iTunes has sold more than 16 billion song downloads. "[The iPod was not] the truly revolutionary advance that launched Apple on the path to dominance in the Internet era," Deutschman declared. "The greatest breakthrough was really the iTunes store, which went live in April 2003. The debut of iTunes marked the beginning of one of the most incredible winning streaks in the history of modern business, a breathtaking eight-year run."

At the same time, Jobs's other company, Pixar, was enjoying similar success. *Toy Story* was only the first in an unbroken string of critically acclaimed hit movies, including *Bug's Life, Toy Story 2, Monsters Inc., Finding Nemo, The Incredibles, Cars, Ratatouille,* and *Wall E.* In fact, *Finding Nemo* became the most successful animated movie to date when it debuted in 2003. Although Jobs had occasional conflicts with Disney management over their deal to market and distribute Pixar films, he listened when they offered to buy the company in 2006. The deal, in which Disney bought Pixar for $7.4 billion in stock, meant that Jobs gave up his title as Pixar

CEO. Instead, he joined Disney's board of directors as its largest single shareholder, with almost seven percent of the company's stock.

Meanwhile, Apple was making so much progress in developing electronic devices that in 2007 they dropped "computer" from the company title, becoming simply "Apple Inc." In 2005 the company had debuted the video iPod, making episodes of many popular television shows available on their iTunes Store. Two years later, with Jobs's usual flair for secrecy and style, Apple debuted the iPhone mobile phone. Unlike many personal digital devices of the time, the iPhone had no writing stylus; instead, it pioneered an unusual touch-screen interface that allowed customers to use two fingers to manipulate data and applications. Although it was the most expensive phone on the market, the iPhone outperformed projections, with 11.6 million sold by 2008. By the end of 2010, almost 90 million iPhones had been sold worldwide; sales almost doubled one year later, by the end of 2011, bolstered by the introduction of the iPhone 4S.

The next big Apple product was the iPad, a tablet computer featuring Apple's distinctive touch-screen interface and fun applications. The tablet computer had been around for almost 20 years, but the iPad was the first to energize the market. Again, Apple provided everything that its customers might need: it designed its own hardware, wrote its own software, sold products through its own stores, and delivered services through iTunes. The iPad sold one million units in its first month alone, with 15 million sold after nine months. In summer 2011, Apple introduced iCloud, an online storage service that integrated with all the company's various products.

Jobs was known for exerting complete control over every aspect of Apple's products. By creating one system designed by Apple, the company was able to integrate its hardware, software, design, content—even the retail store where the products were sold. This approach earned Jobs a reputation as a control freak. But others found value in his constant search for perfection, as Walter Isaacson argued in *Time* magazine, "There proved to be advantages to Jobs's approach. His insistence on end-to-end integration gave Apple, in the early 2000s, an advantage in developing a digital-hub strategy, which allowed you to link your desktop computer with a variety of portable devices and manage your digital content.... The result was that the iPod, like the iPhone and iPad that followed, was an elegant delight, in contrast to the kludgy rival products that did not offer such a seamless end-to-end experience.... In a world filled with junky devices, clunky software, inscrutable error messages, and annoying interfaces, Jobs' insistence on a simple, integrated approach led to astonishing products marked by delightful user experiences."

The iPhone (top), the iPod (left), and the iPad (bottom)—each device revolutionized its segment of the industry and changed people's lives.

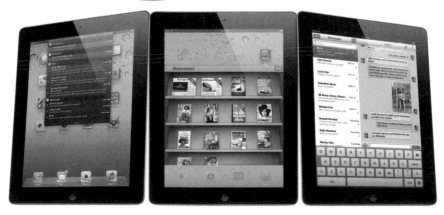

A Lasting Legacy

Jobs was a workaholic accustomed to long hours. But he had also endured several health issues. He first developed kidney stones in 1997; a follow-up exam in 2004 showed he had developed pancreatic cancer. Although most pancreatic cancers are fatal within months, his cancer was a rare form that was treatable with surgery. Still, the experience made him conscious his time was limited. At a rare public speech at Stanford University's 2005 commencement, he told new graduates, "Remembering that you are going to die is the best way I know to avoid the trap of thinking you have something to lose. You are already naked. There is no reason not to follow your heart." He made plans for Apple to continue without him, hiring a chief operations officer to help manage the company and establishing "Apple University" to help employees understand the company's philosophy of management and product development. Still, in 2008 Jobs lost weight and looked ill, and speculation about his health led to a decline in stock prices. In early 2009, he announced he would take a medical leave from Apple to have a liver transplant. He was back at work at Apple offices within two months of his transplant.

By the beginning of 2011, Jobs announced that his cancer had returned and he began another medical leave. That August, he officially stepped down as CEO of Apple. "I've had a very lucky career, a very lucky life," he shared. "I've done all that I can do." Soon after, Apple became the world's most valuable company (in terms of the total value of all its stock).

Jobs died of complications from pancreatic cancer in Palo Alto, California, on October 5, 2011. News of his death led to spontaneous tributes from the public, as piles of flowers, notes, and apples were left at Apple stores around the world. Notable public figures paid tribute as well, including President Barack Obama. "Steve was among the greatest of American innovators—brave enough to think differently, bold enough to believe he could change the world, and talented enough to do it.... Steve was fond of saying that he lived every day like it was his last. Because he did, he transformed our lives, redefined entire industries, and achieved one of the rarest feats in human history: he changed the way each of us sees the world," Obama said. "The world has lost a visionary. And there may be no greater tribute to Steve's success than the fact that much of the world learned of his passing on a device he invented."

Many commentators remarked on the lasting influence Jobs had on technology and its role in our everyday lives. In naming Jobs CEO of the decade in 2009, *Fortune* senior editor Adam Lashinsky remarked that "in the past 10 years alone he has radically and lucratively reordered three

LEFT TO RIGHT: LEONARDO DaVINCi, ALEXANDER GRAHAM BELL, THOMAS EDISON, THE NEW GUY

Jobs's death brought forth eulogies in many different forms, including this comment on his genius by cartoonist Steve Sack.

markets—music, movies, and mobile telephones—and his impact on his original industry, computing, has only grown." Business leader and New York City Mayor Michael Bloomberg observed, "Tonight, America lost a genius who will be remembered with Edison and Einstein, and whose ideas will shape the world for generations to come. Again and again over the last four decades, Steve Jobs saw the future and brought it to life long before most people could even see the horizon."

Some commentators marveled at what Jobs was able to achieve, as in these comments from Harry McCracken in *Time* magazine. "Steve Jobs ... wasn't a computer scientist. He had no training as a hardware engineer or industrial designer," McCracken remarked. "The businesses Apple entered under his leadership—from personal computers to MP3 players to smart phones—all existed before the company got there. But with astonishing regularity, Jobs did something that few people accomplish even once: he reinvented entire industries. He did it with ones that were new, like PCs, and he did it with ones that were old, like music. And his pace only accelerated over the years. He was the most celebrated, successful business executive of his generation.... It's impossible to imagine what the past few

———— " ————

In a speech at Stanford University, Jobs once said that wonderful things happened in his life because he risked failure to do what he loved. "Your time is limited, so don't waste it living someone else's life.... Don't let the noise of others' opinions drown out your own inner voice. And most important, have the courage to follow your heart and intuition. They somehow already know what you truly want to become. Everything else is secondary."

———— " ————

decades of technology, business, and, yes, the liberal arts would have been like without him."

For technology writer Steven Levy, Jobs held a singular place in the history of invention. "If Jobs were not so talented, if he were not so visionary, if he were not so canny in determining where others had failed in producing great products and what was necessary to succeed, his pushiness and imperiousness would have made him a figure of mockery," Levy wrote in *Wired* magazine. "But Steve Jobs *was* that talented, visionary, and determined. He combined an innate understanding of technology with an almost supernatural sense of what customers would respond to. His conviction that design should be central to his products not only produced successes in the marketplace but elevated design in general, not just in consumer electronics but everything that aspires to the high end.... His accomplishments were unmatched. People who can claim credit for game-changing products—iconic inventions that become embedded in the culture and answers to Jeopardy questions decades later—are few and far between. But Jobs has had not one, not two, but *six* of these breakthroughs, any one of which would have made for a magnificent career. In order: the Apple II, the Macintosh, the movie studio Pixar, the iPod, the iPhone, and the iPad. (This doesn't even include the consistent, brilliant improvements to the Macintosh operating system, or the Apple retail store juggernaut.) Had he lived a natural lifespan, there would have almost certainly been more."

Speaking of his work, Jobs once commented, "My goal has always been not only to make great products, but to build great companies." Despite some failures, Jobs built not one but two great companies. By 2011, Pixar had grossed over $7.2 billion in worldwide box office sales, including *Toy Story 3.* the first animated film to make over a billion dollars worldwide. Apple was also left in strong shape, continuing to gain in stock value even

Apple CEO Tim Cooks speaks to employees at a celebration of Jobs's life.

during an economic downturn. Jobs called himself "a tool builder" who wanted to build tools "that I know in my gut and my heart will be valuable." He also noted that "technology is nothing. What's important is that you have a faith in people, that they're basically good and smart, and if you give them tools, they'll do wonderful things with them." Wonderful things happened in his life, he told his Stanford audience, because he risked failure to do what he loved. "Your time is limited, so don't waste it living someone else's life…. Don't let the noise of others' opinions drown out your own inner voice. And most important, have the courage to follow your heart and intuition. They somehow already know what you truly want to become. Everything else is secondary."

MARRIAGE AND FAMILY

Jobs was 23 when he had a daughter with Chrisann Brennan, his on-again, off-again girlfriend since high school. He initially denied paternity and had little involvement with the girl, named Lisa Brennan-Jobs. But they later reconciled and she spent her teen years living with him.

Jobs met Laurene Powell in 1990 when he was giving a lecture at Stanford University, where she was studying for her master's degree in business. They married on March 18, 1991, in Yosemite National Park. After their marriage Powell founded a natural foods company and started College

Track, a program matching mentors with disadvantaged students. She also kept busy raising their three children: son Reed Paul (born 1991) and daughters Erin Siena (born 1995) and Eve (born 1998).

HOBBIES AND OTHER INTERESTS

Growing up in the San Francisco area, Jobs was heavily influenced by the counterculture movement of the 1960s and early 1970s, which challenged authority and sought new means of self-expression. Jobs developed an early interest in Eastern philosophies, particularly Zen Buddhism, that lasted throughout his lifetime. He was also an early experimenter with both vegetarianism and veganism (not eating any animal products, including dairy and eggs) and tried various specialized diets throughout his life. Music, especially that of 1960s icons Bob Dylan and the Beatles, was another lifelong interest. While Jobs was not associated with any particular charities, he did involve Apple in several charitable initiatives, introducing a special red iPod as part of the (Product)RED campaign to benefit the Global Fund to Fight AIDS, Tuberculosis, and Malaria.

HONORS AND AWARDS

National Technology Medal (U.S. Department of Commerce): 1985, for "the creation of a cheap but powerful computer" (with Stephen Wozniak)
Jefferson Award for Public Service (American Institute for Public Service): 1987
Entrepreneur of the Decade (*Inc.*): 1989
Lifetime Achievement Award (Software Publishers Association): 1989
Vanguard Award (Producers Guild of America): 2002 (with Ed Catmull and John Lasseter)
Named #1 Most Powerful Person in Business (*Fortune*): 2007
CEO of the Decade (*Fortune*): 2009
Person of the Year (*Financial Times*): 2010
Inspire Award (AARP): 2012

FURTHER READING

Books

Isaacson, Walter. *Steve Jobs,* 2011

Periodicals

Current Biography Yearbook, 1983, 1998
Financial Times, Dec. 23, 2010, p.11
Fortune, Nov. 23, 2009, p.92

Newsweek, Sep. 5, 2011, p.30; Oct. 10, 2011, p.26
New York Times, Oct. 6, 2011, p.A1
New York Times Magazine, Jan. 12, 1997, p.6
Rolling Stone, June 16, 1994, p.73
Time, Jan. 3, 1983; Oct. 5, 2011
USA Today, Oct. 6, 2011, p.A1

Online Articles

www.businessweek.com
  (Business Week, "Technology Executives Comment on Steve Jobs's
  Death," Oct. 6, 2011)
www.computerhistory.org/highlights/stevejobs
  (Computer History Museum, "Steve Jobs: From Garage to World's Most
  Valuable Company," Dec. 8, 2011)
money.cnn.com
  (Money/CNN, "25 Most Powerful People in Business: #1. Steve Jobs,"
  July 11, 2007)
www.topics.nytimes.com
  (New York Times, "Steve Jobs," multiple articles, various dates)
www.nytimes.com
  (New York Times, "Steven P. Jobs, 1955-2011; Apple's Visionary Rede-
  fined Digital Age," Oct. 5, 2011)
americanhistory.si.edu/collections/comphist/sj1.html
  (Smithsonian Institution: Oral and Video Histories, "Steve Jobs Oral
  History," Computerworld Honors Program International Archives,
  Apr. 20, 1995)
www.time.com/time/topics
  (Time, "Steve Jobs," multiple articles, various dates)
www.wired.com
  (Wired, "Steve Jobs, 1955-2011," "Steve Jobs' Greatest Achievements,"
  "Steve Jobs Through the Years," all Oct. 5, 2011)

WEB SITE

www.apple.com/stevejobs

Jennifer Lawrence 1990-

American Actress

Star of the Hit Movies *Winter's Bone, X-Men: First Class,* and *The Hunger Games*

BIRTH

Jennifer Shrader Lawrence was born on August 15, 1990, in Louisville, Kentucky. Her father, Gary, owned a concrete contracting business, and her mother, Karen, ran a children's camp. She has two older brothers named Ben and Blaine.

YOUTH

Lawrence grew up in the Indian Hills neighborhood of Louisville, Kentucky. Her brothers were very active in sports,

———— " ————

Lawrence's parents were reluctant to allow her to pursue her dream of acting. "My parents were the exact opposite of stage parents," she recalled. "They did everything in their power to keep it from happening. But it was going to happen no matter what."

———— " ————

and her parents encouraged her to participate as well. She tried field hockey and softball, but did not particularly enjoy playing those games. She became a cheerleader instead because she liked to do cartwheels and jump around.

As a young girl, Lawrence liked stories of all kinds. She liked watching movies and TV, reading, and listening to her parents and grandparents tell stories. She decided at a young age that she wanted to become a model or an actress. She acted in plays put on by her church, and also performed in productions of Shakespearean plays at the Walden Theatre in Louisville.

When she was 14 years old, Lawrence convinced her parents to take her to New York City during her spring break from school. The trip was more than a family vacation because she had also convinced her mother to meet with modeling and acting agencies. Her parents were reluctant to allow Lawrence to pursue her dream of acting. They thought her dream was unrealistic and only agreed to the trip because they thought it would help her "get the idea out of her system." "My parents were the exact opposite of stage parents," she recalled. "They did everything in their power to keep it from happening. But it was going to happen no matter what."

As it turned out, the trip did not prove to Lawrence that her acting ambition was foolish; instead, it put her on the path to becoming a professional actor. One day while they were walking around the city, Lawrence and her parents stopped to watch some street performers. They were approached by a man who said he was a photographer and that he was scouting for models for a TV commercial. "This guy was watching me, and he asked if he could take my picture," she explained. "We didn't know that that was creepy, at the time. So we're like, 'Sure.' So he took my mom's phone number, and all of a sudden all these agencies are calling. And that's when it all started."

The calls continued even after Lawrence and her parents returned home to Louisville. She begged her parents to let her return to New York and meet with some of the people who were calling. At first, her parents opposed the idea. They finally agreed after her brothers offered their opinions.

A scene from "The Bill Engvall Show," with Lawrence and Graham Patrick Martin.

Lawrence explained, "My two brothers said, 'Mom went to all our basketball and football games and travelled all around the country for us. She would do it for us if it were sports. This is Jen's sport.'"

That summer, Lawrence's parents allowed her to return to New York for two months. They rented an apartment in the city and had various family members take turns staying there with her, taking her to auditions and meetings. Though her parents expected it to be a temporary arrangement, Lawrence knew it was the beginning of her career. "I just started getting an overwhelming feeling of being exactly where I needed to be exactly when I had to be there. Every time I would leave an agency and stop reading a script, I just wanted to keep going and going."

EDUCATION

Lawrence graduated from Kammerer Middle School in Louisville. She wanted to continue to focus on acting, so she persuaded her parents to allow her to study independently instead of enrolling in high school. She earned a GED in just two years, studying while she worked and went to auditions in New York City and Los Angeles. (A GED, or General Equivalency Diploma, is a certification that a person has the academic skills and knowledge that are typically attained through a high school education.) Earning a GED was one of the conditions required by her parents. They insisted that Lawrence must complete her high school education if she wanted to continue acting.

CAREER HIGHLIGHTS

Lawrence started out as an actor with appearances in television commercials. She also had small guest spots on popular TV shows like "Monk," "Cold Case," and "Medium." Her first larger role was in the 2006 television movie *Company Town,* about a group of government agents who all live in the same neighborhood in Washington, DC. *Company Town* was created as the pilot for a TV series, though the series was never produced. In 2007, Lawrence appeared in the pilot episode for the TV series "Not Another High School Show," a parody of TV shows about the lives of high school students.

Lawrence landed her first role on a TV series in 2007, on the situation comedy "The Bill Engvall Show." Set in a suburb of Denver, Colorado, this family comedy centered on the life of Bill Pearson, played by comedian Bill Engvall. Each episode of the show focused on the challenges Pearson faces as a husband and parent. Lawrence played Pearson's teenaged daughter Lauren, a typical high school student making her way through dating, homework, and life with two brothers. "The Bill Engvall Show" aired for three seasons, from 2007-2009. In 2009, Lawrence won a Young Artist Award for Outstanding Young Performers in a TV Series, which she shared with her co-stars.

Becoming a Movie Actor

Lawrence began appearing in movies while she was still acting on "The Bill Engvall Show." She worked on movies during her breaks from filming episodes of the show and had roles in three movies that were released in 2008. Lawrence had a small part in *Garden Party,* the tragic story of a group of confused teens who are on their own in Los Angeles as they chase their dreams. Her first starring role was in the dark, gritty drama *The Poker House.* In this movie, Lawrence played Agnes, a teenager struggling to raise her younger sisters in the chaotic home of their mother, a prostitute who also runs a gambling operation in their house. In the dark and intense drama *The Burning Plain,* she played Mariana, a troubled young woman trying to overcome her mother's death. In 2009, Lawrence appeared in the movie *Devil You Know,* a tense drama about a former movie star who is blackmailed when she tries to restart her career.

These movies were independent films that were not widely released in theaters, though each role helped Lawrence gain acting experience and

A scene from Winter's Bone.

exposure that would benefit her career. She quickly gained a reputation for playing challenging roles with a maturity and acting ability beyond her years. "When you first start acting, you can't pick and choose," she observed. "Those were the roles I was booking. It was me, the girl from Kentucky with the wonderful family. Everyone was seeing this ability to go to this dark place that I didn't know that I had. I auditioned for every comedy, everything under the sun. I'm not going to pretend that I've been smart to pick these things. I've auditioned for all of those, but the comedies and the lovey-dovey movies didn't pick me."

Winter's Bone

Lawrence's early roles portraying difficult characters in dark dramatic stories led to her breakout role as the star of *Winter's Bone,* released in 2010. This critically acclaimed independent film was based on the 2006 novel by Daniel Woodrell. Lawrence played the role of Ree Dolly, a 17-year-old girl living in the rural Ozark Mountains of southern Missouri. With her drug-dealing addict father in jail, Ree desperately struggles to care for her ailing mother and two younger siblings. After her father goes missing, Ree must find him before the court seizes the family's home and land, which he put up for his bail bond. The harsh realities of Ree's difficult life unfold as she tries to uncover the details of her father's fate.

The role of Ree gave Lawrence an opportunity to showcase her acting ability. Even though *Winter's Bone* was not widely seen by general moviegoers, Lawrence's performance captivated film critics. As *Variety* movie reviewer Justin Chang wrote, "The film's atmosphere of suspicion, foreboding, and everyday misery would be too much to bear if not for the rich emotional anchor supplied by Lawrence. Emphasizing Ree's patience, maturity, and love for her siblings as much as her tenacity and courage, Lawrence delivers a striking portrait of someone who, though looked down upon by many for her youth and gender, alone seems to possess the guts and smarts necessary to survive and possibly even escape her surroundings." Writing in *The New Yorker,* David Denby praised Lawrence's acting: "Her Ree is the head of a household, a womanly girl with no time for her own pleasure, and Lawrence establishes the character's authority right away, with a level stare and an unhurried voice that suggest heavy lifting from an early age. The movie would be unimaginable with anyone less charismatic playing Ree."

For her performance in *Winter's Bone,* Lawrence won a New Hollywood Award in 2010. She was nominated for a host of awards in 2011, including an Academy Award for Best Performance by an Actress in a Leading Role, a Golden Globe Award for Best Performance by an Actress in a Motion Picture—Drama, and a Screen Actors Guild Award, for Outstanding Performance by a Female Actor in a Leading Role. She was also nominated for two Broadcast Film Critics Association Critics Choice Awards, for Best Actress and Best Young Actor/Actress, an Independent Spirit Award, for Best Female Lead, and a Young Artist Award, for Best Performance in a Feature Film—Leading Young Actress. Lawrence's portrayal of Ree Dolly earned her a 2011 National Board of Review Award, for Breakthrough Performance.

Lawrence followed the success of *Winter's Bone* with a part in the 2011 romantic drama *Like Crazy.* This movie tells the story of two university students, one American and one British, who must decide if their love is worth fighting for through complicated government rules and immigration laws. She also appeared in the 2011 dark comedy *The Beaver,* about a psychologically troubled man who only communicates through the use of a hand puppet shaped like a beaver.

X-Men: First Class

Lawrence's next big role was in the 2011 action movie *X-Men: First Class.* This installment of the popular movie series based on the *X-Men* comic books chronicles the origins of the first X-Men superheroes. Lawrence plays the young Raven Darkholme, who will become the mutant superhero known as Mystique. (The role of Mystique as an adult is played in previous X-Men movies by Rebecca Romijn.) Young Raven is insecure

Castmates from X-Men: First Class. *From left: Michael Fassbender as Erik (Magneto), Caleb Landry Jones as Banshee, James McAvoy as Charles (Professor Xavier), Rose Byrne as Moira, Jennifer Lawrence as Raven (later Mystique), and Lucas Till as Havok.*

about her natural appearance—she has bright yellow eyes and a blue body covered in scales. She can change her appearance to duplicate any human, so she chooses to appear most of the time as a "normal" girl. But if she is to fully embrace her superpowers, Raven must learn to fully accept her true self. Raven's self-acceptance is encouraged by her friendship with young Xavier and aided by the discovery of other young mutants.

As the young mutants find each other and come together under the direction of Xavier, they each discover that they are not the only ones with special powers. Learning that they are not alone in the world as freaks and outsiders, the young mutants decide to become the X-Men and use their powers to benefit all mankind. Their first challenge is to stop the beginning of World War III, a crisis that ultimately forces former friends and allies Xavier and Magneto to become sworn enemies. The other mutants choose sides, and the conflict between the X-Men and Magneto's Brotherhood begins.

To become the blue-skinned Raven/Mystique, Lawrence had to undergo an elaborate and time-consuming makeup process. Every day, seven makeup artists painted her body with six layers of blue paint, followed by five layers of spackling, and finished with hundreds of scales that had to be glued on one by one. This process took eight to ten hours each day. For her performance, Lawrence was nominated for two 2011 Teen Choice Awards, for Choice Movie Breakout: Female, and Choice Movie Chemistry, which she shared with her co-stars. Lawrence was also nominated for a 2012 People's Choice Award for Favorite Movie Superhero.

The Hunger Games

After *X-Men: First Class*, Lawrence's next major project was the starring role in the highly anticipated 2012 movie *The Hunger Games*. The movie is based on the first book in the wildly popular three-book series by Suzanne Collins: *The Hunger Games, Catching Fire*, and *Mockingjay*. *The Hunger Games* tells the story of fierce and determined Katniss Everdeen. Katniss is a 16-year-old girl living in the brutal world of Panem, a nation that evolved from the remains of North America after a terrible calamity. Most of the citizens of Panem's 12 districts are forced to work to support the wealthy, tyrannical rulers of the Capitol. Many years before Katniss was born, the people in the districts went to war against the Capitol and suffered a terrible defeat. As part of their surrender, each district was forced to agree to send one boy and one girl to participate in "The Hunger Games," an annual televised competition. The 24 competitors, known as "tributes," are selected by lottery. They are taken to the Capitol and locked in an arena where they must fight one another to the death, until only one is left alive. The winner is awarded riches and freedom. An expert hunter and archer, Katniss becomes a tribute for her district. *The Hunger Games* tells the story of her experiences in the gruesome competition.

> "*The cool thing about Katniss is that every fan has such a personal relationship with her, and they understand and know her in a singular way," Lawrence said. "I'm a massive fan too, so I get it." Even Suzanne Collins was impressed with Lawrence: "I never thought we'd find somebody this perfect for the role."*

The casting of Lawrence as Katniss initially set off tremendous controversy among fans of the books. Many were concerned that Lawrence was completely wrong for the role, because she is too pretty, too old, too tall, too athletic, too pale, and too blonde. As a fan of *The Hunger Games* series herself, Lawrence shared some of the same concerns. "The cool thing about Katniss is that every fan has such a personal relationship with her, and they understand and know her in a singular way. I'm a massive fan too, so I get it." Everyone's fears were eased when Lawrence was approved by Collins, who said, "I never thought we'd find somebody this perfect for the role."

Lawrence was pleased to have the support of author Suzanne Collins and film director Gary Ross. "[Katniss is] incredibly powerful, brave, and tough

Lawrence as Katniss in a scene from The Hunger Games.

and yet she has a tenderness and complexity," Lawrence said. "It was very humbling hearing that Suzanne and Gary feel that I embody those traits." Lawrence threw herself into preparing for the role of Katniss. She learned archery from a former Olympic champion and followed an intense physical training program to prepare for the action scenes and stunts. Already a fan of the books, Lawrence also worked hard on developing her approach to the character that would be portrayed on screen. "I'm really picky about the projects I do. I don't really like stories that don't take you anywhere. That's what a film is, it's a journey. I ask myself, 'What is this character like at the beginning and what must I do to get her to the end?'"

The Hunger Games movie was developed under strict secrecy requirements, and few details were revealed about the movie in advance of its release. Collins explained that the story of the movie does not follow exactly along with the story presented in the book. "When you're adapting a novel into a two-hour movie you can't take everything with you," Collins acknowledged. "The story has to be condensed to fit the new form. Then there's the question of how best to take a book told in the first person and present tense and transform it into a satisfying dramatic experience. In the novel, you never leave Katniss for a second and are privy to all of her thoughts, so you need a way to dramatize her inner world and make it possible for other characters to exist outside of her company.... A lot of things are acceptable on a page that wouldn't be on a screen."

*Katniss (Lawrence) being escorted by Capitol guards,
before the start of the Hunger Games.*

Response to the Movie

The Hunger Games movie was released in March 2012, with Lawrence in the role of Katniss joined by Liam Hemsworth as Gale, Josh Hutcherson as Peeta, Woody Harrelson as Haymitch Abernathy, Elizabeth Banks as Effie, Lenny Kravitz as Cinna, and Donald Sutherland as President Snow. Immediate response from the public was overwhelming, and ticket sales soared as the book's many fans came to see how the movie lived up to their expectations. Critical response was a bit mixed. Many critics noted that the movie showed enough of the characters and the action of the book to satisfy, if not enthrall, the book's fans. Several argued that the filmmakers' desire to secure a PG-13 rating meant that some of the more violent scenes in the book had been toned down—yet they also noted that many horrific and gruesome elements still remained. Several reviewers suggested that the movie failed to explain the reasons behind the characters' actions and also failed to explore the book's larger themes. "The movie shows how," Lisa Schwarzbaum wrote in *Entertainment Weekly*, "but the book shows why."

Many critics offered both criticism and praise of the movie, with special admiration for Lawrence's performance. "This *Hunger Games* is a muscular, honorable, unflinching translation of Collins's vision," Schwarzbaum also wrote. "It's brutal where it needs to be, particularly when children fight and bleed. It conveys both the miseries of the oppressed, represented by the poorly fed and clothed citizens of Panem's 12 suffering districts, and the rotted values of the oppressors, evident in the gaudy decadence of those who live in the Capitol. Best of all, the movie effectively showcases the allure of the story's remarkable, kick-ass 16-year-old heroine, Katniss Everdeen. ... [Jennifer Lawrence] is, in her gravity, her intensity, and her own unmannered beauty, about as impressive a Hollywood incarnation of Katniss as one could ever imagine."

"When you're talking about *The Hunger Games*, it all comes down to Katniss," Kenneth Turan wrote in the *Los Angeles Times*. "Making a successful *Hunger Games* movie out of Suzanne Collins's novel required casting the best possible performer as Katniss, and in Jennifer Lawrence director Gary Ross and company have hit the bull's-eye, so to speak. An actress who specializes in combining formidable strength of will with convincing vulnerability, Lawrence is the key factor in making *Hunger Games* an involving popular entertainment with strong narrative drive that holds our attention by sticking as close to the book's outline as it can manage. ... Lawrence's ability to involve us in [Katniss's] struggle is a key to the effectiveness of *Hunger Games*."

> "[Jennifer Lawrence] is, in her gravity, her intensity, and her own unmannered beauty, about as impressive a Hollywood incarnation of Katniss as one could ever imagine." — Lisa Schwarzbaum, **Entertainment Weekly**

"Relax, you legions of Hunger Gamers. We have a winner. Hollywood didn't screw up the film version of Suzanne Collins's young-adult bestseller," Peter Travers wrote in *Rolling Stone*. "The screen *Hunger Games* radiates a hot, jumpy energy that's irresistible. It has epic spectacle, yearning romance, suspense that won't quit, and a shining star in Jennifer Lawrence, who gives us a female warrior worth cheering. As 16-year-old Katniss Everdeen ... Lawrence reveals a physical and emotional grace that's astonishing. Give her the deed, because she owns this movie. ... My advice is to keep your eyes on Lawrence, who turns the movie into a victory by presenting a heroine propelled by principle instead of hooking up with the cutest boy. That's what makes Katniss revolutionary. May the odds be ever in her favor."

Other Projects

Lawrence's future plans include continuing to act and someday becoming a director. She has a starring role in the 2012 horror movie *The House at the End of the Street,* about a mother and daughter who move into a house near the one where a young girl murdered her parents—and soon learn there is more to that story than anyone knew. She also stars in the 2012 comedy *The Silver Linings Playbook,* about a man who tries to rebuild his life after four years in a mental hospital. Lawrence will also appear in the future *Hunger Games* movies.

Lawrence is philosophical in reflecting on the successes that she has achieved thus far in her career. She believes that her success as an actor is at least partially out of her hands. "I'd love to take credit for it. But I was just like every actress in L.A. that auditions for everything, and those were the roles that picked me. I could try to plan everything—and I have, of course, because I'm controlling—but I've watched my career take shape, and I love what it's done. I never could have designed that in a million years."

"You work so hard for something. Mostly, I'm just really happy that I've been able to do what I love. I know that sounds kind of simple, but I've found something I really love doing and I can do it every day of my life. That's what I'm most excited about. The recognition and the parties are great—it's an honor—but I'm mostly just excited to be here working."

HOME AND FAMILY

When she is not filming a movie, Lawrence divides her time between homes in New York City and Santa Monica, California. She lives with her dog, a Yorkshire terrier named Alden.

SELECTED CREDITS

"The Bill Engvall Show," 2007-2009 (TV series)
Winter's Bone, 2010
The Beaver, 2011
Like Crazy, 2011
X-Men: First Class, 2011
The Hunger Games, 2012

HONORS AND AWARDS

Young Artist Award. 2009, Outstanding Young Performers in a TV Series, for "The Bill Engvall Show" (shared with co-stars)
National Board of Review Award: 2010, Breakthrough Performance, for *Winter's Bone*
New Hollywood Award: 2010, for *Winter's Bone*

FURTHER READING

Periodicals

Entertainment Weekly, Mar. 27, 2011, p.34; Aug. 5, 2011, p.44
Flare, June 2011, p.126
Interview, Nov. 2010, p.84
People, June 6, 2011, p.38
Teen Vogue, May 2011
USA Today, June 9, 2010, p.D1
Wall Street Journal, May 27, 2011, p.D5

Online Articles

www.theglobeandmail.com
  (Globe and Mail, "Thanks for Raising Me, But I'm Going to Take it from
  Here," June 11, 2010)
www.louisville.com
  (Louisville, "Too Young for Methods: Louisville's Academy Award-Nom-
  inated Actress Jennifer Lawrence," Feb. 9, 2011)
www.manhattanmoviemag.com
  (Manhattan Movie Magazine, "Jennifer Lawrence Is the Breakout Star of
  Winter's Bone," June 12, 2010)
louisville.metromix.com
  (Metromix Louisville, "Jennifer Lawrence: Bigger Things," Oct. 14, 2009)

ADDRESS

Jennifer Lawrence
PO Box 6509
Louisville, KY 40206

WEB SITE

jenniferslawrence.com

Bruno Mars 1985-

American Singer, Songwriter, and Music Producer
Creator of the Hit Songs "Just the Way You Are,"
"Grenade," "Nothin' on You," "Forget You," and
"Billionaire"

BIRTH

Bruno Mars was born Peter Gene Hernandez Jr. on October 8,
1985, in Honolulu, Hawaii. His mother, Bernadette Hernandez, a former professional singer and hula dancer, is Filipino
(from the Philippines). His father, Pete Hernandez, a Latin
drummer and singer, is Puerto Rican. Mars has four sisters
and one brother. His father gave him the nickname "Bruno"

when he was two years old because he was chubby like the professional wrestler Bruno Sammartino. Bruno adopted the surname "Mars" later, when people called his stage performances "out of this world."

YOUTH

Mars grew up in a family that loved music. His father was a well-known musician in the Waikiki Beach area of Honolulu. When Mars was very young, his parents, uncles, and other family members frequently performed on stage in a popular musical show produced by his father. Mars decided early on that he wanted to be part of the show. "Yeah, from a very young age I remember watching the show and being completely fascinated. You know, my uncle would be up there playing guitar, my dad would be up there conducting the whole show, my mom would be singing out.... And I'd be like 'I wanna go up there too!'"

> *When Mars was very young, his family frequently performed on stage in a popular musical show. "From a very young age I remember watching the show and being completely fascinated. You know, my uncle would be up there playing guitar, my dad would be up there conducting the whole show, my mom would be singing out.... And I'd be like 'I wanna go up there too!'"*

Mars joined his family on stage when he was just four years old. His first performance was an imitation of Elvis Presley. "My dad put me on stage and I remember singing an Elvis song and that was it," he recalled. "Ever since that moment, I've been addicted." As the youngest Elvis impersonator in Hawaii, Mars quickly became a popular feature in his father's stage shows. His performances attracted so much attention that at one point, his parents were summoned to a family court hearing where they had to prove that young Mars was not being forced to perform. The judge was satisfied that he was not being forced on stage when the little boy got up on a table in the courtroom to sing and dance. Mars's early fame led to a cameo appearance as Little Elvis in the 1992 comedy movie *Honeymoon in Vegas.*

The family stage show ended with the divorce of his parents when Mars was ten years old. After that, he and his brother lived with their father while his sisters lived with their mother.

EDUCATION

Mars attended President Theodore Roosevelt High School in Honolulu, where his favorite classes and activities were in the performing arts. Mars was involved in school musicals and directed one of the school's stage plays. He choreographed performances at school pep rallies and also founded a doo-wop singing group called the Schoolboys. (Doo-wop is a rhythm and blues style of music that was popular in the 1950s. It typically involves several voices singing in close harmony, using words or nonsense syllables that fit the desired rhythm.)

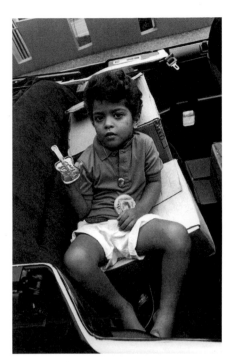

Mars as a four-year-old Elvis impersonator in 1990 in Memphis, Tennessee.

Though the family musical act had been disbanded, Mars continued performing on his own during his teen years. He was featured in a Waikiki Beach musical revue as a Michael Jackson impersonator. In other stage shows, he performed the music of Motown recording stars like the Temptations and the Isley Brothers. When he was 16 years old, Mars was the opening act for a tourist entertainment show called "The Magic of Polynesia," a reference to the large group of islands located in the central and southern Pacific Ocean.

During these years, Mars developed a love of many different styles of music, including Motown, hip-hop, rhythm and blues, reggae, and rock. He also learned to play the guitar and drums. "Hawaii is basically in the middle of the world," he suggested, "so you're exposed to every type of music over there." During high school, music was such an important part of his life that he rarely went anywhere without his guitar or his ukulele. Mars graduated from Theodore Roosevelt High School in 2003.

CAREER HIGHLIGHTS

After high school Mars moved from Hawaii to Los Angeles to live with his brother. Only 17 years old, he began singing in small bars and night clubs.

269

Mars working on a song.

Though he often performed for very small audiences of only a few people, he was able to establish a reputation as a talented singer and musician. In 2004, Mars signed a recording contract with Motown records. At that time, he did not have a clear idea of the kind of record he wanted to make. He received little support from the record label, and after less than a year his contract was cancelled. He later said of this early disappointment, "My heart dropped out. It's not like the movies, where you get signed and you think hit songs are going to come to you and you tour the world. You've got to walk in there knowing exactly who you are."

Becoming a Songwriter

After being released from his contract with Motown, Mars realized that he needed to figure out on his own what kind of music he wanted to create. But meanwhile, he also needed a way to earn a living. Creating music was the only thing he knew how to do. In 2004, Mars stopped trying to make his own record and began to write songs for other more established artists to perform. He formed a songwriting and music production company called the Smeezingtons with two of his friends. "You know, because we were so broke back then I was like, 'I'm gonna forget the artist thing for the moment. We need to eat! So for now let's just concentrate on writing and producing and selling our tracks,'" he remarked. "It was either that or I was going back to Hawaii. After we sold the first track, it opened our eyes. We put the artist stuff on the back burner and took some of the pressure off ourselves."

With the Smeezingtons, Mars wrote many songs that went on to become hits performed by other artists. Some of the hit songs that he wrote during this time are "Long Distance" (recorded by R&B singer Brandy in 2008), "Right Round" (recorded by rapper Flo Rida in 2009), and "Wavin' Flag" (performed by rapper K'Naan in 2009). "Wavin' Flag" became an international hit when it was used as the theme song for the 2010 FIFA World Cup soccer tournament. Because of the amount of time that is usually required to create musical recordings, Mars actually wrote and sold these songs several years before the finished versions were released by the other performers. By 2006, he had become a well-known songwriter.

> *"You know, because we were so broke back then I was like, 'I'm gonna forget the artist thing for the moment. We need to eat! So for now let's just concentrate on writing and producing and selling our tracks,'" Mars remarked. "It was either that or I was going back to Hawaii. After we sold the first track, it opened our eyes. We put the artist stuff on the back burner and took some of the pressure off ourselves."*

While he was writing songs for others, Mars never completely abandoned his dream of making his own record. He created sample recordings known as demos for each of the songs he wrote with the Smeezingtons. The main purpose of these demos was to sell the song to another artist, but Mars also thought that the demos might help him get his own recording contract. "We were just keeping our fingers crossed and hoping that somewhere along the way the [record company] executives were gonna listen to the guy singing on the demo of these songs—ME!—and be like 'This guy is good! Let's sign him!'" Mars admitted. "Which is exactly what happened when the label heard 'Nothin' on You.'" ("Nothin' on You" was later recorded and released by rapper B.o.B.) In 2006, Mars signed his own recording contract with Atlantic Records Elektra. "And that, in a nutshell, is the story of me becoming the solo artist you see today."

Breakout Success

Beginning in 2009, Mars enjoyed a string of successes. His breakout moment came when B.o.B. released "Nothin' on You," a track that showcased a unique mix of R&B and rap. B.o.B. performed the rap and Mars was the featured singer on the track. This was the first time that Mars was exposed to a large listening audience. "Nothin' on You" became an instant hit and was nominated for a host of music awards. These included the 2010 Soul Train Music Award for Song of the Year; two 2010 BET Awards, for Best Collaboration and Video of the Year; and three 2010 BET Hip Hop Awards, for Best Hip Hop Video, Perfect Combo Award, and People's Champ Award. The song also was nominated for awards at the 2010 MTV Video Music Awards, the 2010 Teen Choice Awards, the 2011 Grammy Awards, and the 2011 *Billboard* Music Awards.

The success of "Nothin' on You" was followed by the 2010 release of Travie McCoy's hip-hop/reggae single "Billionaire." Mars wrote "Billionaire" during the time when he was building his career as a songwriter and still struggling to make ends meet. "I was tired of spending half my day worrying about what I can and can't spend on whatever," he recalled. "I would have to worry about, you know, 'I can't afford to get breakfast, so I'll wait until lunchtime to eat.' If I was a billionaire, none of that would matter. I'd be eating diamond cereal." "Billionaire" sold two million singles in the first two months after it was released. Mars once again appeared as the featured singer on the track.

In 2010, Mars had another mega-hit with singer Cee-Lo Green's recording of "Forget You," a Grammy award-winning song that was co-written and co-produced by Mars, who also sang on the track. "Forget You" became a global smash hit that topped the *Billboard* music charts, sold almost four million downloads, and set off a viral video phenomenon. The song became a relationship break-up anthem that *Billboard* magazine called "a true cultural moment." It was nominated for three Grammy Awards in 2011, including Record of the Year and Song of the Year. "Forget You" won the 2011 Grammy Award for Best Urban/Alternative Performance.

By this time, Mars was attracting a lot of attention from the music industry, the media, and music fans. His string of hit records and his performances at the 2010 MTV Video Music Awards and the 2011 Grammy Awards presentation galas had audiences clamoring for more. In 2010, Mars released a four-song EP (extended play) recording called *It's Better That You Don't Understand*. This was his first release as a solo artist. The title refers to his reluctance to talk about the meaning or message that might be found in his music. When asked if his song lyrics are based on his own life experiences, Mars often replies, "It's better if you don't understand, just listen and have a good time."

Mars's first full-length CD included the hit songs "Just the Way You Are," "Grenade," and "The Lazy Song."

Doo-Wops & Hooligans

Mars's EP was closely followed by the 2010 release of *Doo-Wops & Hooligans*, his debut full-length album. Though he dislikes talking about his songs or the lyrics he writes, he has explained the significance of the record's title. "'Doo-wop' is a very special word for me, because I grew up listening to my dad who, as a Fifties rock & roll head, loved doo-wop music. Plus doo-wop, again, is very simple! You know, I could get a guitar, play you just four chords, and sing a thousand doo-wop songs. Because they come from a time back in the day when there were no tricks. You just needed a beautiful melody, you needed a beautiful voice, and you needed to connect. And because to me, 'Just the Way You Are' just feels like it fits into that vibe, that's where the 'doo-wop' side of the title comes in. But, while the 'doo-wop' part is for the women, you also have to remember that I'm a young kid who likes partying and who gets up to some riff-raff sometimes. Which is in turn represented by the 'hooligans' side. So the title basically reflects that you get to hear the two sides of me on this one album."

—— **"** ——

"'Doo-wop' is a very special word for me, because I grew up listening to my dad who, as a Fifties rock & roll head, loved doo-wop music. Plus doo-wop, again, is very simple! You know, I could get a guitar, play you just four chords, and sing a thousand doo-wop songs. Because they come from a time back in the day when there were no tricks. You just needed a beautiful melody, you needed a beautiful voice, and you needed to connect."

—— **"** ——

"Just the Way You Are" was the first single and video released from *Doo-Wops & Hooligans.* The track received heavy radio and video airplay and quickly shot to the top of the music charts. "Just the Way You Are" spent more than 20 weeks ranked as No. 1 by *Billboard,* making it one of the longest reigning debut singles in *Billboard* chart history. Mars credits the song's success to its simplicity. "Well, I'm a big fan of songs like Joe Cocker's 'You Are So Beautiful' and Eric Clapton's 'Wonderful Tonight'— songs that go straight to the point. You know, there's no mind-boggling lyrics or twists in the story—they just come directly from the heart. And to me, 'Just the Way You Are' is one of those songs. There's nothing mind-blowing about it. I'm just telling a woman she looks beautiful the way she is—and let's be honest, what woman doesn't wanna hear those lyrics? I mean, that's why I've been singing those kinda songs to get girls since I was nine years old!" "Just the Way You Are" won the 2011 *Billboard* Top Radio Song Award and the 2011 Grammy Award for Best Male Pop Vocal Performance. In addition, the song was nominated for a 2011 Teen Choice Award and several 2011 *Billboard* Music Awards.

The second single from *Doo-Wops & Hooligans* was "Grenade," another chart-topping hit for Mars. "Grenade" was nominated for a 2011 Teen Choice Award and for three 2011 MTV Video Music Awards. With two blockbuster hit songs in a row, Mars became the first male artist in more than a decade to have his two debut singles reach the No. 1 spot on the *Billboard* Hot 100 list. He continued gathering award nominations with his third single, "The Lazy Song," which was nominated for a 2011 MTV Video Music Award and a 2011 Teen Choice Award. Also in 2011, he released *The Grenade Sessions*, a four-song EP of different versions of "Grenade," including remixes and an acoustic track.

Reflecting on the phenomenal success of his first three singles, Mars said, "You know, I don't make a song for the purpose of the radio or anything like that. I just sit down and write a song." *Doo-Wops & Hooligans* sold more than 2.5 million albums and 15 million singles, including more than 4 million downloads. The album was widely praised by music critics. As music reviewer Jody Rosen wrote in *Rolling Stone*, "*Doo-Wops & Hooligans* proves that Mars is a natural—a lavishly gifted melodist (check the surging 'Grenade') and an engaging singer. It's the year's finest pop debut: 10 near-perfect songs that move from power ballads to bedroom anthems to pop-reggae and deliver pleasure without pretension. Call it bubblegum that eats like a meal."

As *New York Times* critic Jon Caramanica wrote, "There's something to be said for learning a wide repertory at a young age, and also to feel no shame in people-pleasing. It's made [Mars] one of the most versatile and accessible singers in pop, with a light, soul-influenced voice that's an easy fit in a range of styles, a universal donor. There's nowhere he doesn't belong."

Becoming a Star

In 2011, Mars built on his success as a songwriter and recording artist by returning to his roots as a talented stage performer. He toured extensively with such acts as Maroon 5, Travie McCoy, and Janelle Monáe. Mars frequently rejected offers to tour with pop music superstars and perform in large arenas. Instead, he chose to play in smaller venues that allowed him to connect with concert-goers.

Critics liked Mars's live performances as much as his records. According to Sarah Rodman, a music reviewer for the *Boston Globe*, "Because the singer-songwriter-producer traffics in the kind of breezy, flyweight soul pop ephemera that lends itself to Top 40 oversaturation—like his infectious hook for Travie McCoy's 'Billionaire'—it's easy to take for granted the craft involved. Every track on his debut album *Doo-Wops & Hooligans* may not be a knockout … but Mars beefed up the thin spots with an entertaining live show that proved he has the skills, heart, and charisma to go the distance." Perhaps the highest praise came from the *Irish Times* in Dublin, Ireland, whose music critic Brian Boyd wrote, "It can be argued that he is already the most outlandishly successful and talented act of his generation. The phrase 'the new Michael Jackson' may only belong in some demented

Mars performing live.

record company press release, but for once we're looking at someone who could potentially have a seismic effect on the music industry."

In addition to the numerous award nominations for his songs, Mars himself has earned a growing list of nods from the music industry and his fans. In 2011, in recognition of his phenomenal success and diverse talents, *Time* magazine named Mars to its 2011 list of the most influential people in the world. He also won two Teen Choice Awards and was nominated for two BET Awards, an NAACP Image Award, four *Billboard* Music Awards, a Nickelodeon's Kid's Choice Award, and a People's Choice Award.

Mars believes that much of his success comes from the time he spent behind the scenes of the music industry. "I realized that you have to go into this industry as an artist with a clear vision and understanding of who you are. Being so young when I was first signed, I never really had a sense of who I wanted to be. Now things are really working out because everything that I'm singing, writing, and composing is really me," Mars said. "There are no tricks…. It's honesty."

Rapper B.o.B. credits Mars's success to a wide-ranging talent in many different aspects of the music industry. As B.o.B. said in *Time* magazine, "Bruno is part of this new wave of musicians who can do everything: sing, play, write, produce. When he performs live, nothing is prerecorded or fudged. It's a straight-up, classic performance. That's so rare these days." In addition to writing and performing his own songs, Mars still writes and produces music for other artists with his partners in the Smeezingtons. "It's hard to put myself in a box. I just write songs that I strongly believe in and that are coming from inside. [There are] no tricks. It's honesty with big melodies," Mars said. "This is what I'm most excited for—taking these songs and traveling them around the world."

HOME AND FAMILY

Mars currently lives in Los Angeles, California.

SELECTED CREDITS

Songwriting

"Long Distance," 2008 (performed by Brandy)
"Right Round," 2009 (performed by Flo-Rida)
"Wavin' Flag," 2009 (performed by K'Naan)
"Nothin' on You," 2009 (performed by B.o.B.)
"Billionaire," 2010 (performed by Travie McCoy)
"Forget You," 2010 (performed by Cee-Lo Green)

Recordings

It's Better If You Don't Understand, 2010 (EP)
Doo-Wops & Hooligans, 2010
The Grenade Sessions, 2011 (EP)

HONORS AND AWARDS

Soul Train Music Awards: 2010, Song of the Year, for "Nothin' on You"
ASCAP Awards (American Society of Composers, Authors and Publishers): 2011, Top Rap Song, for "Nothin' on You"

Billboard Music Award: 2011, Top Radio Song, for "Just the Way You Are"

Grammy Awards: 2011 (two awards), Best Male Pop Vocal Performance, for "Just the Way You Are" and Best Urban/Alternative Performance, for "Forget You"

Teen Choice Awards: 2011 (two awards), Choice Music: Breakout Artist and Choice Summer: Music Star—Male

100 Most Influential People of the Year (*Time* magazine): 2011

FURTHER READING

Periodicals

Billboard, Oct. 9, 2010, p.24; May 2011, p.77
Current Biography Yearbook, 2011
Entertainment Weekly, Sep. 24, 2010
Forbes, June 6, 2011, p.104
New York Times, Oct. 6, 2010, p.C1
New Yorker, Feb. 14, 2011
Rolling Stone, Nov. 25, 2010, p.34; Jan. 20, 2011, p.48; Feb. 12, 2011
Time, Apr. 21, 2011
USA Today, Sep. 16, 2010, p.D1; Dec. 28, 2010, p.D8; Jan. 25, 2011, p.D2
Village Voice, Aug. 18, 2010

Online Articles

www.bluesandsoul.com
    (Blues & Soul, "Bruno Mars: Out of this World," no date)
www.irishtimes.com
    (Irish Times, "Life on Mars: The Future of Pop Music Is on His Way to Dublin," Mar. 4, 2011)
www.nytimes.com
    (New York Times, "Bruno Mars in Ascension," Oct. 5, 2010)
www.vibe.com
    (Vibe, "The Big Q&A: Bruno Mars Talks Pop Ascension, Damian Marley Collabo, His Song for Nicki Minaj," Oct. 5, 2010)

ADDRESS

Bruno Mars
Atlantic Records
1290 Avenue of the Americas
New York, NY 10104

WEB SITE

www.brunomars.com

Stella McCartney 1971-

British Fashion Designer
Founder of the Stella McCartney Collection of
Clothing and Accessories

BIRTH

Stella Nina McCartney was born on September 13, 1971, in
London, England. Her father, Paul McCartney, is a British guitarist, singer, songwriter, and former member of the world-
famous rock group the Beatles. Her mother, Linda Eastman
McCartney, was an American photographer, author, and entrepreneur. McCartney has an older sister, Mary Anna, and a
younger brother, James Louis. She also has an older half-

sister, Heather, from her mother's first marriage, and a younger half-sister, Beatrice, from her father's second marriage.

YOUTH

As the daughter of famous parents, Stella McCartney grew up in two very different worlds. She enjoyed a normal home life with her family in London, England, but she also travelled the world with her parents and their rock band Wings. Stella was very young when she and her older siblings went on tour with their parents. She spent many nights on the road, sleeping in improvised cribs—usually a hotel dresser drawer lined with pillows and blankets.

> "I went through a period where I thought, 'Do I want to be a landscape gardener? A musician or a photographer? Do I want to do food?' But I really, really loved fashion. It was the thing. I didn't look at films and go, 'Ooh, that's a beautiful planting scheme in the background.' I look at things and say, 'Look at what she's wearing. I love that color.'"

When Stella was ten years old, the family moved from the city to a farm in the rural countryside of West Sussex on the southern coast of England. There they grew their own organic vegetables and raised sheep and horses. Her younger siblings had arrived by then, and she shared one of the small home's two bedrooms with her two sisters. Her brother James slept in the dining room. Within a few years, the family moved to another farm nearby that had a bigger house. In the new house, she was able to have her own bedroom.

Stella grew up with a love of nature and animals. She was a tomboy who never played with dolls, instead preferring to ride her horse, catch frogs, and explore the woods near her family's home. Summers were spent visiting her mother's family in New York. Her parents made sure that their children grew up away from the public world of many celebrity families. Stella knew that her father was a musician, but she did not realize just how famous he was until she saw him perform in concert in Rio de Janeiro, Brazil, for an arena audience of more than 200,000 screaming fans.

As a child, Stella liked to draw pictures of clothing and was interested in fashion design. "I went through a period where I thought, 'Do I want to be a landscape gardener? A musician or a photographer? Do I want to do

*Paul and Linda McCartney with daughters Heather (far left),
Stella (center), and Mary (right).*

food?' But I really, really loved fashion. It was the thing. I didn't look at films and go, 'Ooh, that's a beautiful planting scheme in the background.' I look at things and say, 'Look at what she's wearing. I love that color.'" By the time she was a teenager, she was making her own clothes.

EDUCATION

For elementary and high school, McCartney attended public school in East Sussex, England. She supplemented her regular schoolwork with part-time positions in fashion. In 1986, when she was 15 years old, she worked an internship with renowned French fashion designer Christian Lacroix. Like most fashion interns, McCartney started in the lowest positions. She didn't sew anything or even handle the sewing tools, but she was able to watch and learn about the fashion design industry. Some of her other early learning experiences included a summer position in the fashion department of

British Vogue magazine, internships with other designers, and a stint as a tailor's apprentice in London's exclusive Savile Row. Savile Row shops are known for creating expensive "bespoke" suits for men. Bespoke refers to the tailoring process that is used to create one-of-a-kind custom-fitted suits.

McCartney earned a Bachelor of Arts degree from London's Central Saint Martins College of Art and Design in 1995. Throughout her time there, she struggled against the perception that she was taking advantage of opportunities given to her only because of her parents' fame. McCartney worked hard to prove that she was talented and that she deserved to study at one of the world's most prestigious fashion colleges. Determined to make her own way without help from her parents, she paid for her own expenses by working various jobs, including one as a restaurant dishwasher.

But try as she might, McCartney couldn't always avoid the spotlight. Graduating fashion students traditionally host a runway show to display their final design collections, and McCartney was no different. But unlike most design students, her graduation show was attended by members of the international fashion media. This was due in part to her famous name but also to the models she chose to walk the runway in her show—some of her close friends like Naomi Campbell and Kate Moss, who also happened to be supermodels. McCartney was criticized harshly by her fellow students, who objected to what they saw as an unfair advantage. Her simple response was, "Other students ask their friends to model and I've asked mine." Her graduation show made headlines in fashion publications around the world.

CAREER HIGHLIGHTS

McCartney's career took off immediately after graduation. The media coverage of her student show created great interest in her designs, and she was approached by several large clothing retailers. A Japanese chain with stores in Tokyo and London bought her entire graduation collection, and some of her other early designs were licensed to department store chains in the United Kingdom and the United States.

This initial success was exciting but also presented a big challenge for McCartney. She had constructed all of her early pieces by hand without considering the requirements and restrictions of the manufacturing process needed to make mass market clothing. McCartney had to quickly revise her designs. She made changes in the materials and sewing techniques that she used to create each piece so that the items could be produced in large quantities for department stores. This experience taught her that in order to become a commercial success, she would have to pay more attention to every aspect of her designs. If a finely tailored garment took too long to produce or required costly or rare materials such as antique buttons or lace, then the finished product would be too expensive for most people to buy.

In 1995, McCartney opened a small boutique store in London and launched a line of designs under her own name. The collection was simply called Stella. She made all of the clothing, and she spent a great deal of time involved in the business of running the boutique. She personally ordered materials, cut fabric, sewed the garments, packed them, and sent them to customers. McCartney soon attracted a following among fashion models and celebrities. Her designs were worn by many of her famous friends, including singer Madonna and actors Cameron Diaz and Liv Tyler.

Soon, the business was growing almost faster than McCartney could handle. "I spent so much time on production that the collection was very small. I didn't have time to concentrate on designing." Just when she was at the point of realizing that she would not be able to maintain her design collection by herself, McCartney got an unexpected opportunity that changed her life.

> *Famed* Vogue *editor-in-chief Anna Wintour said of McCartney, "What Stella did was to surprise everybody, by very, very quickly developing her own style. It's very much the way she dresses herself, and you can feel her in all the collections she does. We have so few women designers who are really important in the field of fashion, and it's great to have someone like Stella join the ranks."*

An Unexpected Big Break

In 1997, McCartney was named as the creative director of Chloé, a French fashion house that was established in 1952 and known for designing ready-to-wear luxury clothing. She replaced designer Karl Lagerfield, whom the label had just ousted from the position. McCartney was a controversial choice for creative director because she was only 25 years old and had been out of fashion school for less than two years. Many in the fashion industry criticized her as too young and inexperienced and claimed that she was only hired because of her famous name.

McCartney usually chose not to respond to this type of criticism, but now for the first time, she fired back. "I get so sick of this 'my parents' thing. It's

The end of the runway show: McCartney (center) and models react after the presentation of the Chloe 1998 spring-summer fashion collection presented in Paris, October 1997.

been that way my whole life," she declared. "When I did a good drawing at primary school, it was because my dad was famous. Or if I got a part in a school play, it was because Dad was a Beatle. It's the product that counts. People wouldn't want to work with me if they thought I was a complete loser. Women wouldn't wear our clothes. I don't think the Chloé chiefs would be stupid enough to ride a whole company on me because of who my father is. I'm the breath of fresh air that Chloé needs." The fact was, Chloé was dying as a major fashion label, and McCartney was brought in specifically for her fresh, young perspective.

Major fashion designers of ready-to-wear luxury clothing typically present at least two large collections each year: the spring-summer collection and the fall-winter collection. The collection is presented about six months before the season it was designed for, to give time for stores to order the merchandise and for the designer to ship it to stores. Collections are presented in runway shows, where models walk down a runway wearing the outfits as the designer envisioned them. For the most prestigious fashion houses, the audience for the show would usually be the most influential people, including fashion magazine editors, buyers for major stores, celebrities, and others in the fashion industry. Major shows take place in several cities, including New York, Paris, London, and Milan. Reaction by the influential audience members at the runway shows often shapes the response to the collection.

In her new position at Chloé, McCartney showed ambition, determination, and commitment that quickly earned her a reputation as "Stella Steel." The first Chloé collection launched under her direction was very well received. Her designs revitalized the brand by breaking from the past. McCartney replaced the minimalist, no-frills look of early 1990s fashion with romantic styles that mixed vintage elements with delicate lace and ruffles. She also broke tradition by designing individual pieces of clothing that could be mixed and matched with other fashions. "In the '90s, designers were on this mission to sell 'outfits,' and I felt that was patronizing," she explained. "A woman should be making up her own outfits to reflect her sense of self, instead of becoming what a designer wants her to become."

> *"My greatest honor comes from spotting people in everyday life wearing what I've designed, to get to say to myself, 'Oh, there goes a nice top'—and realize it's mine! When that happens, I am still so totally gobsmacked that anyone would be wearing my clothes."*

The look set off a revolution in the fashion world. Under McCartney's direction, demand for Chloé designs rose to an all-time high, and the label was once again the height of fashion. Famed *Vogue* editor-in-chief Anna Wintour said of McCartney, "What Stella did was to surprise everybody, by very, very quickly developing her own style. It's very much the way she dresses herself, and you can feel her in all the collections she does. We have so few women designers who are really important in the field of fashion, and it's great to have someone like Stella join the ranks."

In recognition of her accomplishments as the head of Chloé, McCartney received the prestigious VH1/*Vogue* Designer of the Year award in 2000. Other nominees for the award that year included veteran designers and fashion legends such as Calvin Klein and Miuccia Prada. McCartney's win was remarkable for a designer who had graduated from fashion school only five years earlier.

Launching the Stella McCartney Label

In 2001, McCartney left Chloé and joined Italian luxury fashion label Gucci. There she launched her own fashion label called Stella McCartney.

As a strict vegetarian and animal rights activist, she initially turned down the opportunity to work with Gucci because the brand was famous for its use of leather and fur. When she was able to negotiate complete control over her designs, McCartney realized that she might be able to influence the fashion industry from the inside. She wanted to prove that luxury clothing and accessories could be made without animal products.

> ———— " ————
>
> *McCartney is committed to cruelty-free fashions that use no leather or fur. "There's no excuse for fur in this day and age," she said. "There's nothing fashionable about a dead animal that has been cruelly killed just because some people think it looks cool to wear."*
>
> ———— " ————

In her debut collection, McCartney tried to break away from the designs she created for Chloé. She wanted to reinvent her own brand by creating new looks. Her first showing in Paris was a failure—fashion editors hated the clothes as well as the production of the runway show. McCartney's designs were considered inappropriate and even trashy, and her show was criticized for its loud music and flashing lights. "Everything was wrong. It was all a bit messy. I was still finding myself as a person and I was trying to find myself as a brand too quickly. I was nervous and I was overthinking things," she recalled. "I was really freaked out. People think I'm strong, but actually I wanted to crawl away."

The failure of her first showing made McCartney even more committed to developing better designs. Her subsequent collections were successful, and by 2002 she had opened the first Stella McCartney store in New York City. Two more stores followed in 2003—in Mayfair, London, and West Hollywood, California. McCartney also began to expand her brand that year, launching her fragrance line with the debut of Stella perfume. In 2004, she began a long-term contract designing a line of active wear for Adidas. In 2005, a special one-time exclusive collection of clothing for retail chain H&M followed. McCartney's line for H&M was placed in 400 stores, and all stores were completely sold out of the entire line in less than an hour.

Branching Out

McCartney continued to expand her collection with the launch of a line of vegan-friendly accessories such as handbags, belts, luggage, jewelry, and shoes. "It's surprising to me that people cannot get their heads around a non-leather bag or shoe," she commented. "They already exist out there,

McCartney puts the finishing touches on a model backstage at the Spring-Summer 2005 Paris show in October 2004.

but unfortunately designers feel that they have to slap a leather trim or sole on them. People need to start looking at the product, and if they like it, that's all that matters. If it has an ethical or ecological edge, that's a huge bonus. We address these questions in every other part of our lives except fashion." McCartney was honored with the Organic Style Woman of the Year Award in 2005. Her commitment to earth-friendly luxury products continued with the launch of CARE, an organic skin care and beauty line. In 2009, she was honored by the Natural Resources Defense Council as a Force for Nature, and *Time* magazine named her among that year's 100 Most Influential People.

By 2010, McCartney had expanded her brand in several directions at once. She created a line of bags and luggage for LeSportsac, launched two more fragrances, and designed a limited-edition collection of children's clothing for GapKids and babyGap stores. She was chosen to design the official outfits for Great Britain's Olympic and Paralympic teams for the 2012 Olympics, marking the first time that a leading fashion designer would create the outfits for both teams.

McCartney also launched Stella McCartney Kids, her own collection of children's clothes, because she had difficulty finding clothing that she liked for her own children. "As a brand with many working parents on the team,

I wanted to create a desirable, fun, wearable kids' collection that was affordable. I feel like all the timeless children's wear is reserved for the expensive brands and that did not sit well with me. Kids and parents, aunts, uncles, friends should all be able to have access to Stella McCartney Kids clothes," she explained. "It's really belittling of the customer to think that anyone from a different price bracket deserves anything less."

> "Designing clothes is not about being famous. It's about dressing people, about giving them something that will provide them with a psychological lift as soon as they try it on. I try to design clothes that will make people feel better about themselves."

McCartney's retail outlets now include 13 Stella McCartney stores in locations around the world, and her collections are distributed in more than 50 countries. She is widely recognized for her talent in designing accessible clothing that women want to wear. Over the course of her career, McCartney has earned a reputation for her ability to create clothes that are fresh, youthful, and modern. Her designs are often described as down-to-earth and wearable, featuring sharp tailoring and unexpected combinations of old and new elements. She is known for mixing many different types of material in her garments and for her signature color palette of soft shades. "I'm a sucker for muted, dirty, old-looking colors. My whole idea for a color palette is when you open an old chest filled with clothes from the 1920s and they've got enough dirt in them that a once-bright color has been taken down a peg or two."

McCartney's status as a leading fashion designer is firmly in place, and her fans include fashion industry professionals, supermodels, pop musicians, and Hollywood stars. But she still insists that her only job is to "anticipate what a woman needs for her wardrobe." As she explained her approach, "Designing clothes is not about being famous. It's about dressing people, about giving them something that will provide them with a psychological lift as soon as they try it on. I try to design clothes that will make people feel better about themselves.

"I try to create something that I would like and which reflects my personality. You're entering a dangerous area when you try to make things for people because you think that's what they want. You do it because you have a love for it. I'm creating stuff for me and my friends," McCartney said. "In fact my greatest honor comes from spotting people in everyday life wearing what I've designed, to get to say to myself, 'Oh, there goes a

Pieces from the Stella McCartney 2012 Fall-Winter collection.

nice top'—and realize it's mine! When that happens, I am still so totally gobsmacked that anyone would be wearing my clothes."

MARRIAGE AND FAMILY

McCartney married magazine publisher Alasdhair Willis in 2003. They have four children, a son named Miller Alasdhair James Willis (born 2005), a daughter named Bailey Linda Olwyn Willis (born 2006), a son named Beckett Robert Lee Willis (born 2008), and a daughter named Reiley Dilys Stella Willis (born 2010).

MAJOR INFLUENCES

McCartney cites her mother as the biggest influence in her life and career. Linda McCartney was a strict vegetarian and animal rights activist who passed those values and ideals on to her children. "Decisions I've based on my beliefs and upbringing have served me well. I feel in my heart that this is the right way to work and it's the right direction to take our business," McCartney explained. "For me, vegetarianism is based on ethics. It's how I was brought up. My mum was very vocal and we were all educated to understand why we weren't eating meat. But actually, now I look at it from all different angles. I think it's very wrong to have the mass murder, every single day, of millions of animals. I find something wrong with that on a spiritual level, an environmental level, and an ethical level."

As a member of PETA and the Vegetarian Society, McCartney is committed to cruelty-free fashions that use no leather or fur. "There's no excuse for fur in this day and age," she said. "There's nothing fashionable about a dead animal that has been cruelly killed just because some people think it looks cool to wear." But McCartney is also realistic about her ideals. "I'm not by any means perfect. I drive a car. I go on planes. But my philosophy has always been 'Something's better than nothing.'

"I am a fashion designer. I'm not an environmentalist.... If I can make you not notice that it happens to be out of biodegradable fake suede, if I can make you not notice that it hasn't killed cows or goats or unborn baby lambs, then I'm doing my job. There should be no compromise for you as a customer. I don't want to do scratchy, oatmeal-colored things, that defeats the object."

Many of McCartney's clothing designs echo her mother's fashion choices. Some of her signature looks include the mix-and-match styles favored by her mother, such as flowing vintage skirts paired with t-shirts featuring pop-culture designs or high-fashion jackets worn over beat-up blue jeans.

"I think, 'if Mum was here, would she like that?' A lot of the things that I do have originated from Mum's way of throwing things together, sort of old and new and not too self-conscious.... I mean, my mum really was the coolest chick in the world."

HONORS AND AWARDS

VH1/*Vogue* Designer of the Year: 2000, for Stella McCartney for Chloé
Woman of Courage Award (Women's Cancer Research Fund): 2003
Glamour Award: 2004, Best Designer of the Year
Star Honoree, Fashion Group International Night of the Stars: 2004
Organic Style Woman of the Year: 2005
Elle Style Award: 2007, Best Designer of the Year
British Style Award: 2007, Best Designer of the Year
Spanish Elle Award: 2008, Best Designer of the Year
Accessories Council Excellence Award: 2008, Green Designer of the Year
Time 100 Most Influential People: 2009
Glamour Woman of the Year: 2009
Force for Nature Award (Natural Resources Defense Council): 2009

FURTHER READING

Books

Aldridge, Rebecca. *Stella McCartney*, 2011

Periodicals

Current Biography Yearbook, 1998
Ecologist, May 2009, p.50
Flare, Sep. 2008, p.146
Harper's Bazaar, Sep. 2002, p.426
InStyle, Apr. 2004, p. 151; Nov. 2009, p.113
New York Magazine, Mar. 10, 2010
New York Times, Apr. 22, 1997, p.B11; Oct. 22, 2009, p.E4; June 20, 2011
New York Times Magazine, Feb. 26, 2012, p.18
New Yorker, Sep. 17, 2001, p.130
NW, Aug. 13, 2007, p.6
Organic Style, May 1005, p.81
Time, Summer 2006, p.16; Sep. 15, 2008, p.56; Apr. 30, 2010
Washington Post, Oct. 16, 1997, p.B1
WWD, Jan. 11, 2012, p.10

Online Articles

www.nytimes.com
   (New York Times, "What Drives Stella McCartney," Feb. 22, 2012)
www.vogue.co.uk/spy/biographies/stella-mccartney-biography
   (British Vogue, "Stella McCartney," May 11, 2011)

ADDRESS

Stella McCartney, Ltd.
Chalegrove House
34-36 Perrymount Road
Haywards Heath
West Sussex RH16 3DN
England

WEB SITE

www.stellamccartney.com

Jerry Mitchell 1959-

American Investigative Reporter
Investigator of Famous Murder Cases from the Civil
Rights Era

BIRTH

Jerry Mitchell Jr. was born in Springfield, Missouri, in 1959.
He was the only child of Jane and Jerry Sr., who served in the
U.S. military as a Navy pilot. Young Jerry, who was nicknamed "Boo" by his parents, spent his earliest years of childhood living on naval bases in California. When his father retired in the mid-1960s, though, the Mitchell family settled in
Texarkana, Texas.

YOUTH

Jerry grew up in a family haunted by illness. He and his parents seemed perfectly healthy, but many members of his father's side of the family suffered from a deadly illness that was so rare that it did not even have a name. Jerry later described the disease as "a monster that [had] lived with my family for more than a century, a monster that first attacks the muscles and then ravages the brain and sometimes bones, a monster that leaves his victims in crumpled heaps, eyes swirling, unable to focus." Symptoms of the disease, which usually appeared before victims reached the age of 50, included severe muscular dystrophy and dementia. The mysterious disease eventually claimed the lives of Jerry's paternal grandfather and all four of his siblings. As Jerry was growing up, his family always lived with the unspoken fear that he or his father might start showing signs of the horrible disease. Their fears were not relieved until the early 2000s, when Jerry and his father participated in a medical research project that revealed that neither man carried the gene responsible for the disease.

> "
>
> *Mitchell grew up in the South during an era of great social turmoil. But the civil rights movement did not really make much of an impression on him. "It's like it took place all around me, but in an alternate universe,"*
> *he later said.*
>
> "

In most other respects, Jerry experienced the normal childhood of a white kid growing up in the American South in the 1960s. His family was heavily involved in church, he got good grades, and his father gave him basic instruction in sports. Jerry Sr. was a pretty stern and hardnosed coach, though. "Dad never let me win at anything," Jerry recalled. "I'll never forget the day I finally beat him in basketball."

Mitchell grew up during an era of tremendous change in the American South. For centuries, southern whites had used segregation (the separation of schools, restaurants, and other facilities by race), to keep African Americans poor, uneducated, and politically powerless. Many white people felt a deep and abiding prejudice against black people. African Americans were often treated as inferior, and they were expected to act subservient. The South had been segregated under what were called "Jim Crow" laws. These discriminatory laws forced the segregation of the races and created "separate but equal" public facilities—housing, schools, transportation, bathrooms, drinking fountains, and more—for blacks and

Scenes from the Jim Crow era: a boy using a segregated water fountain (top) and a Ku Klux Klan night rally with Klansmen burning a wooden cross (bottom).

whites. Although these separate facilities were called equal, in reality those for blacks were miserably inadequate. African Americans usually attended dilapidated, impoverished schools with underpaid teachers. After leaving school, their opportunities for work were often just as limited.

> ———— **"** ————
>
> *"I'm motivated by the fact that people got away with murder," Mitchell said. "And what makes these crimes more egregious is everybody knew they were getting away with it. It was murder with impunity."*
>
> ———— **"** ————

Many African-American people resented the unequal system in which they lived. But the black communities of the American South felt powerless to change things. White men occupied nearly every important political and law enforcement office across the South, and most of them did not want African Americans to gain greater political, economic, or social power. As a result, they used a variety of means to keep black families "in their place." For example, some officials forced African Americans to pass extremely difficult written tests before they would allow them to register to vote. The poll tax—a tax that a person must pay before being permitted to vote—was another popular tool to repress the black vote, because most black people were so poor that they could not afford the expense. Finally, whites used violence and intimidation to make sure that African Americans remained in their inferior position in society.

That began to change during the civil rights era, which flowered across the South during the 1950s and 1960s. During this pivotal period in American history, legendary African-American figures like Martin Luther King Jr., Rosa Parks, John Lewis, and Medgar Evers led activists in a long, difficult, and sometimes deadly struggle for equal civil rights in the United States. This battle was most intense in the South.

The civil rights era generated sickening levels of violence in some parts of the South. Many whites of that period held deeply racist views toward blacks, and they felt free to openly express those feelings at school, church, and places of work. Some whites banded together in white supremacist organizations like the Ku Klux Klan. These groups used violence and intimidation while committing crimes of arson, assault, and murder in an effort to stop the African-American quest for equality. The civil rights movement, though, would not be denied. Thousands of brave African-American demonstrators—aided in some instances by sympathetic white college students and religious leaders from the North—refused to give up. The men and women in the movement persevered in the face of appalling discrimination and violence, and ultimately they were victorious. By the mid-1960s the civil rights movement had spurred the United States to pass a series of laws that outlawed segregation, bestowed equal rights on blacks, guaranteed voting rights, and brought the Jim Crow South crashing down.

Mitchell grew up in the South during this era of great social turmoil. But the civil rights movement did not really make much of an impression on him. "It's like it took place all around me, but in an alternate universe," he later said. Still, his parents made it clear to him that racist talk and attitudes would not be tolerated in their house. "I remember I came home, I was about eight or nine years old, and I said the N-word," Mitchell said. "I learned it from a friend. [My mom] treated me as if it were a capital offense. And I thank God for that. Because she taught me, and my father taught me, about race, and the right ways to treat one another."

EDUCATION

Mitchell earned a bachelor's degree in speech and journalism from Harding University in Searcy, Arkansas, in 1982. He then became a newspaper reporter, but he continued to take classes to further his education. This hard work paid off in 1997, when he received a master's degree in journalism from Ohio State University.

CAREER HIGHLIGHTS

After graduating from college, Mitchell moved to Los Angeles, California, to seek a career as a movie screenwriter. He found little success, though, so he returned to the Southwest in a year or so. Mitchell spent the next few years working for small newspapers in Texas and Arkansas before landing a job in 1986 with the *Jackson (MS) Clarion-Ledger,* a newspaper in Jackson, Mississippi.

Mitchell spent his first few years at the *Clarion-Ledger* working as a general news reporter, but in 1989 he saw a movie that dramatically changed the arc of his career in journalism. He was assigned to cover the opening of the film *Mississippi Burning,* which was loosely based on a Federal Bureau of Investigation (FBI) investigation of a famous civil rights case: a real-life triple murder that had taken place in Mississippi back in 1964. The victims were three civil rights workers named James Chaney, Andrew Goodman, and Michael Schwerner. They had come to Mississippi as part of Freedom Summer, a massive effort by thousands of civil rights activists to register black voters in the South. After their murders, the state of Mississippi refused to file any charges against the suspects. Then the U.S. government stepped in. Federal authorities ultimately convicted seven Ku Klux Klan members of involvement in the murders, but none of them served more than six years in prison. Other key suspects, including alleged ringleader Edgar Ray Killen, went free. Mississippi's legal system was so dominated by whites that investigators were unable to obtain convictions for these crimes. This type of collusion by law enforcement was not uncommon during this period.

Mississippi Burning was criticized in some quarters for being historically inaccurate and failing to acknowledge the bravery of civil rights activists. Nonetheless, the suspenseful film made a huge impression on Mitchell. "I was totally ignorant and stupid of the civil rights movement," he explained. "I always say [the film] was the beginning of my education." Mitchell actually saw the movie with two FBI agents who had been involved on the case. "After the film was over, I wondered aloud why none of these Klansmen had ever been tried for murder," he recalled. "The agents said everyone knew who the killers were, but the state balked at prosecuting, believing convictions were impossible. The agents assured me that these killers were hardly the only ones who had escaped justice in those days."

Reopening Cold Cases of the Civil Rights Era

Mitchell was so inspired by the movie—and so angered by the thought that racist murderers from the civil rights era were still strolling around Mississippi—that he decided to start investigating the state's unsolved murder cases from that period. He did not care that these were "cold cases"—investigations that been closed for years. Mitchell wanted to see these killers brought to justice, and he was prepared to spend a lot of his time and energy trying to uncover evidence that had been missed or covered up by white officials back in the 1960s.

Mitchell decided to start his investigation by examining the secret records of the Mississippi Sovereignty Commission. During the 1960s the agency, which was headed by the governor himself, had been at the forefront of white efforts to stop the civil rights movement. The commission, explained Mitchell, "was a really amazing sort of state-run FBI. Individual states are not supposed to have FBIs in this country, but Mississippi had one, and it was a force for maintaining segregation and otherwise spreading lawlessness, terror, and harassment throughout the state."

Mitchell requested access to the commission's records, but was flatly turned down. These rejections, though, just made him more determined. "When someone tells me I can't have something, I want it a million times worse, right?" he said. "I was told I couldn't have these Sovereignty Com-

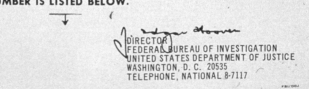

An FBI missing persons poster showing three civil rights workers, Andrew Goodman, James Earl Chaney, and Michael Henry Schwerner, who were murdered by the Ku Klux Klan. Their case was the basis for the movie Mississippi Burning, *which inspired Mitchell to begin investigating civil rights cases.*

A photo of civil rights worker Medgar Evers in Jackson, Mississippi, about 1960.

mission records, and so I began to develop sources which began to leak me these documents."

As Mitchell examined the secret records, he made a startling discovery about one of the most notorious murders ever to take place in Mississippi. On June 12, 1963, the African-American civil rights activist Medgar Evers had been gunned down in his driveway in Jackson. Evers had been active in a variety of civil rights campaigns; at the time of his death, he was a field officer in Mississippi for the National Association for the Advancement of Colored People (NAACP). Nine days after his murder, Byron De La Beckwith, a white fertilizer salesman with known ties to white supremacist groups, was arrested and charged with his murder. De La Beckwith was put on trial twice, but on both occasions he went free because the jurors could not agree on a verdict. These "hung juries," as they were known, came about despite the fact that the prosecution built a strong case against the accused. Court observers blamed the hung juries on the existence of Jim Crow laws that kept blacks out of the jury box. All of the jurors in both trials were white males.

Achieving Justice for Medgar Evers

Mitchell uncovered evidence in the Sovereignty Commission records that the agency had secretly helped De La Beckwith's defense team during his second trial. It had done so by using taxpayer dollars to investigate potential jurors and help De La Beckwith's lawyers pick jurors who would be supportive of their client.

Armed with this knowledge, Mitchell visited De La Beckwith and his wife, Thelma, at their rural home in Signal Mountain, Tennessee. The journalist spent several hours with the couple, during which time De La Beckwith made vicious and hateful statements about blacks and the white "traitors" who had supported their civil rights activism. The elderly racist also hinted—with great pride and satisfaction—that he was Evers's murderer. "I could feel the evil in them," Mitchell said years later when recalling that visit.

Byron De La Beckwith at his home in Mississippi, with a Confederate flag in the background. He was convicted of the murder of Medgar Evers and sent to prison more than 30 years after the crime.

A short time later, Mitchell published a story in the *Clarion-Ledger* detailing his findings about the Sovereignty Commission and its role in De La Beckwith's second murder trial. The article prompted Evers's widow, Myrlie Evers Williams, to ask authorities to reopen the case. They did so in October 1989, and over the next several months a new generation of investigators and prosecutors uncovered important new evidence, including the rifle that De La Beckwith had used to assassinate Evers.

In 1993 De La Beckwith was put on trial once again for Evers's murder. This time, however, he was found guilty by a jury of eight blacks and four whites. When the verdict was announced on February 5, 1994, Mitchell felt a tremendous sense of relief and satisfaction. A few days later, though, he received a frightening phone call from the sheriff who had taken De La Beckwith to jail. "[The sheriff] was telling me, 'you know, when we took Beckwith away he kept saying two words,'" remembered Mitchell. "And I was like, 'Really?' He said, 'Yep, two words.' 'What two words?' 'Jerry Mitchell.' So for a minute I'm just kinda like basking in the glow of what I consider this really great compliment and then the sheriff keeps going and says, 'Now when you drive home, Jerry, you know, you might not want to go the same way [you usually do].'"

Mitchell was terrified by the implication that a racist ally of De La Beckwith might try to kill him for his role in the case, but it did not stop him from continuing his investigations. To the contrary, Mitchell has said that his experience with De La Beckwith encouraged him to look into other long-ago crimes against civil rights activists. De La Beckwith spent the last seven years of his life in federal prison before dying in 2001.

Refusing to Buckle Under Pressure

During the mid-1990s Mitchell's journalistic investigations repeatedly dug up new evidence about Mississippi murders related to the civil rights struggles of the 1960s. His efforts sparked a flurry of new police investigations, trials, and convictions for crimes that had gone unpunished for decades.

Mitchell has admitted, though, that these years were full of uncertainty. Although the *Clarion-Ledger* has been supportive of his journalistic efforts for many years, the reporter acknowledged that his early stories triggered strong hostility from some of the paper's executives. "One of the newspaper's top people did oppose my reporting into these brutal unpunished crimes that brought shame to Mississippi's name," he recalled. "I kept expecting to come in one morning and find my computer gone and my cubicle disassembled and me heading back to my hometown, begging for my old job at the *Texarkana Gazette*." Even though a few of his early stories were rejected, though, Mitchell did not despair. "You know what I did? I'm very sneaky," he said. "I just held onto them. So when that editor was gone, I just resurrected the story and ran it.... Just because an editor kills a story, that doesn't mean it's dead for good."

Mitchell also said that his cold-case sleuthing caused grumbling among some Mississippians—and not just racists whose warped views made them sympathetic to people like De La Beckwith. One common complaint was that Mitchell's stories in the *Clarion-Ledger* were making the state look bad. Other critics expressed resentment, as if they were supposed to feel guilty about things that happened in a bygone era. "Many Southerners—including those who never raised a hand to harm anyone else—would rather move forward in a diverse New South than backtrack to the bad old days of Jim Crow, blatant racism, and murder," explained scholar R. Hayes Johnson in *Human Rights*. "A whole generation of Southerners has been born since the peak of the civil rights movement,

Smoke rises from the firebombed home of civil rights leader Vernon Dahmer.

and many of those younger people—especially whites—are quick to note that they had nothing to do with the crimes and misdeeds of the previous generations."

Mitchell does not have much patience with these complaints, though. In his view, the most important thing to remember is that his reporting helps bring murderers to justice. "I'm motivated by the fact that people got away with murder," he said. "And what makes these crimes more egregious is everybody knew they were getting away with it. It was murder with impunity."

Taking Down a Klan Wizard

In early 1998 Mitchell received information from a secret source about another notorious assassination of the civil rights era—the slaying of Vernon Dahmer in a firebombing of his house in Hattiesburg, Mississippi, on January 10, 1966. Dahmer was a business leader, a civil rights activist, and the president of the local NAACP chapter who was leading the local voters' registration drives. On the night of the attack, the family was at home when several carloads of white Klansmen burst into the house and set it on fire. Dahmer held them off while his wife and children managed to escape, but he died from his severe burns. Authorities ultimately brought 13 white men to trial for involvement in his murder, but only four of them were convicted, and none of the four served more than ten years in prison. The man who ordered the firebombing was Sam Bowers, who had been the "Imperial Wizard" (supreme leader) of an extremely violent offshoot of the Ku Klux Klan in Mississippi during the 1960s. Bowers was put on trial for Dahmer's murder four times, but the jury deadlocked every time, enabling the Klan leader to walk away a free man.

Mitchell talked to an informant about the case. He learned that Billy Roy Pitts, one of the four Klansmen convicted of the Dahmer murder, had never served a day in prison. Instead, Mississippi authorities had let him go, telling everyone that he was in a witness protection program. The journalist quickly tracked Pitts down in Louisiana. Pitts was horrified when Mitchell confronted him. Eager to avoid prison and wracked with guilt over his role in Dahmer's murder, Pitts agreed to testify against Bowers. When prosecutors re-opened the case, they subsequently found other important evidence to use against the Klan leader. Bowers was convicted of murder in 1998, and he spent the last eight years of his life in prison.

The conviction of Bowers gave Dahmer's wife and children a measure of peace that had eluded them ever since his death nearly a half-century ago. "Once this settles in and I get control of my emotions," Vernon Dahmer Jr. told Mitchell, "I am going to the cemetery and pray and tell my father that justice finally came and he can begin to rest in peace."

Uncovering a Murderer's Fake Alibi

Mitchell also began investigating another infamous event of the civil rights era: the 1963 bombing of a black church in Birmingham, Alabama, that killed four young girls. The four girls—Denise McNair, age 11, and Addie Mae Collins, Carole Robertson, and Cynthia Wesley, all age 14—were in the basement of the 16th Street Baptist Church talking about the start of school and getting ready for services when the bomb exploded. Investigators had identified four members of a Ku Klux Klan group as the prime suspects, but they were unable to secure convictions against any of them during the 1960s. In 1977 the case was re-opened, and one of the Klansmen was convicted and sent to prison. Another one died in 1994 as a free man. For many years it appeared that the other two suspects, white supremacists Bobby Frank Cherry and Thomas Blanton Jr., would also avoid prison. In the late 1990s, though, authorities in Alabama opened the case once again.

Blanton and Cherry both main-tained their longstanding claims that they were innocent. Cherry even decided to call Mitchell, who by this time had become one of the best-known journalists in the South, to proclaim his innocence. Mitchell promptly accepted Cherry's offer to come to his home for a chat, and a few days later he spent about six hours visiting with Cherry and his wife. During their con-versation Cherry repeated his long-time claim that he was home watching wrestling on television at the time of the crime. When he returned to his office, Mitchell de-cided to check Cherry's alibi. He instructed an assistant to check and make sure that a wrestling program had in fact been broad-cast on television the day of the bombing. As it turned out, though, none of the stations had carried wrestling that day.

Sam Bowers is helped up the courthouse steps by Deputy Ronald Taylor on his way to court on charges of murder and arson against Vernon Dahmer.

Mitchell's discovery opened the floodgates for investigators. As Cherry's alibi fell apart, they found new evidence that enabled them to make stronger cases against both of the old Klansmen. "For three and a half decades [Cherry's] alibi had basically gone unchallenged, and now, lo and behold his alibi doesn't stand up," said the reporter. "There hadn't been wrestling on [television] for years. And it's always struck me as so stupid. It seems to me if you're a criminal, and you've got your to-do list, it seems like the first thing, num-ber one on the list, would be 'One: Check alibi.' Eh, we're not dealing with people with really high IQs."

In the end, both Cherry and Blanton were convicted of four counts of mur-der in the 1963 Birmingham church bombing. Blanton's conviction came on May 1, 2001, and he remained in prison as of 2012. Cherry received a life sentence on May 22, 2001. He died in prison in November 2004.

Returning to the *Mississippi Burning* Case

At the same time that Mitchell was helping bring the Birmingham church bombers to justice after nearly 40 years, he also undertook a separate investigation into the 1964 murders that had been featured in the movie *Mississippi Burning*. These were the killings of three civil rights workers—James Chaney, Andrew Goodman, and Michael Schwerner—that had first inspired him to dedicate his career to murder cases of the civil rights era.

Mitchell's involvement in the case occurred by chance. During the course of his investigation into the Vernon Dahmer murder, he had learned a secret about Sam Bowers, the Klan Imperial Wizard who had ordered the firebombing of the Dahmer home. In 1983 Bowers had given a secret interview to the Mississippi state archivist, an official responsible for keeping historical records for the state. Bowers had agreed to the interview under the condition that it be sealed from the public until his death. In 1998, however, Mitchell got his hands on a transcript of the interview.

Mitchell was stunned by what he read. During the course of the interview Bowers denied direct involvement in the June 1964 killings of Chaney, Goodman, and Schwerner. The Klan leader added, however, that he organized a campaign of lies to keep the murder investigators from the true mastermind, a Baptist preacher named Edgar Ray Killen. Bowers's scheme worked. Killen was charged with murder in the three killings, but he was acquitted of all charges in 1967. As a result, "I was quite delighted to be convicted and have the main instigator of the entire affair walk out of the courtroom a free man," Bowers said with satisfaction. "Everybody—including the trial judge and the prosecutors and everybody else—knows that that happened."

> *Mitchell has been successful because he refused to let death threats or other forms of intimidation get in his way. "I don't live in fear," he said. "I think it's one of those bridges I had to cross early as a reporter. Am I going to keep reporting on this or not, you know? Just because I get threats, am I going to stop? You know, I decided no. And it does go back to my faith, you know, on a personal level and I've been able to persist at this and thankfully some of these [murderers] have been prosecuted and gone behind bars."*

The burned shell of the station wagon used by the three murdered civil rights workers was found in a swampy area near Philadelphia, Mississippi, 1964. Their killer, Edgar Ray Killen, shown here in court, was convicted after more than 40 years.

Mitchell promptly wrote an article in the *Clarion-Ledger* that exposed Bowers's statements. The paper also published excerpts from the interview detailing Killen's orders to kill the three young activists. This bombshell story convinced state authorities to put Killen on trial again. In 2005 Killen was convicted of three counts of manslaughter and sentenced to three 20-year prison terms. These sentences ensured that the white supremacist would spend the rest of his life behind bars.

Solving Puzzles

Mitchell believes that one of the keys to his journalistic success over the years is that he seems so familiar to the men and women he interviews. "I think they talk to me because I am like them, a white Southerner, raised a Christian," he explained. "Being a Southerner is what enabled me to do these stories. If I'd not had a Southern accent, these Klan guys wouldn't have talked to me. Being willing to go out for barbecue and catfish helped, too."

> Mitchell believes that one of the keys to his journalistic success is that he seems so familiar to the men and women he interviews. "I think they talk to me because I am like them, a white Southerner, raised a Christian," he explained. "Being a Southerner is what enabled me to do these stories. If I'd not had a Southern accent, these Klan guys wouldn't have talked to me. Being willing to go out for barbecue and catfish helped, too."

Another key for Mitchell is that he enjoys the intellectual challenge of finding evidence that will enable authorities to convict killers of yesteryear. "It's like putting a puzzle together," he said. "Sometimes you have pieces and you don't know how they match up. And then years later, you get some more information and suddenly it all makes sense and it all fits together…. I very much work like a detective almost, in terms of trying to piece the case together."

Finally, Mitchell has been successful because he refused to let death threats or other forms of intimidation get in his way. "I don't live in fear," he said. "I think it's one of those bridges I had to cross early as a reporter. Am I going to keep reporting on this or not, you know? Just because I get threats, am I going to stop? You know, I decided no. And it does go back to my faith, you know, on a personal level and I've been able to persist at

Mitchell at his desk in the Clarion-Ledger *newsroom.*

this and thankfully some of these [murderers] have been prosecuted and gone behind bars."

Mitchell also notes that he receives more support from the public than he once did. "When I first started writing about this there were a lot of unhappy people," he admitted. "But as time went on, as there were arrests and there were convictions and those kinds of things, attitudes began to kinda change.... You know, in 1964, there were hardly any African Americans registered to vote in Mississippi. Today in Mississippi there are more [African-American] elected officials than any other state. So you can see, Mississippi has really come a long way. That's not to say it doesn't still have a long ways to go, but it's certainly come a long way."

Becoming One of America's Most Respected Reporters

Mitchell's success in solving cold cases of the civil rights era has inspired many southern states to re-open unsolved murder cases from those years. As of 2011, those investigations have led to a total of 23 convictions for murder and other crimes against civil rights activists and others.

In addition, Mitchell's work has made him one of the nation's most respected journalists. He has received more than 30 national journalism awards, and in 2005 he became the youngest recipient of Columbia University's prestigious John Chancellor Award for Excellence in Journalism. "Mitchell pursued these stories after most people believed they belonged to history, and not to journalism," said famed journalist David Halberstam, who presented the award to Mitchell. "But they did belong to journalism, because the truth had never been told and justice had never been done." Halberstam went on to describe Mitchell as "the most distinguished reporter in the entire country" and "a reflection of what one reporter with a conscience can do."

Mitchell's employers at the *Clarion-Ledger* echo these sentiments. "I just can't say enough about what Jerry has done for journalism and for the history of Mississippi," said *Clarion-Ledger* executive editor Ronnie Agnew in 2007. In recognition of their star reporter's high profile, the newspaper even gave Mitchell his own blog on its website, called "Journey to Justice."

MARRIAGE AND FAMILY

Mitchell lives in Mississippi with his wife and two children.

HOBBIES AND OTHER INTERESTS

Mitchell enjoys working on jigsaw puzzles and listening to music, but he says that he spends most of his free time on writing projects. In 1998 he published a 13-part series in the *Clarion-Ledger* called "The Preacher and the Klansman," which tells the true story of how a preacher and civil rights activist became friends with a former Klansman in Mississippi. Six years later, the newspaper published "Genetic Disaster," a 10-part series in which Mitchell described his family's battle against the rare genetic disease that claimed his grandfather's life. He also continued to write screenplays with an old childhood friend. In 2012 Mitchell announced that he was taking a temporary leave of absence from the *Clarion-Ledger* to complete a book about his work on some of the most notorious murders from the civil rights era.

SELECTED WRITINGS

"The Preacher and the Klansman," 1998
"Genetic Disaster," 2004

SELECTED HONORS AND AWARDS

Outstanding Achievement by an Individual Award (Gannett Newspapers): 1999, 2006
Best Investigative Reporting Award (Gannett Newspapers): 1999
William Ringle Outstanding Achievement Career Award (Gannett Newspapers): 1999
Chancellor Award for Excellence in Journalism (Columbia University): 2005

George Polk Award for Justice Reporting (Long Island University): 2005
Pulitzer Prize for Journalism finalist: 2006
Tom Renner Award for Crime Reporting (Investigative Reporters and Editors): 2006
MacArthur Fellowship (John D. and Catherine T. MacArthur Foundation): 2009
Ralph McGill Medal for Journalistic Courage (University of Georgia): 2009

FURTHER READING

Periodicals

American Journalism Review, Apr.-May 2005
Atlanta Journal-Constitution, June 26, 2005, p.A12
Editor & Publisher, Oct. 30, 2009
Human Rights, Fall 2000, p.18
Jackson (MS) Clarion-Ledger, Aug. 22, 1998
Mother Jones, Jan. 24, 2007
Newsweek, July 4, 2005, p.36
Nieman Reports, Fall 2011, p.17
USA Today, Jan. 17, 2005, p.A4; June 22, 2005, p.A1
USA Today Magazine, July 2011, p.28
Washington Post, Aug. 23, 2009

Online Articles

www.clarionledger.com/apps/pbcs.dll/article?AID=/99999999/special17/60416008
   (Clarion Ledger, "Jerry Mitchell's Entry and Biography," Oct. 22, 2009)
www.journalism.columbia.edu/page/432-2005-chancellor-award-winner-jerry-mitchell/185
   (Columbia Journalism School, "2005 Chancellor Award Winner: Jerry Mitchell," 2005)
www.npr.org/templates/story/story.php?storyId=7399590
   (National Public Radio, "Reporter Jerry Mitchell on Civil Rights-Era Cold Cases," Feb. 14, 2007)
www.pbs.org.newshour/media/clarion/mitchell.html
   (PBS Online NewsHour, "Jerry Mitchell," Apr. 18, 2002)
www.pbs.org/newshour/media/clarion/kc_summer.html
   (PBS Online NewsHour, "Pursuing the Past: A Mississippi Newspaper Investigates Crimes of the Civil Rights Era," June 27, 2005)
civilrightsandthepress.syr.edu/index.html
   (S.I. Newhouse School of Public Communications, Syracuse University, "Hodding Carter Lecture on Civil Rights and the Press," no date)

ADDRESS

Jerry Mitchell
The Clarion-Ledger
PO Box 40
Jackson, MS 39205-0040

WEB SITES

blogs.clarionledger.com/jmitchell/about/
blogs.clarionledger.com/jmitchell/
www.coldcases.org
civilrights.historybeat.com/gn_civilrights_investigations.php

Chloë Grace Moretz 1997

American Film Actress
Star of the Movies *Diary of a Wimpy Kid, Hugo,* and
Dark Shadows

BIRTH

Chloë Grace Moretz was born on February 10, 1997, in Atlanta, Georgia. Her father, McCoy "Mac" Moretz, is a plastic
surgeon, and her mother, Teri (Duke) Moretz, is a nurse practi-
tioner. She has four older brothers: Brandon, Trevor, Colin,
and Ethan. Trevor, an actor and producer who performs under
the name Trevor Duke, also serves as Chloë 's acting coach.

YOUTH

Chloë spent her earliest years in Atlanta. She moved to New York City in 2001 with her mother and Trevor when he was accepted at the Professional Performing Arts High School. She became interested in acting while helping him learn his lines. "When Trevor was 15 and I was five, he'd be practicing his monologues, and I just started memorizing them too," she remarked. "I guess something clicked." Soon she began modeling in national print ads and commercials.

In 2003 her family moved to Los Angeles for her father's medical practice. Chloë continued modeling and at age seven landed her first professional acting job as Violet in two episodes of the television drama "The Guardian." Shortly thereafter she started working in film, landing the role of Molly in the 2005 independent drama *Heart of the Beholder.* Her big break came when she was cast in the 2005 remake of the supernatural slasher movie *The Amityville Horror.*

EDUCATION

Moretz attended school until third grade, at which point she started a distance-learning program at home. She is home-schooled by a private tutor for six hours a day when she is working on a film and taught by her mother when she is not on set. A self-proclaimed "history geek," Moretz has talked about her admiration for Martha Washington as a historical figure and her fascination with the Victorian era of the 19th century. When she gets to college, she hopes to continue studying history, along with other subjects. "I'm hopefully going to Columbia University," she stated. "I want to do a minor in Art History and major in Criminal Psychology. I find criminal psychology incredibly fascinating and scary … how volatile the human mind can be. And I really love classical art."

> *Moretz became interested in acting while helping her older brother Trevor, who was studying acting. "When Trevor was 15 and I was five, he'd be practicing his monologues, and I just started memorizing them too," she remarked. "I guess something clicked."*

CAREER HIGHLIGHTS

Becoming an Actress

Moretz launched her film career at the age of eight with the remake of *The Amityville Horror,* which was re-

A scene from The Amityville Horror, *with Moretz (as Chelsea Lutz) in the right window and Isabel Conner (as Jodie Defeo) in the left window.*

leased in 2005. Her character, Chelsea "Missy" Lutz, befriends the ghost of a young girl named Jodie who had been murdered—along with five other family members—in the same Long Island house into which Chelsea's family has recently moved. This horror movie had gory special effects, disturbing subject matter, and an R-rating, so Moretz was not allowed to see it when it was released. However, critics praised her assured, mature performance, saying that with this role she proved that she was capable of handling dark material, even if she was not old enough to watch the movie. Her believability in *The Amityville Horror* led to offers for several other horror projects, including the zombie movie *Wicked Little Things* (2006), in which she played Emma Tunny, and the supernatural thriller *The Eye* (2008), in which she appeared as young cancer patient Alicia Milstone.

From 2007 to 2010, Moretz was heard as the voice of Darby in the Disney Channel's computer-animated TV series "My Friends Tigger & Pooh." Her character is a brave, six-year-old redhead who, along with her dog Buster, befriends the gang from the Hundred Acre Wood. She also voiced the character in several direct-to-DVD Winnie the Pooh movies. In 2008 she played the voice of Young Penny in the celebrated Disney feature *Bolt,* an animated adventure story starring John Travolta and Miley Cyrus about a dog that believes he has superpowers because he has spent his life on the set of a TV series about a superhero canine.

315

Moretz also continued to perform in live-action pieces, both in movies and on TV. She appeared in the 2006 crime comedy *Big Momma's House 2,* which starred Martin Lawrence as an FBI agent who goes undercover as Big Momma, using this disguise while he's fighting crime. Moretz played Carrie Fuller, part of the family where Big Momma works as a nanny. Despite being panned by critics, the film grossed more than $138 million worldwide. The following year she landed a recurring role as the sweet and talkative Kiki George in the TV drama "Dirty Sexy Money," which ran on ABC from 2007 to 2009. She returned to the silver screen in the 2009 movie *(500) Days of Summer* playing Rachel, the wise-beyond-her-years little sister who offers her lovesick brother sound relationship advice. Critics overwhelmingly praised the romantic comedy as clever, charming, and refreshingly honest. As reviewer Michael Ordoña stated in the *Los Angeles Times,* "*(500) Days of Summer* is something seldom seen: an original romantic comedy. It bristles with energy, emotion, and intellect, as it flits about the dizzying highs and weeping-karaoke lows of a passionate entanglement."

In 2010 Moretz appeared in the comedic film *Diary of a Wimpy Kid,* which is based on the first book in the popular series by Jeff Kinney (for more information on Kinney, see *Biography Today,* January 2011). The *Wimpy Kid* books use humor and cartoon drawings to depict some of the challenges that accompany the transition to middle school. The movie shows the humiliating and intimidating moments in the life of 11-year-old Greg Heffley, both at home and at school. It follows his misadventures with his best friend and sidekick, Rowley Jefferson, as they endure bullies, popularity contests, and gym class, among other trials. Moretz plays Angie Steadman, a student journalist who hangs out under the bleachers reading poetry until she becomes the first girl to notice Greg and Rowley. The movie was a hit with young viewers but received mixed reviews from critics, although many were pleasantly surprised by it. According to Roger Ebert, "It is so hard to do a movie like this well. *Diary of a Wimpy Kid* is a PG-rated comedy about the hero's first year of middle school, and it's nimble, bright, and funny. It doesn't dumb down. It doesn't patronize."

Action and Adventure

Moretz next lit up the silver screen in a leading role as Mindy Macready, also known as Hit-Girl, in the hyper-violent superhero film *Kick Ass* (2010). She became interested in doing an action film after seeing billboards for the movie *Wanted.* She told her mom, "I really want to do an Angelina Jolie-type character. You know, like an action hero, woman empowerment, awesome, take-charge leading role." A month later they re-

Moretz as Angie in a scene from Diary of a Wimpy Kid, *with Rowley (Robert Capron, left) and Greg (Zachary Gordon, middle).*

ceived the script for *Kick-Ass*—the film adaptation of Mark Millar's graphic novel series of the same name. Moretz doesn't usually read movie scripts; instead, her mother reads them first to sort out which are appropriate. This time, her mother knew it was exactly what Chloë wanted. As soon as she found out about the part, Moretz was determined to get the job. "I read it and I freaked out and said, 'I have to be Hit-Girl, Mom!' She was like, 'Okay, well—let's try it,'" she recalled. "So I went out to audition for [director Matthew Vaughn], and I got it ... and then I started training!" Moretz trained in martial arts, gymnastics, and weapons handling to play the pre-teen vigilante. "Every single day I would wake up, do crunches, pull-ups, push-ups and go do my training, then come home and go running and swimming," she remembered. "Somewhere in there, I would fit in school."

The film, and Moretz's role in particular, proved controversial due to the violence and foul language used by Hit-Girl. Moretz was only 11 years old at the time of filming. When asked about the decision to allow Chloë to be part of an adult-oriented production, her mother told the *Sunday Times*, "It definitely pushes boundaries, but Chloë knows the things that Hit-Girl says and does are fictional." She added that she saw it as an opportunity for her to show her grit and athleticism. Moretz has responded to questions about Hit-Girl's use of weapons and obscene language by emphasizing that the character's words and actions are far removed from her own. "If I even uttered a cuss word, I'd be dead. My mom is very strict. It's not real-life. I'm not going around cussing and killing people and pulling out knives."

Kick-Ass was popular with audiences, but critics were divided in their reviews. For example, Chris Hewitt of *Empire* magazine hailed it as "a ridiculously entertaining, perfectly paced, ultra-violent cinematic rush," while Roger Ebert panned it as "morally reprehensible." Critics who liked the film praised Moretz's performance, and *Entertainment Weekly* named her among the Top 10 performers to watch in 2010. The director, Matthew Vaughn, echoed the endorsement. In the voiceover commentary to the *Kick-Ass* DVD, Vaughn asserted "You are watching a star being born." Correspondingly, critics have compared Moretz to actresses Jodie Foster and Natalie Portman, both of whom rose to fame in controversial roles when they were about her age.

Following her attention-getting performance in *Kick-Ass,* Moretz was flooded with film offers. She starred in *Let Me In* (2010), a remake of the Swedish vampire film *Let the Right One In,* as a 250-year-old vampire. Critic Mary Pols of *Time* praised her performance, saying "In her latest, *Let Me In,* the 13-year-old gives a transfixing, delicately intuitive performance as Abby, an ancient vampire trapped in the inconvenient shell of a child's body." The movie received positive reviews by most commentators, including *New York Times* reviewer A. O. Scott, who hailed it as "at once artful and unpretentious, more interested in intimacy and implication than in easy scares or slick effects."

Hugo

Moretz next appeared in the 3-D adventure film *Hugo* (2011), based on the novel *The Invention of Hugo Cabret* by Brian Selznick and directed by the acclaimed filmmaker Martin Scorsese. But to get through the audition, she first had to trick the director. "I heard that [Scorsese] was only really looking at British girls. When I went in I was like: 'I'll do whatever I have to do to be in this movie.'" The casting director agreed not to tell Scorsese that she was an American, and when she delivered a spot-on accent in her audition, he mistook her for a native Brit. Three days later she was cast as Isabelle, a bookish girl growing up in Paris in the 1930s. "I went up to the balcony in my house and screamed at the top of my lungs: 'No way! Oh my gosh!'" she recalled.

Hugo is about a French orphan, played by Asa Butterfield, who lives alone in a Paris train station and keeps the railway clocks running. At the same

A scene from Hugo: *Moretz as Isabelle and Asa Butterfield as Hugo, with the mechanical man.*

time, he is trying to repair the mechanical man left by his late father, a watchmaker. With Isabelle's help, Hugo unlocks the secret that his father had left for him, a discovery that changes his life. To help Moretz prepare for her role, Scorsese asked her to study classic Audrey Hepburn films. "It was really what I based Isabelle off of—that fun girl, kinda naïve but sweet and full of wonderment." She has said that of all the characters she has played, she relates most to the fun-loving yet studious Isabelle. "She just loves reading books and those are her adventures," she explained. "Isabelle is a heightened version of my personality."

Hugo was released in 2011 and met with largely positive reviews. *New York Times* critic Manohla Dargis proclaimed, "It's serious, beautiful, wise to the absurdity of life, and in the embrace of a piercing longing." *Entertainment Weekly* critic Lisa Schwarzbaum called the movie "a haunting, piquant melodrama about childhood dreams and yearnings, enhanced with a pleasant survey course in early film history." Likewise, Todd McCarthy of the *Hollywood Reporter* asserted that "Craft and technical achievements are of the highest order, combining to create an immaculate present to film lovers everywhere." He singled out Moretz's performance for particular praise. "Moretz, with her beaming warmth and great smile, is captivating as a girl who leaps at the chance for some adventure outside of books." *Hugo* was nominated for 11 Academy Awards and won five.

Recent Work

In 2012 Moretz was featured in the Tim Burton film *Dark Shadows* starring Johnny Depp and Michelle Pfeiffer. The movie, which was based on a TV soap opera that aired from 1966 to 1971, is about a vampire who awakens after 200 years and joins his dysfunctional descendants in the 1970s. Moretz plays Carolyn Stoddard, an angst-ridden teenager who loves music and fashion but harbors a dark secret. "Carolyn is just like me but a heightened, ruder version of who I am," she explained. "I'm not that mean to my mom and I don't brood nearly as much as she does, but I understand her." Viewers agreed that Depp's performance as Barnabas Collins was the highlight of the movie. Critical response to the movie overall was mixed, with Manohla Dargis of the *New York Times* deeming it "Burton's most pleasurable film in years" and *Los Angeles Times* reviewer Kenneth Turan criticizing its "woeful lack of concern with story and drama."

> "Everyone around me is so strict about keeping me grounded. My mom won't let anyone treat me like a little princess," Moretz claimed. "Honestly, I don't have the room to go crazy, with four brothers and my mom."

HOME AND FAMILY

The Moretz family works as a team to prevent Chloë from growing up too quickly and to shield her from the negative influences of Hollywood culture. "Everyone around me is so strict about keeping me grounded. My mom won't let anyone treat me like a little princess," she explained. "Honestly, I don't have the room to go crazy, with four brothers and my mom." Chloë has often commented on her mother's no-nonsense parenting style. For example, her mother confiscated her phone and computer when she spent too much time surfing social networks and playing video games. Her mother has also made a conscious effort not to treat her differently because she is a celebrity. "I still get grounded," she admitted. "They make it very apparent that I'm just a normal girl, and if I ever started behaving like I was anything else I'd be out of the business in a flash."

Her brothers are particularly protective when it comes to the subject of dating. "I had a lot of friends and guys that I think are cute and stuff," she explained, "but it doesn't really work out with the family and all. My family's a bit too big and a bit too abrasive." Still, she recognizes the advantages of being the youngest. "The best thing about having four big broth-

The cast of Dark Shadows *(from left): Helena Bonham Carter, Chloë Grace Moretz, Eva Green, Gulliver McGrath, Bella Heathcote, Johnny Depp, Ray Shirley, Jackie Earle Haley, Jonny Lee Miller, and Michelle Pfeiffer.*

ers is you always have someone to do something for you," she teased. "No, no. I think number one would be that they always protect me. There's someone to turn to. It's like having four fathers, basically."

Trevor is an especially important influence in Chloë's life. He is not only her brother, but also her acting coach and manager. He often accompanies her on press appearances and travels with her on location. According to Chloë, Trevor helps her develop her characters and bring her performance to the next level. "The way I like to put it is, it's like a painting. I draw the outline, and he fills it in and makes it perfect," she said. Her mom is also involved in her career. "Mom is everything all at once—hair, make-up, mom, everything. It's pretty crazy," she marveled.

When she is not filming, Chloë lives in a house in Los Angeles with her mother. "It's so cute. It's this little place for Mom and me," she said. She also shares her home with an expanding brood of pets, including three dogs—Fuller, Missy, and Bella—and a cat named Zoe.

HOBBIES AND OTHER INTERESTS

Moretz enjoys a variety of activities, including shopping, going to birthday parties, cooking with her mom, and having sleepovers with friends.

She loves to play video games and to interact with friends and fans on Twitter. She also likes traveling and attending music concerts. For exercise, she enjoys ballet, gymnastics, basketball, and swimming. She is a fan of comic-book films, including *Spider-Man* and *The Dark Knight*, but she has admitted to being terrified of scary movies. She has eclectic musical tastes and has listed Lady Gaga, Adele, and Skrillex as a few of her favorite artists.

Moretz and her sense of style have been noticed by the fashion world, and she has recently been featured in a variety of fashion magazines. "I love fashion! To me, it's another way to express myself," she said. She enjoys participating in photo shoots and attending couture fashion shows, but her mother forbids her from wearing high fashion brands when she is not at a movie premiere or red carpet event. For special events she likes the designers Calvin Klein, Chanel, Dior, and Stella McCartney, and for everyday she likes the labels Topshop, American Apparel, and Urban Outfitters.

Moretz is involved with the Starlight Children's Foundation, a charity that helps children cope with chronic and life-threatening illnesses. As a Star-Power Ambassador for the organization, she uses her celebrity status to brighten the lives of patients through hospital visits and online chats.

SELECTED CREDITS

Movies

Heart of the Beholder, 2005
The Amityville Horror, 2005
Big Momma's House 2, 2006
Wicked Little Things, 2006
The Eye, 2008
Bolt, 2008
(500) Days of Summer, 2009
Diary of a Wimpy Kid, 2010
Kick-Ass, 2010
Let Me In, 2010
Hugo, 2011
Dark Shadows, 2012

Television

"Dirty Sexy Money," 2007-2008
"My Friends Tigger & Pooh," 2007-2010

HONORS AND AWARDS

Scream Awards (Spike TV): 2010, Best Breakthrough Performance—Female, for *Kick-Ass*; 2011, Best Horror Actress, for *Let Me In*

Empire Awards (*Empire* magazine): 2011, Best Newcomer

MTV Movie Awards: 2011 (two awards), Best Breakout Star and Biggest Badass Star, for *Kick-Ass*

Saturn Awards (The Academy of Science Fiction, Fantasy & Horror Films): 2011, Best Performance by a Younger Actor, for *Let Me In*

Young Artist Awards (Young Artist Foundation): 2011, Best Performance in a Feature Film—Young Ensemble Cast, for *Diary of a Wimpy Kid*

Max Mara Face of the Future Awards (Women in Film) 2012

FURTHER READING

Periodicals

Guardian, Dec. 2, 2011, p.5

Interview, Nov. 2011, p.58

Sunday Times, Oct. 24, 2010, p.12

Teen Vogue, Oct. 2010, p.99; Dec. 2011/Jan. 2012, p.138

Time, Oct. 11, 2010, p.59

Variety, Oct. 22, 2010, p.A9

Online Articles

www.interviewmagazine.com
  (Interview, "Another Hit: Chloë Moretz," Oct. 1, 2010; "Chloë Moretz," Jan. 1, 2012)

www.time.com
  (Time, "Young Blood," Oct. 11, 2010)

whosnews.usaweekend.com
  (USA Weekend, "Meet Chloë Moretz, the Precocious Teen Star of 'Kick-Ass,'" Apr. 9, 2010)

www.variety.com
  (Variety, Youth Impact Report 2010, "Chloë Grace Moretz: Gets a Kick Out of Diverse Roles," Oct. 22, 2010)

ADDRESS

Chloë Grace Moretz
William Morris Endeavor
9601 Wiltshire Blvd. Ste. 3
Beverly Hills, CA 90212

WEB SITE

chloemoretz.com

Blake Mycoskie 1976-
American Entrepreneur and Philanthropist
Founder and Chief Shoe Giver of TOMS Shoes

BIRTH

Blake Mycoskie was born on August 26, 1976, in Arlington, Texas. His father, Mike, is a doctor, and his mother, Pam, is a cookbook author. Mycoskie has two younger siblings, a brother named Tyler and a sister named Paige.

YOUTH

Growing up in Arlington, Mycoskie liked to play golf with his father and brother. The three played as often as they could.

———— " ————

Mycoskie explained his decision to leave school by saying, "I realized I loved doing this. I realized I loved the idea of creating something out of scratch and seeing it work and seeing the benefits of that."

———— " ————

Their golf outings usually included plenty of one-dollar bets with each other to see who could make the longest drive or the best putt.

As a young boy Mycoskie wanted to be a truck driver. He thought it would be cool to drive around the country meeting new people and seeing new places. But by the time Mycoskie was a teenager, he had decided that he wanted to become a professional tennis player. He devoted most of his free time to playing tennis, and he stuck to a rigorous training schedule. All of his hard work paid off when he won a tennis scholarship to Southern Methodist University in Dallas, Texas.

EDUCATION

At Southern Methodist University, Mycoskie studied philosophy and finance and played on the university's tennis team. During his sophomore year, he tore his Achilles tendon. This injury meant that he had to use crutches to walk, and so he was unable to continue playing tennis. When he realized that he couldn't carry his laundry to the dorm's laundry room while he was on crutches, Mycoskie thought he probably wasn't the only student who needed help. He got the idea to start a laundry pick-up and delivery service on the university's campus. His EZ Laundry business grew so quickly that in 1998, he left school to run the company full time.

CAREER HIGHLIGHTS

Becoming an Entrepreneur

The success of EZ Laundry helped Mycoskie realize that he wanted to be an entrepreneur. (An entrepreneur is a person who starts a new business, usually using one's own money and often based on one's own idea.) Mycoskie explained his decision to leave school by saying, "I realized I loved doing this. I realized I loved the idea of creating something out of scratch and seeing it work and seeing the benefits of that."

After just one year, EZ Laundry had expanded to several university campuses and had achieved sales of more than one million dollars. Mycoskie

A shot from "The Amazing Race": Paige Mycoskie and Blake Mycoskie (both on the left) arrive at a pit stop in Maui as they pursue the million-dollar prize.

sold EZ Laundry and moved to Nashville, Tennessee. There he started Mycoskie Media, a successful outdoor advertising company that specialized in painting huge ads on the sides of buildings. He sold that company after three years.

In 2002, when Mycoskie was 25 years old, he decided to take a break from business. He moved to Southern California and was chosen to participate in the second season of the CBS reality television competition show "The Amazing Race." His partner for the competition was his sister Paige. The pair finished in third place. "We lost $1 million by four minutes," Mycoskie admitted, "and it was all my fault. I epitomized the cliché that men will never stop and ask for directions."

After being on "The Amazing Race" and seeing firsthand the growing popularity of reality television programs, Mycoskie decided to start his own cable television channel. He worked hard to create Reality Central, a channel dedicated to showing reality programs 24 hours a day, seven days a week. But Mycoskie eventually gave up this idea after competing for three years against the new Fox Reality Channel. His Reality Central went out of business in 2005.

Mycoskie's next business venture was an online driver education program called Driver's Ed Direct. This company was based on the idea that people would prefer to complete required driver education coursework online, at their own pace, rather than in a classroom setting. Mycoskie founded Driver's Ed Direct in 2005. By 2006, he once again wanted to take a break from business. He decided to travel to South America to visit some of the places that he had glimpsed only briefly during "The Amazing Race."

A Big Idea

Mycoskie's South American vacation included an extended stay in Argentina. There he wanted to learn to play polo, a game in which horseback riders try to score points by using a long-handled mallet to hit a ball through the opposing team's goal. Mycoskie also wanted to experience the nation's culture from the perspective of local residents, so he spent time touring many of Argentina's cities and countryside villages.

Near the end of his vacation there, Mycoskie met two women who were volunteering with an organization that distributed donated shoes to residents of Argentina's poorest villages. These women told Mycoskie about all of the problems that people faced when they had no shoes to wear. Children without shoes were often not able to attend school, because shoes were part of the required school uniform. Foot injuries and diseases were widespread among those who had to walk miles to collect fresh water, food, or other necessities. Mycoskie also learned of a terrible disease called podoconiosis, which results from walking barefoot on soil that contains certain minerals. Podoconiosis causes the feet and legs to become extremely swollen, and the damage is permanent.

As Mycoskie learned more about the women's efforts to provide shoes to those who desperately needed them, he began to see a flaw in their organization's plan. Collecting donations of shoes meant that the organization could not control the supply of shoes that they gave away. They had to rely on whatever they were given, even if the donated shoes were already worn out or in the wrong sizes or styles. Sometimes there were not enough shoes donated for all of the children who needed them, meaning that some children were still without shoes while others were given a pair to wear.

Mycoskie realized that the most effective charitable program would be based on a constant, reliable source of shoes. In this way, everyone who needed a pair could get them. He began to form a plan to create a for-profit business that would be able to provide shoes for those in need. Mycoskie decided that he would start a company to make and sell shoes, with the goal of giving away a pair of shoes for every pair sold. Mycoskie called this new model of charitable giving "one for one," a phrase that highlighted the simplicity of his plan.

Founding TOMS

When he decided to start his one-for-one shoe company in 2006, Mycoskie knew nothing about the shoe business. He enlisted the help of his Argentinian polo teacher, Alejo Nitti, who had also become Mycoskie's close friend. Nitti was an elite polo athlete who also knew nothing about making shoes, but he was excited about the chance to give something back to the people of his country. Mycoskie and Nitti began the company in Nitti's family barn, where they worked to develop the business amongst the family's roosters, iguanas, and donkeys.

Mycoskie wanted to create a shoe for American buyers based on the *alpargata*, the traditional shoe of Argentinian workers and farmers. *Alpargatas* are casual shoes made of soft canvas with a sole made of rope. Mycoskie wanted to make a new kind of *alpargata* that would be more durable and more stylish. He imagined a rubber sole on the bottom instead of rope, soft leather inside, and colorful printed cloth on top. With these modern touches and the addition of arch support, Mycoskie thought the shoes would be both comfortable and appealing to fashion-conscious American shoppers.

> "On an early drop in Argentina, after the kids got their shoes, they pulled me around their school to a soccer field. It was full of rocks and sticks that would have mangled their feet if they were playing barefoot....While we gave them shoes for health reasons, I realized they viewed them as equipment," Mycoskie explained. "The most common response we get from the kids and from their parents is that this shoe represents a passport to a better life."

The design of the new shoes began to take shape, but Mycoskie's new company still needed a name. He and Nitti had been working under the slogan "Shoes for a Better Tomorrow." This evolved into "Tomorrow's Shoes" but when this phrase proved to be too long to fit on the shoe labels, it was shortened to simply "TOMS."

Starting Out

To create the first sample shoes, Mycoskie and Nitti enlisted the help of local Argentinian shoemakers. Most of these craftsmen came from families

Two children wearing their new shoes share some food at a soup kitchen in Buenos Aires, Argentina, after receiving their shoes in the first shoe drop, 2006.

that had been making *alpargatas* by hand for generations, with traditional skills passed down from father to son. Mycoskie's idea for new *alpargatas* made with modern materials was met with great skepticism. He and Nitti worked hard to convince shoemakers to give the new design a try. In spite of this early resistance to his idea, Mycoskie was certain that he was on the right track. He explained, "The best sign that it's a truly good idea is no one else believes in it."

After a period of experimentation with different materials and a lot of learning by trial and error, Mycoskie eventually had 250 pairs of TOMS shoes to bring back to the United States. He packed all of the sample shoes in a duffle bag and boarded a plane back to Los Angeles to find buyers. Mycoskie had paid for all of the materials and labor with his own money, based only on his confidence in his ability to sell both the shoes and the one-for-one idea behind TOMS. "It was a small project. It wasn't like I, you know, invested hundreds of thousands of dollars and wrote a big business plan and quit my job and all the dramatic things you think of. Now, later I did all those things. But in the beginning it was a very humble start," Mycoskie said. "People get scared because they think they need a giant loan, but you can start on a very small scale."

Back in Los Angeles, Mycoskie set up a web site to explain the TOMS one-for-one concept and to sell shoes directly to consumers. He also began trying to find stores where TOMS could be sold. But without any knowledge of the retail shoe industry, Mycoskie ran into problems trying to break into the market. Sales were nearly nonexistent until the *Los Angeles Times* ran a story about TOMS and Mycoskie's one-for-one giving program. Sales skyrocketed overnight and the TOMS web site logged more than 2,000 orders in one day. With less than 200 pairs of shoes in stock, Mycoskie scrambled to come up with a plan.

After contacting all 2,000 customers to inform them of a delay in shipping their orders, Mycoskie quickly returned to Argentina to oversee the manufacture of 4,000 pairs of shoes. At that time, TOMS was still relying on local shoemakers working in very small shops. Some of these craftsmen could only complete one part of the whole shoe. Mycoskie and Nitti spent most of their time driving back and forth across Buenos Aires, delivering materials and partially constructed shoes to the next person in the TOMS assembly line.

By the time Mycoskie brought the next batch of shoes back to the United States, TOMS had been featured in *Vogue, Elle, People, Teen Vogue, Time,* and *O* magazines. Mycoskie fielded calls from stores including Nordstrom, Urban Outfitters, and even Whole Foods. Within the first six months, 10,000 pairs of TOMS shoes were sold.

The First Shoe Drop

Mycoskie had planned the first shoe giveaway, or shoe drop, to take place after 10,000 pairs were sold. "When I first used the term 'shoe drop,' someone asked me if anyone ever gets hurt. They thought we were flying by and dropping boxes of shoes, which could be problematic. But that's not what happens." Mycoskie returned to Argentina with his parents, his brother and sister, and several close friends. They travelled the countryside in a bus, stopping in remote rural villages to distribute free shoes to those in need.

Mycoskie described that first shoe drop as one of the most important moments in his life. "The children had been told we were coming, and our local organizers had informed us of the needed shoe sizes. The kids, anticipating a new pair—or their very first pair—of shoes were so eager for our arrival that they would start clapping with joy when they spotted the bus rolling into town. I broke down in tears many times. 'Oh, my God,' I thought, 'This is actually working.' At each stop I was so overcome with emotion that I could barely slip the first pair of shoes on a child without crying with love and happiness."

Mycoskie with recipients of TOMS shoes.

"On an early drop in Argentina, after the kids got their shoes, they pulled me around their school to a soccer field. It was full of rocks and sticks that would have mangled their feet if they were playing barefoot. Growing up as an athlete, I remember being stoked about any new gear that would improve my game. While we gave them shoes for health reasons, I realized they viewed them as equipment," Mycoskie explained. "The most common response we get from the kids and from their parents is that this shoe represents a passport to a better life.

"When I returned from that first shoe drop, I was a different person. I also realized that TOMS wasn't going to be just another business for me. It was going to be my life, in the best sense.... All at once it made a living for me and everyone who worked at TOMS, it brought me closer to the people and places I loved, and it offered me a way to contribute something to people in need. I didn't have to compartmentalize any of my life's ambitions: personal, professional, or philanthropic. They all converged in a single mission."

Mycoskie sold his remaining shares of Driver's Ed Direct and invested the money in expanding TOMS. He hired his first paid employees, including several people who had experience in the shoe industry. Together, this new team dedicated themselves to furthering the one-to-one mission of TOMS.

A Big Break

Mycoskie decided early on that TOMS would have no advertising budget. Instead, the company would rely only on social networking and the comments of satisfied customers. "Most footwear companies spend a fortune on traditional advertising, athlete endorsements, TV commercials and billboards," he explained. "The only way TOMS works is if we spend no money on traditional advertising. All of our marketing comes from social media and word of mouth." But the biggest publicity break still came in the form of a commercial on national television—though TOMS didn't pay for it.

In 2009, AT&T approached Mycoskie with a proposal to feature TOMS in one of its commercials. The commercial focused on the one-for-one concept behind TOMS and how TOMS used AT&T services to run its worldwide operations. The commercial ran for 12 weeks during popular shows such as "Dancing With the Stars," "American Idol," and "Survivor." The commercial was also shown on video screens in 5,000 New York City taxi cabs. It is estimated to have reached hundreds of millions of people. Demand for TOMS shoes exploded after this commercial was aired. As a result, TOMS was able to give away more than 300,000 pairs of shoes in 2009—more than twice as many as were given away in the company's first three years combined.

TOMS has expanded its operations significantly since 2009 and now works with local community health organizations around the world. "Our global shoe giving is now accomplished through humanitarian organizations with deep roots in the communities in which they operate," Mycoskie commented. "They serve children in a holistic way, through health, education, clean water, and more. And they integrate our shoes into their programs for even greater impact. Their ongoing presence means we can get shoes to kids again and again as they grow.

"When I started TOMS, people thought I was crazy," Mycoskie ad-

> "I started TOMS with half a million dollars. If I had taken that money, bought shoes, and distributed them to needy kids, I would have been able to do it only once. But with my business plan, which allows us to give one pair away for each pair we sell, it's a sustainable venture. We can give shoes away every year, grow the business, and help more kids."

mitted. "In particular, longtime veterans of the footwear industry argued that the model was unsustainable or at least untested—that combining a for-profit company with a social mission would complicate and undermine both. What we've found is that TOMS has succeeded precisely *because* we have created a new model. The giving component of TOMS makes our shoes more than a product. They're part of a story, a mission, and a movement anyone can join."

Becoming a Social Entrepreneur

Over the course of his career as the head of TOMS, Mycoskie has changed the way in which businesses can participate in charitable giving. In 2010, TOMS was named as one of the Ten Most Innovative Retail Companies by *Fast Company* magazine. Mycoskie's work has also become a model and an inspiration for a new type of businessperson, called a social entrepreneur. Social entrepreneurs are people who start businesses with the dual goal of making money and helping others at the same time. "I think the term 'social entrepreneur' is very relevant because I believe you can do well by doing good," Mycoskie argued. "TOMS is a for-profit business, and it's important that we have profit so we have sustainability.… The nice thing about TOMS is it being a for-profit business, we're continuing to sell shoes so we can continue to give shoes.

"We've also made it clear to our customers from the very beginning that our company is not like most others in the social-impact sector—we are a *for-profit* company. Our goal is to help people and to make money doing it. We have never hidden that from anyone and in so doing have paved the way for a new type of social venture," Mycoskie explained. "I started TOMS with half a million dollars. If I had taken that money, bought shoes, and distributed them to needy kids, I would have been able to do it only once. But with my business plan, which allows us to give one pair away for each pair we sell, it's a sustainable venture. We can give shoes away every year, grow the business, and help more kids."

Since its creation in 2006, TOMS has given away millions of shoes in 23 countries around the world, including the United States, Argentina, Ethiopia, Haiti, and South Africa. "As we've grown our giving has become more focused on specifically preventing diseases for kids in certain areas of the world," Mycoskie said. "TOMS started as a social experiment but it quickly became a shoe company. Now, it's moving more toward a movement. I want to not only be giving shoes around the world and fulfilling our one-to-one promise but working with doctors and local governments to eradicate Podo [podoconiosis] in 15 to 20 years."

Mycoskie announcing a new One for One program—TOMS eyewear.

In 2011, Mycoskie announced that TOMS was expanding the one-for-one giving model with the launch of the TOMS line of eyewear. For every pair of sunglasses or eyeglasses sold, TOMS will provide medical treatment, prescription glasses, or eye surgeries to a person in need. Also in 2011, he published *Start Something That Matters*. This book outlines his approach to business and provides advice and inspiration for aspiring social entrepreneurs. Mycoskie is donating half of his profits from the sales of the book to his Start Something That Matters Fund, which he created to encourage organizations and projects that make a positive impact on the world.

Mycoskie spends most of his time travelling, either delivering shoes on shoe drops or speaking about his business philosophy. "Often, I'm travelling around the country to speak at companies and universities about our business model. I love teaching people what we do. My goal is to inspire the next generation of entrepreneurs and company leaders to think differently about how they incorporate giving into their business models.

"Increasingly, the quest for success is not the same as the quest for status and money. The definition has broadened to include contributing something to the world and living and working on one's own terms," Mycoskie said. "Start now. Start by helping other people—anyone you can. Do something simple. You don't have to start a business or big initiative right

———— " ————

"The definition [of success] has broadened to include contributing something to the world and living and working on one's own terms," Mycoskie said. "Start now. Start by helping other people—anyone you can. Do something simple. You don't have to start a business or big initiative right away—you can begin just by changing your mindset. Commit to seeing the world through the lens of how you can initiate meaningful change."

———— " ————

away—you can begin just by changing your mindset. Commit to seeing the world through the lens of how you can initiate meaningful change.

"Almost everyone has a passion for something, but sometimes we have trouble saying what it is. It's surprisingly easy to lose touch with our true passions—sometimes because we get distracted with everyday living; sometimes simply because in the usual stream of small talk or transactable business, no one ever asks us about our dreams. That's why it's so important that you first find a way to articulate your passion *to yourself*. When you discover what your passion is, you will have found your story as well."

HOME AND FAMILY

Mycoskie lives on a sailboat in Marina Del Rey, California, but he is rarely there. "I'm home about five or six days a month, and the rest of the time I'm on the road."

HOBBIES AND OTHER INTERESTS

When he is not working, Mycoskie enjoys fly fishing, surfing, sailing, and writing. "Almost every morning I write in my journal. I've been keeping it for a long time—I've filled more than 50 books. I write about what's going on in my personal and spiritual life or what's going on at work. It helps me keep things in perspective, especially when things get crazy or I get stressed or we have obstacles. When I go back a month later and read what I was feeling, I realize that it wasn't that big of a deal—we got through it. And that helps me prepare for the next time that I deal with difficult stuff."

Mycoskie also enjoys reading and is especially interested in biographies. "I read quite a bit when I'm on the road. I've read a lot of business biographies.... The great thing about biographies is the subjects have already been successful, so they're not insecure about their failures."

WRITINGS

Start Something That Matters, 2011

HONORS AND AWARDS

People's Design Award (Smithsonian Institution Cooper-Hewitt National
    Design Museum): 2007
Award for Corporate Excellence (U.S. Secretary of State): 2009

FURTHER READING

Books

Mycoskie, Blake. *Start Something That Matters,* 2011

Periodicals

Business Week, Jan. 26, 2009, p.18
Fortune, Mar. 22, 2010, p.72
Inc., June 2010, pg.112
Los Angeles Times, Apr. 19, 2009; June 12, 2011
Men's Health, Sep. 2008
Newsweek, Oct. 11, 2010, p.50
Texas Monthly, Sep. 2008, p.34
Time, Jan. 26, 2007
Time for Kids, Mar. 2, 2007, p.6
Vogue, Oct. 2006

Online Articles

bigthink.com/ideas/1121
    (Big Think, "Blake Mycoskie on Becoming an Entrepreneur," Apr. 28,
    2008)
www.cnn.com
    (CNN, "Blake Mycoskie: Sole Ambition," Sep. 26, 2008; "These Shoes
    Help Others Get a Step Up," Mar. 26, 2009)
cox.smu.edu/web/guest/blake-mycoskie
    (Cox School of Business, "Blake Mycoskie," no date)
www.fastcompany.com
    (Fast Company, "Blake Mycoskie, Founder and Chief Shoe Giver of
    TOMS Shoes," Oct. 14, 2010)
www.inc.com
    (Inc., "The Way I Work: Blake Mycoskie of Toms Shoes," June 1, 2010)
laist.com
    (LAist.com, "PhiLAnthropist Interview: TOMS Shoes Founder Blake
    Mycoskie Plans to Give Away 300,000 Pairs in 2009," Apr. 15, 2009)

www.openforum.com
  (OpenForum.com, "Trendsetter: TOMS Founder Blake Mycoskie on
  Starting a Movement," Oct. 5, 2011)
online.wsj.com
  (Wall Street Journal, "Sole Man Blake Mycoskie: The TOMS Shoes
  Founder on Business, Buddhism, and Breakfast Burritos," Jan. 7, 2012)

ADDRESS

Blake Mycoskie
TOMS Shoes, Inc.
3025 Olympic Blvd., Suite C
Santa Monica, CA 90404

WEB SITES

www.startsomethingthatmatters.com/about-blake
www.toms.com/blakes-bio

Michele Norris 1961-

American Journalist

Host of the National Public Radio Show "All Things Considered"

Author of the Memoir *The Grace of Silence*

BIRTH

Michele L. Norris was born on September 7, 1961, in Minneapolis, Minnesota. She grew up in Minneapolis with her mother, Elizabeth Norris, and father, Belvin Norris Jr., who were both postal workers.

YOUTH

Dealing with Racial Issues

Norris grew up in a time of transition in race relations in the United States, an issue that affected her childhood and her professional career. The civil rights movement was making significant progress in changing "Jim Crow" laws, which had begun in the late 1800s and lasted until the 1960s. These Jim Crow laws, which were founded on the legal principle of "separate but equal," made it legal to discriminate against African Americans. These laws forced the segregation of the races and created "separate but equal" public facilities for blacks and whites. Restaurants, bathrooms, railroad cars, movie theaters, schools, and other public places were segregated, with one set of facilities for whites and another set of facilities for blacks. Although these separate facilities were called equal, in reality those for blacks were miserably inadequate. African Americans usually attended dilapidated, impoverished schools with underpaid teachers. After leaving school, their opportunities for work were often just as limited. These were the conditions for many African Americans at that time, especially in the South.

> "*What I remember was a wonderfully integrated community where we had friends from all across the color line. What I experienced in south Minneapolis was distinctly at odds with what I saw on the television regarding integration. It just seemed so easy when I looked around my neighborhood. I didn't realize it was anything but easy for my parents. When they first moved in, every family whose property line touched ours moved out.*"

Norris knew that her parents had faced racism and had suffered under these Jim Crow laws. Her father had lived in Birmingham, Alabama, an area of the Deep South that was extremely segregated. If he wanted to go downtown, he would have to plan his trip in advance and take food with him because he might not be able to sit at a restaurant due to his race. "My parents were very careful how they presented those stories," she explained. "They told me some things and they didn't tell me others." Norris spent many summers in Birmingham, and her parents would tell her to be careful. She remembers "getting a lecture … not to look white people in the eye, to be careful when we moved about downtown, never to draw at-

Jim Crow laws, like those that forced this African-American man to drink from the "colored" water cooler, were common when Norris's parents were growing up in the first half of the 20th century.

tention to yourself, to make sure you were dressed a certain way when you always went out in public spaces."

When Norris was growing up in Minnesota, segregation was still common. At that time it was rare for black and white people to live on the same block, and her family was the first black family on her street. Sandy Banks, a writer for the *Los Angeles Times,* described Norris's upbringing like this. "Norris's parents were the first blacks on their block in Minneapolis. Her father was a Navy vet, raised in Birmingham before civil rights arrived, so determined not to be looked down upon that he woke early on snowy days to shovel the driveway and sidewalk before his white neighbors looked outside. Her mother was a fourth-generation Minnesotan who hailed from the only black family in a small northern town." Norris said her parents always made it a point to keep their lawn nice and dress well when going out. She called her family a "Model Minority," determined to prove that their family was as respectable and responsible as any white family. It worked: the whole family got along well with their white neighbors in Minnesota.

Norris doesn't recall very much racial tension in her childhood. However, she still experienced some teasing because of her race. In school, kids made hurtful comments, telling her she had a "kinky little Afro." Nonetheless, she knew that segregation was more deeply entrenched in other parts of the country. "Growing up, I was shielded from what happened," she recalled. "What I remember was a wonderfully integrated community where we had friends from all across the color line. What I experienced in south Minneapolis was distinctly at odds with what I saw on the television regarding integration. It just seemed so easy when I looked around my neighborhood. I didn't realize it was anything but easy for my parents. When they first moved in, every family whose property line touched ours moved out."

Life at Home

When Norris was young, her father had an interesting way of getting her attention. He came home from work every day and called out, "MEE-shell!" She liked the way it sounded so much that she began saying her name the same way, and her family and friends soon caught on.

> *Throughout her childhood, Norris was encouraged to read the newspaper every day. "I grew up in a household where my parents devoured the papers and the evening news and instructed their children to do the same, up to quizzes at the dinner table."*

Throughout her childhood, Norris was encouraged to read the newspaper every day and to value education. "I grew up in a household where my parents devoured the papers and the evening news and instructed their children to do the same, up to quizzes at the dinner table." Her father said she could do anything, as long as she focused on her studies.

Even though Norris's family was respected in her neighborhood and her parents were supportive, family life was not perfect. Her parents divorced when she was a teenager. "There was a silent tornado in our home, and it led to the breakup of my parents' marriage," she said. She lived with her father after the divorce.

EDUCATION

Norris attended Washburn High School in Minneapolis, where she was part of the cheerleading squad and wrote for her high school student newspaper. Her parents' support of her studies helped her to succeed in school and to decide to attend college.

Norris with her father, Belvin Norris Jr.

Norris started college in 1979 at the University of Wisconsin-Madison, where she studied electrical engineering. She was part of a national program called InRoads, which gave scholarships to minority students who did well in math and science classes in high school. While she was studying electrical engineering, she had a C average. Her heart was not in her work, and she said she found her studies "fascinating but isolating." She needed to change direction, and she thought she should study writing. "I always tell the story that, when I was in engineering, I would wind up rewriting the word problems, then maybe I would get to solving the problem," she said. "Engineering was interesting, but it was a diversion. Although it did help me because it teaches you to think logically. So it wasn't a waste of time. But I've always been interested in writing and storytelling and ultimately found my way to my calling."

In 1982, Norris transferred to the University of Minnesota, where she studied journalism. She wrote for the university newspaper, the *Minnesota*

Daily, at that time the fourth-largest student-run paper in the state. In 1985, before she graduated, she dropped out of school to take a job in journalism. She later returned to school and completed her journalism degree at the University of Minnesota in 2005.

CAREER HIGHLIGHTS

Starting Out as a Journalist

Throughout her career, Norris has worked in a variety of jobs in journalism—in television, newspaper, and radio. In 1985, while still attending college in Minnesota, she landed her first professional job—at the CBS TV station, WCCO, where she was an assistant in the newsroom. She didn't work there long, though. In 1985, she landed a job with the *Los Angeles Times.* Over the next eight years, from 1985 to 1993, Norris worked for three of the largest newspapers in the country: the *Los Angeles Times,* the *Chicago Tribune,* and the *Washington Post.*

While working for the *Los Angeles Times,* Norris lived in San Diego, California. One of her first stories focused on why the prices of necessary goods, like food and prescriptions, were much higher in poor neighborhoods than in wealthier ones. Her stories focused on social problems, such as poverty and education. At the *Chicago Tribune,* Norris continued writing about education. She wrote stories about a high school principal's damaged property and a teachers' strike at a local school system. Her passion for education stories flourished at the *Tribune.* At the *Washington Post,* Norris again wrote about social issues. One of her first stories was about a six-year-old boy who lived with his drug-addicted mother. Their house was identified by police as a house where drugs were sold. Norris earned national respect for the series of stories on the boy. She also won the Livingston Award in 1990, which is given to American journalists under the age of 35. The articles were reprinted in the collection called *Ourselves Among Others: Cross-cultural Readings.*

In 1993, Norris was surprised to be asked by ABC News to be a television news correspondent, which means she was an on-screen reporter. She had never worked on TV before, but she jumped at the chance to try something new. Besides, she was proud to bring more racial diversity to the program. "I know what it's like to turn on the TV and not always see people who look like you," she said. The chance to change the face of television gave her work a higher purpose.

During her time with ABC, Norris was a Washington-based correspondent for "World News Tonight," "20/20," "Nightline," and "Good Morn-

Norris at the microphone in the NPR studios while on the air.

ing America." Her stories focused mostly on education, inner-city issues, poverty, and the nation's drug problems. While working at ABC she earned an Emmy Award, an award given for excellence in television, for her coverage of the terrorist attacks on September 11, 2001. She worked at ABC News until 2002.

Moving to National Public Radio

In 2002, Norris became the co-host of "All Things Considered," the longest-running program on National Public Radio (NPR). The job offer came out of the blue. By this point, she was married with children, a big factor in her decision. "It was one of those rare opportunities, in which you could take a gigantic step forward in your career without taking a con-comitant step away from your family," she explained. "I was actually able to stay closer to home because I'm tied to the studio, which meant I would be traveling less." "All Things Considered" is a two-hour news program that airs each weekday on public radio stations around the country during the afternoon drive time, about 4:00 to 6:00 p.m. The award-winning show has been on the air for more than 40 years and now counts more than 13 million listeners. Each show includes the biggest news stories of the day mixed with interviews, commentaries, reviews, and human-interest sto-ries, all enlivened with sound. The show has three hosts, but only two hosts are on at any time; Norris co-hosts "All Things Considered" with Robert Siegel and Melissa Block.

When Norris first started, she was concerned about moving from TV to radio. The staff at NPR really thought about the training she would need and helped her adapt to the responsibilities of being a radio host. One of her bosses, NPR vice president Bruce Drake, praised her ability to report on a wide range of stories. "She's comfortable reporting on everything from Washington politics to popular culture," Drake said. News correspondent Gwen Ifill, who appears on public television (Public Broadcasting System, or PBS), agreed with Drake. "She can see beyond the story to the human element almost instantly. You feel like you're eavesdropping on a private conversation," Ifill said.

> "There's something incredibly powerful about the intimacy of radio and the way that it plays on the listener's imagination," Norris argued. "A soldier knocks on someone's door to deliver bad news. You can describe that in print. You can show that in television. But somehow when you combine the descriptive powers and the ambient sound that they use so well here at NPR to take the listener to that place, it's a very powerful medium."

Norris is the first African-American woman to host a program on NPR, and she likes having another chance to bring racial diversity to the media. She enjoys radio in particular. Norris has suggested that radio is more intimate than print or television journalism because it forces the audience to pay more attention to the story in order to fully understand what is being reported. In print journalism, readers often read the first paragraph to get a general idea of the story, and then they stop and move on to something else. In television journalism, viewers focus on the pictures and video clips more than what the correspondent is saying. Radio journalism is different. "Radio is wonderful because you use the storytelling and descriptive writing that you call upon in print and you enhance that with sound," she declared. "There's something incredibly powerful about the intimacy of radio and the way that it plays on the listener's imagination. A soldier knocks on someone's door to deliver bad news. You can describe that in print. You can show that in television. But somehow when you combine the descriptive powers and the ambient sound that they use so well here at

NPR to take the listener to that place, it's a very powerful medium." It's not only radio in general that Norris enjoys; it's being a part of NPR itself. "I meet someone and after they figure out what I do, they tell me how much NPR means to them."

Norris has said that working at NPR is the hardest job she has ever had. She likes that "All Things Considered" includes the excitement of live reporting on current events, as well as the high production quality of taped pieces about ongoing issues. NPR has given Norris the opportunity to interview famous and influential people, including Oscar winners, American presidents, military leaders, and astronauts. She enjoys the variety.

One story, in particular, led Norris down a new path. During the 2008 presidential campaign between then-Democratic candidate Barack Obama and Republican candidate John McCain, she helped with a series called "The York Project: Race and the '08 Vote." She worked with another NPR reporter, Steve Inskeep, host of the NPR show "Morning Edition." She and Inskeep reported on 15 hours of discussions among a group of voters living in York, Pennsylvania. They wanted to explore the attitudes of York voters regarding race, since Obama was the first black politician to be so close to becoming president. Norris and Inskeep wanted to know how voters' views about race would affect their votes. The two reporters found that the election was an opportunity for voters to reconsider their racial views. "People started talking about race in a different way," Norris said. For their work on "The York Project: Race and the '08 Vote," she and Inskeep were co-winners of the Alfred I. duPont-Columbia University Award.

Returning to Writing

Inspired by the 2008 presidential election, Norris began considering taking a break from NPR in 2009 in order to write a book that focused on people's thoughts about race in general—not just in relation to politics. "I thought there was an interesting conversation about race taking place in the country … and I wanted to swim in that conversation for a while." Norris thought the book would be called *You Don't Say: On Matters of Race and the Consequences of Silence.* "People talk about race one way in public and they often talk about it in a different way in private," she explained, "and I just want to pull back the curtain a little bit." The book was supposed to be a collection of essays about other people.

When Norris began looking into the country's experiences with racism, she also began listening to her own family's stories, especially those about her parents and grandparents. But Norris didn't hear those stories directly from the people involved; instead, she heard them from other family

*Norris with her "All Things Considered" co-host, Robert Siegel,
reporting on the presidential campaign on Super Tuesday 2008.*

members who were tired of hiding the truth. The more she learned, the
more she had to know. "It was like the elders were going through a period
of historic indigestion," she observed. "All these stories and things they
had kept to themselves were coming up and coming out." She kept asking
questions and decided that, instead of writing about the country's history
with racism, she would write a book about her own family's history. Their
stories would relate to racial issues in the United States in general, but she
would be able to learn about her own family along the way.

Writing Her Father's Story

Learning her family stories wasn't always fun. One morning, Norris was
having breakfast with an uncle, who was saying that young people don't understand how much older generations had sacrificed in order to change
racial attitudes to the point that the United States could elect a black president. In the middle of the conversation, her uncle calmly said, "Well, you
know your father was shot." Norris was washing dishes at the time, and she
was so startled that her knees buckled and she sank to the floor. Her father
never told his children or his wife about being shot by a white police officer
in Birmingham, Alabama, after returning from serving in the U.S. Navy during World War II. "Perhaps it was too difficult to go back there in his mind,"
Norris said. So she took it upon herself to learn what he never told her.

Norris decided that her book would become a memoir about her family. Since her father had died more than 20 years before she learned the truth, she had to rely on her investigative skills to find more. She tracked down police records, military documents, and interviews. Once she started researching, she couldn't stop. She learned that the shooting occurred in February 1946, two weeks after her father returned from military service in World War II. Norris's father, uncle, and a friend were in Birmingham, Alabama, an area where racism was deeply entrenched. In this segregated community, the men were in the lobby of a building that housed black professionals.

While Norris's father and the other two black men were waiting for an elevator, two white policemen blocked the elevator entrance with nightsticks. They knocked her father down and put a gun to his chest. Instinctively, Norris's father pushed the gun down just in time for the policeman to shoot him in the leg instead of the chest. Norris's father was not the only one attacked in this way—in a week, about six black veterans were killed by white police officers in Birmingham. Her father's story represents a sordid episode in U.S. history—an example of the United States showing contempt for a group of people who had served in the military to defend their country. "My father was part of a group of men who fought for their country," Norris later said. "They did their part. They participated in the fight for democracy in foreign lands, and they got this crazy idea that they could get a taste of it back home. They loved a country that didn't love them back." She knew this would be an important story to include in her book.

> *"My father was part of a group of men who fought for their country," Norris said. "They did their part. They participated in the fight for democracy in foreign lands, and they got this crazy idea that they could get a taste of it back home. They loved a country that didn't love them back."*

Revealing Her Grandmother's Past

Norris never expected that she would learn something about her grandmother that would startle her as much as her father's story. Iona Brown, Norris's grandmother, was remembered as a well-dressed, elegant woman who was proud of her race. When Norris learned that her grandmother worked as an Aunt Jemima look-alike in the late 1940s and early 1950s, traveling throughout the Midwest to give demonstrations about how to use the pancake mix, Norris was stunned. It may not sound like a bad thing to be an Aunt Jemima look-alike, but in the 1940s and 1950s, Aunt Jemima was drawn to look like a slave woman. The fact that Brown presented herself as a slave did not match the image of the woman Norris remembered from her childhood. When she found a newspaper article with a picture of her grandmother in slave clothes, she didn't know what to think.

Norris's mother never told anyone about this because she was ashamed about the racist presentation of Aunt Jemima. However, Norris was not immediately embarrassed for her grandmother. "I was fascinated because I thought, well wait a minute, she was traveling to small towns in the 1950s, when women didn't really travel at that time," she said. When she dug deeper into this aspect of her grandmother's past, she found that Brown used her tour as Aunt Jemima to give white people a different impression of black people. "She took a job that could so easily have been demeaning, but she did it with great dignity in her own way," Norris said. Brown would focus on the children at her presentations. If they became comfortable with black people, she hoped, they might avoid the racist attitudes of their parents. Norris said her grandmother served as a sort of cultural representative, giving white people a positive view of black people. She was proud to use Brown's story as a part of her memoir.

Norris's work changed the way she thought about her elders. Her research led her to question how well children know the people who raise them? She was unhappy to realize that she hadn't known the most life-changing moments of her father's and grandmother's lives. On top of that, family members who had known these facts kept them from her for most of her life. She understood their silence, though. "It's not because they're dishonest. It's because they want the best for us," she reasoned. "They don't want to weigh us down with their own frustrations." She doesn't look back in anger, but in wonder. She remembered her family's philosophy: "If you want your babies to soar, you don't put rocks in their pockets."

Reaction from the Public

Norris decided to call her book *The Grace of Silence,* which was published in 2010. She settled on the title after learning about her father's shooting. Her father and the other members of her family inspired her because "they set aside their personal grievances in order to help America become a better place, and that is an incredibly graceful act," she said. She hopes the book will help readers think about their own family's history and help them realize the importance of sharing what they have been through.

THE GRACE OF
SILENCE   A Family Memoir

*Michele
Norris*

CO-HOST OF NPR'S
ALL THINGS CONSIDERED

"An insightful, elegant rendering of how the
history of an American family illuminates
the history of our country." —Toni Morrison

Norris's family memoir The Grace of Silence *describes her own
life experiences as well as those of her elders.*

Critics pointed out that Norris used all of her journalistic skills to write *The Grace of Silence.* She interviewed and investigated her way to the truth, just as she has in her career as a journalist. However, because she was investigating her own family's past, there was a deeper appreciation for the type of work she was doing and its emotional toll. As Donna Seaman wrote in *Booklist,* "The result is an investigative family memoir of rare candor and artistry that dramatically reveals essential yet hidden aspects of African-American life…. Norris looks at both sides of every question while seeking truth's razor-edge. But she is also a remarkably warm, witty, and spellbinding storyteller, enriching her illuminating family chronicle with profound understanding of the protective 'grace of silence' and the powers unchained when, at last, all that has been unsaid is finally spoken."

———— **"** ————

"People talk about race one way in public and they often talk about it in a different way in private," Norris explained, "and I just want to pull back the curtain a little bit."

———— **"** ————

Many critics appreciated the way that Norris combined her personal story with events in U.S. history, as in this comment from Lisa Bonos in the *Washington Post.* "She blends the story of her childhood—and her quest to fill in its gaps—with a wider view of Southern race relations immediately following World War II, a period often overshadowed by history's focus on the Martin Luther King era of the 1960s," Bonos wrote. "'What's been more corrosive to the dialogue on race in America over the last half century or so,' Norris asks, 'things said or unsaid?' Her struggle to answer that question becomes a powerful plea to readers to doggedly pursue their families' story lines. She reminds us that speaking candidly about race in America starts not at the president's teleprompter but at our own dinner tables." That view was echoed by Sandy Banks in the *Los Angeles Times.* "Norris displays strong reporting skills and an eye for detail as she renders perfectly a familiar slice of middle-class Midwestern life for black families in the 1960s, when every household had a Bible, a World Book Encyclopedia, and two parents constantly admonishing us to dress well, speak properly, act right," Banks wrote. "Norris has a reporter's instinct for knowing when to get out of the way and let people talk—whether it's the retired white policeman wistfully touting the benefits of segregation or the elderly black woman angrily unpacking ugly memories of Birmingham. She paints a painfully intimate portrait of that city and that era, making clear the toll that official segregation took on 'aspirational Negroes.'"

Race Cards and Other Projects

After Norris published *The Grace of Silence,* she went on a promotional tour, giving readings and discussing the book in both small and large settings. At these events, she gave out postcards and asked people to write about race in just six words. She viewed the cards as a way to start a conversation on this difficult topic. To her surprise, she was overwhelmed with cards and emails. "All over the country people who came to hear about my story wound up telling me theirs," she said. "Despite all the talk about America's consternation or cowardice when it comes to talking about race, I seemed to have found auditorium after auditorium full of people who were more than willing to unburden themselves on this prickly topic."

Norris has commented on the cards and her decision to post many of them on her website. "They are thoughtful, funny, heartbreaking, brave, teeming with anger, and shimmering with hope. Some will make you smile. Others might make you squirm. And there are a few that might make you wonder why they deserve a place on my website's Race Card Wall. Here's the answer. If the intention is to use these cards to get a peek at America's honest views about race, then I must try to honor those people who offer up candor, even if what they share is unsavory or unacceptable in some people's eyes."

In 2011, Norris announced that she was taking a leave of absence from hosting "All Things Considered." Her husband, Broderick Johnson, took a position as a senior advisor in the campaign to re-elect President Barack Obama. Journalists are expected to be impartial and objective in their reporting, and it would be considered a conflict of interest for her to cover political stories related to the campaign while her husband was working for one of the candidates. Norris decided to temporarily leave her hosting duties at "All Things Considered," but she wasn't leaving NPR. She planned to continue to report and produce stories on a special projects basis.

MARRIAGE AND FAMILY

Norris lives in Washington, DC, with her husband, Broderick Johnson, and their two young daughters. Norris met Johnson at a political party in the early 1990s. She later interviewed him and invited him to a board-game party. During a round of the game Scattergories, Norris and Johnson found themselves giving all the same answers. "I looked at him and said, 'I'm marrying that man,'" she said. Norris married Johnson in 1993. She has two small children and an adult stepson, Broddy—Johnson's biological son—who lives in Washington, DC.

HOBBIES AND OTHER INTERESTS

In Norris's free time, she enjoys gardening, writing, and listening to jazz music. It isn't always easy for her to find time to balance her job and her family. Norris said juggling her career and home life can be "like juggling chainsaws ... while riding a skateboard ... during a tornado." Working at NPR has given her more time at home, since she doesn't have to travel as much. When she is home, her favorite thing to do is cook for her family.

WORKS

The Grace of Silence, 2010

HONORS AND AWARDS

Livingston Award for Young Journalists (Mollie Parnis Livingston Foundation): 1990, for coverage of a six-year-old living in a crack house
Emmy Award: 2001, for coverage of 9/11
Outstanding Achievement Award (University of Minnesota): 2006
Salute to Excellence Award (National Association of Black Journalists): 2006, for coverage of Hurricane Katrina
Outstanding Women in Marketing & Communications Award (Ebony Magazine): 2007
Alfred I. Dupont-Columbia University Award (Columbia University): 2008, for excellence in broadcasting (with Steve Inskeep)
Journalist of the Year (National Association of Black Journalists): 2009, for coverage of 2008 presidential campaign
25 Most Influential Black Americans (Essence Magazine): 2009
Power 150 List (Ebony Magazine): 2009

FURTHER READING

Periodicals

Bookmarks, Jan.-Feb. 2011, p.55
Current Biography Yearbook, 2008
Los Angeles Times, Sep. 28, 2010, p.D2
New York Times Book Review, Jan. 30, 2011, p.26
Washington Post, Oct. 6, 2010, p.C1

Online Articles

www.csmonitor.com
    (Christian Science Monitor, "NPR's Michele Norris on Her Family's Hidden History," Sep. 23, 2010)

www.journalismjobs.com
  (Journalism Jobs, Medill-Northwestern University, "Interview with
  Michele Norris," Apr. 2003)
www.npr.org
  (National Public Radio, "Michele Norris: Host, *All Things Considered*,"
  Dec. 2, 2009; "10 Questions: NPR's Michele Norris," 2009)
www.washingtonpost.com
  (Washington Post, "All Things Reconsidered: NPR's Michele Norris Tells
  Her Family's Complete Story," Oct. 6, 2010)

ADDRESS

Michele Norris
NPR
635 Massachusetts Avenue, NW
Washington, DC 20001

WEB SITES

www.michele-norris.com
www.npr.org/people

Francisco Núñez 1965-

American Conductor and Composer
Founder and Artistic Director of the Young People's
Chorus of New York City

BIRTH

Francisco J. Núñez was born in 1965 in New York, New York.
His parents, Emanuel Núñez and Ysmaela Marmolejos, were
both from the Dominican Republic but had emigrated to the
United States before he was born. Francisco is the younger of
their two sons.

YOUTH

Núñez was not very close to his father, who worked as an engineer. Emanuel Núñez wasn't too involved with the family, and he died when Francisco was 14 years old. Marmolejos essentially raised her children as a single parent. Although nobody in her family was formally trained or had made a profession in the arts, they were all very artistic by nature. "My mom always wanted to be a pianist and a ballerina herself," Núñez remembered. "But she had to work, so she left school in seventh grade and worked." In New York, Marmolejos was employed as a seamstress in the garment industry. Although she wasn't able to pursue her dreams of being a professional musician or dancer, she didn't give up her love of music. She bought a beat-up piano at a resale shop, brought it home, and began to teach her sons to play.

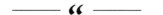

> *When he took part in music competitions, Núñez met kids from all different ethnic and economic backgrounds who shared a common interest in music. "Classical music has always represented an educated sphere, whether you are poor or rich," he said. "And it taught me that you have to work hard to achieve something."*

Núñez was only five years old at the time, but he took to the piano right away and would experiment with it for hours. His mother was delighted. They lived in the Washington Heights area of New York City, which had a high crime rate. "She was afraid of losing us to the streets," he explained. To give her sons something productive to do rather than just hanging out and getting into trouble, Marmolejos began giving them piano lessons and insisting that they put in long hours of practice. It soon became clear that Núñez had an incredible natural talent for music. When his mother had taught him everything she could about the piano, she found more experienced instructors for him. She and her sons frequently traveled back and forth from New York to the Dominican Republic, and in both places, Núñez had a piano and practiced six or seven hours daily. He focused particularly on works by Latin composers.

As his skill increased, Núñez also entered the world of music recitals and competitions. Those experiences changed his life forever. In New York, a huge variety of ethnic groups coexist, but people often remain within their own neighborhoods, sheltered from cultures other than their own, even when the people live nearby. When he took part in music competitions,

Núñez leading practice for a group of students.

Núñez met kids from all different ethnic and economic backgrounds who shared a common interest in music. "Classical music has always represented an educated sphere, whether you are poor or rich," he said. "And it taught me that you have to work hard to achieve something."

In addition to playing music, Núñez was also learning to compose it. At the age of 15 he composed his first serious choral work, entitled "Misa Pequeña." His hard work wasn't only confined to the world of music, though. Because the family didn't have much money, he got his first job at the age of 11, working on Saturdays at a doughnut shop "to make money and afford stuff other kids had," he remembered.

EDUCATION

Núñez attended public and Catholic schools in both the Dominican Republic and New York City. His mother had been such a strong supporter of his musical endeavors throughout his childhood, but when the time came for college, she strongly urged him to study engineering, which she considered a more practical career choice. Núñez did start out in the engineering program at Manhattan College, but he didn't stay there long. He transferred to New York University, where he earned a bachelor's degree in piano performance in 1988. He later earned a degree in music education from the University of Calgary.

EARLY CAREER

Bringing Music to the Children's Aid Society

According to Núñez, music has enriched his life and brought him into contact with people and situations he would never have encountered without it. After graduating from college, he wanted to do something for society that would help other children from poor economic backgrounds to benefit from music, as he had. "I wanted to take kids from neighborhoods where you couldn't play in the street, combine them with kids from other groups, and use music to instill a sense of discipline," he declared.

> *When auditioning children for the YPC, Núñez focused on finding the right attitude and strong parental support. "I'm looking for energy, enthusiasm, and I'm looking for a great parent who loves their child. Singing, we can teach anyone to sing," he explained. "We're not looking to create musicians. We're looking to create great people."*

With this goal in mind, Núñez took a job in 1988 with the Children's Aid Society, a charitable organization founded in 1853 to serve the needs of children in New York City, especially those from the poorest neighborhoods. Although he was basically hired as an afterschool counselor, he had ambitious plans from the start about using music to help the city's children. In 1990, he was given permission by the Society to organize a chorus that would bring together kids between the ages of 12 and 18 from diverse New York neighborhoods to learn and practice music.

There were rough spots to struggle through during the first years of the Children's Aid Chorus. Núñez had to work hard to recruit kids to commit to the program, and there wasn't much support from parents. The students who were involved had little or no knowledge of music, so they had to start with the most basic lessons. When looking for candidates for his program, though, Núñez was always much more concerned with their attitude and interest than in any musical knowledge or raw talent they might have.

Within a few years, the Children's Aid Chorus was achieving great success. The group worked hard, giving numerous performances around the city. By 1997 they had progressed to the point of traveling to Europe to take part in the Prague International Choir Festival and Competition. Just getting to the festival was a challenge, as the cost of the trip came to $1,700 for each child, an expense very few of their families could afford. The group needed to raise about $60,000 to make the trip a reality for the entire chorus. Undaunted, Núñez arranged a series of benefit concerts that successfully raised the needed funds. At the festival, they performed "Ave Maria," by Johannes Brahms, and Stephen Hatfield's "Nukapianguaq," a piece based on chants of the Inuit people. When they returned to New York, they brought home the competition's second-place silver trophy.

CAREER HIGHLIGHTS

Young People's Chorus of New York

When Núñez first started working as the director of music for the Children's Aid Society, he thought he would only do the job for a short while, then move on to some other sort of conducting work. Instead, he stayed in the position for nine years, inspired by his young students and their willingness to "work so hard and sing with such intensity."

Núñez left the Children's Aid Society to develop his dream of a citywide chorus for New York children. The program that had begun as the Children's Aid Chorus was transformed into the Young People's Chorus of New York, commonly known as the YPC. Money to run the program would come from tuition, private donations, and grants from foundations and corporations. Scholarships would be made available to any participant whose family could not afford the tuition. The main chorus would continue to be made up of children between the ages of 12 and 18, but junior choruses for younger children would also be formed. They would begin their first season by performing at some of the city's most famous landmarks, including St. Patrick's Cathedral and Rockefeller Center.

When Núñez had started the Children's Aid Chorus, he had to coax students to make a commitment to it. By the time he formed the YPC, he attracted so many hopeful kids to auditions that only about 1 in 10 could be chosen. A high level of musicianship was part of the overall goal, but when auditioning children, Núñez continued to focus more on finding the right attitude and strong parental support rather than any special talent. "I'm looking for energy, enthusiasm, and I'm looking for a great parent who loves their child. Singing, we can teach anyone to sing," he explained. "We're not looking to create musicians. We're looking to create great people."

Núñez hoped to do that by several means: using music as a vehicle to teach children to be disciplined and focused; helping them develop self-confidence and self-esteem through the mastery of difficult music; and

*Núñez conducting a YPC concert at St. Patrick's Cathedral
in New York City, 2010.*

providing opportunities to make new connections in the world. "Once
they are with us, they make better decisions; it impacts their schoolwork,
and it encourages them to seek out a diverse community," Núñez observed. He took his concern for his students to a very personal level, regularly asking them how things were going at home, if they were keeping up
with homework, or if they needed help or letters of recommendation as
they began applying for admission to colleges.

The YPC grew rapidly, with divisions added for younger children and satel-
lite programs started in several New York schools. As of 2011, there were
more than 1,100 children involved in the YPC program. The vision of music
as a means of cultural exchange is also reflected in the group's repertoire,
which includes music drawn from many traditions, eras, and styles. The
YPC maintains a busy schedule. The group gives regular performances at
Carnegie Hall and serves as the resident choir for the Frederick P. Rose
Hall at the Lincoln Center, as well as the Radio Choir for New York radio
station WNYC. They have traveled to Asia, South America, and Europe to
perform at festivals and competitions. They are considered one of the finest
youth choirs in the world.

The YPC has also served as a model for affiliated programs in Tenafly, New
Jersey, and Erie, Pennsylvania. Núñez has even reached out to bring his vi-

sion to the Dominican Republic, where he organized the National Children's Choir of Santa Domingo. As with the YPC, this choir seeks out children in the poorest neighborhoods. "If you go to the richest schools, you will get more money and be able to hire great people," he said, "But I want to bring the rich and poor together, as we did here. We already created one choir in a gang-run neighborhood, deep in the drug trade. I needed an armed escort. But I believe that music has the power to change society."

"Transient Glory"

In working with children, Núñez wanted both to change their lives and to change something about the world of choral music. Traditionally, the best contemporary composers have not written work intended for children's choruses. It was not seen as an area of serious music. Núñez set out to change that. Part of his plan was to use the YPC to demonstrate that a youth choir could indeed perform very complex, difficult music—and do it with technical excellence. He hoped the YPC would inspire composers to write works that were meant to utilize the unique sound of a youth choir. This would have the added benefit of increasing the selection of works available for youth choruses everywhere to perform.

Núñez called his ambitious project "Transient Glory." He explained the project like this: "transient because it's during a time of a child's voice when it's just before he becomes an adult, and glory because it's a glorious music." In 2001, his friend Ned Rorem, a composer, was hosting a concert of new music. Núñez persuaded Rorem to add the YPC to the concert lineup, and he also convinced four other respected composers to write pieces especially for the youth chorus. The YPC performed original works by Michael Torke, John Tavener, Elena Catch Turnen, and Nora Cora Rosenbaum. This was the beginning of a continuing series of Transient Glory concerts featuring new works by modern composers. "From there it just took off and we started doing concerts each year," Núñez remarked. "But what it did was, it put the children on the map of new music, real music. Even the *New York Times* started to critique it and that was what was unique."

In addition to commissioning new compositions from composers and performing them in concert, the Transient Glory project also involved creating recordings of this music and publishing it. The Transient Glory imprint was created at Boosey & Hawkes, the music publisher where Núñez is an editor. Works were commissioned yearly for concerts and recordings. David Del Tredici, Paquito D'Rivera, Dominick Argento, and Michael Nyman are just a few of the many respected composers who have contributed to the Transient Glory project. "What's unique about this," Núñez commented,

The first CD from the "Transient Glory" project.

"is that composers are studying this instrument [the children's choir] and taking advantage of what this instrument can do." Thanks to his efforts, the YPC has given performances of more than 60 new works in the Transient Glory series as of early 2012.

Núñez certainly had a part in inspiring composers with the warm, rich, expressive sound he has been able to create with the YPC. Reviewing the *Transient Glory* CD in the *American Record Guide,* Lindsay Koob wrote, "The singing of these gifted young folks (predominantly girls, as usual in America) simply blew me away! There are many competent and seasoned adult ensembles out there that would be hard-pressed to match this group's intonation, rhythmic precision, and enthusiastic confidence in these often very tricky pieces." A *New York Times* reviewer commenting on the recording *Transient Glory II* also praised the group: "These young singers are notable for the beauty of their youthfully pure voices and for their technical sophistication."

Awarded the MacArthur "Genius Grant"

In November 2011, Núñez was honored with a grant from the John D. and Catherine T. MacArthur Foundation. Individuals awarded MacArthur grants are given $500,000 over the course of five years to be used in any way they see fit to further their visions. Those selected for the award are typically people of such outstanding talent that it has earned the nickname the "Genius Grant." Upon learning that he was to be honored with a MacArthur grant, Núñez was naturally very pleased—with both the honor of winning the award and with the opportunities it would provide. "I feel that more than the money, the award itself, the title, is going to help me leverage being able to figure new things to do," he explained. "I feel like there is a spotlight that's been placed on the Young People's Chorus, on me, and the choruses all over the country, actually. And we have to do something for the society and to build communities. You know, using the child voice as a way of reaching out to each other."

Work with the YPC keeps Núñez very busy, but he makes it a point to find time to continue his involvement in other aspects of music. He composes music that is noted for its original arrangements and the frequent use of Latin rhythms and melodies. His works include classical pieces for solo instruments, large choruses, and orchestras. From 2003 to 2010, he served as the director of choral activities at New York University. He travels the country working as a guest conductor and a teacher for workshops held at universities and music societies. He works as an advisor and editor at the Boosey & Hawkes music publishing company. He also serves as the conductor for the University Glee Club of New York, a 120-person, elite men's choir that was originally formed in 1894 and has had only had five conductors since then. He has served as the music advisor to the General Consul of the Dominican Republic in New York, and in November 2011, he was given an award from the Dominican Republic for his work with the children of that country. Shortly after, he was also invited to the White

> *Funding for arts education is one of the first things to be eliminated when school budgets are cut, according to Núñez. "All the entertainment that we see is about singing and the arts," he said. "Yet, in schools, there is less and less of it being offered, especially to children of less social economic means. So how do we balance that?"*

Núñez and the YPC share their joy in music.

House in Washington, DC, where he was presented with a National Arts and Humanities Youth Program Award by First Lady Michelle Obama.

Núñez points out that funding for arts education is frequently one of the first things to be eliminated when schools are forced to cut their budgets. "It's unfortunate," he said. "All the entertainment that we see is about singing and the arts.... Yet, in schools, there is less and less of it being offered, especially to children of less social economic means. So how do we balance that?" He believes that it is vital to find ways to do so because music can be such an important catalyst in children's lives, especially for children from disadvantaged backgrounds. And that's equally true for the children in the YPC. "These children, when they hear the applause that [is] not from their parents, but from a general audience of music lovers, people who know music and the applause is so strong. They say, you know what, I've contributed to society and I feel fabulous about myself."

HOME AND FAMILY

In 1993, Núñez married Dianne P. Berkun, who was the director of music at the Brooklyn Friends School, as well as the founder and director of the Brooklyn Youth Chorus. She continues to direct the Brooklyn Youth Chorus and is also the director of one of YPC's junior choruses. She and Núñez have one child, a son named Sebastian, born in 2007. Their marriage has ended.

SELECTED COMPOSITIONS

"Misa Pequeña"
"What Grandpa Told the Children"
"Cantan"
"Canticle: In Remembrance"
"The Sun Says His Prayers"
"Three Dominican Folk Songs"
"Your Heart Goes with Me"

HONORS AND AWARDS

Young Virtuosos International Composition grant
Man of Achievement (*Hispanic* magazine): 2005
One of the 100 most influential Hispanics (*Hispanic Business* magazine): 2005
ASCAP Concert Music Award: 2009
Man of the Year (La Sociedad Coral Latinoamericana): 2009
Choral Excellence Award (New York Choral Society): 2009
Award from the Dominican Republic: 2011
National Arts and Humanities Youth Program Award: 2011
MacArthur Fellowship: 2011

FURTHER READINGS

Periodicals

American Record Guide, Mar. 1, 2004, p.248
Brooklyn Daily Eagle, Aug. 18, 2009
Choir & Organ, Nov.-Dec., 2003, p.38
Latina Magazine, July 2003
New York Times, Apr. 24, 2003; Dec. 13, 2009; Oct. 4, 2011; Jan. 3, 2012, p.E1

Online Articles

nieonline.com/cvaonline/blog
   (Classical Voice America Network, "The Kids Are All Right: Young People's Chorus of New York City at 92nd St. Y," May 9, 2011)
www.huffingtonpost.com
   (Huffington Post, "More Music Please," Feb. 7, 2012)

www.pbs.org/newshour/art/blog
   (PBS, Art Beat, "Conversation: Francisco Núñez, Choral Conductor for
   Kids," Sep. 23, 2011)
online.wsj.com
   (Wall Street Journal, "The Power to Foster Social Renewal through
   Song," Dec. 15, 2011)

ADDRESS

Francisco J. Núñez
Young People's Chorus of New York City
1995 Broadway, Suite 305
New York, NY 10023

WEB SITES

franciscojnunez.com
www.ypc.org/aboutypc/fnunez.html

Manny Pacquiao 1978-

Filipino Boxer and Political Leader
World Boxing Titleholder in Eight Different Weight
Classes
Member of the Filipino House of Representatives

BIRTH

Emmanuel "Manny" Dapidran Pacquiao (PAK-ee-ow) was
born on December 17, 1978, in the Republic of the Philippines. He was born in the town of Kibawe, which is located in
the province of Bukidnon on the island of Mindanao, one of
the largest islands in the Philippines. Altogether, the Philip-

pines consist of more than 7,000 islands clustered in the western Pacific Ocean off the coast of southwest Asia.

Manny's mother is Dionisia Dapidran, who supported her four children by farming, cleaning houses, doing other people's laundry, and selling peanuts and other foods as a street vendor. His father is Rosalio Pacquiao, who worked as a farm hand and manual laborer. He abandoned his wife and children when Manny was a small child.

YOUTH

Although Pacquiao was born in Kibawe, at age two his mother moved the family to an isolated mountain settlement called Tango. The village was located in a densely forested section of the Philippine province of Sarangani. "The jungle was the greenest of green and was populated with every multicolored bird you can imagine," he recalled in his memoir, *Pac-Man.* "I can still clearly recall how very difficult it was for my family to trudge up and down the rocky, dirt-covered road several times a week to get everything we needed to survive. While helping my mother, sister, and brothers lug the heavy buckets of water and the old burlap bags of rice and flour on the steep road, I loved to hear the songs these birds sang."

> *Pacquiao's family was very poor, which left him with little time to play or engage in other ordinary childhood pursuits. "I had no concept of toys, television, household appliances, or even a bed that most of us today would consider necessities," he said. "My toys were rocks and trees, and my bed was a blanket on a dirt floor."*

The Pacquiao family lived in a one-room thatch-covered hut. Each day Manny and his mother and siblings left their home in search of food and fresh water. He remembered that when he and his brothers and sisters were not at school or carrying supplies from town, "we were cooking, tending my mother's small garden, and doing any number of other chores assigned to us." Years later, he wrote that "I was about 10 years old before I fully appreciated ... how close we were to perishing in the harsh jungle environment."

The family's difficult everyday existence left Pacquiao with little time to play or engage in other ordinary childhood pursuits. "I had no concept of toys, television, household appliances, or even a bed that most of us today

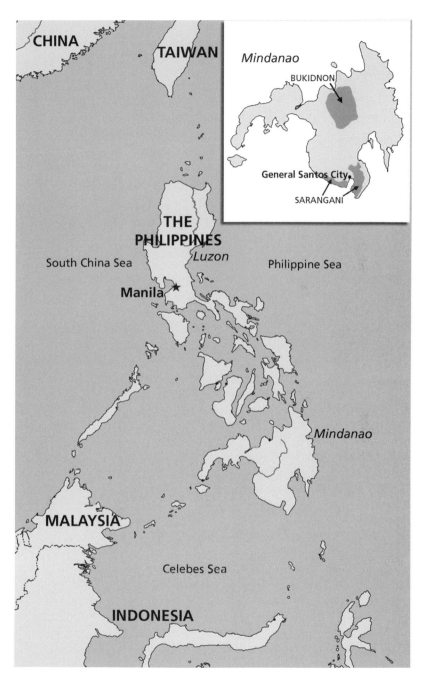

A map of the Philippines, showing portions of China, Taiwan, Malaysia, and Indonesia. The inset map shows the island of Mindanao; the provinces of Bukidnon and Sarangani; and General Santos City.

371

——— " ———

"I could go long stretches without eating, but it always pained me to see my mother, two brothers, and my sister with that vacant and hopeless look of hunger in their eyes," Pacquiao wrote.

——— " ———

would consider necessities," he said. "My toys were rocks and trees, and my bed was a blanket on a dirt floor."

When Pacquiao was 10 years old his mother decided that life on the mountain was just too hard on her children. She packed the family possessions into a few burlap bags and moved her children to General Santos City, a big port city in the south of Mindanao. They settled into one of the city's vast slum neighborhoods, and she found work as a housecleaner and laundress.

All the children pitched in as well, working at whatever odd jobs they could find to supplement their mother's hard-earned but meager earnings. Manny's main contribution came as a street vendor. He became skilled at buying donuts, peanuts, bread, and other food items from street sellers and small stores—then turning around and selling these items to customers at a small profit. "By the time I was 13, I was a one-man traveling grocery store," Pacquiao wrote. "Imagine this small, wiry, hungry boy carrying a box of warm donuts down those dusty, hot streets. The smell was irresistible, and I could easily have chosen to eat all five donuts.... But I knew if I ate them, I would be hungrier later, and so would my family."

Years later, Pacquiao described his daily refusal to give in to temptation and eat those donuts as a defining moment in his youth. "The discipline and willpower those donuts forced me to develop have served me well all my life," he explained. "Patience is a virtue, especially when you are in survival mode."

Starting to Box

Pacquiao's childhood and early adolescence were marked by a lot of scrapes with other kids in his rough and sometimes-violent neighborhood. He did not really think about pursuing a boxing career, though, until age 12, when he saw a televised heavyweight title fight between Mike Tyson and James "Buster" Douglas. Everyone thought Tyson would crush the lightly regarded Douglas, but instead the underdog shocked the world by knocking out Tyson in the 10th round.

The bout made a big impression on Pacquiao. "It was then that I learned that even champions could never count on their wins, that they have to earn them every single time," he wrote. "To this day, I still watch replays of that fight because it still amazes me."

Within a matter of weeks Pacquiao became a regular at the neighborhood boxing ring, which was located in a rundown park down the street. "I fought at this park for two years until I had beaten everyone, including the much bigger and heavier kids," he remembered. "As I trained and gained muscle, there was no one I could not beat."

On His Own in Manila

When Pacquiao was 14 years old he made a momentous choice. He decided to stow away on a ship that was bound for the national capital of Manila, about 500 miles away from General Santos City. Years later, he explained in his memoir that he slipped away to Manila because it would give his mother one less mouth to feed. "I could go long stretches without eating, but it always pained me to see my mother, two brothers, and my sister with that vacant and hopeless look of hunger in their eyes," he wrote.

Pacquiao struggled to survive on the streets of Manila. Some days he would go without food, and he spent many nights sleeping in alleyways or under bridges. As time passed, though, he managed to find work as a gardener, construction worker, restaurant dishwasher, and welder. Whenever he accumulated a little extra money he sent it back to his family.

EDUCATION

Pacquiao's family was so poor that he was forced to drop out of school at age 12. By leaving school he could devote more time to earning money for food and other basic necessities. The decision, though, brought a lot of feelings of regret. He liked his classes, and he enjoyed challenging himself with schoolwork. "[Pacquiao] never cheated during a quiz—he wouldn't try to look sideways, this way or that," recalled one of his elementary school teachers.

Long after Pacquiao became a successful and wealthy boxer, his skimpy educational background continued to bother him. He became so determined to address the issue that he began studying for a General Equivalency Diploma (GED) in the United States. In 2007 he passed his GED test, which is recognized as the equivalent of a regular high school diploma.

CAREER HIGHLIGHTS

Pacquiao continued his boxing training after his arrival in Manila. For a time he even slept at the gym where he trained. At age 16 he decided that he was ready to "turn pro"—become a paid professional boxer.

WEIGHT CLASSIFICATIONS

Professional boxers compete against one another in a series of categories based on weight classifications. The list below shows the maximum weight for each category.

light flyweight	108 pounds
flyweight	112 pounds
super flyweight	115 pounds
bantamweight	118 pounds
super bantamweight	122 pounds
featherweight	126 pounds
super featherweight	130 pounds
lightweight	135 pounds
super lightweight/ junior welterweight	140 pounds
welterweight	147 pounds
super welterweight	154 pounds
middleweight	160 pounds
super middleweight	168 pounds
light heavyweight	175 pounds
cruiserweight	200 pounds
heavyweight	unlimited

Pacquiao's first professional boxing match, on January 22, 1995, was televised on a popular Filipino boxing program called "Blow by Blow," which broadcast several bouts every week. He made his debut as a light flyweight, which is the lightest weight classification in boxing. The left-handed Pacquiao won his first match in a four-round decision. He only made two dollars for the fight—and for each of his next several appearances on "Blow by Blow"—but he still managed to send most of his earnings to his mother to help her provide for his siblings.

Earning His First Two Boxing Titles

Pacquiao won his first 11 bouts. Each time he stepped into the ring, he displayed sharp fighting skills and a sort of boyish enthusiasm that made him a favorite among Filipino boxing fans. Pacquiao lost his 12th match to Rustico Torrecampo in a third-round knockout, but the feisty boxer quickly recovered. He won his next 12 fights—10 by knockout (KO) or technical knockout (TKO), which is when the referee stops the bout because he feels one boxer is too badly injured to keep competing.

Pacquiao's winning streak earned him a title fight against Thailand's Catchai Sasakul, the World Boxing Council (WBC) flyweight champion. Professional boxing includes several different organizations that crown their own champions in the various weight classes. Boxers can hold more than one organizational title at a time, but it is not unusual for a single weight class to have multiple "champions" recognized by different organizations. On December 4, 1998, Pacquiao knocked out Sasakul in the eighth round to earn his first major boxing title.

Pacquiao held the title for nine months, successfully defending his crown in two bouts. But on September 17, 1999, he was knocked out in the third round of a fight against Thailand's Medgoen Singsurat. The loss was a big disappointment to Pacquiao—or Pac-Man, as he was coming to be known by boxing fans.

After losing to Singsurat, Pacquiao skipped the super flyweight and bantamweight divisions and moved all the way up to super bantamweight. Fighting at 122 pounds, Pacquiao won five bouts in a row. These dominating performances gave him an opportunity to win his second major title. In June 2001 organizers of a Las Vegas fight approached Pacquiao. The organizers were planning a fight featuring International Boxing Federation (IBF) super bantamweight champion Lehlo Ledwaba, and they asked Pacquiao if he would be willing to be a last-minute replacement for the scheduled challenger. Delighted at the chance to earn his second major title, Pacquiao quickly agreed, even though he had been told that Ledwaba "was so ferocious that his own managers were sometimes scared to deal with him."

Pacquiao immediately flew to Los Angeles for intensive pre-fight training. Within a day or two of his arrival he began training with Freddie Roach, who owned a fight gym in town. The two men connected immediately, and Roach has remained the boxer's chief trainer since that day.

On June 23, 2001—only two weeks after being offered the fight—Pacquiao scored a sixth-round knockout of Ledwaba. "After the first round, I don't think he knew what hit him," Pacquiao later wrote in his memoir. "I was in a zone and I would not be denied this victory. Part of my iron will was that I was prepared mentally for anything. My vow was just as strong. This was going to be my night."

Building a Better Boxer

Pacquiao defended his IBF super bantamweight title four times before moving up to the 126-pound featherweight division. In his first fight in

Pacquiao raises his arm in victory after defeating Lehlohonolo Ledwaba, June 2001.

that class, he knocked out Mexico's Marco Antonio Barrera on November 15, 2003, to become *The Ring* magazine's world featherweight champion.

Pacquiao's next major fight came in May 9, 2004, when he faced off against Juan Manuel Márquez, who held both the WBA (World Boxing Association) and IBF world featherweight titles at the time. Pacquiao managed to knock the champion to the canvas three times early in the fight, but Márquez came back strong in the later rounds. The fight ended up a draw. One judge scored the champ as the winner, another favored Pacquiao, and the third scored it a tie. The draw became a controversial decision that angered both boxers, each of whom believed that he deserved the win.

In early 2005 Pacquiao moved up yet another weight class in a bid to unseat super featherweight world champion Erik Morales. This March 19 match ended in defeat for Pacquiao, who lost a unanimous decision from the judges. The setback, though, just motivated Pacquiao and Roach to work even harder at developing the boxer's skills. Week after week, they labored to improve the boxer's already amazing hand speed, endurance, and boxing technique. During this time the two men paid particular attention to improving the punching power in Pacquiao's right hand.

> ——— " ———
>
> *"Pac-Man's style still features feverish punches and constant motion," Pablo S. Torre observed in* Sports Illustrated. *"The southpaw lets out a yell with every punch (Boom!) and combination (Boomboomboom!). If he takes a hard shot, he'll bang his gloves together, stick his arms into the air, and grin broadly."*
>
> ——— " ———

On September 10, 2005, Pacquiao knocked out Héctor Velázques in the sixth round to capture the WBC super featherweight crown. This marked the fourth weight class in which Pac-Man had risen to the top of his profession. Four months later, he stepped into the ring against Morales again. By this time Morales had lost his title to another boxer, but he remained a formidable opponent. Determined to avenge his 2005 loss to Morales, Pacquiao applied relentless pressure from the opening bell. He finally knocked Morales out in the 10th round—the first time that Morales had been KO'd in his boxing career.

Pacquiao successfully defended his super featherweight title four more times in 2006-2007, drawing big crowds each time. These triumphs included a unanimous decision over former bantamweight champ Oscar Larios (on July 2, 2006, in Quezon City, Philippines), another knockout of Morales (on November 18, 2006, in Las Vegas), and an easy unanimous decision in a rematch with Barrera (on October 6, 2007, in Las Vegas). These impressive performances resulted in a cascade of special honors from boxing organizations. In addition, growing numbers of boxing experts declared that the hard-hitting Filipino was the best "pound-for-pound" fighter in the world.

Claiming New Titles

On March 15, 2008, Pacquiao renewed his rivalry with Márquez, the fierce boxer who had fought him to a controversial draw back in 2004. This time around, Pac-Man won a narrow split decision in a bout held in Las Vegas. The victory enabled him to retain the WBC and *The Ring* world super featherweight titles.

The rematch with Márquez also provided vivid evidence of the boxer's amazing popularity in his native Philippines. The bout took place at a time when the Philippine army was engaged in a bitter conflict with rebels who wanted to overthrow the government. As the hour approached for the nationally televised Pacquiao-Márquez fight, the army declared a seven-hour cease-fire so that all the troops could watch the bout. Four months after Pacquiao's victory, meanwhile, Filipinos applauded when they learned that the boxer had been selected to be the flag bearer for the Philippines at the 2008 Summer Olympics.

Pacquiao moved up yet another weight class on June 28, 2008, when he stepped into a Las Vegas ring to fight David Diaz, the WBC world lightweight champion. Some observers wondered whether Pac-Man could possibly be as effective a boxer at the heavier weight, but he quickly proved his doubters wrong. He dominated the fight, swarming Diaz with relentless attacks to claim the WBC lightweight belt. The fight ended in the ninth round, when the referee awarded Pacquiao a TKO. Afterwards, Diaz admitted that he had been overwhelmed. "I could deal with the power but not his speed," Diaz said. "His speed was uncontrollable."

On December 6, 2008, Pacquiao moved up a weight class once again to face famed U.S. welterweight Oscar De La Hoya, an Olympic gold medal winner who at one time or another had held titles in six different divisions. De La Hoya was known as one of the all-time greats, but as the match progressed it became clear that it was Pac-Man's night. He defeated De La Hoya with an eighth-round TKO. "We knew we had him after the first round," said Roach. Promoters of the Pacquiao-De La Hoya bout announced that the fight—which was the final fight in De La Hoya's tremendous career—had generated roughly $70 million in pay-per-view television revenue.

Pacquiao won a championship in a sixth weight class on May 2, 2009, when he took *The Ring*'s junior welterweight title from England's Ricky Hatton. He earned this victory with a devastating second-round knockout of Hatton in Las Vegas. Later that year, on November 14, 2009, he added

Pacquiao connects with a right to the head of Oscar De La Hoya during their bout in December 2008.

another championship belt—in a record seventh weight class—when he registered a 12th-round TKO of Puerto Rican fighter Miguel Cotto to claim the WBO welterweight title.

Staying at the Top

After his loss to Pacquiao, Cotto told reporters that "Manny is one of the best boxers we have of all time." Many other people in the boxing world agreed. They pointed out that he had never failed a drug test for performance-enhancing drugs. Observers also noted that even after almost 15 years of professional boxing, he remained at the top of his game. "Pac-Man's style still features feverish punches and constant motion," Pablo S. Torre observed in *Sports Illustrated.* "The southpaw lets out a yell with every punch (Boom!) and combination (Boomboomboom!). If he takes a hard shot, he'll bang his gloves together, stick his arms into the air, and grin broadly."

Pacquiao continued his winning ways in 2010. On March 13, 2010, he defeated welterweight Joshua Clottey in a fight held before 50,000 fans at Texas Stadium in Dallas. Eight months later, on November 13, 2010, he

Pacquiao battles Antonio Margarito, November 2010.

faced Antonio Margarito for the vacant WBC world super welterweight title. Pacquiao beat Margarito so badly that the fighter was forced to spend time in the hospital for a fractured eye socket. The Margarito fight actually upset Pacquiao, who took it easy on his opponent in the later rounds because he was concerned about his health. "Instead of knocking out the guy, he asks him, 'Are you OK?'" recalled Roach. "I told him he should have knocked him out. He said, 'It's a sport, and I didn't have to hurt him; I beat him up enough.' What can you say to that?"

The victory over Margarito made Pacquiao the first boxer in history to win eight world titles in eight different boxing weight classes. Pacquiao did not keep the WBC super welterweight crown for long, though. After he decided to return to welterweight fighting, the WBC decided to leave the title open.

On May 7, 2011, Pac-Man easily defended his WBO welterweight belt against American challenger Shane Mosley, winning by unanimous decision. "He has exceptional power, power I have never been hit with before," said Mosley. But six months later, on November 12, 2011, Pacquiao barely beat his old foe Márquez in a controversial split decision. Many people who watched the fight asserted that Márquez had actually deserved the win.

After the fight, Pacquiao experienced a renewal of his religious faith. He had been going through a difficult period. He and his wife, Jinkee, had been fighting a lot, and right before his fight against Márquez she was ready to file for divorce. He had been drinking, cheating on his wife, and gambling. Pacquiao decided to give up his vices: he stopped drinking and womanizing, and he sold the casino he owned in Manila and a large cock-fighting operation. He also began attending daily Bible study sessions with Jinkee and others. He has since credited this new devotion to his faith with saving his marriage and making him a better fighter.

Pacquiao's next fight took place in June 2012, and the result was as controversial as that of his recent fight against Márquez. Pacquiao lost the WBO welterweight title to Timothy Bradley in a controversial split decision. The decision stunned and angered much of the audience at the fight and was immediately criticized by many media representatives, who had scored the fight in favor of Pacquiao. Then the WBO Championship Committee announced that a panel of independent professional judges would watch the video and score the event. After reviewing the video, the panel announced that they unanimously agreed that Pacquiao should have won the match. The WBO does not have the power to overturn the original decision, however, and the original decision stands. "After everything he's done for boxing, Manny Pacquiao is the last person who should have been cheated like this," Bryan Armen Graham wrote in *Sports Illustrated.* "He deserved better. When a shortage of marketable stars threatened the sport's popularity in the late aughts, the effortlessly charismatic Pacquiao emerged as the sport's biggest international star. Propelled by a quasi-messianic desire to stamp out poverty in his native Philippines ... Pacquiao became the most socially important boxer since Muhammad Ali. There won't be another one like him anytime soon."

Pacquiao's plans for future fights are uncertain at this time. He has the right to a rematch against Bradley in November, but there has also been talk of a fight against Juan Manuel Márquez, Miguel Cotto, or Floyd Mayweather.

Pacquiao has acknowledged that his days as a professional boxer are probably drawing to a close. After all, the bout against Bradley was his 60th professional match, with 54 victories (he has four losses and two draws in his other six bouts). Many of the millions of people who count themselves as Pac-Man fans recognize that the day is coming when their hero will finally hang up his gloves. They hope, however, to still be treated to another epic Pac-Man bout or two before he steps away from the ring.

A Legend in the Philippines

Pacquiao has fans all around the world, but he remains most popular in his native land. "In the Philippines," a Filipino journalist told National Public Radio, "I would say Pacquiao is like Elvis meets Justin Bieber meets Michael Jordan meets Bill Clinton." Signs of Pacquiao's stardom in the Philippines are everywhere. Posters and photos of the boxer can be found in many homes, and the Philippine government honored him by putting his image on a postage stamp. In October 2011 the Philippine military even promoted him to the position of lieutenant colonel in the Philippine Army Reserves. "Manny is our people's idol and this generation's shining light," declared Philippine President Gloria Macapagal-Arroyo in 2008. "He is our David against Goliath, our hero and the bearer of the Filipino dream.... You can feel the excitement throughout the country every time he is in the ring."

Pacquiao's tremendous popularity among his fellow Filipinos is due in large part to his boxing accomplishments, of course. His generous and playful personality is also a major factor, though. Pac-Man takes pride in being a role model for his young fans. "I never believed that you had to say bad things about your opponent to make yourself bigger," he told *USA Today*. "You can be popular, or be a champion, without trash-talking."

Pacquiao also is renowned for using his wealth to help poor individuals and communities in the Philippines. "He knows he came from nothing," explained one of his countrymen. "He knows what it is like to be poor, to beg for food and money. In the Philippines, you cannot afford to forget your roots."

In the Political Arena

Whenever Pacquiao retires from boxing, it appears that he will remain in the public eye. In early 2007 he began a second career in Filipino politics by announcing his intention to run for a seat in the Filipino House of Representatives. He actually lost his first election campaign, though. In May 2007 he was defeated by incumbent Darlene Antonino-Custodio, a wealthy and politically connected congresswoman who managed to turn her opponent's personal popularity against him. She convinced voters that Pacquiao's inspiring story might be stained if he was to get involved in the often messy business of politics.

The election-day loss surprised Pacquiao, but it did not stop him from trying again. In 2009 he formed a strong political organization to help his cause,

Pacquiao with his wife, Jinkee (left), takes his oath as Congressman of the district of Sarangani on June 28, 2010.

and on May 10, 2010, he won election to represent the district of Sarangani in Congress. "I want to help people, especially in my province," he said. "There are a lot of poor people. When I'm old, I want my name, Manny Pacquiao, to be known not only as a good boxer but a good public servant."

MARRIAGE AND FAMILY

Pacquiao and his wife, Jinkee, have four children. They divide their time between big estates in General Santos City and Los Angeles.

HOBBIES AND OTHER INTERESTS

Pacquiao engages in a wide assortment of activities and hobbies. In addition to his work as a boxer and politician, he has become a major media star on Filipino television. He hosts a game show called "Manny Prizes" and even starred for a time on a sitcom called "Show Me da Manny."

Pacquiao is also famous for his love of karaoke and singing. "When I listen to music, all the stress is gone," he explained. "I feel stronger." He has recorded several hit songs in the Philippines, and in April 2011 he and songwriter Dan Hill teamed up to record a new version of Hill's 1977 hit song "Sometimes When We Touch." "The singing thing with Manny is so tender," Hill said. "This guy, such a powerful man in the ring, is unafraid to sing an emotional, sentimental song like 'Sometimes.'"

HONORS AND AWARDS

WBC (World Boxing Council) World Flyweight Champion: 1998
IBF (International Boxing Federation) World Super Bantamweight Champion: 2001
The Ring World Featherweight Champion: 2003
The Ring World Super Featherweight Champion: 2005
WBC (World Boxing Council) World Super Featherweight Champion: 2005
Fighter of the Year (Boxing Writers Association of America): 2006, 2008, 2009
Fighter of the Year (*The Ring*): 2006, 2008, 2009
Boxer of the Year (*Sports Illustrated*): 2008, 2009
Boxer of the Year (World Boxing Council): 2008, 2009
WBC (World Boxing Council) World Lightweight Champion: 2008
100 Most Influential People (*Time* Magazine): 2009
The Ring World Super Lightweight Champion: 2009
World Boxing Organization (WBO) World Welterweight Champion: 2009
ESPY Fighter of the Year (ESPN): 2009, 2011
Athlete of the Decade, 2000-2009 (Philippine Sportswriters Association): 2010
Fighter of the Decade, 2000-2009 (Boxing Writers Association of America): 2010
Fighter of the Decade, 2000-2009 (HBO): 2010
WBC (World Boxing Council) World Super Welterweight Champion: 2010

FURTHER READING

Book

Pacquiao, Manny, with Timothy James. *Pacman: My Story of Hope, Resilience, and Never-Say-Never Determination,* 2010

Periodicals

GQ, Apr. 2010
Los Angeles Times, Oct. 24, 2011; Nov. 12, 2011
Maclean's, May 23, 2011
New York Times, Sep. 18, 2010; Nov. 15, 2010; May 2, 2011; May 9, 2011
Sports Illustrated, Dec. 8, 2008, p.110; Nov. 22, 2010, p.26; May 16, 2011, p.31

Time, Nov. 16, 2009, p.44
USA Today, Nov. 12, 2010; Nov. 15, 2010; May 5, 2011; May 9, 2011

Online Articles

espn.go.com
  (ESPN, "All Hail the New King," June 29, 2008; "Manny Pacquiao," Sep. 7, 2011; "Pacquiao Follows New, Spiritual Path," June 10, 2012; "Timothy Bradley Wins Split Decision," June 10, 2012)
www.npr.org
  (National Public Radio-NPR—All Things Considered, "Manny Pacquiao: Boxer Who Packs a Political Punch," Feb. 16, 2011)
www.npr.org
  (National Public Radio-NPR—Morning Edition, "Pacman: Last of the Great Boxers?" May 11, 2011)
www.sportsillustrated.cnn.com
  (Sports Illustrated, "Pacquiao Deserved Better than Unjust Ending against Bradley," June 10, 2012)
www.usatoday.com
  (USA Today, "Religious Awakening Helps Pacquiao Regain Control of Life," June 6, 2012)

ADDRESS

Manny Pacquiao
House of Representatives
Quezon City, Philippines
Rm. SWA-403, local 7952, 4424064

WEB SITES

www.mannypacquiao.com
www.mp8.ph

AnnaSophia Robb 1993-

American Actress
Star of the Hit Movies *Because of Winn-Dixie, Bridge to Terabithia, Charlie and the Chocolate Factory, Race to Witch Mountain,* and *Soul Surfer*

BIRTH

AnnaSophia Robb was born on December 8, 1993, in Denver, Colorado. She is the only child of Dave and Janet Robb.

YOUTH

Growing up in Denver, Robb liked gymnastics. She also liked making up stories and creating different characters to act out.

> *Robb's first acting job, in a commercial for McDonald's Happy Meals, was not the most glamorous role, but she was overjoyed at the chance to act on TV. "We ate cold french fries and old Chicken McNuggets for a really long time," she remembered. "But I thought it was just the best job ever."*

Robb decided when she was about three years old that she wanted to become an actor. "I saw kids on TV, and I really wanted to act. And I loved performing in front of people," Robb explained. Because she was so young, her parents did not take her acting ambition seriously. "At first my mom was like, 'Yeah, whatever, every little girl wants to be in the movies.'"

Robb was persistent and never wavered from her dream of becoming an actor. She was so focused on achieving her goal that she eventually convinced her parents to let her try acting. "I just love to perform. That's all I can ever remember wanting to do," she recalled. "When I was about eight, I begged my mom for an agent because that's how I heard actors got started." Her mother finally agreed. Robb got an agent and enrolled in a workshop to learn basic acting skills. After she completed the workshop, she met a producer who invited her to come to Los Angeles and try out for roles.

Robb's first trip to Los Angeles included more than 40 auditions and led to her first real acting job in a television commercial for McDonald's Happy Meals. Robb recalled that while it was not the most glamorous role, she was overjoyed at the chance to act on TV. "We ate cold french fries and old Chicken McNuggets for a really long time," she remembered. "But I thought it was just the best job ever."

EDUCATION

At first, Robb was homeschooled to accommodate her schedule of acting and going to auditions. She later enrolled in public school in Denver. Although she was often away from home while working on movies, Robb enjoyed attending public school. "I think it's important, because I want to have a regular life. It helps keep everything in perspective," she commented. "It's nice. I'm removed from the L.A. scene."

Robb's favorite subjects were current events and history. She was a member of her school's French club and the cross-country team. She studied with a tutor when she was away from home, but still stayed in touch with her regular teachers in Denver. She got assignments and turned in homework by e-mail. Juggling schoolwork, acting, and other obligations was sometimes a challenge for Robb. "I have to have structure in my day. I need to focus on one thing or the other. I'm actually pretty bad at multi-tasking," she admitted. "Going to school, trying to do homework, trying to read a script and do interviews on the phone and all that. It's hard to balance but it's worth it."

CAREER HIGHLIGHTS

After various television commercials and smaller parts, Robb landed the title role in the 2004 television movie *Samantha: An American Girl Holiday.* She played Samantha, a character based on the popular line of American Girl dolls and books. The story takes place around the beginning of the 20th century, when nine-year-old Samantha is sent to live with relatives after the death of her parents. In her new home, she struggles with her grandmother's expectations of proper behavior and the radically different attitudes of her aunt. As she makes new friends and tries to fit in with her new family, Samantha learns about life and faces challenges she never imagined possible. For her performance as Samantha, Robb was nominated for a 2005 Young Artist Award for Best Performance in a TV Movie, Miniseries or Special—Leading Young Actress.

Because of Winn-Dixie

Robb's breakout role was in the 2005 film *Because of Winn-Dixie,* based on the Newbery Award-winning book published in 2000 by Kate DiCamillo. In this movie, Robb stars as Opal, a lonely young girl who moves to a small town with her father (played by Jeff Daniels). Her mother abandoned the family when Opal was very young, and her father refuses to talk about it. Seven years have passed since her mother left, and both Opal and her father still struggle with the loss. One day, while exploring her new town, she finds a stray dog at the supermarket. She takes him home and names him Winn-Dixie, after the store where she found him. Winn-Dixie seems to have a special influence on people, and soon Opal's father begins to tell her about her mother and the reasons why she left. As she learns about life, love, and loss, Opal realizes that she has found a new family among various townspeople, including a pet store clerk, the town librarian, and an eccentric old woman who everyone feared was a witch.

Robb remembers when she got the phone call telling her she had the part. "I started screaming! I was jumping up and screaming and running around. I was so excited because I had only been acting for about a year, and I had gotten my first big film. So I was really excited." *Because of Winn-*

Scenes from Robb's early movies:
Because of Winn-Dixie *(top)*, Samantha:
An American Girl Holiday *(middle)*,
and Charlie and the Chocolate Factory
(bottom).

Dixie pleased both moviegoers and film critics. According to Claudia Puig, a movie reviewer for *USA Today*, "What seemed to be a simple story of a girl and her dog becomes a much deeper tale about loss and companionship. But the movie doesn't moralize or dwell too long in serious emotional terrain....*Winn-Dixie* is a welcome relief: a whimsical family film about longing and belonging told with gentle humanity." Robb received a 2006 Young Artist Award nomination for Best Performance in a Feature Film (Comedy or Drama)—Leading Young Actress.

Charlie and the Chocolate Factory

In 2005, Robb appeared as Violet Beauregarde in the movie *Charlie and the Chocolate Factory*. The story is based on the 1964 book by Roald Dahl. Robb plays one of five children who win the once-in-a-lifetime opportunity to tour the mysterious and famous candy factory owned by Willy Wonka (played by Johnny Depp). At the end of the tour, one of the lucky children will be chosen to receive a special prize. Robb's character, the gum-chewing Violet, is extremely competitive, strong willed, and determined to claim the prize. But as the tour progresses, the children learn that the factory is not exactly what it appears to be, and there are surprises in store for each of them. By the end of the story, Violet and the other children learn important lessons about life and the dangers of always getting what you want.

Charlie and the Chocolate Factory was a hit with moviegoers around the world. The movie's success gave a boost to Robb's career and helped her land starring roles in her next two movies.

Bridge to Terabithia

Robb's next major role was in the 2007 movie *Bridge to Terabithia*, based on the Newbery Award-winning book published in 1977 by Katherine Paterson. In this movie, Robb plays Leslie Burke, a smart, creative, imaginative tomboy who becomes best friends with fellow loner Jess Aarons (played by Josh Hutcherson) after defeating him in a race at school. Leslie and Jess create an imaginary forest kingdom called Terabithia, which is accessible only by swinging across a creek on a rope that hangs from a tree. Jess and Leslie spend most of their free time together in Terabithia, making up stories and pretending to fight monsters. Leslie helps Jess learn about courage, strength, and true friendship. These qualities prove invaluable to Jess when he must come to terms with a terrible tragedy that he feels responsible for causing.

The movie was well regarded by movie critics and viewers. "[*Bridge to Terabithia* is] a thoughtful and extremely affecting story of a transformative

Robb and Josh Hutcherson in a scene from Bridge to Terabithia.

friendship between two unusually gifted children," wrote *New York Times* movie reviewer Jeannette Catsoulis. "Consistently smart and delicate as a spider web, *Bridge to Terabithia* is the kind of children's movie rarely seen nowadays." For her performance in *Bridge to Terabithia,* Robb was nominated for the 2008 Broadcast Film Critics Association Critics Choice Award for Best Young Actress. She won two Young Artist Awards in 2008, for Best Performance in a Feature Film—Leading Young Actress, and Best Performance in a Feature Film—Young Ensemble Cast, which she shared with her co-stars. *Bridge to Terabithia* also provided Robb with the chance to explore singing, as she recorded the song "Keep Your Mind Wide Open" for the movie's soundtrack.

Race to Witch Mountain

In 2009, Robb starred as Sara in the Disney movie *Race to Witch Mountain,* a follow up to the movies *Escape to Witch Mountain* (1975) and *Return from Witch Mountain* (1978). Sara and her brother Seth (played by Alexander Ludwig) are two otherworldly teens with paranormal powers. They are on the run from evil government agents, assassins, and scientists. They enlist the help of reluctant but heroic taxi driver Jack Bruno (played by Dwayne

Johnson, also known as The Rock), who doesn't believe in the supernatural. As the unlikely trio set off on a high-speed race to save the world, Bruno learns the truth about Sara and Seth and is forced to change his beliefs about what is real.

Race to Witch Mountain was a hit with moviegoers, although the film received mixed reviews from critics. Joe Leydon, a movie reviewer for *Variety*, noted that the film "strikes a deft balance of chase-movie suspense and wisecracking humor, with a few slam-bang action set-pieces that would shame the makers of more allegedly grown-up genre fare." Writing in the *New York Times*, reviewer A.O. Scott called *Race to Witch Mountain* "modest and diverting, rough and bland, with some good actors and so-so special effects."

Soul Surfer

Robb went on to star as Bethany Hamilton in the 2011 movie *Soul Surfer*. This film, based on Hamilton's 2004 book *Soul Surfer: A True Story of Faith, Family and Fighting to Get Back on the Board,* tells the true story of her recovery from a terrible shark attack when she was 13 years old. The story begins with the attack and its immediate aftermath, in which Hamilton lost her arm along with 60 percent of her body's blood supply. Though she was not expected to survive the massive blood loss, the story unfolds as Hamilton works to recover and adapt to living with one arm. She eventually begins surfing again, overcoming a host of challenges along the way. In her triumphant return to competitive surfing, Hamilton faces off against her arch rival in a national tournament. (For more information on Hamilton, see *Biography Today*, April 2005.)

The role proved to be a challenging and life-changing experience for Robb, who became close friends with Hamilton while making the movie. To prepare for the role, Hamilton taught Robb how to surf. "It's a really rigorous sport, but once you do it, you're kind of hooked. I've fallen in love with the ocean," she explained. She also said that she learned much more than surfing from Hamilton. "I've learned so much from her, which I'll keep with me for the rest of my life," Robb said. "It's an amazing story of the human spirit and how we can live our dream through any hardship. Bethany never felt bad for herself. She does more with one arm than I can do with two."

The movie received mixed reviews from critics. *Variety* movie reviewer Rob Nelson praised *Soul Surfer* as "a kind-hearted coming-of-age drama with killer waves." *Christianity Today* movie reviewer Carolyn Arends called Robb "strong in the central role, capturing both Bethany's resiliency and her vulnerability with natural charisma." Owen Gleiberman's comments

Robb starred as real-life surfing champ Bethany Hamilton in Soul Surfer.

in *Entertainment Weekly* were a bit more mixed. "*Soul Surfer*, while formulaic in design, is an authentic and heartfelt movie. At first, you think you're watching *Jaws* remade as a Miley Cyrus drama," he wrote. "But as Bethany recovers from her cataclysmic wound, AnnaSophia Robb's performance comes to life. She gives Bethany's belief in God a concrete depth and understanding. When Bethany gets up on that surfboard again, refusing to wear a prosthetic limb, her pluckiness hits home because we see that she's out to impress no one in the world but herself." For her portrayal of Hamilton in *Soul Surfer*, Robb was nominated for a 2011 Teen Choice Award.

Looking to the Future

Following the successes of her recent films, Robb plans to continue making movies that connect with audiences. "Probably one of the hardest parts, but most satisfying too, is just trying to find and create a character that's real and then just put on that character's clothes and really get into the mindset," she explained. "I try to get into the mind of my character. I have to feel what they feel, so the character is real. Good acting isn't really acting, it's 'being.'" Robb's approach to acting is based on her desire to tell stories that are meaningful, rather than purely entertaining. "Anything that's really worthy of doing and is a good script and has good people and a good director, and can help people or teach someone a lesson, I think is worth doing."

HOME AND FAMILY

Robb lives with her parents in Denver, Colorado.

HOBBIES AND OTHER INTERESTS

In her free time, Robb enjoys many different sports, including swimming, running, surfing, snowboarding, and kickboxing. She also enjoys hanging out with her friends, listening to music, and going to the movies. Robb is also committed to humanitarian work in human rights, animal rights, and environmental conservation. She works with the Dalit Freedom Network, and has traveled to India on behalf of the organization. Whenever she can, Robb tries to encourage young people to become actively involved in changing the world. She said, "Show people that you care about them because we really need to start welcoming everybody around us not just our friends and family. We need to start opening up to the world and become one community."

SELECTED CREDITS

Samantha: An American Girl Holiday, 2004
Because of Winn-Dixie, 2005

Charlie and the Chocolate Factory, 2005
Bridge to Terabithia, 2007
Race to Witch Mountain, 2009
Soul Surfer, 2011

HONORS AND AWARDS

Young Artist Award: 2008 (two awards), Best Performance in a Feature Film—Leading Young Actress, and Best Performance in a Feature Film—Young Ensemble Cast, shared with cast, both for *Bridge to Terabithia*

FURTHER READING

Periodicals

Current Events, Feb. 12, 2007, p.6; Mar. 28, 2011, p.6
Foam, Apr. 2011, p.33
Girls' Life, Apr./May 2009, p.48
Nylon, May 2009
Portrait, Jan. 2007
TC Magazine, Winter 2008, p.24
Teen Vogue, Apr. 2007, p.143; May 2011, p.87

Online Articles

news.christiansunite.com
(Christians Unite, "An Interview with AnnaSophia Robb, 11-Year-Old Star of Because of *Winn-Dixie,*" Feb. 21, 2005)
www.kidzworld.com
(Kidz World, "AnnaSophia Robb Bio—Get the Look," no date)
www.lateenfestival.com
(LA Teen Festival, "AnnaSophia Robb: A Young Star on the Move," Issue 10)
www.radiofree.com/profiles
(Radio Free, "AnnaSophia Robb," Feb. 5, 2007)

ADDRESS

AnnaSophia Robb
Untitled Entertainment
350 South Beverly Drive
Suite 200
Beverly Hills, CA 90212

WEB SITE

www.annasophiarobb.com

Jaden Smith 1998-

American Actor
Star of the Hit Movie *The Karate Kid*

EARLY YEARS

Jaden Christopher Syre Smith was born on July 8, 1998, in Los Angeles, California. His father, Will Smith, is an actor, producer, and rapper. His mother, Jada Pinkett Smith, is an actor and singer. Smith has a younger sister, Willow, and an older half-brother, Trey, from his father's first marriage.

Smith made his acting debut when he was five years old. He appeared as Reggie in six episodes of the television comedy

"All of Us," which aired on the CW network from 2003 to 2007. Smith was homeschooled by his mother until 2009, when he began attending classes at the New Village Leadership Academy in Calabasas, California. He enjoys playing video games, listening to rap music, writing rap lyrics, and hanging out with his friends. "I go to the movies a lot, you know? I love vampire movies. I like kung-fu movies too. I love horror movies and comedies too. *Twilight*, all those, I love those movies."

MAJOR ACCOMPLISHMENTS

The Pursuit of Happyness

Smith landed his first movie role when he was just seven years old in the drama *The Pursuit of Happyness*, based on a real-life story. Smith played Christopher, the five-year-old son of Chris Gardner, the film's main character (played by his father, Will Smith). *The Pursuit of Happyness* tells the story of how Gardner became a self-made millionaire after working his way out of poverty. When his wife leaves him and their young son, he struggles to make ends meet but soon finds himself unemployed and with no place to live. He and his son survive on the streets of 1980s San Francisco by sleeping in shelters or bus stations, bathing in public restrooms, and finding refuge wherever they can. With few job prospects, Gardner decides to take an unpaid internship at a prestigious stock brokerage firm. Though there is no salary, he hopes the position will lead to a paying job that could provide a secure future for himself and his son. The story focuses on one pivotal year in the lives of Gardner and his son as they endure the hardships of being homeless while working towards a better life.

Smith became interested in the role of Christopher after his father had been cast as Gardner. In talking to his father about the movie, Jaden asked if he might be able to play the part. His father said, "You don't just get the job because you're my kid. You'll have to audition like everyone else, and you may not get it, that's how it works." Jaden went to the audition with his mother, where he learned that he would be competing for the role against 100 other young actors. The film's director liked Smith, and he got the part.

> "I go to the movies a lot, you know? I love vampire movies. I like kung-fu movies too. I love horror movies and comedies too. *Twilight*, all those, I love those movies."

The Pursuit of Happyness was a major hit when it was released in 2006. The

Smith in a scene from The Pursuit of Happyness
with his father and co-star, Will Smith.

movie was the top box office moneymaker during its opening weekend and received glowing reviews from movie critics. Reviewers were particularly impressed with Jaden Smith's performance. The role was challenging for an actor as young as Smith was at the time, and the story was difficult and emotional as father and son struggled with life on the streets. A *USA*

399

Today movie reviewer praised Jaden's ability to show the complexity of the character. "He plays this resilient boy in a way that indicates an innate intelligence. He seems to sense how down-and-out they are; you can read his fear, and even his occasional anger. He's not a sunny Pollyanna of a child, but he's not a cynic, either. It's as if he realizes that the only way to survive is to keep his head down and persevere."

Smith's portrayal of Christopher earned a 2007 MTV Movie Award for Breakthrough Performance and a 2007 Teen Choice Award for Choice Movie: Chemistry, which he shared with his father. That same year, Smith was also nominated for a Teen Choice Award for Choice Movie: Breakout Male, an NAACP Image Award for Outstanding Supporting Actor in a Motion Picture, and a Black Reel award for Best Breakthrough Performance.

Appearing alongside his father in *The Pursuit of Happyness* convinced Jaden that he wanted to pursue a career as an actor. "After I did that movie, I was like 'yeah, wow, this is something that I might like to do.'" Smith went on to play the role of eight-year-old Jacob in the 2008 remake of *The Day the Earth Stood Still*. In this science fiction drama, an alien space traveler named Klaatu and a robot named Gort arrive on Earth and threaten to destroy the human race. With all life on Earth at stake, Jacob and his stepmother must convince Klaatu that humans deserve to survive. For his performance as Jacob, Smith won a 2009 Saturn Award for Best Performance by a Younger Actor from the Academy of Science Fiction, Fantasy and Horror Films.

In 2009, Jaden and his sister Willow became youth ambassadors for Project Zambi, a charitable program that works to raise awareness of the millions of children who are affected by the AIDS epidemic in Africa. "Willow and I joined Project Zambi to represent all the kids out there who want to make the world a better place," he said. "We want to encourage kids everywhere to lend a hand and join us in spreading the word about how much children who have been orphaned by AIDS in Africa need our help."

The Karate Kid

When he was 12 years old, Smith won his first starring role, in the remake of the 1984 movie *The Karate Kid*. This martial arts drama focuses on the story of Dre, played by Smith. After his father dies, Dre and his mother leave Detroit and move to Beijing, China, for her new job. Dre was popular and had a lot of friends in Detroit, but in China he is an outcast. He struggles to understand the Chinese culture and society and finds that he just doesn't fit in. It seems that all of Dre's new schoolmates know kung-fu,

Scenes from The Karate Kid.

and the school bullies don't hesitate to use their skills against him. A particularly savage beating motivates Dre to begin studying martial arts. Dre's teacher is a former martial arts master (played by Jackie Chan) who is now the maintenance man at the apartment building where Dre lives. As Dre's fighting skills progress, he decides to enter a tournament where he ultimately must prove himself by facing the relentless bully Cheng.

Smith couldn't wait to get to work on the movie. "I've always really been interested in martial arts. I started taking karate when I was three. So when my dad mentioned this idea to remake the movie, there's no way I was going to pass that up!" To prepare for the role, Smith began an intense martial arts training program. He practiced three hours a day for four months before filming started. The fight scenes were his favorite parts of the movie. "The tournament at the end of the movie was the most fun and the hardest to shoot because I had to constantly fight every day. It was exhausting. But it was also really cool."

All of Smith's hard work paid off, and *The Karate Kid* became an international phenomenon when it was released in 2010. The movie was a box-office sensation that grossed more than $350 million worldwide and made Smith an instant star. Though the movie received mixed reviews from critics, Smith was praised for his talents as an actor and a martial artist. A reviewer for *Film Journal* described *The Karate Kid* as a "formulaic but savvy reboot of the four-film series [that] makes for a solid children's movie, bolstered by exotic locales and a genuinely talented young star.... Smith seems at once in conscious control and emotionally spontaneous. He has a great, subtle way of showing the doubt beneath Dre's blustery bravado, and of seeming like a genuinely irritating 12-year-old and not a ham-fisted, obnoxious movie 12-year-old."

Smith's performance in *The Karate Kid* was recognized with a host of award nominations. *Entertainment Weekly* named Smith a Top Celebrity of 2010. In 2011, he was nominated for an NAACP Image Award for Outstanding Actor in a Motion Picture, an MTV Movie Award for Biggest Badass Star, and two Teen Choice Awards for Choice Summer Movie Star: Male and Choice Red Carpet Fashion Icon: Male. Smith also shared with Jackie Chan a People's Choice Award nomination for Favorite On-Screen Team. Smith won a 2011 Young Artist Award for Best Performance in a Feature Film—Leading Young Actor and shared the 2011 BET Young Stars Award with his sister Willow.

Along with starring in *The Karate Kid*, Smith also recorded "Never Say Never," a song on the movie's soundtrack that he performed with pop singer Justin Bieber.

Jaden with his family: mother Jada Pinkett Smith,
sister Willow Smith, and father Will Smith.

Other Projects

Smith's next movie is *After Earth*, a science fiction adventure story in which he will once again star opposite his father. The two play a father and son who live 1,000 years after cataclysmic events forced humans to evacuate their planet. When their space ship crashes on Earth, the pair is forced to explore the vacant planet. *After Earth* is scheduled for release in 2013.

After completing that project, Smith plans to appear in more movies. "Yes, definitely, I want to be an actor. I want to travel around the world and meet new people. It's pretty cool going to different cities and seeing different stuff." But he isn't limiting himself to just acting, and would also like to record more music. "I just like rapping, and I've always been good at poetry," he claimed. "I love both. I'll be writing rhymes in a director's chair when I'm older."

HONORS AND AWARDS

MTV Movie Award (MTV): 2007, Breakthrough Performance, for *The Pursuit of Happyness*

Teen Choice Award: 2007, Choice Movie: Chemistry, for *The Pursuit of Happyness*, shared with Will Smith

Saturn Award (Academy of Science Fiction, Fantasy & Horror Films): 2009, Best Performance by a Younger Actor, for *The Day the Earth Stood Still*

Top Celebrity of 2010 (*Entertainment Weekly*): 2010
Young Artist Award (Young Artist Foundation): 2011, Best Performance in
    a Feature Film—Leading Young Actor, for *The Karate Kid*
Young Stars Award (BET): 2011, shared with Willow Smith

SELECTED CREDITS

The Pursuit of Happyness, 2006
The Day the Earth Stood Still, 2008
The Karate Kid, 2010

FURTHER READING

Periodicals

Daily Variety, Apr. 5, 2011, p.1
Ebony, July 2010
Entertainment Weekly, Apr. 23, 2010, p.70; Dec. 10, 2010, p.84
Jet, Dec. 15, 2008, p.38; June 28, 2010, p.28
USA Today, June 4, 2010

Online Articles

www.biography.com
    (Biography, "Jaden Smith," no date)
www.kidzworld.com
    (Kidzworld, "Jaden Smith Bio," no date)

ADDRESS

Jaden Smith
Overbrook Entertainment
450 North Roxbury Dr., 4th Floor
Beverly Hills, CA 90210

WEB SITE

www.jadensmith.com

Hilda Solis 1957-

American Political Leader
Four-Term Congresswoman from California
U.S. Secretary of Labor

BIRTH

Hilda Lucia Solis was born on October 20, 1957, in Los Angeles, California. She was the third child born to Raul Solis and Juana Sequiera Solis. She has four sisters and two brothers.

YOUTH

Solis's parents were both immigrants to the United States. Her father was born in Mexico, where he worked in a shop and was active with a labor union. (Labor unions are organizations created to make sure that workers get fair pay and treatment.) Upon coming to the United States, he settled in the Los Angeles area and began working at a plant where batteries were recycled. He became a member of the International Brotherhood of Teamsters, the union that served workers at the plant. He was active in the union's struggle to get better health care for employees.

Solis's mother had a similar story. Born in Nicaragua, she also headed north in search of a better quality of life. She found work at a toy factory near Los Angeles, where she worked shifts as long as 10 hours. She joined the United Rubber Workers Union and was outspoken about the poor working conditions at the factory. She and her husband met during classes they had to take in order to attain U.S. citizenship.

> **Solis's father taught his children "to stand up for your rights, and regardless of who you are and where you come from, to hold your head up high with dignity and respect."**

Solis believes that her family benefited greatly from her parents' membership in the unions. Without protection from the unions, both of her parents probably would have been fired for their efforts to improve working conditions. Furthermore, the unions ensured that they were paid decently and received good benefits. Therefore, even though they came to the United States with very little, they were able to save some of the money they worked so hard to earn. They purchased a home in La Puenta, a working-class area just east of the city of Los Angeles.

La Puenta represented security and upward mobility for the Solis family, yet it was also an area with many problems. Many residents were unemployed and lacked adequate housing. Everyone in the area suffered from the effects of significant air and water pollution. The Puente Hills Landfill, a gigantic landfill some 22 stories deep, sat over the water table that supplied the region. If the wind blew in the right direction, the stench from the landfill was easy to smell at the Solis home. The pollution from this landfill inspired Solis's later work to protect the poor from environmental toxins. The Puente Hills Landfill is still in operation today and is currently the largest active landfill in the United States, taking in more than 10,000 tons of garbage a day.

The Solis family was better off than many in La Puenta, but life was not easy. Hilda Solis had to grow up quickly. When she was ten years old, her

Solis grew up near the Puenta Hills Landfill, the largest active landfill in the United States and the source of a tremendous amount of pollution in East LA and the surrounding area.

mother had twins and had to return to an overnight shift at her factory job soon afterwards. Solis was the one in charge of the infant twins and her other younger siblings when her mother was out. She developed a mature, serious attitude at a young age. She remembered her father telling his children how important it was "to stand up for your rights, and regardless of who you are and where you come from, to hold your head up high with dignity and respect."

EDUCATION

Solis attended La Puenta High School. Her counselor there tried to steer her away from college, telling her she should consider becoming a secretary instead, but Solis disregarded that advice. After graduating from La Puenta High, she enrolled at California State Polytechnic University. With the help of government funding, she became the first person in her family to attend college. In addition to her studies, she also worked as an interpreter for the Immigration and Naturalization Service. In 1979, she graduated with a Bachelor of Arts degree (BA) in political science. She then entered a master's program at the University of Southern California (USC) to study public administration.

While working on her master's degree, Solis was determined to get some experience in the nation's capitol. She sent out about 100 letters inquiring

——— " ———

"There are so many people I knew when I was growing up who were not even paid the minimum wage," Solis recalled. "People wouldn't know where to go to lodge a complaint. And if you didn't speak good English, forget it."

——— " ———

about internships with various federal agencies in Washington, DC. Her efforts paid off: she was offered a job working for President Jimmy Carter in the White House Office of Hispanic Affairs. There, she gained valuable experience in the way government works and also got a broader perspective about what life was like for Latinos beyond the Los Angeles area.

The experience of working for the Carter administration was very important to Solis. A classmate of hers who also worked for Carter at that time said, "I think being at the White House empowered her to say: 'You can do anything you want to do if you work hard.'" Solis completed her studies at the University of Southern California and earned her Master of Public Administration degree (MPA) in 1981.

FIRST JOBS

In 1981 President Jimmy Carter, a Democrat, left office, and Ronald Reagan, a Republican, became president. During a change in administration like this, many staffers lose their jobs as the new president brings in his own team. Solis was asked to stay on in Washington, working as an analyst in the Office of Management and Budget. She accepted the position, but only a few months passed before she found herself uncomfortable with the conservative Republican politics of the Reagan administration. She left the job and returned to California.

Back in her home state, Solis returned to the area around eastern Los Angeles, where she lived and worked throughout her political career. She also turned her attention to education, becoming director of the California Student Opportunity and Access Program in 1982. This organization helps disadvantaged youths to prepare for college. In 1984, she won her first elected position when she was voted in as a member of the Rio Hondo Community College board of trustees. She was re-elected in 1989. While on the board at Rio Hondo, Solis worked to upgrade the quality of the college's vocational training and to increase the number of women and minority members on the faculty.

In 1991, Solis was named a commissioner on the Los Angeles County Commission on Insurance. She was appointed to the position by Gloria

*As a California state senator, Solis fought for the rights of workers.
She helped to investigate an illegal garment factory in El Monte
that enslaved these workers, and others, from Thailand.*

Molina, the Los Angeles County Supervisor. Molina was a powerful political mentor who could help advance her career. Solis also gained valuable
experience working as chief of staff for Art Torres, a California state senator.

CAREER HIGHLIGHTS

Serving in the California State Legislature

In 1992, Solis was elected to the California State Assembly. Her family gave
her support on the most basic level—her mom even cooked burritos for the
volunteers working on her campaign. One of her first actions in the assembly was to vote for legislation that made it illegal to smoke in any California
workplace. By doing that, she sent a clear signal that she wasn't afraid to
take a stand against big-business interests, including the tobacco industry.

In 1994, Solis became the first Latina to be elected to the California State
Senate. As a senator, she increased her reputation as a hard worker and as
a staunch labor supporter. She was also named the chairwoman of the
Senate Industrial Relations Committee. Not long after she took office, state
authorities discovered an illegal garment factory operating in El Monte,
California. Inside, 72 people from Thailand were being held in terrible con-

ditions and forced to work. Solis gave her support to a very thorough investigation of the matter that led to much better enforcement of the laws protecting garment workers.

In 1996, Solis supported legislation that raised California's minimum wage from $4.25 to $5.75 an hour. Her background helped her feel sympathy for people who work for low wages and for those who are easy victims of employers who want to exploit them. Solis wanted to protect these workers. "There are so many people I knew when I was growing up who were not even paid the minimum wage," she recalled. "People wouldn't know where to go to lodge a complaint. And if you didn't speak good English, forget it."

This pro-labor, pro-worker stance did not make Solis popular with everyone. Big business interests sometimes view workers' rights and protections as barriers to higher profits. Even those politicians who did not agree with her thought highly of her, however. "We obviously didn't see eye to eye," said Rob Hurtt, a conservative senator who served at the same time as Solis. "But she was respectful. I'll give her credit; she was a very hard worker and she knew her stuff."

Working for Environmental Justice

The voters liked Solis and reelected her to the California senate in 1998. The following year, she was the author of Senate Bill 115, a bill that defined the term "environmental justice." Environmental justice refers to the fact that environmental problems disproportionately affect poor people and people of color. People in poor areas are much more likely to be the victims of toxic waste dumping and other forms of pollution than are people in more well-to-do areas. For example, Solis's district was home to 17 gravel pits and numerous abandoned gas stations, both of which can cause significant pollution; 5 landfills; 4 Superfund sites, which are places polluted with particularly toxic substances, eligible for federal funding for cleanup; and the San Gabriel Basin, which is one of the most polluted water sources in the United States.

Senate Bill 115 was the first of its kind to be signed into law. It required the California Environmental Protection Agency to adopt environmental justice standards, and it paved the way for more such laws to be written and passed. Because of her work for environmental justice, Solis was honored with the John F. Kennedy Profile in Courage Award in 2000. She was the first woman ever to receive the prestigious award. In a statement released by the John F. Kennedy Library, she was praised for her willingness to take on "entrenched economic interests as she sought relief for minority communities that suffered the ill effects of haphazard enforcement of environmental laws." Solis gave the $25,000 cash portion of the prize to environmental groups in her area.

Serving in the U.S. House of Representatives

Solis's advocacy for workers, unions, and the environment had made her a favorite of the voters in her district. In 2000, she decided to run in the primary election for a seat in the U.S. House of Representatives, representing the 31st Congressional District. (District boundaries were later redefined, and then she represented the 32nd District.) Running for the U.S. House of Representatives meant she was challenging incumbent Democrat Matthew G. Martinez, who had held the office for nine terms. Some people in the community felt that Solis was being disrespectful by challenging the long-established congressman. Yet others felt that Martinez was out of touch with district voters and their needs. While the Democratic Party wouldn't endorse Solis's challenge to Martinez, she did win the support of many key people in the Latino community. She beat Martinez decisively in the primary, with a winning margin of 69 to 31 percent. With no Republican challenger in the general election, she won that contest as well and returned to Washington, DC as a member of the U.S. Congress.

Solis's main goals in Congress were the improvement of access to affordable health care for all workers, safeguarding the environment, improving the lives of working families, and protecting immigrants' rights. She was known to be closely allied with Nancy Pelosi, another Democratic congresswoman from California who was also the Speaker of the House. Solis served in many special capacities.

"People have to be reminded that unions played a very historic role in our economy," Solis asserted. *"If you didn't have unions, you wouldn't have Saturdays and Sundays [off]; you wouldn't be paid a minimum wage, be guaranteed paid overtime and sick leave and a pension. Believe it or not, we still have these issues come up."*

She was chair of the Congressional Hispanic Caucus Task Force on Health and the Environment and co-chair of the Congressional Women's Caucus. She was a member of numerous important committees, including the House Natural Resources Committee, the House Energy and Commerce Committee, the Education and the Workforce Committee, and the

In a show of labor support, U.S. Congresswoman Solis adds her name to a display expressing support for hotel workers who were negotiating a union contract.

House Select Committee on Energy Independence and Global Warming. She was reelected in 2002, 2004, 2006, and 2008.

Throughout her time in Congress, Solis consistently worked for the good of the environment and for job creation and workers' rights. She was considered both idealistic and tough. In 2003, she helped to start a federal study about how to conserve the health of the water sources in her district. In 2005, she voiced her opposition to the Central American Free Trade Agreement (CAFTA). She compared it to the North American Free Trade Agreement (NAFTA), which in her words, resulted in "750,000 jobs lost in the United States and little progress in improving workers' rights in Mexico." In 2007, she lent her support to the Green Jobs Act, which was intended to train workers for environmentally friendly work.

Becoming Secretary of Labor

During the primary elections leading up to the 2008 presidential election, the race for who would become the Democratic candidate for president gradually narrowed down to two candidates: Barack Obama and Hillary Clinton. Solis was a strong supporter of Clinton, who lost the race to Obama. When Obama was nominated as the Democratic candidate, he immediately asked for Solis's support for his campaign. Her endorsement of his candidacy was seen as a very important factor in winning the Latino vote. After he won the presidential election, Obama nominated Solis as Secretary of Labor on December 18, 2008. She recalled Obama telling her that if she took the job, he wanted her to be "the voice for working families and organized labor."

There was little opposition to her nomination, and on February 24, 2009, Solis was confirmed by the Senate as the U.S. Secretary of Labor. As such she became part of the Cabinet, the group of the president's top advisors who lead the major departments of the U.S. government. Solis was the first Latina to serve in the Cabinet. Upon taking office, she assumed responsibility for making sure laws regulating safe working conditions were enforced and companies that broke them were penalized. She also took responsibility for the Department of Labor's $10.5 billion budget (now about $12.8 billion). It

—— " ——

Solis brings a methodical approach to her work, according to a former professor who has known her since her college days. "[Solis is] a person who is very organized, who will lay out a plan of action, and quietly carry it through. I think that's what has made her effective: She's not a show-boat person, she's not a talker. ... And she does things without grandstanding it, she does things quietly."

—— " ——

was a difficult time to be the Secretary of Labor. The economy was troubled and unemployment was very high. Nevertheless, Solis brought a positive attitude to her new position and a commitment to finding ways to create new jobs and continuing to protect the rights of workers.

When Obama was elected president, he succeeded George W. Bush, whose policies had been strongly pro-business. Solis felt that during the Bush administration the Department of Labor had been neglected, or even restrained from carrying out key parts of its mission to protect workers. Almost as soon as she took office, she declared herself the "new sheriff in town" and set out to establish a high standard for workplace safety.

In her first year alone, Solis took the following actions: she hired 250 new workplace inspectors to ensure safety rules were being followed; she increased funding to the U.S. Occupational Safety and Health Administration (OSHA), a governmental agency that exists to ensure worker safety; and she imposed a huge fine on BP, a large and powerful oil company, for

—— " ——

"As the first Latina to serve in a U.S. President's cabinet, I am committed to ensuring that the nation's Latino communities are part of America's effort to outcompete the world," Solis stated. *"Achieving that requires good communication, and ensuring that Latinos have the information they need to do their jobs safely, provide for their families, and share in the country's economic recovery."*

—— " ——

violations of safety regulations that took place in 2005, before she was in office. At $87 million, the fine was four times larger than any that had ever been previously imposed by the Department of Labor. It came in response to BP's failure to make repairs that were needed at a Texas oil refinery. BP failed to maintain and repair equipment at the refinery, investigators found, which caused a massive explosion that killed 15 people and injured 170. Solis wanted to send a message that workers were more important than any company's profits. "An $87 million fine won't restore those lives, but we can't let this happen again," she stated.

Solis supported the Employee Free Choice Act (EFCA), a piece of legislation that was designed to make it easier for workers to form unions. Big business interests generally disliked EFCA, while labor interests considered it vital. One of the more controversial aspects of EFCA was the "card check" measure. This would have forced employers to officially recognize the existence of a union once more than half of its employees signed cards indicating their support. Yet even some Democrats disliked the card check measure, saying it made it impossible for employees to remain anonymous about whether or not they had voted to unionize. In July 2009, the card check provision was written out of EFCA, but the act still found little support in Congress.

On April 5, 2010, Solis faced her first significant workplace disaster as Secretary of Labor. At the Upper Big Branch Mine in West Virginia, an explosion occurred about 1,000 feet underground. Despite rescue efforts, 29 of the 31 miners working at the site lost their lives. It was the worst mining accident to occur in the United States since 1970. Solis went to Upper Big Branch herself to inspect conditions and do whatever she could to help rescue operations. "In times like these," she said, "one thinks two things: First, why is this even happening? Mine accidents are pre-

President Barack Obama looks at a map of the Upper Big Branch Mine during a meeting in the Oval Office on mine safety with Solis and top staffers.

ventable. No one should have to go through all this. And second: What more could we have done?"

Reaching Out

The Department of Labor is entrusted with the safety and well-being of all U.S. workers. But Solis is particularly interested in reaching out to groups who find themselves on the fringes of mainstream society, including the Latino community. In March 2011, the Latino news and information company impreMedia announced that Solis would be featured in a monthly column distributed by their service, called "Tu Trabajo." It would function as a forum where Latino audiences could ask questions and learn about programs and services available to them through the Department of Labor. "As the first Latina to serve in a U.S. President's cabinet, I am committed to ensuring that the nation's Latino communities are part of America's effort to outcompete the world," Solis stated "Achieving that requires good communication, and ensuring that Latinos have the information they need to do their jobs safely, provide for their families, and share in the country's economic recovery."

Solis put the Department of Labor to work for many other marginalized segments of society as well. For example, in July 2011 she announced that

—— " ——

"Getting Americans back to work, expanding opportunities, ensuring the safety of workers, and protecting their right to keep what they earn—these are all top priorities for my department," Solis said.

—— " ——

$20 million in grants would be made available to prisoners being released from jail. Ex-convicts often have a hard time readjusting to life outside prison and have a harder-than-average time finding work. As a result, they often end up drifting back into crime and returning to jail. The Department of Labor grants funded programs that help ex-convicts succeed at their jobs and function well in society. The program makes good economic sense as well as humanitarian sense, Solis pointed out. Studies have shown that workers who have been in jail tend to value their jobs more highly because they know it is difficult for them to find employment. They have been shown to work harder and be more productive than many workers who have not done jail time. If they succeed as working members of society, they will not end up costing taxpayers money by needing to be on welfare or living in homeless shelters.

In September 2011, Solis revealed a plan to spend $2.2 million on the "Add Us In" initiative. The goal of Add Us In is to open up more job opportunities for disabled people by helping businesses and communities find ways to make jobs more accessible for the disabled. This is important because the unemployment rate is significantly higher for disabled people than for those who are not disabled.

In the following month, Solis announced that $32.5 million would be spent on grants to fight child labor internationally. On the same day that news was made public, the Department of Labor also released three reports detailing the situation on child labor around the world. More than 215 million children are believed to be used as forced labor around the world, and more them half of those children are engaged in dangerous work. Solis stated her belief that with "increased education and awareness, and critical assistance to families and governments, we can help make exploitative child labor a thing of the past." Solis also hosted a panel discussion on child labor and how to fight it, bringing together authorities on the subject from around the world.

On the matter of illegal immigration, Solis believes it is wrong to focus only on stern enforcement of existing laws to keep immigrants out. She feels it is vital to take a more realistic and humanitarian approach to the

Secretary of Labor Solis meets with an autoworker
while touring a Jeep plant in Toledo, Ohio.

problem, one that takes into consideration the hardships endured by these immigrants and their families. She believes this can be done without endangering national security. She has stated her belief that "immigrant workers should be documented, allowing them to enjoy the rights and to exercise the responsibilities of U.S. citizens. We can heighten national security while bringing millions of hard-working immigrants out of the shadows and into full citizenship. But first we have to give up the illusion that enforcement alone can solve our immigration crisis."

Creating Jobs and Protecting Workers

As Secretary of Labor, Solis brings a methodical approach to her work, according to a former professor who has known her since her college days. "Hilda is not a very extroverted person; she's the kind of person who is a very methodical plotter, in the best sense of the word, not 'plotter' in the sense of conspiracy. But, a person who is very organized, who will lay out a plan of action, and quietly carry it through. I think that's what has made her effective: She's not a show-boat person, she's not a talker, she's a kind of person that does. And she does things without grandstanding it, she does things quietly."

Solis has said that when she accepted the position as Secretary of Labor, she really did not understand just how important the job was. She has found that she has much more influence than she expected to have. "Getting Americans back to work, expanding opportunities, ensuring the safety of workers, and protecting their right to keep what they earn—these are all top priorities for my department," she said. She emphasized the vital role the Department of Labor plays in protecting workers. "We take for granted much of what we have, and if we erode those protections, we're going to see more casualties and more fatalities. People have to be reminded that unions played a very historic role in our economy. If you didn't have unions, you wouldn't have Saturdays and Sundays [off]; you wouldn't be paid a minimum wage, be guaranteed paid overtime and sick leave and a pension. Believe it or not, we still have these issues come up."

HOME AND FAMILY

Solis met Sam H. Sayyad while living in Washington, DC when she was working on her master's degree. They married in June 1982. Sayyad owns an auto-repair shop not far from their home in El Monte, California. They have no children. Solis is Roman Catholic.

HOBBIES AND OTHER INTERESTS

Solis has very little free time, but she enjoys salsa dancing when she gets the chance. She also enjoys riding her bike, taking her nieces and nephews to Disneyland, and listening to music, especially jazz.

HONORS AND AWARDS

John F. Kennedy Profile in Courage Award (John F. Kennedy Library Foundation): 2000
Distinguished Public Health Legislator of the Year Award (American Public Health Association): 2007

FURTHER READING

Periodicals

Current Biography Yearbook, 2009
Hispanic, June 2000, p.20
National Journal, Sep. 10, 2010
Sierra, June 2004, p.44

Online Articles

articles.latimes.com
(Los Angeles Times, "Hilda Solis' Belief in Unions Runs Deep," Jan. 9, 2009, and "Patt Morrison Asks: U.S. Secretary of Labor Hilda Solis," Sep. 3, 2011)

www.nytimes.com
  (New York Times, Steven Greenhouse, "As Labor Secretary, Finding Influence in Her Past," July 5, 2009)
www.nytimes.com/pages/topics/
  (New York Times, multiple articles, various dates)
www.time.com
  (Time, "Labor Secretary: Hilda Solis," Dec. 22, 2008)
www.usnews.com
  (U.S. News and World Report, "10 Things You Didn't Know about Hilda Solis," Feb. 13, 2009)
usatoday.com
  (USA Today, Hilda Solis, "There Are Jobs Out There," Sep. 3, 2010)
www.washingtonpost.com
  (Washington Post, "People in the News: Hilda L. Solis, Secretary of Labor," no date)
www.washingtonpost.com/whorunsgov
  (Washington Post, WhoRunsGov, "Hilda Solis," no date)

ADDRESS

Hilda Solis
U.S. Department of Labor
Frances Perkins Building
200 Constitution Ave., NW
Washington, DC 20210

WEB SITES

www.dol.gov/_sec
www.allgov.com/Official/Solis__Hilda
www.facebook.com/hildasolis

Emma Stone 1988-

American Actress

Star of the Hit Movies *Easy A*; *Crazy, Stupid, Love*; *The Help*; and *The Amazing Spider-Man*

BIRTH

Emily Jean Stone was born on November 6, 1988, in Scottsdale, Arizona. Her mother, Krista, was a homemaker. Her father, Jeff, operated his own construction company. She has one brother, named Spencer. Stone changed her first name to Emma when she became an actress, in order to avoid confusion with another actress named Emily Stone.

YOUTH

Stone grew up in Scottsdale, Arizona. As a young girl, she enjoyed watching movies with her parents, especially comedies. "My dad showed me the classics—*Animal House, The Jerk*—and I connected comedy to my happiness," she explained. "I think I was drawn to comedy originally because when I was really young, by the time I was eight I had seen movies like *The Jerk, Animal House,* and *Planes, Trains & Automobiles* with my dad, and I knew them by heart. I loved them and my dad loved them, and we would laugh together, and I would think, 'This is love.' I just wanted to make people feel like that." She also shared her mother's love of sketch comedy. "My mom loved 'Saturday Night Live' and Gilda Radner. She would do Gilda Radner impressions and she showed me old 'Saturday Night Live' shows when I was about seven."

> "By the time I was eight I had seen movies like **The Jerk, Animal House,** *and* **Planes, Trains & Automobiles** *with my dad, and I knew them by heart. I loved them and my dad loved them, and we would laugh together, and I would think, 'This is love.' I just wanted to make people feel like that."*

When she was 11 years old, Stone began acting in community theater productions with the Valley Youth Theater in Phoenix, Arizona. She appeared in 16 plays, including *Alice in Wonderland, Cinderella, The Little Mermaid,* and *The Princess and the Pea.* She was also a member of an improvisation comedy troupe. (Improvisation is a form of comedy that is not planned or scripted. Instead, performers respond to situations, characters, and each other by making things up as they go along.) Stone has said that her childhood experiences performing comedy helped her later in her acting career. "I think every kid should have access to something like that, because it's not only great training for acting, but for life. Learning improv skills is kind of like being on the debate team, you know? You learn life lessons." She also enjoyed writing and performing her own original sketch comedy pieces.

Though Stone always knew that she wanted to be a performer, it took a while for her to figure out what kind of performing artist she most wanted to be. Throughout her childhood, she explored different performance styles, as she explains here. "I wanted to do comedy, and then I thought I wanted to do theater, so I wanted to do musical theater, and then I took voice lessons for like eight years, and I sucked at singing, so I was like, 'Alright, nevermind.'" By the time she was a teenager, Stone had decided on a career as an actor.

Stone decided when she was 14 years old that she wanted to move to Hollywood. When she told her parents what she wanted to do, at first they would not even consider allowing it. In order to show her parents how serious she was about going to Hollywood, Stone carefully prepared a persuasive argument. "When I was 14 years old, I made this PowerPoint presentation, and I invited my parents into my room and gave them popcorn. It was called 'Project Hollywood 2004' and it worked."

Stone at the 2011 Teen Choice Awards.

EDUCATION

Stone attended Sequoya Elementary School and Xavier College Preparatory High School in Arizona. Her schooling changed at age 15, when she moved to California and began pursuing a full-time career as an actor. At that time, Stone left traditional high school and enrolled in online classes so that she could complete her school work on a more flexible schedule that allowed her to go to more auditions.

CAREER HIGHLIGHTS

In January 2004, when she was 15 years old, Stone moved to Los Angeles with her mother. She hired an acting agent and began auditioning for roles. After eight months, she still had not landed any acting jobs. Stone took a part-time job at a bakery that made treats for dogs. Her job was to bake dog cookies, and she soon discovered that she had no talent for the work. "I think three people called my specific dog cookies inedible to their dogs. I'm not a super-talented dog baker."

Stone's first year in Los Angeles was more difficult than she imagined it would be. "It's definitely a shock to go from being 15 and in high school to working. There's no real cushion there. There's no preparation at all. You learn by doing," she explained. "I don't know why I had to do it right then.... I was having breakdowns—'What am I doing? I'm 15 years old! I have no friends! I'm not in school—why did I need to do this?' But I kept pushing through it, and I'm so glad I got rejected for so long because things fall into your lap when you least expect it.... So follow your gut. Your gut will tell exactly what to do when you need to do it."

Starting Out

In 2005, Stone got her first acting job. She was cast as a contestant on a proposed VH1 reality competition show called "In Search of the New Partridge Family." The original "Partridge Family" television showed aired in the 1970s. It was about a single mother and her five children who perform together as pop musicians. The winners of the new VH1 competition would be cast in a remake called "The New Partridge Family" TV show. Stone filmed the pilot episode of the reality competition, but VH1 decided not to create the series. Though this show did not work out, she said the experience was extremely valuable. "I met a lot of people that ended up having a big effect on my life. It all kind of changed from there."

> "It's definitely a shock to go from being 15 and in high school to working. There's no real cushion there. There's no preparation at all. You learn by doing," Stone explained. "I was having breakdowns—'What am I doing? I'm 15 years old! I have no friends! I'm not in school—why did I need to do this?'"

One of the people that Stone met during that time became her new manager and helped her get more acting jobs. She soon landed guest roles on popular TV shows like "Malcolm in the Middle," "The Suite Life of Zack and Cody," and "Medium." She auditioned for the role of Claire on "Heroes" but lost the part to actress Hayden Panettiere. Stone recalls being devastated when she was not chosen for that role. She learned the news by overhearing a conversation while she waited outside the audition room. "I could hear that, in the other room, a girl had just gone in and they were saying, 'You are our pick.... On a scale of one to ten, you're an 11.' I went home and just had this meltdown."

Though she did not get the part on "Heroes," the rejection motivated Stone to try even harder on her next audition. She was cast in a 2007 TV series called "Drive," a drama-action series about a group of people who were competing in an illegal cross-country road race. The show only lasted one season, but the experience ultimately led to Stone winning her break-out role in the movie *Superbad*.

Becoming a Movie Actor

Stone's first movie role was in the 2007 comedy *Superbad*, the story of two high school seniors who want to do something cool and daring before they graduate. Although they are underage, they decide to try to buy alcohol and bring it to a party thrown by Jules, played by Emma Stone. On the way to Jules's house, the two join forces with another friend, meet up with a couple of strange local police officers, and get into a series of misadventures. *Superbad* was a box office hit that quickly became a cult classic.

Stone was thrilled to be part of the movie. "The script was so hysterical to me, so I was just excited to be a part of something that was that funny and in line with my humor, because that's so rare." Though she had only a supporting role, playing Jules gave Stone the chance to show off her acting talent and comedic abilities. Her performance in *Superbad* earned her the 2008 Young Hollywood Exciting New Face Award.

After *Superbad*, Stone began to receive more job offers, leading to roles in a string of movies. In the 2008 movie *The Rocker*, she played Amelia, a bass guitar player in an amateur rock band. That same year, she appeared in *The House Bunny* (2008), the story of a former Playboy bunny who becomes a sorority house mother and proceeds to give all of the sorority members beauty and lifestyle makeovers. Stone played Natalie, the sorority's quick-witted president. Then in 2009, she appeared in the romantic comedy *Ghosts of Girlfriends Past*. This movie tells the story of a man who tries to talk his brother out of getting married and is subsequently visited by three ghosts, one of which is played by Stone. The ghosts give him glimpses of his past, present, and future romantic relationships, causing him to think about the way he has been living his life. These roles broadened Stone's appeal and helped her to land her first starring role, in the action movie *Zombieland*.

Zombieland

In the 2009 comedy-horror movie *Zombieland*, Stone played Wichita, one of the survivors of a catastrophe that turned most humans into zombies. With the world in ruins, Wichita joins up with three other survivors for a road trip across America to find a place that is free from zombies. The movie became an instant cult hit, and Stone was nominated for a 2010 Teen Choice Award for Choice Movie Actress: Comedy. A writer for movie review web site Rotten Tomatoes said, "Emma Stone is rapidly carving a niche for herself as a young actress with good comic chops."

Scenes from several of Stone's early movies: Superbad *(top),* The Rocker *(middle), and* Zombieland *(bottom).*

For Stone, the experience of filming an action movie presented new challenges. "I'm shockingly terrible at action movies. I tore my muscle three days in just running, and then I was limping around everywhere.... I was limping like a zombie. I'm dead serious. We're running from zombies, and I'm limping in the same fashion that they limp. It was just awful." Stone also found herself genuinely frightened in some of the movie's scenes, even though she knew the zombies weren't real. "On the second day, [costar Abigail Breslin] and I had to be chased by something like 30 zombies and it was two o'clock in the morning and I was really overtired. I started getting these paranoid thoughts that one of them was really crazy. I was like, 'How do you know you can trust these people?!' So we're running from these people and shooting at them and in my mind I'm thinking, 'What if one of them snaps and attacks me?' I got myself into a paranoid tizzy about it."

> —————— " ——————
>
> *"I'm shockingly terrible at action movies," Stone said about filming* **Zombieland**. *"I tore my muscle three days in just running, and then I was limping around everywhere.... I was limping like a zombie. I'm dead serious. We're running from zombies, and I'm limping in the same fashion that they limp. It was just awful."*
>
> —————— " ——————

Easy A

Stone's next project was the 2010 teen comedy *Easy A*. In this movie, Stone starred as Olive Penderghast, an uncool high school student who gains a bad-girl reputation after one tiny lie grows bigger each time it is repeated on the gossip grapevine. Olive soon finds that she has been branded as the school slut, although she is actually still a virgin. Instead of trying to correct the misunderstanding, Olive decides to take advantage of her new status by working the school's rumor mill. Stone said the message of *Easy A* is that gossip and rumors are not always true. "No matter how true something may seem, we don't really know if it's fact or fiction."

Easy A became a hit with moviegoers and critics as well. "Whatever else it accomplishes, the sassy high school comedy *Easy A* commands attention for the irresistible presence of Emma Stone, playing a good girl who pretends to be bad," Stephen Holden wrote in the *New York Times*. "Her performance is the best of its type since Alicia Silverstone's star turn several high school generations ago in Amy Heckerling's 1995 hit *Clueless*." Re-

Easy A *was Stone's first big film.*

viewer Elizabeth Weitzman predicted a successful future for Stone in the *New York Daily News*: "Expect to hear much more about Emma Stone, who's thoroughly charming as misguided heroine Olive Penderghast."

For her performance in *Easy A*, Stone earned a 2010 Golden Globe nomination for Best Performance by an Actress in a Motion Picture Comedy or Musical. She was nominated for 2011 MTV Movie Awards for Best Female Performance and Best Line from a Movie, and she won the MTV Movie Award for Best Comedic Performance. During its "Thankful Week," MTV News named Stone "the actress we're most thankful for in 2010." Stone also won a 2011 Teen Choice Award, for Choice Movie Actress: Romantic Comedy.

In fall 2010, Stone fulfilled one of her lifelong goals by hosting "Saturday Night Live." "I've never been so happy in my entire life," she said of that experience. "Walking into Studio 8H and seeing pictures of Gilda Radner and Bill Murray and Steve Martin and Jan Hooks and Eddie Murphy and Molly Shannon and everyone I've ever admired in this exact room on this exact stage—I mean, beyond."

Stone followed the success of *Easy A* with a starring role in the 2011 romantic comedy *Crazy, Stupid, Love*. This movie tells the story of Cal (played by Steve Carell), a man who tries to enter the dating world after his wife leaves him. He finds a mentor, Jacob (played by Ryan Gosling), who is willing to teach him how to pick up women. The lessons seem to be going well until Jacob meets Hannah, played by Stone. Hannah is the one woman for whom Jacob's playboy techniques are completely ineffective. Things get complicated as relationships become intertwined and everyone struggles to figure out what they really want. Though the movie received mixed reviews from critics, Stone was praised for her performance. Movie reviewer David Denby wrote in the *New Yorker* that Stone "has a direct, clearheaded way about her that suggests the confidence of a potential star. She's the strongest thing in the movie."

> **"**
>
> *"The Emma Stone Character represents a kind of young American female role (and role model) in precious short supply these days—one who likes herself and cherishes her options," film critic Lisa Schwarzbaum wrote in* **Entertainment Weekly.** *"That a generation of young women and men are learning from the real Stone's bright example is more valuable still."*
>
> **"**

Also in 2011, Stone made a cameo appearance in the romantic comedy *Friends with Benefits*. She appeared in one scene, in which she broke up with the lead character Dylan, played by Justin Timberlake.

The Help

Stone's first dramatic role was in the highly anticipated 2011 movie *The Help*, a film adaptation of the 2009 bestselling novel of the same name by Kathryn Stockett. The book was a worldwide phenomenon that ranked on bestseller lists for more than 100 weeks. The story of *The Help* takes place in the early 1960s in Jackson, Mississippi. It focuses on the relationships between African-American maids and their white employers during the turbulent and tense early days of the civil rights movement. Stone plays Eugenia "Skeeter" Phelan, an ambitious young writer who wants to learn about the life experiences of the maids who work for her friends. Though it was unheard-of and incredibly risky for whites and blacks to talk about the racial tensions of that time, Skeeter manages to convince two maids to let her interview them. The story unfolds as the women begin to speak openly about their lives.

Though *The Help* was a bestselling novel and many readers eagerly awaited the movie version, a great deal of controversy also surrounded the project. *The Help* was praised by many film critics but heavily criticized by others. Some in the African-American community objected to the story as an oversimplification of the terrible racial discrimination that occurred in the time and place shown in the movie. Others thought the story was too condescending and implausible and did not provide a complete picture of the times or the lives of the African-American characters, especially black women.

"Many audiences, especially African-American viewers, are exhausted with seeing black actresses as maids. It was a role to which many black actresses were regulated to for decades, and *The Help* brings back old Hollywood memories that some would rather forget," Clay Cane wrote for BET. "Regardless of mammy stereotypes, *The Help* needed some help with its janky, watered-down storyline and its Disneyfied version of the Jim Crow South. Predictably, the movie focuses more on the rich, racist characters versus the heart of the film, the impoverished domestic servants and their untold stories. There should've been fewer Southern tea parties and poolside gatherings and more of the gritty realities of being a maid in the '60s. For a film that is set in pre-civil rights Mississippi, it is too bright and cheery, cheapening the horrific experiences of legalized racism.... In moments, the film works, but overall it was another clichéd civil rights film

Scenes from The Help.

with all of the typical elements: the ultra-racist evil white person, ... the sympathetic Southern woman suffering from white guilt, a sassy black rebel and a flock of obedient Negros."

But many others enjoyed and defended the film, including Peter Rainer, a critic for the *Christian Science Monitor*. "*The Help* too often feels like a civics lesson.... I would defend *The Help*, simplistic though it is, against the charge that some have leveled against it for being 'patronizing.' It's true that, by framing the maids' stories through Skeeter's lens, the film implicitly overvalues the historical contribution of whites to the civil rights movement [but] ... there are not so many stirring, full-fledged black characters on the screen, particularly black female characters, that we should feel it necessary to downgrade the few that we have by playing the blame game."

Amidst the controversy, Stone's performance was praised as believable and honest. Matt Stevens, a critic for *E! Online,* wrote that the movie provides "a clear understanding of Southern Culture and manages to stitch together the many patches of this crazy quilt, even if some pieces don't fit perfectly.... Stone, too, is stellar as the plucky, progressive Skeeter." David Denby observed in the *New Yorker*, "Stone makes it clear that Skeeter's break with her friends is produced as much by ambition for a hot literary subject as by moral disapproval. She is one of the few actresses playing a working writer who have actually seemed like one." As Owen Gleiberman wrote in *Entertainment Weekly*, "I've loved Stone as a wide-eyed comic sprite, but here, playing a young woman more no-nonsense than anyone around her, she doesn't just sparkle—she holds the movie together."

The Amazing Spider-Man

Stone next appeared in *The Amazing Spider-Man,* a new version of the superhero story. With director Marc Webb at the helm and Andrew Garfield as Peter Parker/Spider-Man, Stone co-starred as Gwen Stacy, his girlfriend. The movie *The Amazing Spider-Man* tells the origin story of the superhero. Abandoned by his parents, raised by his aunt and uncle, an outcast at school, Peter Parker has a difficult but normal life as he tries to understand who he is, what happened to his parents, and how he feels about Gwen, a fellow student. But when he is bitten by a spider and develops superpowers, he has to figure out how to use his powers and become a hero.

Gwen is an iconic character in the comic book series—she was Spider-Man's first true love and was killed after being taken hostage by the Green Goblin. As Stone soon learned, Gwen is very important to the legions of Spider-Man fans, who were very concerned about her portrayal. "There's a

*Stone (Gwen Stacy) and Andrew Garfield (Peter Parker)
in a scene from* The Amazing Spider-Man.

part of me that really wants to please people that love Spider-Man or Gwen Stacy and want her to be done justice," Stone said. "I hope they'll give me license to interpret her my way. But that fan base, I'm one of them, so I completely understand why they would be judgmental of certain things. I try not to look [at stories on the Internet] because I do care and I don't want to psych myself out. I kinda have to stay off the Internet. I'm not thick-skinned enough. I get too sensitive. I don't want it to affect what I'm doing."

The Amazing Spider-Man was released in 2012, not that long after a recent *Spider-Man* movie trilogy (2002-2007) directed by Sam Raimi and starring Tobey Maguire as Spider-Man and Kirsten Dunst as Mary Jane Watson, a later girlfriend. Reviews of the new movie were surprisingly mixed, from very negative to very positive. The proximity to the earlier series was one sticking point, with several critics commenting that the new version was both too similar to and inferior to the earlier movies. Many also commented that the new movie's greatest purpose seemed less about creating a new vision of the superhero, and more about just making money. "This *Spider-Man* feels like one of those unnecessary software versions, more Spider-Man 1.5 than Spider-Man reborn," Manohla Dargis wrote in the *New York Times.* "Spider-Man's ethos remains—'With great power comes great responsibility'—but these days you can't see his superhero heart and soul for his branding." That view was echoed by Ty Burr in the *Boston Globe.* "Is there a reason we need a new *Spider-Man* movie 10 years after Sam Raimi and Tobey Maguire got it done properly?" Burr asked. "Only if you're Sony Pictures and the lawyers say you have to keep the movies coming or the rights will revert to Marvel Comics. That's correct, *The Amazing Spider-Man* is a contract extension, which is exactly how it plays on the screen. Dumbed down, tarted up, and almost shockingly uninspired, it's the worst superhero movie since *Green Lantern.*"

Those reviews contrasted greatly with others that were much more appreciative. They tended to emphasize the story's depth of character and romance-driven plot, saying the movie was as much a coming-of-age story as a crime-fighting action story. "As a new chapter in the superpowered arachnid saga, it stands on its own quite nicely, focusing more on human emotions than on a panoply of special effects," Claudia Puig wrote in *USA Today.* "The casting of Garfield as Spidey and Emma Stone as Gwen Stacy is inspired. He's appealingly awkward and boyishly handsome. She's radiant and self-assured. Together they set off sparks. There are no forced theatrics, no upside-down kisses, just unadulterated chemistry." Peter Travers shared this view in *Rolling Stone.* "The core of the new movie is the love story," Travers wrote. "Webb never loses touch with the film's emotional through line. And he allows time and space for Garfield and Stone, both stellar, to turn a high-flying adventure into something impassioned and moving. A *Spider-Man* that touches the heart. Now that really is amazing."

The emotional depth of the movie was also what captivated *Entertainment Weekly* contributor Lisa Schwarzbaum. "Five minutes into *The Amazing Spider-Man,* I got bitten. With pleasure. A friskier, sweeter-natured variation on the story Sam Raimi told in his recent trilogy, with greater emphasis on human relations than on special effects, this Spidey reboot refreshes an old story through the on-trend notion of making a Marvel superhero less … super-heroic. With an effortlessly winning Andrew Garfield now in the title role and the irresistible Emma Stone by his side as Gwen Stacy, the most delicious high school girlfriend a bug- and love-bitten young man could hope to woo, *The Amazing Spider-Man* may be the first big-ticket, big-budget, big-action-sequence comic-book movie that also doubles as a lilting coming-of-age indie," Schwarzbaum wrote. "Any time [Garfield] shares a scene with the radiant Ms. Stone … well, the two are a chemistry experiment gone as blindingly right as reptilian Dr. Curt Connors' little lab test goes terribly wrong. What's most amazing in *The Amazing Spider-Man* turns out to be not the shared sensations of blockbuster wow! the picture elicits, but rather the shared satisfactions of intimate *awww.*"

Other Plans

Stone has earned a reputation as a talented comedic and dramatic actor and is widely recognized as a rising star among younger actors. Lisa Schwarzbaum, a film critic for *Entertainment Weekly,* summarized her star potential by describing the types of roles she typically chooses. "The Emma Stone Character represents a kind of young American female role (and role model) in precious short supply these days—one who likes herself and cherishes her options. That a generation of young women and men are learning from the real Stone's bright example is more valuable still."

While she enjoys acting in movies, Stone also enjoys working behind the scenes. "I really want to produce eventually because I love movies so much," she said. "It's really incredible to see something that you got to be a part of become something that people really respond to and are grateful is around." Stone has achieved her childhood dream of becoming an actor, and she is ready for whatever the future brings. "I rely on my instincts and intuition, and I feel it's so imperative for people to follow not the path, but their path."

HOME AND FAMILY

In 2009 Stone moved to New York City, where she lives with her dog Alfie. "I feel like I'm home for the first time, I really do. Arizona never felt like home, except for my family, and L.A. never felt like home except for my friends. And here, feels like the place I was always meant to live."

HOBBIES AND OTHER INTERESTS

In spite of her early failure as a baker of dog cookies, baking is now a serious hobby for Stone. She plans to work an internship at a gourmet bakery someday.

SELECTED CREDITS

Superbad, 2007
The Rocker, 2008
The House Bunny, 2008
Ghosts of Girlfriends Past, 2009
Zombieland, 2009
Easy A, 2010
Crazy, Stupid, Love, 2011
Friends with Benefits, 2011
The Help, 2011
The Amazing Spider-Man, 2012

HONORS AND AWARDS

Young Hollywood Awards: 2008, Exciting New Face, for *Superbad*
MTV Movie Awards: 2011, Best Comedic Performance, for *Easy A*
Teen Choice Award: 2011, Choice Movie Actress: Romantic Comedy, for
Easy A

FURTHER READING

Periodicals

Entertainment Weekly, July 9, 2010, p.50; Apr. 22, 2011, p.56; Aug. 12, 2011,
p.32
Teen Vogue, Sep. 28, 2008, p.195; Oct. 2010, p.76
Us Weekly, Sep. 27, 2010, p.72
Vanity Fair, Aug. 2011, p.83
Vogue, Mar. 2011, p.538

Online Articles

www.accesshollywood.com
(Access Hollywood, "Rising Star: Emma Stone," June 4, 2008)
www.ew.com
(Entertainment Weekly, "Emma Stone's Hot Summer: With *The Help*
and *Crazy, Stupid, Love* in Theaters, the Actress' Career Is on Fire. Allow
Us to Fan the Flames," Aug. 5, 2011)
www.nowtoronto.com
(Now Toronto, "Emma Stone," Sep. 9, 2010)
www.rottentomatoes.com
(Rotten Tomatoes, "Emma Stone Talks *Zombieland*—RT Interview," Oct.
7, 2009)
www.snmag.com
(Saturday Night, "Emma Stone: Coolest Chick We Know," July 2008)

ADDRESS

Emma Stone
William Morris Endeavor Entertainment, LLC
9601 Wilshire Blvd., 3rd Fl.
Beverly Hills, CA 90210

WEB SITES

thehelpmovie.com/us
www.sonypictures.com/homevideo/easya

Justin Verlander 1983-

American Professional Baseball Pitcher for the
Detroit Tigers
Winner of the 2011 American League MVP Award
and the Cy Young Award

BIRTH

Justin Brooks Verlander was born on February 20, 1983, in
Manakin Sabot, Virginia. His father, Richard Verlander, worked
as a pole climber for a telecommunications company and later
served as president of a local labor union. His mother, Kathy
Verlander, stayed home to care for Justin and his brother, Ben,
who is nine years younger.

YOUTH

Justin grew up on the outskirts of Richmond, Virginia, in what he once described as "a small, everybody-knows-everybody town." He always enjoyed playing sports, especially baseball, and developed a strong throwing arm at an early age. Unfortunately for his opponents, though, young Justin pitched with great velocity and terrible accuracy. "I started pitching when I was seven or eight," he remembered. "In Little League, I walked a lot of hitters, and I hit a ton of kids. They were all totally an accident. A couple of kids quit because I hit them a few times. A few kids were crying on deck before they faced me. They knew I might hit them in the head or something."

> "I started pitching when I was seven or eight," Verlander remembered. "In Little League, I walked a lot of hitters, and I hit a ton of kids. They were all totally an accident. A couple of kids quit because I hit them a few times. A few kids were crying on deck before they faced me. They knew I might hit them in the head or something."

By the time he was 13, Justin was so overpowering as a pitcher that his father no longer felt safe catching for him. His parents sent him to train at the Richmond Baseball Academy, which was run by former Major League Baseball (MLB) scout Bob Smith. As Justin's pitching skills continued to improve, the Verlanders also made sure that their son did not become arrogant. At one game, Justin recalled, "some parent asked me if I was any good, and I said, 'Yeah, I'm the best.' And my parents told me I couldn't be like that, that I had to be humble. That stuck with me."

EDUCATION

By the time he began pitching for Goochland High School, Verlander had fixed his accuracy problem. He struck out 144 batters in 72 innings and posted an incredible 0.38 earned run average or ERA (the average number of earned runs given up by a pitcher per nine innings pitched) during his high school career. Despite his outstanding statistics and a fastball clocked at 93 miles per hour, however, he was passed over for the MLB draft. "Senior year of high school I had strep, and I came out on opening day when all the scouts were there," he explained. "I was throwing 83 when I was supposed to be throwing 93. By the time I got [my pitching speed] back up there [later in] the season, no one was there to see it."

After graduating from high school in 2002, Verlander accepted an athletic scholarship to attend Old Dominion University in Norfolk, Virginia. He was the star pitcher on the school's baseball team for three seasons, compiling a 21-18 win-loss record and striking out 427 batters in 335 2/3 innings. Over the course of his college career, Verlander added 15 pounds to his lanky, 6-foot-5-inch frame, pushed the speed of his fastball to over 100 miles per hour, and started developing tricky changeup and curveball pitches. By the time he left Old Dominion in 2004, without completing his degree in communications, Verlander was considered one of the nation's top baseball prospects.

CAREER HIGHLIGHTS

Major League Baseball—The Detroit Tigers

Verlander was selected second overall in the 2004 MLB amateur draft by the Detroit Tigers, a historic franchise that had set a new American League (AL) record by losing 119 games in 2003. He signed a contract with the team that October that included a $3.12 million signing bonus.

After becoming a millionaire at age 21, Verlander could afford to pay up on a deal he had negotiated with a friend back in tenth grade. "I wanted a chocolate milk that cost 50 cents, and I didn't have the money," he remembered. "So I said, 'How about I give you 1 percent of my signing bonus if you give me 50 cents now?' He found a napkin, wrote it up, and I signed it. I forgot about it, but after I signed [with the Tigers], he comes over and whips out this old napkin. I'm like, Oh my God! My bonus was three-point-something million. Was a chocolate milk worth $3,000? I want to say yes. I was parched."

Verlander launched his professional baseball career in 2005 at the Tigers' Class A minor-league affiliate in Lakeland, Florida. He posted a 9-2 record with an impressive 1.67 ERA and struck out 104 batters in 86 innings. His strong start earned him a promotion to the Tigers' Class AA affiliate in Erie, Pennsylvania, where he went 2-0 with a 0.28 ERA and struck out 32 batters in 32 innings. Verlander went on to be named a Minor League All-Star by *Baseball America* and Minor League Starting Pitcher of the Year by MLB.com. He was even called up to the big leagues to start two games for the Tigers that season. His first major-league appearance came on July 4, 2005, in a game the Tigers lost to the Cleveland Indians.

Winning Rookie of the Year Honors

While Verlander was working his way up through the minor leagues in 2005, the big-league Tigers posted a disappointing 71-91 record. Team

Verlander throwing during batting practice for the first time in spring training in Lakeland, Florida, while still in the minor leagues, 2005.

owner Mike Ilitch fired manager Alan Trammell and replaced him with veteran manager Jim Leyland. During spring training for the 2006 MLB season, Leyland was so impressed by Verlander that he added him to the Tigers' roster as the team's fifth starter. Verlander joined a promising rotation that included up-and-coming young pitchers Nate Robertson and Jeremy Bonderman, veteran Kenny Rogers, and reliever Joel Zumaya.

To the amazement of many baseball fans, the rookie emerged as the best of the bunch. Verlander notched 10 victories by midseason and barely missed earning a spot on the All-Star Team. He finished the year with the fourth-best record in the American League at 17-9, and he added a solid 3.63 ERA and 124 strikeouts in 186 innings. Verlander's impressive debut helped the Tigers clinch a playoff spot with a 95-67 record. The team went on to beat the New York Yankees 3 games to 1 in the best-of-5 AL Division Series, then swept the Oakland Athletics 4-0 in the best-of-7 AL Championship Series. Verlander started and won Game 2 in both series.

Detroit then advanced to the World Series for the first time in 22 years, where the Tigers faced the St. Louis Cardinals. Game 1 featured a showdown between two rookie pitchers, Verlander and the Cards' Anthony Reyes. While Reyes shut down the Tigers' bats, Verlander's outing was ruined by a series of defensive lapses, and the Tigers lost the game 7-2. Verlander took the mound again in Game 5, with the Tigers down 3 games to 1 and facing elimination. He made a throwing error in the fourth inning that led to a St. Louis rally. The Tigers lost the game 4-2 and were knocked out of the World Series. Still, Verlander insisted that he had enjoyed the experience. "This has been nothing but fun, getting to know these guys and getting to be a part of this team. I couldn't ask for more in my rookie year," he declared. "The total end result, I would change a little bit. But in the long scheme of things, excluding this, I wouldn't change a thing. This has been an unbelievable run."

Despite the disappointing result of the World Series, Verlander's rookie season was a tremendous success. He

—— " ——

"This has been nothing but fun, getting to know these guys and getting to be a part of this team. I couldn't ask for more in my rookie year," Verlander declared. *"The total end result, I would change a little bit. But in the long scheme of things, excluding this, I wouldn't change a thing. This has been an unbelievable run."*

—— " ——

Verlander pitching during Game 1 of the World Series,
October 2006—his rookie season.

won the AL Rookie of the Year Award in a landslide, earning 26 of 28 first-place votes and 133 points. Verlander was outside washing his car when members of the team called to tell him he had received what he called "the ultimate honor." "I was pretty excited, but I had to go out and finish washing my car—can't leave the soap on there," he joked.

Over the course of his rookie season, Verlander impressed many people with his attitude as well as his talent. "He can hit triple digits with his fastball, has a very good changeup and curveball, and can throw all three for strikes," said teammate Nate Robertson. "No hitter I've ever talked with wants to face stuff like that. Plus he's receptive, wants to learn, and works hard. If he can keep doing this, especially when he hits valleys, he's going to be special."

Still, some observers expressed concerns about the extent to which the Tigers relied upon Verlander's young arm. They worried that fatigue from the long season might result in an injury that could threaten his promising career. After all, Verlander pitched 77 more innings in 2006 than he had in 2005; many experts recommend that young pitchers only increase their total innings by about 30 per year. Critics noted that Verlander's performance declined toward the end of the regular season, when he lost 5 of his final 8 decisions.

Verlander admitted that he suffered some physical effects of overwork, but he claimed that the experience helped him learn how to better condition his body for the demands of an MLB season. "After a start, the next day I'm real sore. I feel like crap. It's a weird feeling. You're tired, and your shoulder feels sore, dull," he related. "I'd say from about the halfway point, it was all downhill. It was a battle. It was a blessing in disguise. I'm lucky I didn't get hurt, but I went into that offseason and I knew what I needed to do."

Coming into His Own

Verlander's hard training during the offseason paid off in 2007. He started off his second MLB season by throwing his first career no-hitter against the Milwaukee Brewers on June 12, 2007. Determined to avoid interfering with Verlander's concentration as the young ace retired batter after batter, Tigers catcher Ivan (Pudge) Rodriguez made a point of not going out to the mound to talk to him during the game. "I didn't talk to him, I just left him alone," Rodriguez remembered. "Then, in the ninth inning, he tried to come over and talk to me and I told him, 'You know what? Go away. Just do what you've been doing. You're fine. You don't have to change anything.'" Verlander later claimed that his no-hitter had been inspired by his younger brother,

Verlander posing with fans after his first no-hitter, 2007.

who had pitched a no-hit high school game a few weeks earlier. "My parents called to tell me," he noted. "I'm the older brother, so I had to top him."

Verlander went on to post a stellar 18-6 record in 2007. His win total ranked sixth in the American League. He also struck out 183 batters in 201 2/3 innings with a 3.66 ERA, which helped him earn his first appearance in the MLB All-Star Game. Verlander's strong performance was not enough to take the Tigers back to the World Series, however. The team finished the year with an 88-74 record and missed the playoffs.

The 2008 season turned out to be a rough one for both Verlander and his team. Verlander's record dropped to 11-17, while his ERA increased to 4.84. He struck out 20 fewer batters than the year before (163) and walked 20 more (87), while pitching the same number of innings. He blamed his struggles on mechanical problems with his pitching motion as well as mental fatigue. "For two years, this game was easy," he acknowledged. "Just go out there and throw and—not that I wasn't giving it my all, because I was—win 17, win 18. Hey, what can go wrong? And then the next year, bam! Things catch up with you. This game has a way of taking you down in a hurry. It was an eye-opener." Meanwhile, the Tigers posted a disappointing 74-88 record and finished fifth in their division.

> *Verlander claimed that his first no-hitter was inspired by his younger brother, who had pitched a no-hit high school game a few weeks earlier. "My parents called to tell me," he noted. "I'm the older brother, so I had to top him."*

Verlander returned to form in 2009 and turned in the best season of his young career. He went 19-9 with a 3.45 ERA and struck out 269 batters in 240 innings. He led all starting pitchers in the American League in victories, strikeouts, and innings pitched. His strong performance helped him earn a second selection to the All-Star Team and a third-place finish in voting for the Cy Young Award, which is presented annually to the best pitcher in each league.

Despite Verlander's contributions, the Tigers collapsed down the stretch and barely missed making the playoffs with a 86-77 record. "October was tough. You've got the whole season, then this huge letdown toward the very end. I had never experienced anything like that," Verlander stated. "We had the team. To be honest with you, man, I wish we could go back and have another chance to make those playoffs. I believe we matched up well against anybody."

During the offseason, Verlander signed a five-year, $80-million contract extension with the Tigers that made him one of the highest-paid pitchers in the game. He had another outstanding year in 2010, posting the fourth-best record in the league at 18-9 and lowering his ERA to 3.37. He also struck out 219 batters in 224 1/3 innings and made his third appearance in the All-Star Game. The Tigers' record dropped to 81-81 despite Verlander's stellar showing, however, and the team failed to make the playoffs once again.

Becoming the Best

From the outset, the 2011 season showed signs of being a very special one for Verlander. He notched his 1,000th career strikeout in April against the Chicago White Sox. Then, on May 7, he threw his second career no-hitter against the Toronto Blue Jays. Verlander dominated that game so completely that he was one eighth-inning walk away from pitching a perfect game (allowing no runners on base). He also maintained his velocity throughout the game, throwing a 100 mile-per-hour fastball to the very last batter. The whole experience gave him a tremendous boost in confidence. "I had a different feeling in that game," he recalled. "I just felt very calm and relaxed. And I remember thinking, 'Let's try to carry this over for the rest of the season.'"

Verlander's confidence showed every time he took the mound in 2011, and he came tantalizingly close to no-hitters on several other occasions. "In the past I've gotten away with my stuff and making a lot of mistakes. This year I feel like I've just found myself to be more mentally prepared and physically prepared," he explained. "It's hard for me to put a finger on what I know, but it's there. Time. Experience of pitching at this level for a while now. You log it all away, and it opens up a new game to you, almost."

By midseason, baseball analysts agreed that Verlander had brought his game to a new level, and many argued that he was the best pitcher in baseball. He showed more maturity on the mound, trusting his ability to make pitches and not letting an occasional mistake bother him. Although the average speed of his fastball (95.3 miles per hour) remained the highest of any MLB pitcher, he mixed in more off-speed pitches. By pacing himself, he was often able to throw progressively faster pitches as games wore on. "There were times early in his career when he would overthrow," said Tigers General Manager Dave Dombrowski. "He realizes now that throwing harder

Teammates rush out as Verlander and Detroit Tigers catcher Alex Avila celebrate another no-hitter, May 2011.

isn't always the solution. If you can throw 93 to 95 on the outside corner enough and you have a plus curve and a plus changeup, that's pretty good. Of course, when you dial it up to 100 when you need it, that's good too."

By the end of the 2011 season, Verlander led the league in nearly every statistical category for pitchers. He posted the best record at 24-5, the lowest ERA at 2.40, the most strikeouts at 250, and the most innings pitched at 251. He became only the 11th pitcher in the American League ever to win the elusive "triple crown" by leading in victories, ERA, and strikeouts in the same season. Verlander's incredible season earned him a slew of awards. He made the All-Star Team for the fourth time, was named *Baseball Digest* Pitcher of the Year and MLB Players' Choice Player of the Year, and won the Cy Young Award as the best pitcher in the American League by a unanimous vote.

Claiming the Most Valuable Player Award

Many baseball analysts and Tigers fans also considered Verlander a leading candidate for the American League's Most Valuable Player (MVP) Award. No one doubted that he played a vital role in the Tigers' success, as the team posted a 95-67 record for the season and won the AL Central Division. Yet some people argued that the MVP award should go to a player who took the field every day, rather than a pitcher who only appeared in one out of every four or five games. For this reason, the last starting pitcher to claim the MVP award was Roger Clemens in 1986. Verlander believed that he deserved as much consideration for the award as any other player. "Pitchers are players," he stated. "It's the Most Valuable Player Award." His supporters also pointed out that Verlander had faced 969 hitters during the 2011 season, while Boston Red Sox outfielder Jacoby Ellsbury—also considered a leading MVP candidate—had only appeared at the plate 729 times.

The MVP debate continued throughout the playoffs, as the Tigers beat the New York Yankees 3 games to 2 in the AL Division Series. Verlander started Game 1 against Yankees ace C.C. Sabathia, but the highly anticipated pitchers' duel never materialized. The game was postponed due to heavy rain after two innings with the score tied 1-1. When the game resumed the next day, neither pitcher returned to the mound, and the Tigers lost 9-3. Verlander faced Sabathia once again in Game 3. He pitched 8 innings, allowed 4 runs, and struck out 11 batters, as the Tigers won the game 5-4.

> "I love the Tigers. The fans there have seen me grow up not only as a person but as a player. I feel a sense of belonging there, and I think the fans feel that connection as well."

In the AL Championship Series, the Tigers lost to the powerful Texas Rangers 4 games to 2. Verlander started Game 1 against Texas, but lengthy rain delays limited his time on the mound to 4 innings. He allowed 3 runs and took the loss as the Tigers went down by a score of 3-2. Verlander pitched again with his team facing elimination in Game 5. He went 7 innings, struck out 8 batters, and allowed 4 runs, but ended up winning the game 7-5. Unfortunately, Detroit was eliminated in Game 6 when the series returned to Texas. "Day in and day out, we go through it as a family," Verlander said afterward of his teammates. "To come up a bit short is tough."

Verlander's disappointment at missing a chance to pitch in the World Series was eased somewhat when he received the American League MVP Award. He thus became the 10th pitcher in history to win both the Cy Young and the MVP award in the same season, and only the second pitcher (after Don Newcombe) ever to have won both of those awards as well as Rookie of the Year honors. Verlander was proud to claim the MVP trophy on behalf of all pitchers. "I think this set a precedent," he said. "I'm happy

Verlander pitching against the Texas Rangers in Game 5 of the 2011 American League Championship Series. The Tigers lost the series four games to two.

the voters acknowledged that we do have a major impact in this game and we can be extremely valuable to our team and its success."

By the end of the 2011 season, Verlander had posted a remarkable 107 career victories in only 6 full seasons in the majors. "He works hard and has the desire to be the best," said Tigers Manager Jim Leyland. "There is nobody I'd rather have on the mound in a must-win game." Even though Detroit did not quite reach the World Series, Verlander feels confident about his team's future chances. "I still think our owner and our management is going to put us in a position every year where we can win. That's one of the things I look at when I think about being in Detroit for a while. I'm an extremely competitive guy in everything I do, and I want to win at all costs," he noted. "I love the Tigers. The fans there have seen me grow up not only as a person but as a player. I feel a sense of belonging there, and I think the fans feel that connection as well."

HOME AND FAMILY

During the offseason, Verlander lives in a townhome on a golf course in Lakeland, Florida. His favorite room is his "man cave," where he plans to display his Cy Young and MVP trophies. "I have a humongous couch with a 12-foot TV projector and a Ping-Pong table," he said. "I guess I'm going to find some space for some hardware."

HOBBIES AND OTHER INTERESTS

In his free time, Verlander enjoys playing golf, watching movies, and playing video games. His all-time favorite movies are the baseball-related *Field of Dreams* and *The Rookie,* but he also likes the *Spider-Man* series and other action movies. He was excited to be featured on the cover of the *Major League Baseball 2K12* video game. Verlander also hosts a weekly poker game and occasionally plays competitively in casinos. "I just like to have fun," he noted. "I like to hang out with the guys a lot and just live my life."

Verlander also participates in a number of charity functions with the Tigers, including the Tigers Dreams Come True Program, the Detroit Tigers Autographed Memorabilia Donation Program, the Tigers Winter Caravan, and the Children's Miracle Network.

HONORS AND AWARDS

Minor League All-Star (*Baseball America*): 2005
Minor League Starting Pitcher of the Year (MLB.com): 2005
American League Rookie of the Year Award: 2006

American League All-Star Team: 2007, 2009, 2010, 2011
American League Cy Young Award: 2011
American League Most Valuable Player Award: 2011
Pitcher of the Year (*Baseball Digest*): 2011
MLB Players' Choice Player of the Year: 2011

FURTHER READING

Periodicals

Baseball Digest, Sep. 2006, p.60; May 2007, p.56; Jan.-Feb. 2012, p.22
New York Times, Sep. 18, 2009; Nov. 22, 2011
Sporting News, Mar. 15, 2010, p.52; Sep. 12, 2011, p.36
Sports Illustrated, Aug. 28, 2006, p.50; May 28, 2007, p.14; Sep. 19, 2011,
    p.62
Sports Illustrated Kids, Aug. 2011, p.18
USA Today, June 26, 2006; June 20, 2007; July 8, 2011; Oct. 5, 2011; Nov. 16,
    2011

Online Articles

www.baseball-reference.com/bullpen/Justin%20Verlander
    (Baseball Reference, "Justin Verlander," no date)
www.mensjournal.com/justin-verlander
    (Men's Journal, "Shut Up and Throw the Ball," Apr. 16, 2012)
sportsillustrated.cnn.com/2012/writers/joe_lemire/05/02/justin.verlander
    .velocity/
    (Sports Illustrated, "How Justin Verlander Is Defying Conventional Wis-
    dom," May 2, 2012)

ADDRESS

Justin Verlander
Detroit Tigers
Comerica Park
2100 Woodward Ave.
Detroit, MI 48201

WEB SITES

detroit.tigers.mlb.com
sportsillustrated.cnn.com/baseball/mlb/players/7590
espn.go.com/mlb/player/_/id/6341/justin-verlander

Abby Wambach 1980-

American Soccer Player with the U.S. Women's
National Team
Gold Medalist at the 2004 and 2012 Olympic Games

BIRTH

Mary Abigail Wambach (pronounced WAHM-bahk), known
as Abby, was born on June 2, 1980, in Rochester, New York.
Her parents, Peter and Judy Wambach, own a garden supply
store. Abby is the youngest of seven children in her family.
Her siblings, who range from 2 to 11 years older, are Beth,
Laura, Peter, Matthew, Patrick, and Andrew.

YOUTH

As the youngest member of a very active family, Abby grew up playing a variety of rough-and-tumble games on the cul-de-sac where they lived. "My mom would literally lock us out of the house and say go play," she recalled. "We wouldn't be able to come in, not even to pee."

Starting when Abby was five or six, her brothers would dress her up in makeshift hockey pads and make her stand in front of a net while they fired slapshots at her. She also demonstrated her fearless nature in neighborhood basketball and football games. "One of the first experiences where I knew she'd be better than most was a game of football," her brother Matthew remembered. "I threw the ball to one of the neighbors and Abby tackled him. She got up and he was on the ground, groaning. She was 11 or 12."

> As the youngest member of a very active family, Abby grew up playing a variety of rough-and-tumble games on the cul-de-sac where they lived. "My mom would literally lock us out of the house and say go play," Wambach recalled. "We wouldn't be able to come in, not even to pee."

Abby was first introduced to soccer when her sister Beth checked out a book from the library about the sport. She joined her first girls' soccer team at the age of four. After she scored 27 goals in 3 games, however, Abby was moved to a boys' team. "Boys aren't going to let you win, no matter what," she noted. "I had to learn to use my body because the boys were stronger than I was." Even after changing leagues, Abby continued to excel on the soccer field. As she got older and went back to girls' leagues, she played for the Rochester Spirit Soccer Club and was selected to the Olympic Development Team U-16 National Team.

EDUCATION

Wambach attended Our Lady of Mercy, an all-girls Catholic high school in Rochester. She starred in both soccer and basketball, playing varsity all four years in each sport. On the soccer field, she scored 142 goals during her high school career, including an amazing 39 goals as a senior in 1997. She was selected as a High School All-American in both 1996 and 1997, and as a senior she was named High School Player of the Year by the Na-

Wambach playing for the University of Florida Gators in 2000.

tional Soccer Coaches Association of America. Wambach enjoyed representing Mercy on the soccer field, although she regrets that her high
school team never won a state championship. Mercy made it to the state
finals in 1997, but the team blew a 3-goal lead and lost the title. "That in a
lot of ways motivates me to continue being better because that's something I know I didn't accomplish," she stated.

After graduating from high school in 1998, Wambach accepted a scholarship to play soccer at the University of Florida. She made an immediate

impact as a freshman, scoring 19 goals to help the Gators claim the National Collegiate Athletic Association (NCAA) national championship. During her senior season in 2001, Wambach led all NCAA Division I players with 31 goals and 13 assists for 75 points (a player's points in soccer are calculated by doubling the number of goals scored and then adding assists). Her performance helped lift the Gators to an appearance in the Final Four of the NCAA tournament.

By the time she completed her college soccer career, Wambach held school records for goals scored (96), game-winning goals (24), assists (49), and points (241). She also ranked as the Division I career leader in points per game (3.17) and goals per game (1.29). She was named Southeastern Conference (SEC) Player of the Year in both 2000 and 2001—becoming the first player ever to claim the honor two years in a row—and was selected as an NCAA All-American three times.

When Wambach left Florida in 2002, she was a few credits short of completing her degree in leisure-services management. But she wanted to take advantage of an exciting opportunity to continue playing soccer in a newly formed professional league, the Women's United Soccer Association (WUSA). "I didn't realize until late in my college career that it was actually something I could do after college, maybe for a living and as a career," she recalled. "Even then, you still had to be the best in the world."

CAREER HIGHLIGHTS

Professional Soccer—The WUSA

Wambach was selected with the second overall pick in the 2002 WUSA draft by the Washington Freedom. She joined a team that was led by one of the legends of women's soccer—Mia Hamm. Wambach considered Hamm a mentor and felt that playing alongside the veteran helped her polish her skills. Although both Hamm and Wambach were known as goal-scorers, their styles of play were very different. Hamm was a small, fast, elusive striker who usually dribbled around opponents to score goals. Wambach, on the other hand, was a tall, physical, high-leaping striker who usually scored after receiving passes in front of the opponent's goal. "She is a mass of woman," said fellow WUSA player Brandi Chastain. "You can't move her very easily, and once she gains position, it's almost impossible to get around her."

Wambach turned in a phenomenal rookie season, leading the Freedom in goals (10), assists (9), and points (29). She was selected to play in the All-Star Game and was named Most Valuable Player (MVP) in that contest, and she easily won the league's Rookie of the Year Award. "I feel like I'm still in the middle of this tornado that's just struck in terms of my career just taking off," she said.

Wambach had an even better year in 2003. She scored 13 goals, added 7 assists, and tied with Hamm for the league lead in scoring with 33 points. The formidable offensive duo took the Freedom all the way to the WUSA championship, known as the Founders Cup. Wambach scored both of her team's goals in the final match, including the game-winner in sudden-death overtime, and was named MVP of the tournament. Unfortunately, the WUSA went out of business just a few weeks after the Freedom's triumph in the 2003 Founders Cup. The fledgling league simply did not attract enough fans and sponsorship money to continue operating. Its failure put an end to women's professional soccer in the United States for six years.

> "She is a mass of woman," said fellow WUSA player Brandi Chastain. "You can't move her very easily, and once she gains position, it's almost impossible to get around her."

International Soccer—The U.S. Women's National Team

The demise of the WUSA was a big disappointment for Wambach. During her short-lived pro soccer career, however, she also got an opportunity to play for the U.S. Women's National Team (WNT). The WNT would play in the FIFA Women's World Cup, held every four years beginning in 1991, and the Olympic Games, held every four years including 1996. Both of these international events are tournaments with a series of games, with teams eliminated along the way, that lead up to a final match for first place. Led by such well-known players as Mia Hamm, Julie Foudy, Joy Fawcett, Michelle Akers, and Kristine Lilly, the American squad had won the first-ever FIFA Women's World Cup tournament in 1991 and had also earned a gold medal in the 1996 Olympics. Team USA's memorable defeat of China in the 1999 World Cup final—an event watched by 90,185 fans (a world record for a women's sporting event) at the Rose Bowl in California—had also given a big boost to girls' soccer programs all across the United States.

When Wambach was invited to play with the WNT in 2002, she was thrilled to take the field with some of her childhood heroes. Despite scoring five goals in her first seven international matches, however, she was left off the

*Wambach (left) moves the ball around a German defender
at the 2003 Women's World Cup semifinal match.*

WNT roster in spring 2003. Coach April Heinrichs told her that she needed to improve her fitness and play with greater intensity if she hoped to make the team for the 2003 World Cup tournament that fall. "She needed to put it in black-and-white terms for me, and I think a light bulb went off in my head," Wambach remembered. "I wasn't playing my best soccer when I had this talk with April and we both knew it. But I knew something April didn't know—that I was going to start playing better."

Wambach worked hard over the next few months, and her commitment paid off during her tremendous 2003 WUSA championship season. Impressed by her MVP performance in the Founders Cup, Heinrichs selected Wambach as a member of the American team that would compete for the 2003 FIFA Women's World Cup. She appeared in her first World Cup match—a 3-1 U.S. victory over Sweden—on September 21, 2003. Two days later she scored her first World Cup goal in a 5-0 win over Nigeria. She scored again in Team USA's next match, a 3-0 victory over North Korea, and tallied her third goal of the tournament in the WNT's 1-0 victory over Norway in the quarterfinals. Unfortunately, the American squad lost to eventual champion Germany 3-0 in the semifinals. This defeat was a big blow to Wambach and the other American players. Wambach, however, was able to take pride in the fact that she was named U.S. Soccer's Female Athlete of the Year in recognition of her outstanding performance.

Winning an Olympic Gold Medal

Following the disappointing conclusion of the 2003 Women's World Cup, Wambach was determined to capture a gold medal at the 2004 Summer Olympics in Athens, Greece. Her mission gained even more importance when three of the biggest stars of American women's soccer—Mia Hamm, Joy Fawcett, and Julie Foudy—announced that they planned to retire afterward. The WNT spent seven months training together in preparation for the Olympic tournament, and Wambach relished every moment she spent with her legendary teammates. "Every time they talk on the soccer field, I'm listening," she noted. "I just want to absorb as much information from them as I possibly can. If I don't, I'll be cheating myself and the rest of the future of this team."

As the Olympic tournament got underway, Wambach once again proved to be a dangerous scoring threat. She scored a goal in each of the first two matches to help the United States defeat Greece 3-0 and Brazil 2-0. She also received yellow cards (penalties) in both contests, however, which meant that she had to sit out the third match against Australia. Her teammates struggled to a 1-1 tie without her. Team USA still advanced to the quarterfinals, where Wambach scored her third goal of the tournament to help beat Japan 2-1. After defeating Germany 2-1 in the semifinals, the American women squared off against Brazil in the gold medal match.

> "I don't think you'd ever use a word like timid about Abby," said teammate Mia Hamm. "She just kind of embraces life and goes for it and doesn't apologize for it. From that standpoint, every single day is high speed with Abby, and it is infectious. It gave us older players that youthful enthusiasm that carried us through."

The United States and Brazil played an intense, evenly matched game. With the score deadlocked at 1-1 at the end of regulation time, the two teams were forced to play a 30-minute overtime period. In the 22nd minute, Kristine Lilly lofted a corner kick toward the front of Brazil's goal. Wambach jostled for position and headed the ball into the net. It was her fourth goal of the tournament, and it turned out to be the game-winner for the United States. It was especially meaningful for Wambach to help send her star teammates into retirement with a gold medal. "To be able to play, to be able to win a gold medal, to be able to score the winning goal in the gold-medal game for these women, the women who have given me my way of life, who have given me my job in a lot of respects.... This is the best thank you I could give them," she stated. "It's a dream come true."

Wambach's teammates were eager to give her credit for lifting the United States to victory. "I don't think you'd ever use a word like timid about Abby," said Hamm. "She just kind of embraces life and goes for it and doesn't apologize for it. From that standpoint, every single day is high speed with Abby, and it is infectious. It gave us older players that youthful enthusiasm that carried us through." By the end of 2004, Wambach had scored 31 goals in 30 international matches—the highest per-game average in history. In honor of her remarkable Olympic performance, she earned the U.S. Soccer Female Athlete of the Year Award for the second straight year.

Emerging as the Team Leader

Once the longtime leaders of the WNT retired, Wambach emerged as the top player for the American squad. "Mia was the one. Now Abby's the one," Lilly explained. "Now they're going to be gunning for her." Despite getting more attention from opposing defenses, however, Wambach continued to perform well against international competition. During the 2005 season she scored 4 goals and added 5 assists in the 8 games in which she played. The following year she led Team USA in scoring with 17 goals and 8 assists. Her two most important goals came in a North American regional qualifying victory over Mexico. The win enabled the American squad to qualify for the 2007 FIFA Women's World Cup tournament.

In the first round of the World Cup tournament, Wambach scored a goal as Team USA battled North Korea to a 2-2 tie. In some respects the American squad was relieved to manage a tie, because they did not have Wambach for a significant stretch of the game. She collided with an opposing player midway through and sustained a cut on her head that required 11 stitches. While she was getting patched up in the locker room, she could not wait to return to action. "I was yelling at the doctors to get it done quicker," she remembered. "I cursed some bad words and hurried up and got my jersey on and ran as fast as I could."

Three days later Wambach scored both American goals in a 2-0 victory over Sweden. After Team USA defeated Nigeria 2-1 to reach the quarterfinals, she scored her fourth goal of the tournament to help the American squad beat England 3-0. In the semifinals, however, Wambach and her teammates were shut out by Brazil 4-0 to dash their hopes for a World Cup championship. It was the worst-ever defeat for the WNT. Although Wambach came back to score 2 more goals to help Team USA win the con-

During this game against North Korea in the 2007 Women's World Cup, Wambach cut her head while colliding with another player, left the field to get 11 stitches, and then returned to the game.

461

solation game against Norway—giving her 6 goals in 6 matches—she was still deeply disappointed in the result. At the end of the year, she received U.S. Soccer Player of the Year honors for the third time.

In 2008 the WNT played 22 games in preparation for the Olympic Games in Beijing, China. Wambach led the team with 13 goals and 10 assists during that period. In Team USA's last exhibition match before the Olympic tournament, however, she crashed into Brazilian defender Andréia Rosa and broke two bones in her leg. Wambach knew right away that the injury was serious. "My knee was pointing up and my foot was pointing in a little bit of a different direction," she explained. The following day she underwent surgery to insert a titanium rod in her leg.

The injury forced Wambach to miss the Olympics. Yet she felt confident that her teammates would prevail in her absence. "I wasn't freaked out about what was ahead, what was in store for the team," she declared. "Yes, I know I'm a very important player for the team. But in the moment, it made me realize even more how insignificant one player is in a team environment. It really does take a team to win championships. There is no doubt in my heart, no doubt in my mind, no doubt in my soul this team can win a gold medal." True to her prediction, Team USA defeated Brazil in the finals to claim the gold medal.

Heading for the World Cup

After nearly a year of recovery and rehabilitation, Wambach returned to international competition in 2009. On July 19 she scored her 100th career goal in international play during a 1-0 victory over Canada in her hometown of Rochester. The milestone placed her behind only Mia Hamm (with 158 career goals) and Kristine Lilly (with 129) on the all-time list of American scorers. By the end of 2010 she had scored 117 goals in 149 international games, a tally that gave her the best goals-per-game ratio in U.S. history. Perhaps most amazingly, 46 of those goals (nearly 40 percent) were struck with her head rather than her feet. Wambach was widely considered to be the best "header" in the world—male or female.

Wambach also returned to professional soccer in 2009 in the newly created Women's Professional Soccer (WPS) league. She joined her old WUSA team, the Washington Freedom, late in the season but still managed to score 8 goals, including 3 game-winners. During the 2010 season Wambach netted 13 goals, including 5 game-winners. Prior to the start of the 2011 season, the Freedom franchise moved to Florida and was renamed magicJack (after the data storage device company that served as its main sponsor). Wambach scored 4 goals in 5 games before leaving to join the WNT in preparation for the FIFA Women's World Cup.

As the 2011 World Cup tournament approached, Wambach desperately wanted to bring home a trophy to make up for the disappointments of 2003 and 2007. "My career will not be complete without a World Cup championship," she declared. "I take it personally that I haven't won one, and I'll be heartbroken if we walk away without one."

At the same time, though, Wambach realized that her role on the team was beginning to change. Under new head coach Pia Sundhage, the WNT moved to a possession-oriented, ball-control offense that emphasized short passes. The team thus moved away from the long passes that had set up many of Wambach's goals over the years. Under the new style, Wambach only scored 1 goal in 10 games in 2011 leading up to the World Cup tournament. "I'm not going to sit here and say I don't want to score," she said. "What I'm going to say is that I would prefer winning to scoring. I've been fortunate to score many goals in the World Cup, and we haven't won one. So I'll set up goals. If I have to watch my teammates score goals and we win the championship, I couldn't care less."

> *At the 2011 World Cup tournament, Wambach wanted to bring home a trophy to make up for the disappointments of 2003 and 2007. "My career will not be complete without a World Cup championship," she declared. "I take it personally that I haven't won one, and I'll be heartbroken if we walk away without one."*

Falling Short in the Final Match

The United States opened the 2011 World Cup tournament with a 2-0 win against North Korea and followed up with a 3-0 victory over Colombia. In the third match, however, Team USA lost 2-1 to Sweden. Wambach broke her scoring drought in that game by putting the ball into the net off her shoulder in the 67th minute of play. But the loss meant that the United States faced a tough quarterfinal matchup against Brazil—the team that had knocked the American women out of contention for the 2007 World Cup.

The United States jumped out to an early lead when Brazilian defender Daiane deflected the ball into her own goal. In the 68th minute, however,

U.S. defender Rachel Buehler received a red card for fouling Brazilian star Marta, the five-time FIFA Player of the Year. Marta made the penalty kick to tie the score at 1-1, and Team USA was forced to play shorthanded (10 players vs. 11) for the remainder of the game. When Marta scored again 2 minutes into the 30-minute overtime period, it appeared as if the U.S. team might endure another early exit from the World Cup tournament. But with time running out, Wambach took a crossing pass from teammate Megan Rapinoe and headed it into Brazil's goal to tie the score 2-2 and force a shootout. All 5 American kickers scored, while U.S. goalkeeper Hope Solo made a key save against the third Brazilian kicker, Daiane, to preserve the epic, come-from-behind victory.

Team USA thus advanced to face France in the semifinals. The score was tied 1-1 until the 79th minute of play, when Wambach scored another header off a corner kick from Lauren Cheney. The United States went on to win 3-1 to advance to the World Cup finals for the first time since 1999. "We've achieved our goal. We're in the final," Wambach said afterward. "We want to complete it. We want to be world champs." Many Americans felt optimistic about the WNT's chances in the final when they learned that the opponent would be Japan, which was winless against the United States in 25 matches.

Wambach and her teammates came out strong and played some of their best soccer of the tournament against Japan. Although the Americans had dozens of great scoring opportunities, they did not get a goal until the 69th minute on a tough shot by Alex Morgan. The Japanese came right back to tie the score 12 minutes later following a defensive mistake by the U.S. squad. Wambach finally worked her way free of the smothering Japanese defense to score yet another header in the 104th minute of play. It was her fourth goal of the tournament and the 13th World Cup goal of her career, which placed her third on the all-time list. Japan refused to give up, however, and evened the score at 2-2 just a few minutes later. The World Cup championship was ultimately decided in a shootout, which Japan won 3-1. Wambach was the only American shooter to make her penalty shot. For her outstanding performance, she received the Silver Ball Award as the second-best player in the tournament (behind Japan's Homare Sawa) and the Bronze Boot Award as the third-leading goal scorer.

Despite the accolades, Wambach was devastated by the loss. "There are really no words. We were so close," she stated. "Obviously, we wanted to bring home the Cup; we felt we played well enough to do that. Obviously, the Japanese proved to be stronger-willed in the end." Upon returning home to the United States, Wambach and her teammates were gratified to

During the 2011 Women's World Cup game against France, the score was tied 1-1 when Wambach headed the ball off a corner kick past France's goalkeeper.

find hundreds of fans waiting to greet them at the airport in New York. The crowds were cheering and waving American flags. "It brought my spirits up more than anything could have," she acknowledged. "I'm so disappointed for my teammates, myself, I'm so disappointed for our country because I really feel we had it, and it was so close. Coming home to this type of reception is truly one of the best things that ever happened."

The 2012 Olympics

Wambach continued to play with the U.S. Women's National Team in preparation for the 2012 Olympic Games. The main location for the Olympics was London, England, but soccer games were held throughout the United Kingdom. In the first round, the U.S. started out by facing France. Just 13 minutes into the game France scored two goals in a 3-minute span, and Wambach came back with a goal 5 minutes later with a header off a corner kick; the U.S. went on to win 4-2. It was Wambach's 139th goal of her career, her first goal of this Olympic contest, and her

———— " ————

"This win feels like everything has come full circle," Wambach said after the Olympics gold medal match. "I'm so proud of this team for never giving up. It was a team effort for this entire tournament and it shows what it takes to win championships—it's teamwork and loyalty and trusting in each other."

———— " ————

fifth lifetime Olympic goal. Next up was Colombia, and the U.S. controlled that match. In a physical contest, the U.S. showed superior skill and athleticism and won 3-0, including a goal from Wambach. The U.S. then played Korea DPR (the Democratic People's Republic of Korea, also known as North Korea), winning 1-0 on another goal from Wambach and moving on to the next round. The team celebrated their win on the field by doing a worm dance.

In the quarterfinals, the U.S. faced New Zealand. Wambach continued to dominate, scoring the first goal of an eventual 2-0 win. She then joined a team celebration of cartwheels to honor the U.S. women's gymnastics team. "We obviously don't do it quite as well," she admitted. "But we wanted to send a shout out to all the gymnasts." Many soccer observers noticed that she was playing a very physical game, despite all the wear and tear of her years of play. "Wambach's strength has always been her willingness to be aggressive," Sam Borden wrote in the *New York Times*. "She is unafraid to jump in the chaotic mix beneath a high cross and she never shies away from contact if a ball is bouncing near the goal…. Since the Olympic tournament began, Wambach has been the most indispensable American threat."

The team moved on to face Canada in the semifinals in what many called one of the most dramatic, exciting, and emotional games in Olympic history. The Canadian team was very organized and applied constant pressure on the U.S. Canadian forward Christine Sinclair scored 3 times, and each time the U.S. answered with a goal of their own to tie the game—including one from Wambach on a penalty kick. The game went into overtime, and Alex Morgan scored the game-winning goal at the 123-minute mark, just moments before the game would go to penalty kicks.

For the gold medal match, the U.S. team faced Japan. Many viewed it as a rematch of the World Cup just a year earlier, calling it a chance for the Americans to exact revenge for their loss. The U.S. Women's National Team did just that, outscoring Japan 2-1 to win the gold medal. It was the Americans' fourth win in the five soccer competitions that have been held in the

Wambach celebrating on the field with an American flag immediately after the U.S. won the gold medal match.

Olympics—since the 1996 Games, when soccer was added to the Olympics, the U.S. has won four gold medals and one silver, losing to Norway in 2000. Midfielder Carli Lloyd scored both goals and goalkeeper Hope Solo made a series of spectacular saves to defeat a Japanese team playing with their usual speed and discipline. "The teams put on a back-and-forth, don't-turn-your-head soccer showcase, proving again that these are the two premier teams in the world," one analyst wrote for ESPN. Soccer commentator Sam Border offered a similar view in the *New York Times.* "For more than a year, the United States women's soccer team spoke of redemption and revenge," Borden wrote. "But when the Olympic gold medal match was finally over, and the Americans were hugging and shrieking and laughing together in a pile, there was also an obvious sense of relief. Who could blame them? Yes, the United States got its payback for the wrenching defeat in last summer's Women's World Cup final, but its 2-1 victory over Japan was what most of this team's biggest matches are: Tense and dramatic, with the Japanese poking and pushing for an equalizer until the final whistle as the United States did everything it could to stay strong."

It was a huge win for the whole team, as Wambach said later. "This was a year's worth of work and the sacrifices all of us have had to make for our friends and families, for the players that didn't make the roster, this goes out to all of our fans that cheered us on last summer and were equally as heartbroken as we were," she said. "This year has been trials and tribulations, we lost to Japan a few times, and this win feels like everything has come full circle. I'm so proud of this team for never giving up. It was a team effort for this entire tournament and it shows what it takes to win championships—it's teamwork and loyalty and trusting in each other."

By the end of the Olympics, Wambach had 143 career goals, with 9 Olympic goals—including 5 at the 2012 Olympics. She then stood as the 2nd highest goal scorer in the history of the U.S. Women's National Team, after Mia Hamm. The team has a series of games planned in late 2012, but after that, Wambach's long-term plans remain uncertain. She has said in the past that she hoped to continue playing professional soccer, but in 2012 the WPS suspended the season, then announced it was folding.

Planning Ahead

Wambach has said that when her soccer career concludes, she hopes to continue reaching out to people internationally. "I want to travel the world in a different capacity," she explained. "Not as a soccer player but as a humanitarian, a philanthropist. I want to own restaurants, own real estate, stuff that I'm working now to afford and achieve."

HOME AND FAMILY

Wambach, who is single, lives in Hermosa Beach, California. She shares her home with a skateboard-riding English bulldog named Kingston.

HOBBIES AND OTHER INTERESTS

In her spare time, Wambach enjoys listening to music, playing video games, surfing, mountain biking, and camping.

HONORS AND AWARDS

High School All-American: 1996, 1997
National High School Player of the Year (NSCAA): 1997
NCAA All-American: 1998, 1999, 2000, 2001
SEC Player of the Year: 2000, 2001
WUSA Rookie of the Year: 2002
WUSA Founders Cup Champion: 2003 (with Washington Freedom)
WUSA Founders Cup MVP: 2003
U.S. Soccer Female Athlete of the Year: 2003, 2004, 2007, 2010, 2011
Olympic Women's Soccer: 2004, gold medal (with U.S. Women's National Team); 2012, gold medal (with U.S. Women's National Team)

Associated Press Female Athlete of the Year: 2011
FIFA World Cup Silver Ball: 2011
FIFA World Cup Bronze Boot: 2011

FURTHER READING

Periodicals

Current Biography Yearbook, 2011

Houston Chronicle, July 14, 2011, Sports, p.1

New York Times, July 8, 2007, p.L8; July 17, 2011, p.L1; July 18, 2011, p.D1; Aug. 9, 2011, p.B11

Newsday, July 19, 2011

Sports Illustrated, Oct. 1, 2007

Sports Illustrated for Kids, Sep. 2011, p.13

St. Louis Post-Dispatch, July 6, 2011

USA Today, Sep. 18, 2003, p.C10; July 8, 2005, p.C10; June 6, 2011, p.C2; July 7, 2011, p.C1; July 13, 2011, p.C1

Online Articles

espn.go.com
(ESPN, "Closure for U.S.: Beating Japan 2-1 at Wembley Brings Closure to a Yearlong Mission of Revenge" and "U.S. Tops Japan for Soccer Gold," Aug. 10, 2012)

soccernet.espn.go.com
(ESPN, "Wambach Leads by Example," Aug. 12, 2004)

www.topics.nytimes.com
(New York Times, "Abby Wambach," multiple articles, various dates)

www.nytimes.com
(New York Times, "United States Wins Women's Soccer Gold," Aug. 9, 2012)

www.democratandchronicle.com
(Rochester Democrat-Chronicle, "Abby Wambach Eager to Win a World Cup," June 28, 2011)

www.sportsillustrated.cnn.com
(Sports Illustrated, "Lloyd leads U.S. women to gold medal victory over Japan 2-1" and "U.S. women's fourth gold medal a team effort in the truest sense," Aug. 9, 2012)

content.usatoday.com/topics/index
(USA Today, "Abby Wambach," multiple articles, various dates)

www.usatoday.com
(USA Today, "U.S. women hold off Japan to claim third consecutive
gold," Aug. 9, 2012)

ADDRESS

Abby Wambach
U.S. Soccer Federation
1801 South Prairie Avenue
Chicago, IL 60616

WEB SITES

www.abbywambach.com
www.ussoccer.com/teams/wnt/abby-wambach
www.gatorzone.com/soccer/bios

Florence Welch 1986-

British Singer and Musician
Lead Singer of the Musical Group Florence + the Machine

BIRTH

Florence Leontine Mary Welch was born on October 28, 1986, in Camberwell, a southern district of London, England. She was the oldest of three children born to Nick Welch, who worked in advertising, and Evelyn Welch, an American-born professor of art history and Renaissance studies. She has two younger siblings, Grace and John James.

YOUTH

Music was a big part of Welch's life when she was growing up. She joined her school choir and at 10 or 11 played the lead female role in a school production of the musical *Bugsy Malone.* Her father recalled that usually parents were only interested in watching their own children, "but when Florence sang, the whole audience was suddenly fully engaged. I remember thinking: 'Cripes, she's got a voice—this is serious.'" She also sang at various family funerals, including one for her grandfather Colin Welch, the noted satirist and newspaper editor. Although she did not play an instrument, she was already writing songs by the time she was 13. "My first songs were about imaginary break-ups," she recalled. "I'd never even had a boyfriend and it was all very flowery and poetic." She also had a fascination with dark and spooky things, including witches, vampires, werewolves, graveyards, and paintings of religious martyrs.

> "
>
> *Welch was already writing songs by the time she was 13. "My first songs were about imaginary break-ups," she recalled. "I'd never even had a boyfriend and it was all very flowery and poetic."*
>
> "

Welch was 13 when her parents divorced. Soon after, her mother married a widowed neighbor and the two families moved in together. With three older stepsiblings in the mix, there was a lot of tension in the house. (She also gained a fourth stepsibling when her father remarried.) With all the family drama, Welch rebelled. She stayed out late at parties held in abandoned buildings, where she learned to sing loudly to cut through the noise. As she grew older, her lyrics also grew darker. "I've always been attracted to dark imagery," she noted. "I used to believe in vampires and werewolves. I get night terrors, panic attacks. Even as a kid, I'd be more inclined to write about a flower dying than blossoming." She formed a band called the Toxic Cockroaches with a schoolmate and also took voice lessons. "It was too constraining for me," she recalled. "When I was told to preserve my voice by not partying or talking loudly, I thought, WRONG GIRL. There was no freedom for me in singing classically."

EDUCATION

Welch completed her secondary education at Alleyn's School, a private school in Dulwich, southeast London. She was diagnosed with dyslexia, a reading disability, and dysmetria, a problem judging distances, but she still

Welch has become known for her creative approach to costumes for all her shows.

earned good grades. In high school in Great Britain, students study specific subjects for their last two years and then take tests in order to qualify for college. Welch earned A-levels (Advanced Level) in several subjects, including art, English, and history. She entered the Camberwell College of Arts, part of the University of the Arts London. She planned to study illustration, but instead much of her work tended towards installations and performance art. She famously created a six-foot piece making fun of herself in fake flowers. She was more focused on college bands than college classes, however, and left after 18 months to focus on her music career.

CAREER HIGHLIGHTS

Breaking into the Music Business

Welch was 19 when she and her band signed a contract with a music manager. It wasn't a good match, and when she discovered she could get out of the contract by resigning from the band, she left the group. "I just didn't have a nice time," she recalled. "I didn't play an instrument, so I always thought I had to be a singer in a band ... then I found the drums." She sang on and off at area clubs until she found her manager, DJ-promoter Mairead Nash, by singing to her in a nightclub ladies' room. With a friend, keyboard player and producer Isabella Summers, Welch began writing songs and putting together demo recordings. They nicknamed each other "Florence Robot" and "Isabella Machine." When Welch began performing their songs live, she shortened "Florence Robot/Isa Machine" to Florence + the Machine. The name stuck, even though the lineup of musicians who formed "the Machine" has rotated and changed since then.

Welch spent the next two years experimenting with musical styles and seeking the right record company. "I used to make 10-minute songs about stationery and dead swans," she recalled. "I felt like a bit of a fraud when the record companies were taking me out for dinner. I didn't actually know what I could offer them, and I felt they had a certain idea of what they wanted me to be." By 2008, she signed with a record label, Island Records, that was willing to let her make music the way she wanted. She wrote lyrics inspired by "that feeling you get when you wake up in the morning with that creeping unknown dread that follows you around all day." Her songs often transposed lyrical images with strong percussion to create music that was both primal and thoughtful. Welch added another unique sound to her group when a harpist walked by the studio where she was working one day. "We figured why not get him in to actually play it," she remembered, "and it sounded so great that we just decided to use it on

Lungs *was Florence + the Machine's debut album.*

everything." In the summer of 2008 the group toured Europe in a camper van, opening for American electronic rock group MGMT.

In June 2008 Florence + the Machine released their first single, "Kiss with a Fist." Welch wrote the song when she was 17, using images of physical violence to portray the extreme feeling of young love. The song hit the British charts and the group performed it on British television. Welch had not even completed an album when she got her first major recognition. In February 2009 she received the BRIT Awards' Critics' Choice prize for the British artist most likely to break through in the coming year. Soon after, she and songwriting partner Isa Summers began writing a song by banging on studio walls with their hands. The result was "Dog Days Are Over," the group's next single and a worldwide breakout hit. "I said to Isa: 'This is it, this is what I want to do,'" Welch recalled. "That song represents the whole album coming together for me."

In July 2009 Florence + the Machine released their first album, *Lungs,* in the United Kingdom. It debuted at No. 2 on the British charts—kept out of the top spot only by the recently deceased Michael Jackson—and stayed on the charts for 28 weeks before finally hitting No. 1. The artist described her sound as "choral, gospel, chamber pop with heavy tribal drum stylings," and it was further distinguished by her powerful voice. That year *Lungs* was nominated for the Mercury Music Prize, a prestigious award for the year's best album voted on by British musicians and industry insiders. In 2010, *Lungs* won the Brit Award for album of the year. "That was a big moment for us," Welch noted. "You don't create music to win awards, but it is very nice when it happens."

Finding an American Audience

In October 2009 *Lungs* was released in the United States. Over the next year, songs from the album were all over American radio and television. "Dog Days Are Over" hit No. 21 on *Billboard*'s Hot 100 chart and was covered on the popular musical television show "Glee." Other Florence + the Machine songs appeared on the American TV shows "Grey's Anatomy," "Community," "90210," and "Gossip Girl"; Welch even performed on an episode of the latter show. Another song from the album, "Heavy in Your Arms," was chosen for the soundtrack to the popular 2010 film *The Twilight Saga: Eclipse.* By the end of 2010, *Lungs* had hit No. 2 on *Billboard*'s Alternative Album chart and No. 1 on their Heatseekers Albums chart for new and developing acts.

Welch made an impression on audiences through live performances as well, especially her appearance at the 2010 MTV Music Awards, where she had been nominated for Video of the Year and Best Rock Video. Her stage appearance, during which she rose from lying on a rotating platform to belt out "Dog Days Are Over," was the talk of the evening. The singer reflected on her ability to become larger-than-life on stage and attributed it to watching her mother, an art professor. "She's not a performer," Welch explained. "But when she gets on stage to give a lecture she becomes this heightened version of herself. She can suddenly hold the whole room rapt. I think that's where it comes from." For Welch, performing was a way to express her deepest, most heart-felt emotions. "You can feel things violently. It's a beautiful word. I'm such a non-violent person, too. I keep so much inside. I'm the least aggressive person ever. I can't argue. ... Music is my way out. I keep things locked up and never say anything."

Florence + the Machine opening a concert for U2 in Miami, Florida, 2011.

The year 2011 brought a lot of success for Welch and Florence + the Machine. The group began headlining their own U.S. shows, and they opened several U.S. concerts for the Irish rock group U2. Florence + the Machine was also nominated for the Grammy Award for Best New Artist. At the Grammys show, Welch performed live with star singers Yolanda Adams, Christina Aguilera, Jennifer Hudson, and Martina McBride in a tribute to the Queen of Soul, Aretha Franklin. By the end of 2011, *Lungs* had sold over 3.5 million copies worldwide.

By that point Welsh was ready to record her second album. Although she had offers to record with the hottest American producers in Los Angeles, she decided to remain in England and continue working with producer-songwriter Paul Epworth, noted for his work on British singer Adele's smash album *21*. The second Florence + the Machine album, *Ceremonials*, debuted in fall 2011. "I wanted it to be more dark, more heavy, bigger drum sounds, bigger bass, but with more of a whole sound," she said of the album. "So it sounded like a whole project rather than a scrapbook of ideas, which, for better or for worse, the first one was. That was a real specific thing: I wanted to work in one place with one producer." She also wanted to highlight the members of her band—synthesizer player Isa Summers, drummer Chris Hayden, harpist Tom Moth, guitarist Rob Ackroyd, pianist Rusty Bradshaw, and bass player Mark Saunders. "This time I

*The Chanel fashion show at Paris Fashion Week, with Welch
singing from inside a clam shell, October 2011.*

really wanted to give the music space to breathe and for the band to be able to experiment." The album debuted at No. 6 on the *Billboard* album chart and earned Welch Brit Award nominations for album of the year and best female solo artist.

Becoming a Fashion Icon

In addition to her success in the music world, Welch soon became a favorite of fashion designers. Becoming a fashion icon was not something she would have foreseen. "I was a short, chubby kid," she remembered. "It wasn't until I was 17 that I really grew into myself and started wearing the clothes I wanted to wear." She experimented with vintage clothes, found glamorous gowns like those she had admired as a child, and had a stage of wearing Goth clothes, with "bat-wing costumes" and black lipstick. She tried many different hair colors before fixing on bright red, which set off her blue eyes and pale, porcelain skin. Style mavens appreciated her dramatic flair and fondness for using vintage clothing, including many pieces found at flea markets the day of her performances. "I didn't construct the image deliberately but as the music got more overpowering, I felt I needed to compete with it," she explained. "I wanted something that would put me in a more dramatic place and it just happened as I toured." Her costumes became an important part of her stage persona. "What I wear on stage really can affect my performance, from how I move to how I feel," she said. "When I'm on stage it's really part of my armor, it makes me feel connected to my home and to myself. Besides, dressing up is just fun. It makes life better."

By 2011, Welch had been embraced by many noted designers. She was invited to sit in the front row at fashion shows by Valentino and Givenchy, and Gucci designed several outfits for her 2011 tour. She performed at the Metropolitan Museum's Costume Institute Gala, which honored the late designer Alexander McQueen, singing for an audience filled with celebrities like Madonna, Jay-Z, and Paul McCartney. In fall 2011 designer Karl Lagerfeld, the lead designer for the Chanel fashion house, recruited her to sing at his Paris fashion week show, which she did from inside a giant clam shell. Even when Welch wore a couture gown to the Grammys

"I love singing, and I love playing music. So it's a real joy for me to get up there, and I'm grateful every time I step on the stage that I'm allowed to do it.

that some critics disliked, designers appreciated her daring. In response to the criticism, she said, "People can say a million bad things about wearing that Givenchy dress and I would not care! I was so lucky to have on something so beautiful that day. If you know yourself and you know what you like then don't worry about it." For the singer, music and fashion had become two different ways to express herself. "Music to me is so internal. It's physical and it's emotional," she explained. "Whereas fashion is so much about the external that it's almost like a break. It's not inner turmoil. It's total escapism."

Welch and her group continued their conquest of the music world in 2012. They made an appearance on the noted acoustic performance show "MTV Unplugged," and the subsequent album, also titled *MTV Unplugged,* hit the *Billboard* album chart. The show was part of a more mature image Welch was developing. "I think, now, I feel a bigger sense of responsibility to the fans. To the people who come to see me play." The show attempted to capture Welch's joy in live performance. "I think it's that sense of wanting to make people let go," she explained. "What I really like seeing from the stage is people having their own moments, when people are doing some performance of their own." Florence + the Machine headlined their own tour in 2012, appearing all across the United States, Australia, and Europe. They were also scheduled for several festival appearances, including a featured performance at Chicago's noted Lollapalooza festival.

Whether through her recordings or on stage, Welch hoped to transport her listeners to another place, a world of heightened emotion. She wanted her music to be "something overwhelming and all-encompassing that fills you up, and you're either going to explode with it, or you're just going to disappear." Performing allowed Welch to experience that heightened emotion, and to share it with her fans. "I'm just an emotional creature.... I want to make people feel something good. It's essential. You should lift people." Although her rise to the top of the music world was swift, she hoped for a long career as a musician, bringing pleasure to her listeners. "I love singing, and I love playing music. So it's a real joy for me to get up there, and I'm grateful every time I step on the stage that I'm allowed to do it."

HOME AND FAMILY

Welch has been so busy recording and touring that as of 2012 she had not had time to find her own place to live. She still lives with her mother, stepfather, and extended family in her childhood home in London, and while on tour she was often accompanied by her sister. She has said that some day she would like to settle down and have children, but "I love singing. So I wouldn't want to give it up. I just think, hopefully, I would be able to fit all that in. At some point."

FAVORITE MUSIC

Welch's first influences were Disney movie musicals, especially *The Little Mermaid*; as a young girl she also discovered her father's classic rock CDs, including the Smiths, the Velvet Underground, and especially Grace Slick of Jefferson Airplane. As a teenager, she got into the local garage-punk scene and enjoyed punk-influenced bands like Green Day and Hole. She also listened to a lot of classic soul music, particularly Etta James, Nina Simone, and Billie Holliday. She has also acknowledged the influence of British female singers like Kate Bush and Annie Lennox of the Eurythmics, to whom she has been compared. Her own music collection contains all different sorts of music, including popular songs by Beyoncé and rappers Jay-Z and Kanye West. The singer made this analogy about her musical tastes: "I can't just have one painting—I need to cover the wall in paintings. It's the same with music. I want to mix everything together to create more."

480

HOBBIES AND OTHER INTERESTS

Although she left art school early, Welch still enjoys drawing and sketching. She brings sketchbooks along with her on tour and has considered returning to school to finish her illustration degree. She's also involved in several charities, specifically charities for sick children and teens.

RECORDINGS

Lungs, 2009
Ceremonials, 2011
MTV Unplugged, 2012

HONORS AND AWARDS

BRIT Awards (British Phonographic Industry): 2009, Critics' Choice Award; 2010, MasterCard British Album of the Year, for *Lungs*
MTV Video Music Award: 2011, best art direction, for "Dog Days Are Over"
NME Awards (*NME* magazine): 2012 (two awards), Best Solo Artist and Best Track, for "Shake It Out"

FURTHER READING

Periodicals

Billboard, Oct. 8, 2011
Entertainment Weekly, Apr. 13, 2012
Evening Standard (London), Oct. 24, 2008, p.41
Flare, Jan. 2012, p.66
Glamour, Nov. 2010, p.218
Guardian (England), Oct. 29, 2011
Interview, June/July 2009, p.46; Oct. 2011, p.68
Mail on Sunday (London), July 26, 2009, p.6
Rolling Stone, Dec. 23, 2010, p.32; Nov. 10, 2011; Nov. 24, 2011, p.42; July 21, 2012
Sunday Times (London), Sep. 20, 2009, p.14; Feb. 19, 2012
Sydney Morning Herald (Australia), August 1, 2009, p.4
Teen Vogue, Oct. 2009, p.74
USA Today, Oct. 31, 2011

Online Articles

www.billboard.com
    (Billboard, "Florence and the Machine," no date)

www.dailymail.co.uk
  (London Daily Mail, "Florence Welch: 'I Was Awkward, Intense, and Ridiculously Self-Conscious,'" Apr. 30, 2011)
www.ew.com
  (Entertainment Weekly, "Florence Welch: The Soundtrack of My Life," Apr 13, 2012)
www.kidzworld.com
  (Kidz World, "Florence and the Machine Bio," May 28, 2012)
www.npr.org
  (National Public Radio, "Florence and the Machine: From Delicate to Fierce," Apr. 7, 2010)

ADDRESS

Florence Welch
FATM Fan Mail
PO Box 67541
London, EC2P 2GL
United Kingdom

WEB SITE

www.florenceandthemachine.net

Rita Williams-Garcia 1957-

American Author of Novels for Young Adults
Winner of the 2011 Coretta Scott King Award for
One Crazy Summer

BIRTH

Rita Williams-Garcia was born Rita Williams on April 13, 1957, in Queens, New York. Her father, James Williams, had a career in the army and served in the Vietnam War for two years. Her mother, Essie Williams, was a domestic servant who volunteered with an anti-poverty program during the Vietnam War era. Williams-Garcia has an older brother, Russell Williams, and an older sister, Rosalind Rogers.

YOUTH

Williams-Garcia spent her early years in an apartment in Far Rockaway, a neighborhood in the Queens borough of New York City. Because of her father's military obligations, the family moved eight times before she was 12 years old. They lived in Arizona, California, and Georgia before eventually moving back to Jamaica, New York, a predominantly African-American neighborhood in Queens.

Williams-Garcia had few toys when she was young but remembers playing with wooden alphabet blocks frequently, which contributed to her early interest in words. She also engaged in imaginative play and told herself stories to pass the time. She was a very observant child, teaching herself to read at an early age by looking at billboards, cereal boxes, and her sister's textbooks. "My mother discovered I could read when we went to the Red Cross for our shots," she explained. "I knew all of the letters on the eye chart and could produce their sounds. When I figured out the sounds made words and the words made pictures—well, at two and a half, I was hooked." By age four she was writing adventure stories and nursery rhymes.

———— **"** ————

"My siblings and I indulged in now-vanishing pastimes," Williams-Garcia recalled. "We played hard. Read books. Colored with crayons. Rode bikes. Spoke as children spoke. Dreamed our childish dreams. If our parents did anything for us at all, they gave us a place to be children and kept the adult world in its place—as best as they could."

———— **"** ————

Williams-Garcia has shared many fond memories of growing up in Seaside, California, where she spent countless hours playing kickball, roller skating, and "dirt clod fighting" outdoors. "My siblings and I indulged in now-vanishing pastimes," she recalled. "We played hard. Read books. Colored with crayons. Rode bikes. Spoke as children spoke. Dreamed our childish dreams. If our parents did anything for us at all, they gave us a place to be children and kept the adult world in its place—as best as they could." Her parents had firm rules and high expectations for their children, providing a home environment that the author has described as "a safe place for us to dream and achieve." They also instilled in them a sense of social responsibility. For example, Rita and her siblings would come to the rescue of kids who were bullied at school or in the neighborhood.

Williams-Garcia has cited her mother, known as Miss Essie, as the most influential figure in her life, crediting her as an artistic inspiration. "She frightened me, made me laugh, and loved to paint things in weird colors—napalm orange, chartreuse, and aqua. She encouraged me to be creative and to see objects and situations beyond their physicality," the author explained. In addition to Miss Essie's creative spirit, Williams-Garcia has also discussed her mother's strength of character and no-nonsense parenting style, which included physical punishment. "My mother was clear about do's and don'ts, so you couldn't plead ignorance or miscommunication. Miss Essie was quite the communicator," she stated.

In 1969, when Williams-Garcia was 12 years old, the family left California for Georgia. After six months in the South, they moved back to Queens, settling in the neighborhood of Jamaica. She recalls experiencing culture shock during this transition. "We had no backyard to play in, no great outdoors," she revealed. "School was hardly a safe-haven. Fighting for the underdog became a thing of the past. We learned quickly to mind our own business. During those times, my journal became my confidant. I wrote in it faithfully." Her love for words grew as she entered adolescence, and she grew hungry for literature featuring female African-American protagonists. At the time, she found only the books *Mary Ellen, Student Nurse* and *Amos Fortune, Free Man,* both of which she enjoyed. Wanting more, however, she read the biographies of two important historical figures: Sojourner Truth, a slave who escaped and became an abolitionist and women's rights activist, and Harriet Tubman, an escaped slave who helped other slaves find freedom along the Underground Railroad.

Around the same time, Williams-Garcia developed the habit of jotting down story ideas in a notebook throughout the day. In the evening, after she had completed her homework, she would write at least 500 words of her continuing autobiographical novel. She also kept a diary. "I laugh when I read my early work," she said, "but writing it developed my writing rhythm. It helped that writing was my own thing and I looked forward to doing it." In seventh grade she began spending afternoons and weekends in the library reading *The Writer's Market, The Writer's Handbook,* and other guides on how to get published. She mailed out a manuscript every week to publishers and quickly accumulated a stack of rejection letters. When she was 14, however, her hard work began to pay off—she sold her first story to *Highlights* magazine and her second to *Essence* when she was a college student.

EDUCATION

As a student, Williams-Garcia was very conscientious and always eager to demonstrate her knowledge. In elementary school, this self-described

Williams-Garcia working at her writing desk.

geek would often spend her recess time writing stories and poems. "I was a proud little nerd with my hands clasped on my desk ready to rocket in the air when the teacher asked a question. My classmates wanted to kill me," she joked.

Williams-Garcia attended Hofstra University in New York, determined to try new things—eating liver, scheduling a dental appointment, and taking dance classes. She soon became a serious dancer studying under choreographers Alvin Ailey and Phil Black. "I had a gift for dance but was too shy to pursue it in high school," she admitted. "Before long I was taking classes in school, then jumping on the LIRR [train] to take classes at Alvin Ailey's and Phil Black's in Manhattan. I lived in leotards."

Another new thing Williams-Garcia decided to try was studying economics. "I truly believed blacks needed to have an active role in the distribution of capital within their communities, and I planned to be at the forefront of this movement," she remembered. For three years, she temporarily abandoned writing in favor of other activities, including political activism, a leadership role in a dance company, and community outreach with her sorority, Alpha Kappa Alpha. She eventually changed her academic focus, graduating from Hofstra in 1980 with a Bachelor of Arts degree (BA) in liberal arts.

During her senior year, Williams-Garcia took a fiction workshop led by noted authors Richard Price and Sonia Pilcer, which revived her interest in creative writing. At the same time, she was involved in a volunteer tutoring initiative to help high school girls who were reading below their grade level. She combined her writing ambitions with her outreach work to produce a draft of what would become her first novel, *Blue Tights*. She created her protagonist, Joyce, in an effort to awaken the girls to a love of reading. "Contemporary urban black girls were hard to find in literature in the early 80s," she explained. "They

weren't non-existent—just hard to find. Honestly, if I had found Alice Childress or Rosa Guy's novels, *Blue Tights* wouldn't have been written.... Since I couldn't find the right book to speak to a group of girls I worked with in college, I came up with Joyce, her big butt and low self-esteem. The girls in my group didn't want to read about a victimized, heroic girl or a 'good' girl. They wanted a real girl. They wanted to identify."

In the early 1990s Williams-Garcia went back to school part-time to pursue a graduate degree. In 1997 she earned a Master of Arts degree (MA) in creative writing from Queens College. "I can't tell you how I balanced writing, my job, school, and family," she said of her graduate school experience. "None of these things are possible without the support and understanding of my family."

CAREER HIGHLIGHTS

Blue Tights

After finishing her bachelor's degree in 1980, Williams-Garcia planned "to take my manuscript, get an agent, sell it, find an island, and write the Pulitzer Prize-winning novel." In the meantime, she took a clerical job in the mailroom of a marketing software company in Manhattan and sent out her manuscript—*Blue Tights, Big Butt*—to various publishers, only to receive a pile of rejection letters. Editors noted that the main character was not a positive role model and was overly concerned with her physical appearance. Despite these criticisms, she continued to try to sell her novel for three years before tucking it away. She meanwhile accepted a new job within her firm as a promotional writer, married Peter Garcia, and started a family.

In the mid-1980s the marketing firm eliminated her writing position, and Williams-Garcia took an administrative job within the company. Deciding

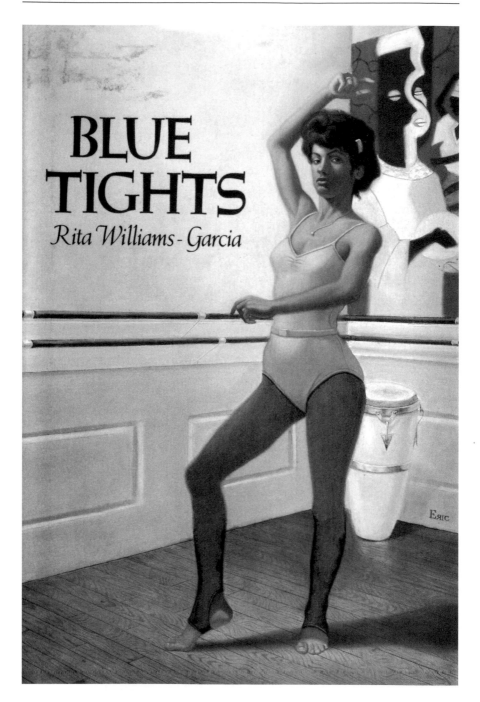

Williams-Garcia worked on her first novel, Blue Tights, *for almost 10 years before it was published.*

it was time to write again, she dusted off her manuscript, made some revisions, and looked for publishers who might be interested in realistic depictions of adolescence. She sent a query letter to Rosemary Brosnan of Lodestar Books that asked: "What would you do if ... your ballet teacher tells you your butt's too big for *Swan Lake*?" Brosnan was immediately intrigued. She met with Williams-Garcia in 1986 to discuss a revision strategy and then guided her through an extensive editing process. "*Blue Tights* needed work," Brosnan admitted in *Horn Book Magazine*, "but there was something about it that was clearly unique, and the author had a fresh, vibrant voice."

Blue Tights was published in 1988 and received a warm welcome by reviewers. The novel follows the life of Joyce Collins, a voluptuous 15-year-old with a gift for dance, as she struggles with self-esteem and her place within her family and urban community. After her ballet teacher remarks that she does not have a dancer's body, she joins an African-American troupe that accepts her for who she is, which allows her to achieve success and independence. *Blue Tights* won several awards and was a hit with critics, who remarked on the novel's uplifting ending, powerful subject matter, and believable characters. As Rudine Sims Bishop stated in *Horn Book Magazine*, "Williams-Garcia has created in Joyce a credible teenager—headstrong, confused, self-absorbed, but capable of positive growth and change. Young-adult readers will recognize something of themselves and appreciate the honesty of her story."

Writing for Young Adults

Williams-Garcia did not start off intending to write for a teenage audience. In contrast, she idolized authors Toni Morrison and Alice Walker, and she hoped to write postmodern fiction for adults. When she told Brosnan that *Blue Tights* would be her last young adult novel, she truly meant it. That changed, however, when the idea for another character came to her. "I was born to write stories," she said. "When I'm not working, I'm daydreaming. Plotting out the next story. Listening to understand my character." As it turned out, that next character was also an African-American teen, and the author has since come to view writing for young people as her passion and her mission. "I find young people interesting. They have such potential," she stated. "Their thoughts and actions matter and have great consequences. There is nothing simple about their lives, which makes for fertile ground."

Williams-Garcia was inspired to write her next book after she ran into an acquaintance from school, a young man who was now working at a fast-food restaurant. He had dropped out of college despite showing a lot of potential. This encounter prompted her to write *Fast Talk on a Slow Track* for "those bright young men who couldn't accept failure as a part of learning." The novel is about Denzel Watson, a class valedictorian who has breezed through high school and is headed to Princeton. Facing potential failure for the first time, he opts to attend community college instead, where he knows he can pass with minimal effort. Although he is not portrayed as an honorable character, the reader comes to understand that he is struggling with self-doubt. After getting a taste for life on the street by selling candy door-to-door, he ultimately decides to study at Princeton. The book was published in 1991 to positive reviews and was named a Best Book for Young Adults by the American Library Association.

Williams-Garcia's next work, *Like Sisters on the Homefront* (1995), is considered her breakthrough novel. "Of all my books, I believe *Like Sisters on the Homefront* was the story that I enjoyed telling," she stated. "I knew it would have profound meaning for my readers.... They have all connected with the characters and the story." The novel centers on 14-year-old Gayle, who becomes pregnant with her second child. At her mother's insistence, Gayle undergoes an abortion and is sent to Georgia to live with her Uncle Luther, a minister, and his family. While there, Gayle grows very close to her great-grandmother, whose strong will and stubbornness mirror her own. Critics hailed the book for its authentic dialect, memorable characters, and dynamic narrative style. It was featured on the recommended reading lists of *School Library Journal, Publishers Weekly,* and the American Library Association, among other organizations, and it received an honorable mention from the Coretta Scott King Award committee. In 1997 Williams-Garcia garnered the PEN/Norma Klein Award for a New Children's Fiction Writer in recognition of her first three books.

After publishing her first picture book, *Catching the Wild Waiyuuzee* (2000), to favorable reviews, Williams-Garcia returned to writing for an adolescent audience with *Every Time a Rainbow Dies* (2001). The story centers on Thulani, a shy 16-year-old boy who witnesses a rape. He intervenes on the victim's behalf and eventually falls in love with her. The book received a warm reception from critics. "Well-observed and subtle, Williams-Garcia's latest novel artfully interplays harsh urban realities with adolescent innocence," wrote Nell D. Beram in *Horn Book Magazine.* The American Library Association included *Every Time A Rainbow Dies* on its Top 10 Best Books for Young Adults in 2002.

Williams-Garcia's next book, *No Laughter Here* (2004), tackles sensitive subject matter through the eyes of fifth-graders Akilah and Victoria, the latter of whom has just returned from a summer in Nigeria. Victoria's fami-

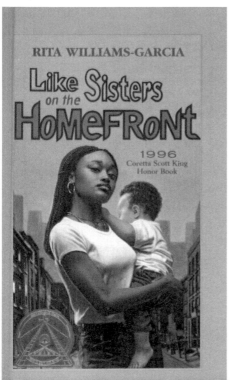

The award-winning novel
Like Sisters on the Homefront
*(top); and Williams-Garcia working
with a high school student who is
sharing a graphic novel version of
the same book (bottom).*

ly made the trip to her birthplace for what they described as a "special celebration to mark her coming of age." While there, she undergoes female genital mutilation, a cultural practice prevalent in some parts of Africa. During this procedure, part or all of the external female genitalia is removed. Many major groups, including the World Health Organization, the United Nations Commission on Human Rights, and the American Medical Association, have called for an end to this practice, which has zero health benefits and can cause serious physical complications. According to the World Health Organization, 100 to 140 million females worldwide are currently living with the consequences of genital mutilation. *No Laughter Here* demonstrates how the trauma of this procedure has affected Victoria, whose once-sparkling personality has faded to the point that she barely speaks. A commentator for *Kirkus Reviews* called the novel "unapologetic, fresh, and painful," and other reviewers admired the grace and skill with which Williams-Garcia related this powerful and delicate narrative.

> "I find young people interesting. They have such potential," Williams-Garcia stated. "Their thoughts and actions matter and have great consequences. There is nothing simple about their lives, which makes for fertile ground."

In 2005 Williams-Garcia left her day job to concentrate on writing full-time. After 25 years of writing during her subway commute and on her lunch hour, she suddenly had significantly more time to devote to her craft. "There's something to be said for finally being in the life you were meant to have," she affirmed. "I write every day except for Sunday." Despite having more time, Williams-Garcia has said that her next novel, *Jumped* (2009), was the hardest to write. "Getting through *Jumped* was a trek through the desert. I thought I'd have this thing wrapped up in six months, tops. It took two years to submit the manuscript to my most patient editor," she lamented. "*Jumped* went through editing and was placed on the publisher's calendar for release two years later. So altogether, it's been four years from spark to print.... So many drafts. So many restarts."

Jumped addresses the issue of female-initiated peer violence and the idea of bystander responsibility. Narrated from the varying perspectives of its three central characters, the novel documents the events of a school day during which Leticia overhears Dominique threaten to beat up Trina after school. Leticia must decide whether or not to get involved in the conflict between the angry tough girl and the oblivious pretty girl. Critics noted the author's well-observed characterizations and the lingering impact of her message. "Teens will relate to Leticia's dilemma even as they may criticize her motives, and the ethical decision she faces will get readers thinking about the larger issues surrounding community, personal responsibility, and the concept of 'snitching,'" noted Meredith Robbins in *School Library Journal*. *Jumped* was a finalist for the 2009 National Book Award.

Winning the Coretta Scott King Award

Williams-Garcia created her most recent novel, *One Crazy Summer* (2010), as a work of historical fiction aimed at middle-school readers. It follows three sisters—11-year-old Delphine and her younger siblings Vonetta and Fern—as they travel to Oakland, California, to visit their estranged mother. The story takes place in 1968, an era of radical social change in America, and depicts the Black Panther movement. The Black Panthers group was a militant political party that played a significant role in the civil rights movement, a movement to ban racial discrimination and segregation in the United States. Founded in Oakland in 1966, the Black Panthers sought to protect the African-American community from racism and police brutality, and they were willing to use violence to establish social, political, and economic equality for minorities. The Black Panthers' calls for a revolutionary war against the U.S. government came to the attention of local police and the FBI. These law enforcement officials considered them a threat to the internal security of the nation. But in addition to their violent activities, the Black Panthers created a number of community programs, including free breakfasts for low-income families, clothing drives, and health screenings to test for sickle cell anemia, an inherited blood disorder affecting people of African descent. They also hosted recreational activities for children such as arts and crafts, physical fitness, and literacy.

One Crazy Summer depicts the Black Panther movement from a child's point of view. "I grew up in the 1960s and wanted to share a part of that time with my readers. If we think of the Black Panthers at all, we rarely remember their work with and for children," the author explained. Through Delphine's eyes, the reader experiences the pivotal changes of that period in history as she and her sisters attend a summer camp sponsored by the Black Panthers.

One Crazy Summer earned Williams-Garcia admiration from critics, who praised her ability to interweave themes of family and identity with broader social issues. "Regimented, responsible, strong-willed Delphine narrates in an unforgettable voice, but each of the sisters emerges as a distinct, memorable character, whose hard-won, tenuous connections with their mother

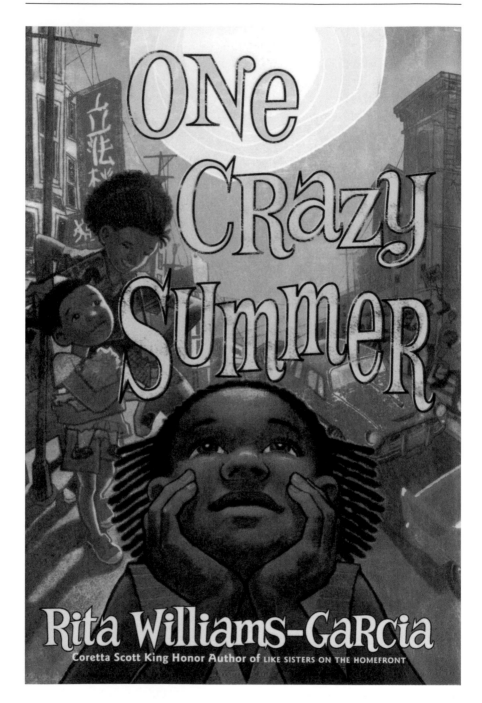

One Crazy Summer *won a host of awards, including the Coretta Scott King Author Award and the Scott O'Dell Award for Historical Fiction.*

build to an aching, triumphant conclusion," wrote Gillian Engberg in *Booklist.* "Set during a pivotal moment in African-American history, this vibrant novel shows the subtle ways that political movements affect personal lives; but just as memorable is the finely drawn, universal story of children reclaiming a reluctant parent's love." Reviewer Teri Markson offered similar praise in *School Library Journal.* "Emotionally challenging and beautifully written, this book immerses readers in a time and place and raises difficult questions of cultural and ethnic identity and personal responsibility. With memorable characters (all three girls have engaging, strong voices) and a powerful story, this is a book well worth reading and rereading."

One Crazy Summer also earned Williams-Garcia a host of awards. She won the 2011 Coretta Scott King Author Award and the Scott O'Dell Award for Historical Fiction. In addition, the novel was selected as a finalist for the National Book Award and was named a Newbery Honor Book. "[*One Crazy Summer*] was selected because it is thought-provoking and features complex, well developed characters," said Jonda C. McNair, chair of the Coretta Scott King Awards jury.

Williams-Garcia has frequently confronted serious issues in her books. But she has maintained that her main focus is on developing characters. "Although my stories are contemporary and realistic, I don't write specifically about issues. I write about my characters' lives," she said. As critic Carla Sarratt stated in an interview for the website the *Brown Bookshelf,* "Rita connects with her characters and shows us that connection so that we feel as if we really know [them].... She studies people and imagines what if and out of those what if moments, a story is born." While most of her characters and storylines are the result of daydreams, she injects little pieces of herself into each of her characters. For example, she was an avid dancer like Joyce in *Blue Tights,* and she sold candy door-to-door like Denzel in *Fast Talk on a Slow Track.* "The characters have to become part of Rita; they need to talk to her before she can write," affirmed Brosnan, her longtime friend and editor. Despite writing about controversial or sensitive topics like sexual assault and bullying, she considers herself an optimist. "I'm always very hopeful about the generation that's coming up and the avenues that are opening up and how people are discovering that they can make an impact. I'm a very happy, hopeful person."

Advice to Young Writers

Williams-Garcia teaches in the Writing for Children and Young Adults Master of Fine Arts (MFA) program at the Vermont College of Fine Arts. In addition, she holds an annual short story contest for young authors between the ages of 12 and 19 to help develop new talent. She encourages

> ―――― " ――――
>
> *Williams-Garcia encourages aspiring writers to read as much as possible, to study the techniques that authors use for effective storytelling, and to spend at least 15 minutes a day writing. "Write for your own joy to get into the habit of flexing those muscles," she urged. "Writing a little bit each day will grow into a sustained ability. Just write!"*
>
> ―――― " ――――

aspiring writers to read as much as possible, to study the techniques that authors use for effective storytelling, and to spend at least 15 minutes a day writing. "Write for your own joy to get into the habit of flexing those muscles," she urged. "Writing a little bit each day will grow into a sustained ability. Just write!" In addition, she has emphasized the importance of paying attention to the surrounding environment using all five senses. "As you engage your senses to the world around you, your word choices and images will become all the more lively and multi-dimensional," she maintained. Finally, she has stressed the importance of understanding grammar to develop good habits and clear, concise sentence structure. She envisions herself focusing on community outreach in the future. In fact, she predicted that "20 years from now, I'll probably direct my resources and energy toward creating a space for other people to write. Most likely, young people."

MARRIAGE AND FAMILY

In the early 1980s Rita married Peter Garcia, with whom she had two daughters, Michelle and Stephanie. Peter served in the Persian Gulf War of 1990-91 when the children were young. The couple later divorced, but Peter remains a close and supportive friend. "Back while I was trying to do everything (work, write, school), my ex-husband kicked in as 'Super Dad,'" she stated. "The marriage didn't hold, but the co-parenting is forever." She lives in Jamaica, Queens, New York.

FAVORITE BOOKS

Williams-Garcia's list of favorite young adult books includes *Skellig,* by David Almond; *A Wrinkle in Time,* by Madeleine L'Engle; *Island of the Blue Dolphins,* by Scott O'Dell; and *The Hobbit,* by J.R.R. Tolkien. As a child, she read the books of Beverly Cleary and particularly enjoyed Louise Fitzhugh's novel *Harriet the Spy.* She has cited Jamaica Kincaid, Gayle Jones, and Toni Cade Bambara as her favorite authors.

Williams-Garcia with two high school students at a book signing.

HOBBIES AND OTHER INTERESTS

Williams-Garcia likes to visit schools to talk to students about her career. Like her character Gayle in *Like Sisters on the Homefront,* she hates to fly, and she refuses to travel by air during the winter months. In her spare time, she enjoys sewing, knitting, playing chess or Tetris, jogging, and boxing at the gym. She loves art, especially the works of Pablo Picasso, Vincent Van Gogh, and 20th-century collage artist Romare Bearden. While she is developing the characters for her books, she often listens to music as inspiration. She enjoys many musical genres, including soul, be-bop, gospel, Afro-Brazilian, reggae, and ska. Moreover, she admires such vocalists as Aretha Franklin, Nancy Wilson, Alicia Keyes, Johnny Hartman, and Frank Sinatra. "I love vocalists because I can't carry a note pinned to my sweater," she joked.

SELECTED WRITINGS

Blue Tights, 1987
Fast Talk on a Slow Track, 1991
Like Sisters on the Homefront, 1995
Catching the Wild Waiyuuzee, 2000

Every Time a Rainbow Dies, 2001
No Laughter Here, 2004
Jumped, 2009
One Crazy Summer, 2010

HONORS AND AWARDS

Books Recommended for Reluctant Readers (American Library Association): 1988, for *Blue Tights*; 1992, for *Fast Talk on a Slow Train*; 1996, for *Like Sisters on the Homefront*

Books for the Teen Age (New York Public Library): 1989, for *Blue Tights*; 2002, for *Every Time a Rainbow Dies*

Best Books for Young Adults (American Library Association): 1991, for *Fast Talk on a Slow Track*; 1995, for *Like Sisters on the Homefront*; 2002, for *Every Time a Rainbow Dies*; 2005, for *No Laughter Here*; 2010, for *Jumped*

Best Books for Young Adults (*School Library Journal*): 1995, for *Like Sisters on the Homefront*

Best Books for Young Adults (*Publishers Weekly*): 1995, for *Like Sisters on the Homefront*

Fanfare Award (*Horn Book*): 1995, for *Like Sisters on the Homefront*

NCSS-CBC Notable Books in the Field of Social Studies (National Council for the Social Studies-Children's Book Council): 1996, for *Like Sisters on the Homefront*

PEN/Norma Klein Award for a New Children's Fiction Writer (PEN American Center): 1997, for three books, *Blue Tights, Fast Talk on a Slow Track,* and *Like Sisters on the Homefront*

Best Children's Books for the Year (Bank Street College): 2001, for *Catching the Wild Waiyuuzee*

Top 10 Black History Titles for Youth (*Booklist*): 2004, for *No Laughter Here*

Youth Editors' Choice Award (*Booklist*): 2009, for *Jumped*

Coretta Scott King Author Award (American Library Association): 2011, for *One Crazy Summer*

Scott O'Dell Award for Historical Fiction (American Library Association): 2011, for *One Crazy Summer*

FURTHER READING

Periodicals

Booklist, Feb. 15, 1996, p.1002
Horn Book Magazine, Sep./Oct. 2009, p.479; Mar./Apr. 2011, p.151; July/Aug. 2011, pp.86 and 94.
School Library Journal, May 2010, p.22

Online Articles

www.thebrownbookshelf.com
(Brown Bookshelf, "Rita Williams-Garcia," Feb. 4, 2008; 28 Days Later archive, 2008)
cynthialeitichsmith.blogspot.com/2009/03
(Cynsations, Cynthia Leitich Smith, "Author Interview: Rita Williams-Garcia on *Jumped*," Mar. 27, 2009, scroll to correct date)
www.hofstra.edu
(Hofstra College of Liberal Arts & Sciences: In Focus, "Rita Williams-Garcia '80: Liberal Arts Major," no date, In Focus—University Relations archive)
archive.hbook.com/magazine/articles/2011/jul11_brosnan.asp
(Horn Book, "Rita Williams-Garcia," July-Aug. 2011)
www.loc.gov
(Library of Congress 2011 National Book Festival, "Rita Williams-Garcia," 2011, National Book Festival archive, Kids and Teachers site, Meet the Authors category)
www.myshelf.com
(MyShelf.com, "Rita Williams-Garcia," Feb. 2003, Have You Heard archive, 2003)
www.nationalbook.org
(National Book Foundation, "Rita Williams-Garcia: *One Crazy Summer*," 2010, National Book Awards 2010 archive, Young People's Literature category)
comminfo.rutgers.edu/professional-development/childlit/AuthorSite/index.html
(Rutgers University, Kay E. Vandergrift's Learning about the Author and Illustrator Pages, "Learning about Rita William-Garcia: Biography," Sep. 1996)

ADDRESS

Rita Williams-Garcia
Author Mail, 18th Floor
HarperCollins Children's Books
10 East 53rd Street
New York, NY 10022

WEB SITES

www.ritawg.com
www.harpercollins.com/authors/19042/Rita_WilliamsGarcia

Photo and Illustration Credits

Front Cover photos: Adele: PR Newswire/Newscom; Steve Jobs: Mark Richards/ ZUMA Press/Newscom; Jennifer Lawrence: Movie still: THE HUNGER GAMES © 2012 Lionsgate. Photo by Murray Close; Hilda Solis: U.S. Department of Labor.

Adele/Photos: PR Newswire/Newscom (p. 11); Carmen Valino/PA Photos/Landov (p. 13); Dana Edelson/NBC/NBCU Photo Bank via AP Images (p. 16); XL Recordings/Columbia Records (p. 18); MTV/PictureGroup (p. 20).

Rob Bell/Photos: Courtesy of Rob Bell and Mars Hill Bible Church (pp. 23, 25, 26); Romain Blanquart/MTC/Landov (p. 28); DVD cover: RAIN © 2002 Nooma. © 2005 by Flannel.org. Published by Zondervan. All rights reserved. (p. 31); Courtesy of Rob Bell and Mars Hill Bible Church (p. 34).

Big Time Rush/Photos: AP Photo/Seth Wenig (p. 39); PRNewsFoto/Nickelodeon, Stewart Shining/via Newscom (p. 41); PRNewsFoto/Nickelodeon, Ben Watts/via Newscom (p. 44); CD cover: BIG TIME RUSH © 2010 Nickelodeon/Columbia/Sony Music Entertainment (p. 47); Kevork Djansezian/Getty Images for Nickelodeon/ KCA2011 (p. 49).

Judy Blume/Photos: Courtesy Random House, Inc. Photo © Sigrid Estrada (p. 51); Romain Blanquart/Detroit Free Press/MCT/Newscom (p. 53); Book cover: ARE YOU THERE GOD? IT'S ME, MARGARET. By Judy Blume. Published in the U.S. by Ember (Random House, Inc., New York). All rights reserved. Text © 1970, copyright renewed 1988 by Judy Blume. Cover art © 2009 by Dana Edmunds/Jupiter Images. Cover design by Kenny Holcomb. (p. 56); Book cover: IT'S NOT THE END OF THE WORLD by Judy Blume. Published in the U.S. by Delacorte Press (Random House, Inc., New York). All rights reserved. Text © 1972, copyright renewed 2003 by Judy Blume. Cover art © 2009 by Laurence Mouton/Vccr. Cover design by Kenny Holcomb. (p. 59); Book cover: STARRING SALLY J. FREEDMAN AS HERSELF by Judy Blume. Published by Yearling (Random House, Inc., New York). All rights reserved. Text © 1977 by Judy Blume. Cover art © 2004 by Susy Pilgrim-Waters. (p. 62); Audio book cover: OTHERWISE KNOWN AS SHEILA THE GREAT by Judy Blume. Published by Listening Library (P 2000 Random House, Inc., New York). All rights reserved. Text © 1972 by Judy Blume. Cover illustration © Peter H. Reynolds. (p. 65); Book cover: FOREVER by Judy Blume. Published by Simon Pulse (Simon & Schuster, New York). All rights reserved. Text © 1975, copyright renewed 2003 by Judy Blume. Cover designed by Russell Gordon. Cover photograph © 2007 Jupiter Images. (p. 67); ZUMA Press/Newscom (p. 69).

Cheryl Burke/Photos: FayesVision/WENN.com/Newscom (p. 75); ABC/Craig Sjodin (p. 79); Adam Larkey/ABC via Getty Images (p. 80); ABC/Adam Taylor (p. 84).

Chris Daughtry/Photos: Brendan McDermid/Reuters/Landov (p. 87); Market Wire Photos/Newscom (p. 90); Ray Mickshaw/WireImage (p. 92); Album cover: LEAVE THIS TOWN © 2009 RCA Records/Sony Music Group (p. 95); RCA Records/Sony Music Group (p. 96).

Ellen DeGeneres/Photos: Noel Vasquez/Getty Images for Extra (p. 101); Photofest (p. 103); © Touchstone Television/Photofest (p. 105); © ABC/Photofest (p. 107); Official White House Photo by Chuck Kennedy (p. 109); Movie still: FINDING NEMO © Disney/Pixar. All rights reserved. (p. 111).

Drake/Photos: ZUMA Press/Newscom (p. 115); © CTV Television Network/Photofest (p. 117); AP Photo/Chris Pizzello (p. 119); Dana Edelson/NBC/NBCU Photo Bank via Getty Images (p. 122); Album cover: TAKE CARE © 2012 Universal Republic/UMG. All rights reserved. (p. 124).

Kevin Durant/Photos: AP Photo/Alonzo Adams (p. 127); AP Photo/Denis Poroy (p. 130); Larry Smith/Icon SMI/Newscom (p. 132); Otto Greule, Jr./Getty Images (p. 135); Martin Levison/Minneapolis Star Tribune/MCT/Newscom (p. 137); Don Emmert/AFP/Getty Images/Newscom (p. 140); John G. Mabanglo/EPA/Landov (p. 142).

Dale Earnhardt Jr./Photos: John Harrelson/Getty Images for NASCAR (p. 147); Racing Photo Archives/Getty Images (p. 149); Jeff Siner/MCT/Landov (p. 152); Jonathan Ferrey/ALLSPORT/Getty Images (p. 154); Mark Wallheiser/RTR/Newscom (p. 157); Jerry Markland/Getty Images for NASCAR (p. 158); Todd Warshaw/Getty Images (p. 161); Geoff Burke/Getty Images for NASCAR (p. 164).

Zaha Hadid/Photos: Udo Hesse/akg-images/Newscom (p. 167); Christopher Pillitz/Getty Images (p. 169); Vitra Company Fire Station by Zaha Hadid, Weil am Rhein, Germany, 10/04/2006. Author: en:User:Sandstein, a.k.a. User:TheBernFiles. http://en.wikipedia.org/wiki/File:Vitra_fire_station,_full_view,_Zaha_Hadid.jpg (p. 171); The Contemporary Art Center, Cincinnati OH, 12/06/2006. Author: Lanskeith17 http://en.wikipedia.org/wiki/File:Contemp_Art_Center.JPG (p. 173); View Pictures/ UIG via Getty Images (p. 175); The rear (riverside) view of the Glasgow Riverside Museum, 2/15/2012. Author: Bjmullan http://en.wikipedia.org/wiki/File:Riverside_Museum_rear_view.JPG (p. 177); Graham Barclay/Bloomberg via Getty Images (p. 179).

Josh Hamilton/Photos: John Sleezer/MCT/Landov (p. 183); AP Photo/St. Petersburg Times/Jonathan Newton (p. 186); Ezra Shaw/Getty Images (p. 188); AP Photo/Rusty Kennedy (p. 192); Ron Jenkins/Fort Worth Star-Telegram/MCT via Getty Images (p. 195); AP Photo/Jeff Roberson (p. 197).

Heidi Hammel/Photos: NASA/Bill Ingalls (p. 201); Roger L. Wollenberg/UPI/Newscom (p. 204); NASA/JPL (p. 207, top and bottom); NASA/HST (p. 209); H.A. Weaver, T.E. Smith/Space Telescope Science Institute/NASA (p. 211, top); Hubble Space Telescope Comet Team/NASA (p. 211, bottom); NASA/MSFC/David Higginbotham (p. 214, top); NASA (p. 214, bottom).

Josh Hutcherson/Photos: Daniel Deme/EPA/Landov (p. 217); © Studio Ghibli/Walt Disney Pictures/Photofest (p. 219); Movie still: BRIDGE TO TERABITHIA © Buena Vista Home Entertainment, Inc. and Walden Media, LLC. All rights reserved. (p. 221); © New Line/Photofest. Photo by Sebastian Raymond (p. 223); Movie still: THE HUNGER GAMES © 2012 Lionsgate. Photo by Murray Close (pp. 225 and 226).

Steve Jobs/Photos: David Paul Morris/Getty Images (p. 231); Kimberly White/Reuters/ Landov (p. 235); SSPL/Getty Images (p. 237, top); Terry Schmitt/UPI/Landov (p. 237, bottom); Movie still: TOY STORY © Disney. All Rights Reserved. (p. 240); AP Photo/Ben Margot (p. 242); © Apple Inc. All rights reserved. (p. 245); Cartoon by Steve Sack. Reprinted with permission, Minneapolis Star Tribune (p. 247); © 2011 Apple Inc. All rights reserved. (p. 249).

Jennifer Lawrence/Photos: Michael Buckner/Getty Images for Jameson (p. 253); Very-Funny Productions/Album/Newscom (p. 255); Movie still: WINTER'S BONE © 2010 Roadside Attractions/DVD distributed by Lionsgate (p. 257); Murray Close/TM and © 2011 Twentieth Century Fox Film Corporation. All rights reserved. (p. 259); Movie still: THE HUNGER GAMES © 2012 Lionsgate. Photo by Murray Close (pp. 261 and 262).

Bruno Mars/Photos: Jason Merritt/Getty Images (p. 267); Catherine McGann/Getty Images (p. 269); PRNewsFoto/Renaissance Hotels via AP (p. 270); CD cover: DOO-WOPS & HOOLIGANS © 2010 NEK/New Elektra/Warner Atlantic Elektra Corporation (p. 273); John Shearer/WireImage (p. 276).

Stella McCartney/Photos: EPA Photo/EPA/Hugo Philpot/Newscom (p. 279); David Montgomery/Getty Images (p. 281); AP Photo/Michel Euler (p. 284); Eric Ryan/ Getty Images (p. 287); Photos from the Winter 2011 Collection, Stella McCartney .com (p. 289).

Jerry Mitchell/Photos: Courtesy of the John D. & Catherine T. MacArthur Foundation (p. 293); Photo by John Vachon, FSA/OWI Collection, Prints & Photographs Division, Library of Congress, LC-USF33-001112-M1 (p. 295, top); Rolls Press/Popper foto/Getty Images (p. 295, bottom); MPI/Getty Images (p. 299); Michael Ochs Archive/Getty Images (p. 300); AP Photo/Jeff Guenther (p. 301); AP Photo/File (p. 303); AP Photo/Hattiesburg American/Kim Harris-Guillory (p. 305); AP Photo/Jack Thornell (p. 307, top); AP Images/Rogelio Solis (p. 307, bottom); Courtesy of the John D. & Catherine T. MacArthur Foundation (p. 309).

Chloë Grace Moretz/Photos: Vera Anderson/WireImage (p. 313); © MGM/Dimension Films/Photofest (p. 315); Movie still: DIARY OF A WIMPY KID. Photo: Rob McEwan © 2010 Twentieth Century Fox Film Corporation. All rights reserved. DIARY OF A WIMPY KID®, WIMPY KID™ and the Greg Heffley design™ are trademarks of Wimpy Kid, Inc. All rights reserved. (p. 317); Movie still: HUGO © 2011 Paramount Pictures and GK Films. All rights reserved. (p. 319); © Warner Bros. Pictures/ Photofest (p. 321).

Blake Mycoskie/Photos: Donato Sardella/WireImage (p. 325); Tony Esparza/CBS/ Landov (p. 327); AP Photo/Ali Burafi (p. 330); PRNewsFoto/TOMS Shoes/via Newscom (p. 332); Michael Kovac/Getty Images for TOMS (p. 335).

Cumulative General Index

This cumulative index includes names, occupations, nationalities, and ethnic and minority origins that pertain to all individuals profiled in *Biography Today* since the debut of the series in 1992.

Places of Birth Index

The following index lists the places of birth for the individuals profiled in *Biography Today*. Places of birth are entered under state, province, and/or country.

Birthday Index

February (continued)

Day	Name	Year
20	Adams, Ansel	1902
	Barkley, Charles	1963
	Cobain, Kurt	1967
	Crawford, Cindy	1966
	Hernandez, Livan	1975
	Littrell, Brian	1975
	Rihanna	1988
	Verlander, Justin	1983
21	Carpenter, Mary Chapin	1958
	Hewitt, Jennifer Love	1979
	Jordan, Barbara	1936
	Lewis, John	1940
	Mugabe, Robert	1924
22	Barrymore, Drew	1975
	Fernandez, Lisa	1971
	Gorey, Edward	1925
	Singh, Vijay	1963
23	Brown, Claude	1937
	Dell, Michael	1965
	Fanning, Dakota	1994
24	Borgman, Jim	1954
	Jobs, Steve	1955
	Vernon, Mike	1963
	Whitestone, Heather	1973
25	Voigt, Cynthia	1942
26	Thompson, Jenny	1973
27	Clinton, Chelsea	1980
	Gonzalez, Tony	1976
	Hunter-Gault, Charlayne	1942
	King, Mary-Claire	1946
28	Andretti, Mario	1940
	Chu, Steven	1948
	Mallett, Jef	1962
	Napoli, Donna Jo	1948
	Pauling, Linus	1901

March

Day	Name	Year
1	Bieber, Justin	1994
	Ellison, Ralph Waldo	1914
	Murie, Olaus J.	1889
	Nielsen, Jerri	1952
	Rabin, Yitzhak	1922
	Zamora, Pedro	1972
2	Gorbachev, Mikhail	1931
	Hamilton, Laird	1964
	Roethlisberger, Ben	1982
	Satcher, David	1941
	Seuss, Dr.	1904
3	Hooper, Geoff	1979
	Joyner-Kersee, Jackie	1962
	MacLachlan, Patricia	1938
4	Armstrong, Robb	1962
	Morgan, Garrett	1877
5	Margulis, Lynn	1938
6	Ashley, Maurice	1966
	Howard, Tim	1979
7	McCarty, Oseola	1908
8	Prinze, Freddie Jr.	1976
	Rowland, Pleasant T.	1941
10	Guy, Jasmine	1964
	Miller, Shannon	1977
	Underwood, Carrie	1983
	Wolf, Hazel	1898
11	Buckley, Kelsie	1995
	Madden, Benji	1979
	Madden, Joel	1979
	Scalia, Antonin	1936
12	Hamilton, Virginia	1936
	Hiaasen, Carl	1953
	Nye, Naomi Shihab	1952
13	Van Meter, Vicki	1982
14	Dayne, Ron	1977
	Hammel, Heidi	1960
	Hanson, Taylor	1983
	Jones, Quincy	1933
	Williamson, Kevin	1965
15	Ginsburg, Ruth Bader	1933
	Hahn, Joe	1977
	White, Ruth	1942
	will.i.am	1975
16	O'Neal, Shaquille	1972
	Ramos, Jorge	1958
17	Hamm, Mia	1972
	Nureyev, Rudolf	1938
18	Blair, Bonnie	1964
	de Klerk, F.W.	1936
	Griese, Brian	1975
	Queen Latifah	1970
19	Blanchard, Rachel	1976
	Brashares, Ann	1967
20	Bennington, Chester	1976
	Lee, Spike	1957
	Lowry, Lois	1937
	Rogers, Fred	1928
	Sachar, Louis	1954
21	Gilbert, Walter	1932
	O'Donnell, Rosie	1962

September (continued)   **Year**

King, Stephen 1947
Nkrumah, Kwame 1909
22 Richardson, Dot 1961
Sessions, Michael 1987
23 Jenkins, Jerry B. 1949
Nevelson, Louise 1899
Oudin, Melanie 1991
Warrick, Earl 1911
24 George, Eddie 1973
Ochoa, Severo 1905
25 Gwaltney, John Langston 1928
Locklear, Heather 1961
Lopez, Charlotte 1976
Murphy, Jim 1947
Pinkney, Andrea Davis 1963
Pippen, Scottie 1965
Reeve, Christopher 1952
Smith, Will 1968
Walters, Barbara 1931
26 Mandela, Winnie 1934
Stockman, Shawn 1972
Williams, Serena 1981
27 Handford, Martin 1956
Lavigne, Avril 1984
28 Blake, James 1979
Cray, Seymour 1925
Duff, Hilary 1987
Pak, Se Ri 1977
29 Berenstain, Stan 1923
Durant, Kevin 1988
Farro, Josh 1987
Guey, Wendy 1983
Gumbel, Bryant 1948
30 Hingis, Martina 1980
Moceanu, Dominique 1981

October   **Year**

1 Carter, Jimmy 1924
McGwire, Mark 1963
2 Leibovitz, Annie 1949
3 Campbell, Neve 1973
Herriot, James 1916
Richardson, Kevin 1972
Simpson, Ashlee 1984
Stefani, Gwen 1969
Winfield, Dave 1951
4 Cushman, Karen 1941
Forman, James 1928
Kamler, Kenneth 1947

Meissner, Kimmie 1989
Rice, Anne 1941
Simmons, Russell 1957
5 Fitzhugh, Louise 1928
Hill, Grant 1972
Lemieux, Mario 1965
Lin, Maya 1959
Roy, Patrick 1965
Tyson, Neil deGrasse 1958
Winslet, Kate 1975
6 Bennett, Cherie 1960
Lobo, Rebecca 1973
7 Holmes, Priest 1973
Ma, Yo-Yo 1955
McAdams, Rachel 1976
8 Jackson, Jesse 1941
Mars, Bruno 1985
Ringgold, Faith 1930
Stine, R.L. 1943
Winans, CeCe 1964
9 Bryan, Zachery Ty 1981
Senghor, Léopold Sédar 1906
Sorenstam, Annika 1970
Williams, Tyler James 1992
10 Earnhardt, Dale Jr. 1974
Favre, Brett 1969
Saro-Wiwa, Ken 1941
11 Freedman, Russell 1929
Murray, Ty 1969
Perry, Luke . . . .?1964
Wie, Michelle 1989
Young, Steve 1961
12 Bloor, Edward 1950
Childress, Alice . . . .?1920
Hutcherson, Josh 1992
Jackman, Hugh 1968
Jones, Marion 1975
Maguire, Martie 1969
Ward, Charlie 1970
13 Ashanti 1980
Carter, Chris 1956
Kerrigan, Nancy 1969
Rice, Jerry 1962
14 Daniel, Beth 1956
Maines, Natalie 1974
Mobutu Sese Seko 1930
Usher 1978
15 Donovan, Marion 1917
Iacocca, Lee A. 1924

Biography Today

General Series

For ages 9 and above

B iography Today **General Series** includes a unique combination of current biographical profiles that teachers and librarians — and the readers themselves — tell us are most appealing. The **General Series** is available as a 3-issue subscription; hardcover annual cumulation; or subscription plus cumulation.

Within the **General Series**, your readers will find a variety of sketches about:

- Authors
- Musicians
- Political leaders
- Sports figures
- Movie actresses & actors
- Cartoonists
- Scientists
- Astronauts
- TV personalities
- and the movers & shakers in many other fields!

"Biography Today **will be useful in elementary and middle school libraries and in public library children's collections where there is a need for biographies of current personalities. High schools serving reluctant readers may also want to consider a subscription."**
— *Booklist,* American Library Association

"Highly recommended for the young adult audience. Readers will delight in the accessible, energetic, tell-all style; teachers, librarians, and parents will welcome the clever format [and] intelligent and informative text. It should prove especially useful in motivating 'reluctant' readers or literate nonreaders."
— *MultiCultural Review*

"Written in a friendly, almost chatty tone, the profiles offer quick, objective information. While coverage of current figures makes *Biography Today* a useful reference tool, an appealing format and wide scope make it a fun resource to browse." — *School Library Journal*

"The best source for current information at a level kids can understand."
— Kelly Bryant, School Librarian, Carlton, OR

"Easy for kids to read. We love it! Don't want to be without it."
— Lynn McWhirter, School Librarian, Rockford, IL

ONE-YEAR SUBSCRIPTION

- 3 softcover issues, 6" x 9"
- Published in January, April, and September
- 1-year subscription, list price $66. **School and library price $64**
- 150 pages per issue
- 10 profiles per issue
- Contact sources for additional information
- Cumulative Names Index

HARDBOUND ANNUAL CUMULATION

- Sturdy 6" x 9" hardbound volume
- Published in December
- List price $73. **School and library price $66 per volume**
- 450 pages per volume
- 30 profiles — includes all profiles found in softcover issues for that calendar year
- Cumulative General Index, Places of Birth Index, and Birthday Index

SUBSCRIPTION AND CUMULATION COMBINATION

- $110 for 3 softcover issues plus the hardbound volume

For Cumulative General, Places of Birth, and Birthday Indexes, please see www.biographytoday.com.

1992

Paula Abdul
Andre Agassi
Kirstie Alley
Terry Anderson
Roseanne Arnold
Isaac Asimov
James Baker
Charles Barkley
Larry Bird
Judy Blume
Berke Breathed
Garth Brooks
Barbara Bush
George Bush
Fidel Castro
Bill Clinton
Bill Cosby
Diana, Princess of
    Wales
Shannen Doherty
Elizabeth Dole
David Duke
Gloria Estefan
Mikhail Gorbachev
Steffi Graf
Wayne Gretzky
Matt Groening
Alex Haley
Hammer
Martin Handford
Stephen Hawking
Hulk Hogan
Saddam Hussein
Lee Iacocca
Bo Jackson
Mae Jemison
Peter Jennings
Steven Jobs
John Paul II
Magic Johnson
Michael Jordan
Jackie Joyner-Kersee
Spike Lee
Mario Lemieux
Madeleine L'Engle
Jay Leno
Yo-Yo Ma
Nelson Mandela
Wynton Marsalis
Thurgood Marshall
Ann Martin
Barbara McClintock
Emily Arnold McCully
Antonia Novello

Sandra Day O'Connor
Rosa Parks
Jane Pauley
H. Ross Perot
Luke Perry
Scottie Pippen
Colin Powell
Jason Priestley
Queen Latifah
Yitzhak Rabin
Sally Ride
Pete Rose
Nolan Ryan
H. Norman
    Schwarzkopf
Jerry Seinfeld
Dr. Seuss
Gloria Steinem
Clarence Thomas
Chris Van Allsburg
Cynthia Voigt
Bill Watterson
Robin Williams
Oprah Winfrey
Kristi Yamaguchi
Boris Yeltsin

1993

Maya Angelou
Arthur Ashe
Avi
Kathleen Battle
Candice Bergen
Boutros Boutros-Ghali
Chris Burke
Dana Carvey
Cesar Chavez
Henry Cisneros
Hillary Rodham Clinton
Jacques Cousteau
Cindy Crawford
Macaulay Culkin
Lois Duncan
Marian Wright
    Edelman
Cecil Fielder
Bill Gates
Sara Gilbert
Dizzy Gillespie
Al Gore
Cathy Guisewite
Jasmine Guy
Anita Hill
Ice-T
Darci Kistler

k.d. lang
Dan Marino
Rigoberta Menchu
Walter Dean Myers
Martina Navratilova
Phyllis Reynolds
    Naylor
Rudolf Nureyev
Shaquille O'Neal
Janet Reno
Jerry Rice
Mary Robinson
Winona Ryder
Jerry Spinelli
Denzel Washington
Keenen Ivory Wayans
Dave Winfield

1994

Tim Allen
Marian Anderson
Mario Andretti
Ned Andrews
Yasir Arafat
Bruce Babbitt
Mayim Bialik
Bonnie Blair
Ed Bradley
John Candy
Mary Chapin
    Carpenter
Benjamin Chavis
Connie Chung
Beverly Cleary
Kurt Cobain
F.W. de Klerk
Rita Dove
Linda Ellerbee
Sergei Fedorov
Zlata Filipovic
Daisy Fuentes
Ruth Bader Ginsburg
Whoopi Goldberg
Tonya Harding
Melissa Joan Hart
Geoff Hooper
Whitney Houston
Dan Jansen
Nancy Kerrigan
Alexi Lalas
Charlotte Lopez
Wilma Mankiller
Shannon Miller
Toni Morrison
Richard Nixon

Greg Norman
Severo Ochoa
River Phoenix
Elizabeth Pine
Jonas Salk
Richard Scarry
Emmitt Smith
Will Smith
Steven Spielberg
Patrick Stewart
R.L. Stine
Lewis Thomas
Barbara Walters
Charlie Ward
Steve Young
Kim Zmeskal

1995

Troy Aikman
Jean-Bertrand Aristide
Oksana Baiul
Halle Berry
Benazir Bhutto
Jonathan Brandis
Warren E. Burger
Ken Burns
Candace Cameron
Jimmy Carter
Agnes de Mille
Placido Domingo
Janet Evans
Patrick Ewing
Newt Gingrich
John Goodman
Amy Grant
Jesse Jackson
James Earl Jones
Julie Krone
David Letterman
Rush Limbaugh
Heather Locklear
Reba McEntire
Joe Montana
Cosmas Ndeti
Hakeem Olajuwon
Ashley Olsen
Mary Kate Olsen
Jennifer Parkinson
Linus Pauling
Itzhak Perlman
Cokie Roberts
Wilma Rudolph
Salt 'N' Pepa
Barry Sanders
William Shatner

Elizabeth George
  Speare
Dr. Benjamin Spock
Jonathan Taylor
  Thomas
Vicki Van Meter
Heather Whitestone
Pedro Zamora

1996

Aung San Suu Kyi
Boyz II Men
Brandy
Ron Brown
Mariah Carey
Jim Carrey
Larry Champagne III
Christo
Chelsea Clinton
Coolio
Bob Dole
David Duchovny
Debbi Fields
Chris Galeczka
Jerry Garcia
Jennie Garth
Wendy Guey
Tom Hanks
Alison Hargreaves
Sir Edmund Hillary
Judith Jamison
Barbara Jordan
Annie Leibovitz
Carl Lewis
Jim Lovell
Mickey Mantle
Lynn Margulis
Iqbal Masih
Mark Messier
Larisa Oleynik
Christopher Pike
David Robinson
Dennis Rodman
Selena
Monica Seles
Don Shula
Kerri Strug
Tiffani-Amber Thiessen
Dave Thomas
Jaleel White

1997

Madeleine Albright
Marcus Allen

Gillian Anderson
Rachel Blanchard
Zachery Ty Bryan
Adam Ezra Cohen
Claire Danes
Celine Dion
Jean Driscoll
Louis Farrakhan
Ella Fitzgerald
Harrison Ford
Bryant Gumbel
John Johnson
Michael Johnson
Maya Lin
George Lucas
John Madden
Bill Monroe
Alanis Morissette
Sam Morrison
Rosie O'Donnell
Muammar el-Qaddafi
Christopher Reeve
Pete Sampras
Pat Schroeder
Rebecca Sealfon
Tupac Shakur
Tabitha Soren
Herbert Tarvin
Merlin Tuttle
Mara Wilson

1998

Bella Abzug
Kofi Annan
Neve Campbell
Sean Combs (Puff
  Daddy)
Dalai Lama (Tenzin
  Gyatso)
Diana, Princess of
  Wales
Leonardo DiCaprio
Walter E. Diemer
Ruth Handler
Hanson
Livan Hernandez
Jewel
Jimmy Johnson
Tara Lipinski
Jody-Anne Maxwell
Dominique Moceanu
Alexandra Nechita
Brad Pitt
LeAnn Rimes
Emily Rosa

David Satcher
Betty Shabazz
Kordell Stewart
Shinichi Suzuki
Mother Teresa
Mike Vernon
Reggie White
Kate Winslet

1999

Ben Affleck
Jennifer Aniston
Maurice Ashley
Kobe Bryant
Bessie Delany
Sadie Delany
Sharon Draper
Sarah Michelle Gellar
John Glenn
Savion Glover
Jeff Gordon
David Hampton
Lauryn Hill
King Hussein
Lynn Johnston
Shari Lewis
Oseola McCarty
Mark McGwire
Slobodan Milosevic
Natalie Portman
J.K. Rowling
Frank Sinatra
Gene Siskel
Sammy Sosa
John Stanford
Natalia Toro
Shania Twain
Mitsuko Uchida
Jesse Ventura
Venus Williams

2000

Christina Aguilera
K.A. Applegate
Lance Armstrong
Backstreet Boys
Daisy Bates
Harry Blackmun
George W. Bush
Carson Daly
Ron Dayne
Henry Louis Gates Jr.
Doris Haddock
  (Granny D)

Jennifer Love Hewitt
Chamique Holdsclaw
Katie Holmes
Charlayne Hunter-
  Gault
Johanna Johnson
Craig Kielburger
John Lasseter
Peyton Manning
Ricky Martin
John McCain
Walter Payton
Freddie Prinze Jr.
Viviana Risca
Briana Scurry
George Thampy
CeCe Winans

2001

Jessica Alba
Christiane Amanpour
Drew Barrymore
Jeff Bezos
Destiny's Child
Dale Earnhardt
Carly Fiorina
Aretha Franklin
Cathy Freeman
Tony Hawk
Faith Hill
Kim Dae-jung
Madeleine L'Engle
Mariangela Lisanti
Frankie Muniz
*N Sync
Ellen Ochoa
Jeff Probst
Julia Roberts
Carl T. Rowan
Britney Spears
Chris Tucker
Lloyd D. Ward
Alan Webb
Chris Weinke

2002

Aaliyah
Osama bin Laden
Mary J. Blige
Aubyn Burnside
Aaron Carter
Julz Chavez
Dick Cheney
Hilary Duff

Billy Gilman
Rudolph Giuliani
Brian Griese
Jennifer Lopez
Dave Mirra
Dineh Mohajer
Leanne Nakamura
Daniel Radcliffe
Condoleezza Rice
Marla Runyan
Ruth Simmons
Mattie Stepanek
J.R.R. Tolkien
Barry Watson
Tyrone Willingham
Elijah Wood

2003

Yolanda Adams
Olivia Bennett
Mildred Benson
Alexis Bledel
Barry Bonds
Vincent Brooks
Laura Bush
Amanda Bynes
Kelly Clarkson
Vin Diesel
Eminem
Michele Forman
Vicente Fox
Millard Fuller
Josh Hartnett
Dolores Huerta
Sarah Hughes
Enrique Iglesias
Jeanette Lee
John Lewis
Nicklas Lidstrom
Clint Mathis
Donovan McNabb
Nelly
Andy Roddick
Gwen Stefani
Emma Watson
Meg Whitman
Reese Witherspoon
Yao Ming

2004

Natalie Babbitt
David Beckham
Francie Berger
Tony Blair

Orlando Bloom
Kim Clijsters
Celia Cruz
Matel Dawson Jr.
The Donnas
Tim Duncan
Shirin Ebadi
Carla Hayden
Ashton Kutcher
Lisa Leslie
Linkin Park
Lindsay Lohan
Irene D. Long
John Mayer
Mandy Moore
Thich Nhat Hanh
OutKast
Raven
Ronald Reagan
Keanu Reeves
Ricardo Sanchez
Brian Urlacher
Alexa Vega
Michelle Wie
Will Wright

2005

Kristen Bell
Jack Black
Sergey Brin & Larry
   Page
Adam Brody
Chris Carrabba
Johnny Depp
Eve
Jennie Finch
James Forman
Wally Funk
Cornelia Funke
Bethany Hamilton
Anne Hathaway
Priest Holmes
T.D. Jakes
John Paul II
Toby Keith
Alison Krauss
Wangari Maathai
Karen Mitchell-
   Raptakis
Queen Noor
Violet Palmer
Gloria Rodriguez
Carlos Santana
Antonin Scalia
Curtis Schilling

Maria Sharapova
Ashlee Simpson
Donald Trump
Ben Wallace

2006

Carol Bellamy
Miri Ben-Ari
Black Eyed Peas
Bono
Kelsie Buckley
Dale Chihuly
Neda DeMayo
Dakota Fanning
Green Day
Freddie Highmore
Russel Honoré
Tim Howard
Cynthia Kadohata
Coretta Scott King
Rachel McAdams
Cesar Millan
Steve Nash
Nick Park
Rosa Parks
Danica Patrick
Jorge Ramos
Ben Roethlisberger
Lil' Romeo
Adam Sandler
Russell Simmons
Jamie Lynn Spears
Jon Stewart
Joss Stone
Hannah Teter
Brenda Villa
Tyler James Williams
Gretchen Wilson

2007

Shaun Alexander
Carmelo Anthony
Drake Bell
Chris Brown
Regina Carter
Kortney Clemons
Taylor Crabtree
Miley Cyrus
Aaron Dworkin
Fall Out Boy
Roger Federer
Will Ferrell
America Ferrera
June Foray

Sarah Blaffer Hrdy
Alicia Keys
Cheyenne Kimball
Keira Knightley
Wendy Kopp
Sofia Mulanovich
Barack Obama
Soledad O'Brien
Jamie Oliver
Skip Palenik
Nancy Pelosi
Jack Prelutsky
Ivan "Pudge"
   Rodriguez
Michael Sessions
Kate Spade
Sabriye Tenberken
Rob Thomas
Ashley Tisdale
Carrie Underwood
Muhammad Yunus

2008

Aly & AJ
Bill Bass
Greta Binford
Cory Booker
Sophia Bush
Majora Carter
Anderson Cooper
Zac Efron
Selena Gomez
Al Gore
Vanessa Hudgens
Jennifer Hudson
Zach Hunter
Bindi Irwin
Jonas Brothers
Lisa Ling
Eli Manning
Kimmie Meissner
Scott Niedermayer
Christina Norman
Masi Oka
Tyler Perry
Morgan Pressel
Rihanna
John Roberts Jr.
J. K. Rowling
James Stewart Jr.
Ichiro Suzuki
Karen P. Tandy
Marta Tienda
Justin Timberlake
Lee Wardlaw

2009

Elizabeth Alexander
Will Allen
Judy Baca
Joe Biden
Cynthia Breazeal
Michael Cera
Miranda Cosgrove
Lupe Fiasco
James Harrison
Jimmie Johnson
Heidi Klum
Lang Lang
Leona Lewis
Nastia Liukin
Demi Lovato
Jef Mallett
Warith Deen
   Mohammed
Walter Dean Myers
Michelle Obama
Omarion
Suze Orman
Kenny Ortega
Robert Pattinson
Chris Paul
Michael Phelps
Rachael Ray
Emma Roberts
Robin Roberts
Grayson Rosenberger
Dinara Safina
Gloria Gilbert Stoga
Taylor Swift
Shailene Woodley

2010

Beyoncé
Justin Bieber
Charles Bolden
Drew Brees
Ursula M. Burns
Robin Chase
Hillary Rodham Clinton
Gustavo Dudamel
Eran Egozy & Alex
   Rigopulos
Neil Gaiman
Tavi Gevinson
Hugh Jackman
Jesse James
LeBron James
Taylor Lautner
Chuck Liddell
Mary Mary
Christianne Meneses
   Jacobs
Melinda Merck
Stephenie Meyer
Orianthi
Alexander Ovechkin
Brad Paisley
Keke Palmer
Paramore
Candace Parker
David Protess
Albert Pujols
Zoë Saldana
Sonia Sotomayor
Caroll Spinney
Kristen Stewart

2011

Usain Bolt
Chris Bosh
Robert Bullard
Steven Chu
Chris Colfer
Suzanne Collins
Paula Creamer
Lucas Cruikshank
Jason Derülo
Nina Dobrev
Andy Goldsworthy
Jay-Z
Angelina Jolie
Victoria Justice
Elena Kagen
Jeff Kinney
Lady Antebellum
Miranda Lambert
Liu Xiaobo
Monica Lozano
Jane Lubchenco
Mike Lupica
Charles Martinet
Bridgit Mendler
Lea Michele
Janelle Monáe
Melanie Oudin
Sarah Palin
Aaron Rodgers
Laurie Santos
Ryan Sheckler
Esperanza Spalding
Mark Zuckerberg

2012

Adele
Rob Bell
Big Time Rush
Judy Blume
Cheryl Burke
Chris Daughtry
Ellen DeGeneres
Drake
Kevin Durant
Dale Earnhardt Jr.
Zaha Hadid
Josh Hamilton
Heidi Hammel
Josh Hutcherson
Steve Jobs
Jennifer Lawrence
Bruno Mars
Stella McCartney
Jerry Mitchell
Chloë Grace
   Moretz
Blake Mycoskie
Michele Norris
Francisco Nuñez
Manny Pacquiao
AnnaSophia Robb
Jaden Smith
Hilda Solis
Emma Stone
Justin Verlander
Abby Wambach
Florence Welch
Rita Williams-Garcia